THE DIGITAL YOUTH NETWORK

The John D. and Catherine T. MacArthur Foundation Series on Digital Media and Learning

Engineering Play: A Cultural History of Children's Software, by Mizuko Ito

Hanging Out, Messing Around, and Geeking Out: Kids Living and Learning with New Media, by Mizuko Ito, Sonja Baumer, Matteo Bittanti, danah boyd, Rachel Cody, Becky Herr-Stephenson, Heather A. Horst, Patricia G. Lange, Dilan Mahendran, Katynka Martínez, C. J. Pascoe, Dan Perkel, Laura Robinson, Christo Sims, Lisa Tripp, with contributions by Judd Antin, Megan Finn, Arthur Law, Annie Manion, Sarai Mitnick, David Schlossberg, and Sarita Yardi

The Civic Web: Young People, the Internet, and Civic Participation, by Shakuntala Banaji and David Buckingham

Connected Play: Tweens in a Virtual World, by Yasmin B. Kafai and Deborah A. Fields

The Digital Youth Network: Cultivating Digital Media Citizenship in Urban Communities, by Brigid Barron, Kimberley Gomez, Nichole Pinkard, and Caitlin K. Martin

INAUGURAL SERIES VOLUMES

These edited volumes were created through an interactive community review process and published online and in print in December 2007. They are the precursors to the peer-reviewed monographs in the series.

Civic Life Online: Learning How Digital Media Can Engage Youth, edited by W. Lance Bennett

Digital Media, Youth, and Credibility, edited by Miriam J. Metzger and Andrew J. Flanagin

Digital Youth, Innovation, and the Unexpected, edited by Tara McPherson

The Ecology of Games: Connecting Youth, Games, and Learning, edited by Katie Salen

Learning Race and Ethnicity: Youth and Digital Media, edited by Anna Everett

Youth, Identity, and Digital Media, edited by David Buckingham

THE DIGITAL YOUTH NETWORK

Cultivating Digital Media Citizenship in Urban Communities

Brigid Barron, Kimberley Gomez, Nichole Pinkard, and Caitlin K. Martin

with contributions by Kimberly Austin, Tene Gray, Amber Levinson, Jolie Matthews, Véronique Mertl, Kimberly A. Richards, Maryanna Rogers, Daniel Stringer, and Jolene Zywica

The MIT Press
Cambridge, Massachusetts
London, England

MIT Press books may be purchased at special quantity discounts for business or sales promotional use. For information, please email special_sales@mitpress.mit.edu.

This book was set in ITC Stone by the MIT Press. Printed and bound in the United States of America.

Library of Congress Cataloging-in-Publication Data

The Digital Youth Network : cultivating digital media citizenship in urban communities / Brigid Barron, Kimberley Gomez, Nichole Pinkard, and Caitlin K. Martin; with contributions by Kimberly Austin, Tene Gray, Amber Levinson, Jolie Matthews, Véronique Mertl, Kimberly A. Richards, Maryanna Rogers, Daniel Stringer, and Jolene Zywica.
    p. cm — (The John D. and Catherine T. MacArthur Foundation series on digital media and learning)
Includes bibliographical references and index.
ISBN 978-0-262-02703-8 (hardcover : alk. paper)
1. Computer literacy—Illinois—Chicago. 2. Digital Youth Network (Chicago, Ill.) 3. Social media—Study and teaching (Middle school)—Illinois—Chicago. 4. Middle school students—Counseling of—Illinois—Chicago. I. Barron, Brigid. II. Digital Youth Network (Chicago, Ill.)
QA76.9.C64D524   2014
004.009773'11—dc23
2013034774

10 9 8 7 6 5 4 3 2 1

CONTENTS

SERIES FOREWORD

In recent years, digital media and networks have become embedded in our everyday lives and are part of broad-based changes to how we engage in knowledge production, communication, and creative expression. Unlike the early years in the development of computers and computer-based media, digital media are now *commonplace* and *pervasive*, having been taken up by a wide range of individuals and institutions in all walks of life. Digital media have escaped the boundaries of professional and formal practice and of the academic, governmental, and industry homes that initially fostered their development. Now they have been taken up by diverse populations and noninstitutionalized practices, including the peer activities of youth. Although specific forms of technology uptake are highly diverse, a generation is growing up in an era when digital media are part of the taken-for-granted social and cultural fabric of learning, play, and social communication.

This book series is founded upon the working hypothesis that those immersed in new digital tools and networks are engaged in an unprecedented exploration of language, games, social interaction, problem solving, and self-directed activity that leads to diverse forms of learning. These diverse forms of learning are reflected in expressions of identity, in how individuals express independence and creativity, and in their ability to learn, exercise judgment, and think systematically.

The defining frame for this series is not a particular theoretical or disciplinary approach, nor is it a fixed set of topics. Rather, the series revolves around a constellation of topics investigated from multiple disciplinary and practical frames. The series as a whole looks at the relation between youth, learning, and digital media, but each contribution to the series might deal with only a subset of this constellation. Erecting strict topical boundaries would exclude some of the most important work in the field. For example, restricting the content of the series only to people of a certain age would mean artificially reifying an age boundary when the phenomenon demands otherwise.

This would become particularly problematic with new forms of online participation, where one important outcome is the mixing of participants of different ages. The same goes for digital media, which are increasingly inseparable from analog and earlier media forms.

The series responds to certain changes in our media ecology that have important implications for learning. Specifically, these changes involve new forms of media *literacy* and developments in the modes of media *participation*. Digital media are part of a convergence between interactive media (most notably gaming), online networks, and existing media forms. Navigating this media ecology involves a palette of literacies that are being defined through practice but require more scholarly scrutiny before they can be fully incorporated pervasively into educational initiatives. Media literacy involves not only ways of understanding, interpreting, and critiquing media, but also the means for creative and social expression, online search and navigation, and a host of new technical skills. The potential gap in literacies and participation skills creates new challenges for educators who struggle to bridge media engagement inside and outside the classroom.

The John D. and Catherine T. MacArthur Foundation Series on Digital Media and Learning, published by the MIT Press, aims to close these gaps and provide innovative ways of thinking about and using new forms of knowledge production, communication, and creative expression.

ACKNOWLEDGMENTS

This work is the result of years of sustained collaboration, including many people and organizations beyond the authors and contributors. The editors and authors recognize foremost the students, parents, teachers, and administration of the Renaissance Academy school site. Without their enthusiasm for the Digital Youth Network (DYN) program, their flexibility throughout design implementations and iterations, and their willingness to have researchers in and out of the classroom, this work would not have been possible.

Over the three years of our research, DYN mentors allowed us access to their classrooms, after-school spaces, and online learning environments; helped us to collect and understand students' work; and connected us with students and their families. The mentors also participated in the research efforts, adding material to our case portraits and reading the chapters in this book, strengthening the story through their insights, additions, and corrections. They were co-presenters of the work at conferences and were the first to turn research findings into redesigns and iterations of the DYN program. Though many of the mentors are named in the book, we again thank them here for their invaluable contributions: Mike Hawkins, Benjamin Shapiro, Pierre Tchetgen, Asia Roberson, Raphael Nash, Simeon Viltz, Rob Price-Guma, Tiffanie Jackson, Jeanine Holmes, Paula Hooper, Karla Thomas, Hondo Lawrence, Jennifer Steele, Erica Vaughn, Avri Coleman, Jovia Armstrong, and LeAnne Sawyers. Special thanks are due Tene Gray, the director of professional development, and Akili Lee, a cofounder of DYN.

The research in this book was initially funded by the John D. and Catherine T. MacArthur Foundation as part of the digital media and learning initiative. We thank in particular our program officer and director of education at the foundation, Constance M. Yowell, for her recognition of the value of supporting the systematic documentation of the environment and learning outcomes in projects such as DYN. A midproject research workshop held at Stanford University and attended by DYN mentors, two teachers, and members of both research teams was made possible with funds from a National Science Foundation CAREER award (REC-238524) given to Brigid Barron that included funds for teacher-educator workshops focused on learning across setting and time. Finally, from 2009 to 2013 funding for the analysis of data and the writing of this book was also provided by the National Science Foundation through the Learning in Informal and Formal Environments (LIFE) Center (REC-0354453, REC-0835854), which is co-led by Brigid Barron.

The inception and implementation of the DYN program at Renaissance Academy was funded by the John D. and Catherine T. MacArthur Foundation. DYN was made possible at the school as a direct result of the leadership of the University of Chicago's Urban Education Institute, including Tim Knowles and Linda Wing, who helped to create an environment supportive of DYN. Special thanks are owed to Tony Bryk for creating the initial conditions for a center focused on the intersection of research and practice that enabled the creation of school environments inviting to design-based research.

We thank all members of the stellar research team that came together from the University of Illinois at Chicago, the University of Chicago, Stanford University, and DePaul University, including the chapter authors as well as contributors Paula Hooper, Lori Takeuchi, Hongmei Dong, and Sandra Vaughan. We also acknowledge the following people for their contribution to this work: Stacy Beardsley, Jared Washington, Shayne Evans, Rodney Bly, Connie Clark, Kristen Hernandez, Darrell Johnson, Tracy Lee Edwards, Carol Love, Katrina Salaam, Will Spots, and Cynthia Taitt.

Karen Jarsky helped us to maintain a consistent voice across authors and to ensure that the content was accessible to a range of readers from different perspectives. Editors and designers at MIT Press helped to make the production of this book possible. Colleagues and anonymous reviewers—including Susan Goldman, Shirley Brice Heath, Na'ilah Nasir, Jane Margolis, Jean Ryhoo, Roy Pea, Lissa Soep, Joseph Polman, and Heather Horst—provided encouragement and feedback along the way, and we thank them. We thank Mimi Ito for her support of the research program reported in this manuscript. A special word of thanks goes to Alan Collins, who was the first to encourage us to put the research in book form and who has been a cheerleader throughout.

Finally, the contributing authors thank their individual families for their patience and support through the numerous night and weekend writing sessions required to bring this project to completion, particularly in the final months, when substantial work took place to incorporate the advice from both named and anonymous reviewers.

NOTES ON THE TEXT AND FIGURES

This is not a traditional edited volume that brings together contributions from a set of independent scholars around a cohesive topic. Each author was a member of the core research team, and the form and content of the majority of chapters were collaboratively constructed. Lead chapter authors typically took on more writing responsibility, but the effort involved in writing and rewriting was frequently distributed among the entire writing team. The case material that connects chapters represents the most coordinated analysis, so we don't identify individual case writers, although there were several for each. When possible, we had Digital Youth Network case learners and mentors review the case material for accuracy and to approve the content.

DYN chose to use the names of the adult mentors, teachers, and administrators mentioned in this book, while all students mentioned and the school are referred to by pseudonyms. All adults are identified first by their full name, and then referred to as they were within the DYN environment: mentors were commonly referred to by their first names while school teachers and program administrators were usually addressed more formally.

The conceptualization and design of the technobiographical timeline representations (found in case narratives B–E) came out of prior research by the Stanford team in 2000 as part of Barron's Learning in Informal and Formal Environments Center research. These representations were developed as theory-building tools based on an ecological perspective on learning and came out of a need to represent and account for the strikingly social and distributed nature of learning activities across time and home, school, community, and online settings. The content for these representations is based on observational and interview data and the visualizations were initially drafted with paper and pencil and then re-represented in a professional design program. The elegance of these representations could not have been achieved without the graphic design talent of Caitlin K. Martin, one of the authors and lead researchers on the project. These representations evolved again for this project, and we have found them to be a useful tool to coordinate our collaboration with the mentors and to communicate with our research communities. Members of the research team took the photographs used throughout the book.

Because DYN is an ongoing, dynamic, and constantly evolving program, we refer to it in the past tense when we are talking about our research findings and the model of the program at the time of the three years of research.

INTRODUCTION: THE DIGITAL MEDIA LANDSCAPE

Kimberley Gomez, Brigid Barron, and Nichole Pinkard

There is an emerging cultural image of a "digital native"—most often portrayed as a technically savvy, digitally empowered teen, deeply immersed, often simultaneously, in activities mediated by an array of devices, from cell phones and iPods to gaming equipment, cameras, and computers. Some believe that members of the "Net generation" are more creative, dynamic, socially networked, and technologically sophisticated than earlier generations. This idea is fueled by powerful exemplars of young people who have staked a claim as innovators and entrepreneurs within rapidly expanding networked systems. Take the case of Heather Lawver, who at age fourteen launched the *Daily Prophet*, a Web-based newspaper dedicated to the production and editing of original fictional material related to J. K. Rowling's *Harry Potter* series. Or consider Ashley Qualls, who at age fourteen started whateverlife.com, a site offering layout templates and HTML tutorials to help other teens personalize their MySpace pages. She left high school to run the business full time, repeatedly turned down purchasing offers of more than a million dollars, and at the age of seventeen was able to use advertising revenue from the site to buy a house for her family. And there is Blake Ross, who built his first website at age ten, began programming in middle school, and secured an internship with Netscape when he was fifteen. He and his collaborators later developed the popular open-source Web browser Firefox and launched it when he was nineteen years old. Finally and perhaps most famously, there is Mark Zuckerberg, who drew on years of programming experience—including the creation of an intranet for his father's dental office when he was a teen—to create Facebook while a sophomore at Harvard.

These impressive stories, portrayed widely in the media, demonstrate how technologies can set the stage for significant levels of creative agency. What they leave mostly unexplained is how these young people managed to develop both their vision and the expertise that allowed them to achieve it. A close look at the life histories of other young innovators reveals the essential role of access to learning opportunities, a range of tools, and networks of collaborators. However, recent research suggests that not many teens have access to opportunities, tools, and/or networks of collaborators to develop these kinds of skills and particularly not in underserved communities. In this book, we make the argument that this need not be the case. We do so by telling the story of a creative community intentionally designed to bridge divides in access to learning opportunities. We suggest that this access can increase the odds that youth are able to employ diverse digital tools to advance their own goals and those of their communities. Before turning to a more detailed discussion of the Digital Youth Network, we provide a snapshot of what recent research tells us about equity and learning, emerging definitions of new literacies, and why all this matters.

THE MYTH OF THE DIGITAL NATIVE

Our own research led us to a high-tech community in Silicon Valley, where we found some young people like Blake Ross and Ashley Qualls who helped us to understand on a deeper level how they found pathways to expertise (Barron, Martin, Takeuchi, et al. 2009). For example, we met Jonathan, who at age thirteen managed two online businesses, ran a computer consulting business, and served as the back-end web developer for a nonprofit educational organization. At home, he had sixteen computers in various states of working order, shelves full of programming books, and office space—shared only by the family's pet hamster—to house these resources. He learned to program from his father, his school classes, an online course, and reading and playing around on his own. We also met twelve-year-old Layla, who began participating in an online math community during middle school, which encouraged her to participate in a programming elective at her school and to establish her own math club once she entered high school. She maintained her interests in programming and mathematics, combining them in a substantial project that was recognized in a national science competition.

Despite the fact that it was not difficult to find young people such as Jonathan and Layla in Silicon Valley, we found very different stories in a neighboring community only ten miles away (Barron, Walter, Martin, et al. 2010). The teens we interviewed there had the creativity, interest, and ideas that we saw in the technologically immersed subcommunities in Silicon Valley, but they had minimal home access to computer technology and attended schools that did not offer opportunities to learn about subjects such as programming or web design. In fact, we were impressed with how resourceful some of these teens were in exploiting the tools they did have access to in order to create, amplify, and share broadly what they imagined despite the lack of both social and material resources. Most schools in the United States have been slow to embrace new technologies, and when technologies are available in schools, the use is uneven (Gomez, Gomez, and Gifford 2010; Warschauer and Matuchniak 2010) so home is still the most frequent access site for most teens (Lenhart and Madden 2005). In a study of highly engaged youth in Silicon Valley, we found that their development of expertise is closely linked to the breadth and depth of expertise within their social network, including their families (Barron, Martin, Takeuchi, et al. 2009). Parents in particular play a number of significant roles in advancing their children's technological fluency. They advance their children's learning when they collaborate with them, learn from them, broker outside learning opportunities, provide nontechnical support, or hire them to do technical work. They also play instrumental roles when they share their technical expertise through informal teaching processes or provide their children with learning resources such as books or digital media tools.

Many youth do not have families who possess deep levels of technical expertise, so schools are an important site for bridging the digital experience divide. However, when it comes to building high-level computing knowledge, schools do not seem to be meeting that need for youth. Jane Margolis and her colleagues (2008) offer a compelling and highly nuanced glimpse into the continuing disparities across ethnicity, gender, and family income. In a study of three Southern California high schools, they address concerns around access to and use of technology. In keeping with the late 1990s hue and cry regarding racial disparities in opportunities for access to computers in schooling, they investigated the availability of computers and other technologies to students as well as the nature of students' interactions with technological tools and ideas.

Consistent with other research (e.g., Warschauer 2003, 2006), Margolis and her colleagues found that physical access to computers (the original disparity that spurred calls for reduction of the "digital divide") is less of an issue than it was a decade ago. However, they also found that although minority students participate in computer classes, these students are more likely to be in classes that offer only low-level intellectual and social experiences with computers. They argue that real access—access that prepares students to communicate, produce, and design with technology—should be a clear goal for all students. The pattern they saw in Southern California shows these opportunities available primarily to students in well-funded schools in affluent, predominately white communities. Margolis and her colleagues frame their argument with an analogy to segregation policies that blocked opportunities for African American children to learn to swim. Just as the opportunity to participate regularly in safe swimming was critical in saving the lives of minority children and freeing them from the shallow end of the pool, equal access to high-quality experiences with computers is essential if they are to participate meaningfully in many occupations, educational arenas, and society in general—things that exist well beyond the figurative shallow end of opportunity. Recent uprisings in the Middle East were in large part organized and sustained through social media—ordinary citizens in the Middle East who had access to technology, and the skills to leverage that access, gave voice to their dream of a different world. The opportunity to give voice to hopes and dreams and to critique the governmental and entertainment media hegemony is an important, empowering, and, we would argue, necessary experience for all students. Knowing how, knowing when, and knowing where to access and build important technological skills are perhaps more critical than ever for this generation.

Lisa Delpit has argued that minority students need opportunities to develop their critical thinking skills and to have opportunities to be trained in knowledge economy skills. "Let there be no doubt: a 'skilled' minority person who is not capable of critical analysis becomes the trainable, low-level functionary of the dominant society, simply the grease that keeps the institutions which orchestrate his or her oppression running smoothly. On the other hand, a critical thinker who lacks the 'skills' demanded by employers and institutions of higher learning can aspire to financial and social status only within the disenfranchised underworld" (1995, 19).

A recently published study by Mizuko Ito and colleagues (2010) confirms wide disparities in how youth participate in digital media landscapes. This broad-based ethnography affirms that today's young people are constantly connected but do not necessarily have clear understandings of the potential power of this connectedness. It found that youth primarily leverage digital media to extend their social worlds, explore information, expand their understandings, and direct their learning. The online world provides them places to determine independently what they want to know, who they want to befriend, and how they want to be known. Some enter virtual worlds and outfit avatars as a means of trying on alternate selves. Some use Twitter to follow the latest news from their friends and celebrities. Some chat with online friends in other countries. Through this "messing around," according to the researchers, they begin to develop new technical and literacy skills. A minority of these young people, such as Ashley Qualls and Blake Ross, go beyond messing around and learn to create new uses and spaces within existing technologies as well as their own tools. Ito and her colleagues refer to this genre of participation as "geeking out."

The Ito study does not directly consider issues of race/ethnicity, socioeconomic status, or any other demographic variable relative to experiences with technology; the authors' goal was to paint a broad portrait of youth engagement. However, a review of empirical studies of computing and access confirms the variability among both youth and adults in how digital resources are used. Like many other resources, computing goods are not distributed equally across socioeconomic groups in the United States. Although this "digital divide" was originally defined in terms of physical access to computers, more recent definitions reflect a multidimensional construct that also captures inequities in use of and expertise in computing tools (DiMaggio, Hargittai, Celeste, et al. 2004; Hargittai and Hinnant 2008). The ways that technologies are used have been shown to vary by family income, age, ethnicity, gender, education level, and geographic location. These variables are frequently associated with differences in access to tools, formal or informal learning opportunities, and a knowledgeable social network (Barron, Walter, Martin, et al. 2010; Hargittai and Hinnant 2008; McFarlane 2010; Purcell, Heaps, Buchanan, et al. 2013; Warschauer and Matuchniak 2010). Patterns of participation in engineering or computer science college majors also reveal persistent disparities between males and females and between majority and minority ethnic groups (Camp 1997; National Science Board 2012).

DEFINING NEW LITERACIES AND THE ACTIVITIES THAT NURTURE THEM

The New London Group (1996), an interdisciplinary group of scholars, has suggested that our understanding of literacy must move far beyond text-based reading and writing and traditional oral communication forms. Pointing to the sociocultural nature of language, the group argues that we must consider the social outcomes of learning and making use of multiple forms of literacy (e.g., reading and writing text and using or creating images and graphics), or multiliteracies, particularly with respect to the global nature of twenty-first-century work and interactions. Social outcomes of learning include but are not limited to opportunities to create words and images for personal benefit or to share with others, opportunities to communicate with those who are close by or far away, and opportunities to participate in civic and community activities.

Members of the New London Group urged researchers, designers, and practitioners in particular to provide opportunities for students to learn and make use of what they describe as "available designs." If children are well versed in the languages of film, photography, and gesture, for example, they will have these languages to call upon as they make choices about who they want to communicate with and what they would like to draw on to effectively communicate thoughts, feelings, and ideas. In some cases, for example, written language may take a backseat to oral and visual representations of information. Members of the New London Group and likeminded researchers contend that the twenty-first-century global landscape will increasingly require young people to be producers and transformers of information in order to demonstrate their facility with digital technologies and with the grammars of available designs.

Related concerns about defining new skills led the National Science Foundation to ask the Computer Science and Telecommunications Board of the National Research Council to initiate a study of information technology literacy. The increasing ubiquity of information technology in daily life underscores the importance of empowering all citizens to participate actively in this new era, and the National Science Foundation was interested in understanding how to reach this goal. The result of the committee's work is a report entitled *Being Fluent with Information Technology* (National Research

Council 1999). Here, the committee defines a tripartite approach to fluency with information technology—for which they use the term *FITness*. FITness gives equal attention to intellectual capabilities, domain-general information technology concepts, and contemporary information technology skills rather than conflating the term *literacy* with current understandings of skill development and skillful use of technologies. Areas of FITness range from higher-level thinking (including sustained reasoning, management of complexity, and collaboration) to understanding basic principles and ideas of computers, networks, and information and using today's computer applications and hardware.

Carol Disalvo and Jonathan Lukens (2009) seek to expand the definition of technological fluency to include another critical dimension—speculative design. Speculative design is focused on the exploration and investigation of possible social and political futures. At base, it provides a starting point for design. From this starting point, images, text, and other representations may emerge as well as a process for communicating using these representations. Through speculative design, students and others can connect to community information that may stimulate discussion, critique, imitation, and new ways of thinking.

Since the advent of the seminal New London Group and National Research Council reports, multiple efforts have been made to define and distill the new literacies (or fluencies), skills, and capabilities that students will need as communication technologies continue to advance. These literacies, skills, and capabilities have been referred to as "twenty-first-century learning skills" (e.g., Binkley, Erstad, Raizen, et al. 2012; North Central Regional Educational Laboratory and the Metiri Group 2003; Partnership for 21st Century Skills 2009), "twenty-first-century competencies" (Pelligrino and Hilton 2012), and "digital media literacies" (Jenkins 2009). What these efforts share is their aim to capture the important intersection of knowledge and the ever-increasing presence of new technologies. A recent National Research Council synthesis report offers a tripartite classification scheme of twenty-first-century competencies that include cognitive, interpersonal, and intrapersonal domains (Pellegrino and Hilton 2012). Within each of these categories, multiple clusters of competencies are defined—including creativity, critical thinking, collaboration, appreciation for diversity, and information literacy. Although these skills can certainly be employed using text-based tools, youth are increasingly leveraging the affordances of Web 2.0 visualization technologies, social media sites, and social learning networks (Richards and Gomez 2011) as well as creating videos and blogs online. In this vein, Henry Jenkins (2009) outlines the necessary skills for what he terms "participatory culture," including a willingness to engage in collaborative work, knowledge of how to manage information, self-direction of one's own learning, meaningful interaction with valuable tools, and the building of collective intelligence.

NEW LITERACIES AND THE FUTURE OF WORK

The relationship between these new literacies and the future of work is becoming increasingly clear. Frank Levy and Richard Murnane's volume *The New Division of Labor: How Computers Are Creating the Next Job Market* (2004), describes a growing employment sector across the globe referred to as "information labor." The US workforce—and arguably the international work force—is becoming increasingly digitalized, and information-processing skills will be essential for certain segments of it. Contrary to concerns that many jobs (in particular low-level jobs) will be replaced by computers and robots, Levy and Murnane argue that some jobs are not easily performed by computers and thus will continue as they are now. However, they do suggest that computers and other digital technologies will now augment many forms of work. If their predictions hold true, then we will see a new form of digital divide around technology use separating those who know what to do with these technologies (how to communicate, how to engage in high-level intellectual tasks, etc.) from those with the rudimentary skills often taught in schools (Margolis, Estrella, Goode, et. al. 2008; Warschauer and Matuchniak 2010).

For the foreseeable future, job growth will be dominated by two sectors: professional and related occupations, on the one hand, and service occupations, on the other. Both of these sectors, Levy and Murnane (2004) argue, will demand strong communication skills for sharing complex ideas across diverse communities. Workers will need to be skillful in expert thinking: the twenty-first-century economy will require its members to think creatively and critically while responding and adapting to rapidly changing situations. "Knowledge workers," as Peter Drucker (1998) has described them, must be able to engage in complex communication across social, cultural, and geographic boundaries. They will be expected to be skillful in collaboration and will have regular opportunities and expectations to do so.

Researchers are beginning to find that disparities in computing expertise shape life options over time. As with other forms of literacy, it is possible that those who already have the most skills and knowledge will continue to accrue more, while others are left behind (Barron, Walter, Martin, et al. 2010; Warschauer and Matuchniak 2010). The so-called Matthew effect—that is, the rich get richer and the poor get poorer—has been amply documented in educational settings (Adams 1990; Rigney 2010; Stanovich 1986). With respect to reading, for example, children who struggle to learn to read continue to read less than their classmates, and as a consequence their vocabulary, background knowledge, and fluency in decoding and comprehension are hindered. In turn, the divide between the more and less literate grows wider. With computing, deep engagement in digital media hobbies can similarly lead to expertise development, self-efficacy, and new forms of creative agency—all critical pieces of necessary twenty-first-century skills. In the absence of these interests and of the opportunities to develop them, these skills cannot emerge. Ensuring equitable access for all is essential.

ADDRESSING DIVIDES THROUGH INTENTIONAL DESIGN: THE DIGITAL YOUTH NETWORK

In this volume, the Digital Youth Network (DYN) is offered as an object lesson for illustrating what it means to create structures, materials, pedagogy, and experiences that support technology use for all and to provide opportunities for youth to develop the critical and technical skills (Watkins 2012) necessary to participate in the emerging knowledge economy. As we argued earlier in this introduction, few students around the country have little more than very limited and aperiodic opportunities to engage in productive and intellectually rigorous digital media experiences—that is, ones that involve collaboration, critique, debate, and analysis. Even fewer have opportunities to engage in such interactions and experiences while actually using the digital technologies that increasingly predominate the early-twenty-first-century landscape. Recent studies of economically disadvantaged and minority students' technology-related schooling experiences suggest that there is a mismatch between the technology they experience, however infrequently, and the advanced technology dominating the employment landscape. What seems clear is that many students generally and poor and many minority students more specifically will not be prepared for the particular types of work that now dominate the employment landscape (Margolis, Estrella, Goode, et al. 2008; Warschauer and Matuchniak 2010).

There has been a fundamental organizational failure in this country to bridge spaces where youth can or do use digital tools. Youth view school, after-school, home, and community spaces (e.g., the library) as separate domains that by and large do not interact with or impact each other. Though these spaces may be technically connected through broadband and wireless access, they have not been linked in ways that meaningfully allow youth to span them conceptually and artifactually. DYN was designed to build bridges across settings. Its aim is to create access and equitable opportunities to computation that can be leveraged if kids and parents so desire. Using in-school and out-of-school programs as well as an online social learning network tool, Remix World (Richards and Gomez 2011; Zywica, Richards, and Gomez 2011), DYN has reached across spaces and beyond the constraints of the school day to address these inequities for African American youth attending public schools on the South Side of Chicago.

In her 2002 essay arguing for more politically aware information technology development practice and theory, Norwegian educational researcher Eevi Beck posed the question "What constitutes political action through computing?" The DYN response has been to provide opportunities for youth to become part of a community that helps them view technology critically, create it on their own, and use their creations to advocate for better futures for themselves and their communities—in short to "produce creative expressions of issues of concern" (Disalvo and Lukens 2009). DYN program developers equate skill development with opportunity, access, and knowledge building. They have determined that preparing students for the twenty-first century means creating an environment in which they can demonstrate literacy with new forms of media, in which knowledge and skill development are expected, and in which the audience that these students will interact with is, and will be, the world.

Projects that involve the production of personally meaningful artifacts can offer motivation that drives persistence and the setting of learning goals as designers work to create what they have imagined (Barron 2006). Today's youth are often drawn to projects involving web design, game design, robotics, programming, animation, and video production, which are likely to nurture these capabilities (Barron 2006; Resnick, Rusk, and Cooke 1998; Walter, Forssell, Barron, et al. 2007). Design-oriented activities play a special role in learning to adapt computing tools for one's own purposes (Bers 2006; Kafai 1995; New London Group 1996; Papert 1980); during design projects, learners frequently encounter implementation challenges that provide them with opportunities to develop the knowledge, skills, and intellectual capabilities that underlie the technological fluency we described earlier (National Research Council 1999). These authentic challenges also frame the development of a set of dispositions and capabilities that are so necessary in today's workforce, including prototyping, modeling, and iterating (Balsamo 2010).

In this volume, we offer evidence that it is possible through intentionally designed programs such as the DYN to begin to bridge the participation gap (Jenkins 2009; Watkins 2012) by increasing students' experiences with conceptualizing and producing digital media artifacts. However, we also claim that to move students beyond consumption of the myriad messages and images that exist in print and digital form requires support for and access to examples, guidance, and tools. In this regard, we discuss in later chapters DYN's model of leveraging pedagogically and artistically skilled adults to support students' experiences with a number of different types of design, including design that is grounded in critical perspectives on media and design that reflects students' developing skills in using and creating technology. In learning to make use of available designs, DYN students engage in reflective analysis and interpretation of issues that are of cultural, civic, and social concern. They engineer solutions for planning and troubleshooting during game design and robotics projects. As described in the remainder of this volume, DYN participants learn how to use technology skillfully to produce multimedia artifacts and to reflect on and critique the work produced by others in their local and online communities. Armed with digital media knowledge and skills, they are able to use technology to express their ideas, hopes, dreams, concerns, and passions—they become digital media citizens.

DOCUMENTING DYN

Reports of unequal access to and uses of technology are generally not coupled with new ideas for solutions. To develop a more equal technological playing field, we need empirical accounts of contexts that provide students with intellectually challenging access to computers and other technologies. Rich descriptions of *what is possible* as well as theoretical accounts of *how it comes to be possible* are critical if we are to move underserved children out of the shallow end of computing. This book provides such an analysis, and we hope it speaks to an unusually broad audience. Through detailed narratives of learners, mentors, and activities, we hope to inspire others who participate in the design of learning environments, whether as designers, educators, or policymakers. In addition, we intend the book to speak to the research communities we are part of and, with this in mind, we include a great deal of data analysis as well as recent scholarship on learning. Our theoretical goal was to better understand the social conditions and consequences of persistent engagement in technologically mediated design activities. A focus on engagement, in contrast to an exclusive focus on knowledge acquisition, is consistent with contemporary theories of learning that conceptualize moments of learning as part of a process of identity development rather than as isolated, discrete events (Beach 1999; Nasir 2002; Wenger 1998). Practice-linked identities typically emerge when learners view their own engagement in a practice as an important part of who they are (Nasir and Hand 2006), and when this connection is made, learners often adopt observable, self-sustaining strategies of continued learning (Barron 2006). This kind of persistence, along with a host of other dispositional qualities and interpersonal capacities, is increasingly recognized as important for learning. To make progress on documenting how these hard-to-measure qualities changed with experience, we designed a longitudinal study that followed the entire cohort of learners for three years. We collected qualitative and quantitative data that would inform our accounts of the development of expertise, social learning dispositions, and creator identities. We report our measures and findings in detail in order to contribute to broader efforts focused on expanding the field's repertoire of assessment methods (e.g., see National Research Council 2012). We also carried out more detailed observations of nine learners and their participation in DYN. Our research is guided by a learning ecology framework (Barron 2006) that foregrounds the fact that adolescents are simultaneously involved in many settings and are active in creating activity contexts for themselves within and across these settings.

This definition of a learning ecology shares with that of information ecologies the idea that both relational and material resources are important in any sociotechnical ecology (J. Brown 2000; Nardi and O'Day 1999). In order to investigate these highly personalized learning dynamics, we considered it important to document and represent choices about participation across time and place, the evolution of projects, and the establishment of learning partnerships. We share these detailed narratives and visualizations of facets of engagement as complements to our quantitative metrics and broader accounts of learning interactions. It is our intent to represent these facets of engagement in a form that might speak to educators and researchers alike.

Using this combination of methods has been time and resource intensive. We were fortunate to have funding from the MacArthur Foundation, supplemented with funds from the National Science Foundation through the Learning in Informal and Formal Environments (LIFE) Science of Learning Center. This combined funding supported our interdisciplinary, multisite team as we spent three years documenting the DYN environment and student development and another three years analyzing our data and writing up the results in book form.

THE CHAPTERS AHEAD

Our book is organized into three main sections. In the first section, this introduction is followed by an account of the history of DYN and this research project. In chapter 1, we lay out the programmatic goals and pedagogical stance for developing digital media literacies, and we describe the use of school-day classes, after-school "pods," and a virtual social networking environment designed to achieve these goals. In chapter 2, we share our research questions and strategies. In the second section of the book, we introduce the nine students we followed closely from sixth through eighth grade and present the findings from our three-year study. In chapter 3, we discuss the role of mentors who lead the DYN program and highlight how a model of professional development emerged to help them become flexible in their hybrid roles as teachers-mentors. In chapter 4, we focus on the practices DYN mentors developed to engage learners in identifying major catalysts for participation. In chapter 5, we focus on the ways that learner identities as social, critical, and constructive digital media citizens were supported. In chapter 6, we turn to the less planned but equally important processes that sustained learning, including the development of personal projects and learning relationships. In chapter 7, we report on the quantitative data that we collected from the whole cohort, focusing on change over time for more-engaged and less-engaged DYN participants, and from a comparative study involving a sample of eighth graders from Silicon Valley. Chapter 8 describes some of the challenges we documented and the opportunities that these challenges present for future designers. Interspersed among the chapters in this section, we provide expanded narratives of

DYN members that help illustrate the chapter themes and the variability in interests we saw. The learning portraits of Calvin, Maurice, Ruby, and Michael show the unique ways that DYN participants' families, friends, prior interests, and future goals came to play a part in how they chose to engage with the DYN. We share the ways that the relationships they built with mentors were consequential for their learning and report on the self-created projects and roles that sustained their development inside and outside the DYN. In the third section of the book, we summarize our findings and discuss implications for future research and practice. Chapter 9 provides suggestions for designers of informal spaces or hybrid programs. Chapter 10 summarizes what was learned from our dual analytic focus on learners and the DYN environment and draws out implications for future research. Chapter 11 concludes the book with a progress report on duplicating the DYN program on a larger scale and bridging the divides associated with access to tools, a knowledgeable social network, and learning opportunities for large numbers of urban minority and disadvantaged teens.

INTERPRETATION OF THIS WORK

In the end, these chapters illustrate that careful attention to the design of technology-driven in-school and out-of-school learning environments creates a set of important opportunities where youth are able to leverage technology to express their societal understandings creatively, to develop an awareness of their work in the broader community, and to make media designed to critique societal and civic issues. At the same time, there are many lenses one can use to understand the DYN. One can view it as a hybrid program spanning both in-school and after-school spaces; a unique approach to bridging pop culture and the development of multiple digital literacies; a model for one-to-one computing designed to address the digital divide; or a exemplar of the use of new technologies. Although each of these lenses provides a perspective on the work, the DYN team viewed the work primarily through the lens of community development. The founding goal for DYN was to create a community that needed the literacies they were developing on a daily basis. DYN is an example of the importance of building communities where all members view the literacies being taught as essential tools for developing and possessing the social capital valued in the multitude of communities they inhabit on a daily basis. The DYN team believed that by focusing on developing literacies that the students found immediately valuable, the students would put in the time and effort to deepen these literacies and as a consequence develop literacies that would serve them in the future. To achieve this goal, DYN needed to create bridges that linked the different communities where students spent their time (e.g., in-school classrooms, after-school programs, online social networks, friendships groups, home). In this way, students were able to view their digital literacies as valuable tools for interacting across all of these spaces rather than yet another form of literacy that they needed to switch on and off as they moved through their day. Hence, the unique aspect of DYN wasn't the development of workshops, but the development of multiple performance spaces where students' work was celebrated, showcased, and discussed, simultaneously enabling the student creators to earn social capital and encouraging them to expand their horizons of what is possible and valued in the intersecting spaces that occupied their day from their first design activities in the morning to their last Remix World posting of the night.

The DYN's ability—collectively with school leaders, teachers, and parents—to create links across these spaces allowed urban youth with varied identities (e.g., the academic, the rapper, the gamer, the musician, the writer, the dreamer, the builder, the social activist, the critic, etc.) to find some aspect of digital media that engaged them individually and connected them to one another. Because this work was done with African American youth on the South Side of Chicago and the positive results of the effort shared in this book stand in contrast to research descriptions of the contemporary digital divide, it may be tempting to summarize this model as a successful approach to meeting minority youth's digital literacy needs. Although we believe this focus on urban youth in underserved communities to be one aspect of the model, we also strongly believe the model has resonance for the development of literacies, both digital and traditional, for all youth.

At its core, the DYN model issues the challenge of breaking down long-term educational outcomes into near-term achievable milestones that students find desirable and actionable today. Building the skills, knowledge, and dispositions to achieve these milestones will lead the students down pathways of learning that allow them to reside proudly in all the communities they call home.

BRIDGING DIVIDES BY DESIGN: DEFINING A RESEARCH AGENDA

THE DIGITAL YOUTH NETWORK LEARNING MODEL

Nichole Pinkard and Kimberly Austin

> My whole journey on these issues started with my own experience of being an African American female eighth grader in public school and being exposed to computer programming.
>
> —Nichole Pinkard, DYN internal program interview, 2011

Both this book and the Digital Youth Network learning model were informed by multiple years of research documenting the implementation of DYN at Renaissance Academy, an urban public charter middle school serving approximately 140 African American students in sixth through eighth grade. In this chapter, we describe the origins of the school and the DYN program and then lay out the learning model that emerged from the work carried out there.

DYN AT RENAISSANCE ACADEMY

In 1998, the University of Chicago Center for Urban School Improvement (USI) opened Renaissance Academy, a K–8 charter school in a predominantly low-income African American neighborhood on the South Side of Chicago (see box 1.1). University of Chicago charter schools were established to offer a pathway to college for students living in underserved areas on the city's south side and to operate as a research and practice ecosystem. Parents across the city could apply for enrollment, and enrollment decisions were made by a random lottery system. From its inception, Renaissance Academy was a space where research and practice together addressed urban schools' core teaching and learning challenges through daily collaborative efforts by teachers, specialists, and researchers. One example of this collaboration was the development of the Strategic Teaching and Evaluation of Progress (STEP) Literacy Assessment, a product still used nationally today and created by teachers and researchers at

USI in order to develop a better method for discussing development of student literacy in the K–3 grades. In addition to a focus on literacy, from its inception Renaissance Academy had a technology focus and within five years of existence became a site for the Information Infrastructure System (IIS) research group. The IIS work—led by Anthony Bryk and Louis Gomez, implemented through USI, and supported by the John D. and Catherine T. MacArthur Foundation and the Hewlett Foundation—was a collaborative partnership between researchers from four academic institutions, local and community practitioners including school administrative staff, and commercial ventures. The program was intended to help advance classroom instruction and promote organizational change through the creation and integration of technology-based tools and social practices for their effective use (Bryk, Gomez, Joseph, et al. 2006). Existing course-management software such as PowerSchool and First Class were used to collect and manage student data, and new systems were designed, with teachers as design partners, to help transform data into specific and actionable information that teachers could understand and make use of. IIS was intended to support teachers in more formative reflective practices rooted in evidence and to catalyze better coordination at the organizational level.

A number of important by-products of the IIS work helped to set the stage for DYN. Renaissance Academy teachers began their tenure at the school knowing they would be design partners in research and implementation; would be working with program designers, researchers, colleagues, and new technologies; and would be using data to inform and guide their practice. Each teacher was provided a laptop, and through weekly professional development the teachers became comfortable with and knowledgeable about technology as a tool in the classroom and as a tool for daily tasks such as email, documentation of student work, and so on. Renaissance Academy parents and students similarly knew they would be part of an ongoing research effort that would collect student data and use them to iterate design and development of the learning environment. The IIS project also ensured a sound and reliable technology infrastructure, including laptop carts, a wireless network, on-site technical support, and a technology-integration specialist. This combination of supports enabled

---

BOX 1.1
Renaissance Academy Zip Code Demographics

Size:	2.33 square miles with approximately 30,000 people (2010)
Population:	93.8% African American (2010)
Median household income:	$28,122 (compared to $53,966 in the state [Illinois] and $50,221 in the United States) (2010)
College degree or higher:	12.2% (2000)

Source: All information from US Census Bureau n.d.

teachers to focus on technology integration without all the usual worries of whether the equipment and software would work in their classroom.

A Central Figure to Blend Research and Practice

The DYN story is not only one of organizational implementations, but of personal relationships formed over years of collaboration—specifically the relationships cultivated by first author Nichole Pinkard, PhD, an African American woman who traces her advanced degree in computer science to her eighth-grade basketball coach's encouraging her to take his programming class. Her work developing literacy software for youth in underserved populations led to an understanding of the critical importance of attending directly to the specific context of learning. Pinkard left a tenure-track position to work at USI to have more opportunity to apply research in context. At USI, she was the lead designer on the IIS project. Through her work with IIS at Renaissance, Pinkard became part of the integral school community, building relationships with the principal and administrative staff, teachers, students, and parents. Bringing her experiences full circle, she coached the girl's after-school basketball team.

Youth interested in becoming competitive basketball players quickly come to understand the knowledge and skills they need to dribble, shoot, and pass the ball. As they develop these skills, they also recognize that they must be able to read the floor, run plays, and predict opponents' actions (Nasir 2002). This process is culturally meaningful and ripe with powerful opportunities for youth of varying ability levels to participate and develop their skills while interacting with one another. Everyone is a teacher and a learner simultaneously; with hard work, everyone has the ability to be a player. As described earlier, however, few comparable affinity spaces exist for urban youth to learn digital media literacy in the same way they learn basketball literacy. And if opportunities are scarce for urban minority and low-income youth to be a part of digital media cultures of participation, how will they understand the necessary skills and tools? How will they see possible pathways to success? How will they build their interest and drive to learn more? These beliefs and questions about learning and technology and Pinkard's place in the Renaissance environment led her to see opportunities for increased intervention—namely, the development of the Digital Youth Network.

The Emergence of the DYN

In 2005, the K–8 student population outgrew the Renaissance Academy school building, and the middle school grades (sixth through eighth) moved to a new site. The middle school teachers had come to embrace technology in the classroom as a result of their work with IIS and were interested in maintaining a high level of technological access and involvement within their school-day classes. IIS funding was used to implement a robust wireless network in the middle school, with its own technical support team, editing stations, digital projectors in each classroom, and laptops. Because the middle school building had no elevator, multiple laptop carts were required to service the different floors, resulting in enough carts to provide laptops for two-thirds of the middle school students. Together, USI[1] and the school devised a plan to implement a one-to-one laptop program for Renaissance Academy, ensuring that each child, regardless of income, had his or her own computer to use at school and at home. Working together, USI and Renaissance devised specifications for the program and convinced parents who were able to contribute $250 each year to cover the extra costs. With these resources in place, students and teachers began incorporating computers into the school's daily life, including an introductory class for sixth graders where they learned basic web design and Internet safety.

Pinkard recognized that true integration would not happen until all students became creators of media and that this development would not happen within the boundaries of the traditional classes. Hence, a need for an innovative approach using after-school time to develop students' digital media literacies. In 2005, Pinkard received a pilot grant from the MacArthur Foundation to develop a digital media after-school program for Renaissance Academy. Her first hire, Akili Lee, was a recent computer science graduate from Northwestern University who had grown up in Chicago and brought to the table his connections with digital media artists throughout the city in areas such as spoken word, digital video, digital music, and animation. Lee's connections with practicing citywide digital artists and Pinkard's trust and collaboration with members of the Renaissance Academy community, including both teachers and administrative staff, helped to make the program a success, and so the DYN staff's talents were brought into the school day, incorporating digital media into elective classes and core curriculum. Further funding from the Macarthur Foundation allowed DYN to operate as a blended during- and after-school program at Renaissance Academy, growing to incorporate curriculum, professional development, performance spaces, and an online social learning network (see figure 1.1). DYN and school leadership worked together at the outset to allocate space for DYN programs, to hire artists without teaching certificates to come into the classroom, and to offer enthusiastic support for less-traditional activities that expanded beyond the walls of the classroom and beyond the school day. It is important to track the history of the program at Renaissance Academy to stress that a strong technology infrastructure and the collaborative partnership between DYN and the school were critical to the program's successful implementation.

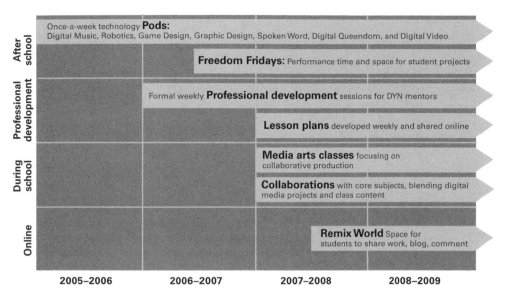

FIGURE 1.1

Snapshot of different DYN model components introduced across the first four years of DYN at Renaissance Academy.

THE DYN MODEL

The DYN learning model has emerged through review of existing literature on multi-literacies (Jenkins 2009; New London Group 1996; Partnership for 21st Century Skills 2004, 2009) and reflections on DYN program implementation from one year to the next. It has continuously evolved through cycles of implementation, research, and feedback in an attempt to best reach project goals and meet the needs of students, mentors, and the school. A deliberate attempt to remedy the participatory gap discussed earlier, the model has an intentional focus on digital media literacy development and incorporates the organic processes for learning found in affinity spaces. Four core questions guided the work:

- What does it mean for youth to be digital media literate?
- How do we know if youth are digital media literate?
- How do we develop mentors and teachers to cultivate youth digital media literacy?
- How do we motivate youth to intrinsically want to develop digital media literacy?

The DYN learning model can best be explained as a collection of overlapping affinity spaces within a larger community context. Through a mix of during-school, after-school, and online spaces, DYN provides youth opportunities to develop and apply digital media literacy in ways that are personally and academically meaningful to them. Guided by more experienced student peers and professional adult artists who are also mentors trained in elements of pedagogy, students produce digital artifacts, share their products, and demonstrate digital media skills and understandings. The DYN learning model is specifically organized to allow students to share, showcase, and critique media projects within the DYN community. Interactions between the learner, peers, and adult mentors result in an environment in which the possession and demonstration of one's digital media literacy increases status and social capital. The perception of digital media literacy as valuable social capital, attainable through individual work and participation in DYN programs, motivates many youth in the DYN community. They see a reason to put in the work to deepen their digital media skills and, when ready, to showcase their work to peers, mentors, and teachers. One student's work, in turn, often inspires a peer to comment or put forth the effort to improve and showcase his or her own work and skills.

The DYN learning model consists of five important components, each of which is discussed in detail in this chapter: modes of digital media communication; integrated learning spaces; regular opportunities to showcase work; skilled mentors; and an artifact-driven curriculum (see figure 1.2). Before diving into the model, we first describe the intended outcome of student participation: the creation of a digital media citizen.

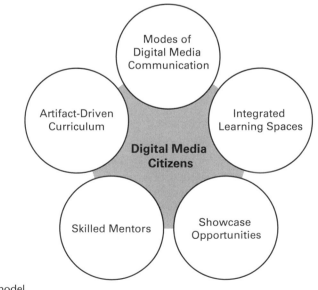

FIGURE 1.2
DYN learning model.

WHAT IS A DIGITAL MEDIA CITIZEN?

The ultimate goal of the DYN learning model is to prepare students for productive careers, prosperous lives, and civic engagement in the twenty-first century. Three dispositions are cultivated that together are referred to as "digital media citizenship." The curriculum demands that students become (1) critical consumers of digital media; (2) constructive producers of digital media; and (3) social advocates for better futures.

Critical Disposition

DYN encourages students to be critical consumers by developing the ability to understand how different types of digital media are constructed and how they are influenced by language, culture, gender, and ethnicity on the part of both the creator and the audience. This understanding includes an appreciation of a designer's responsibility to his or her audience. Rather than simply accepting what is seen and heard through media messages, students develop the ability to critique the information, question the authorship, and take into account multiple points of view.

Constructive Disposition

DYN encourages students to be constructive producers of digital media artifacts as they learn and apply various techniques and tools and take on multiple roles across different types of media construction. They learn from their own design process through the organization, assessment, revision, and archiving of project work. They see themselves as creators of digital media and seek out new opportunities and resources to advance new learning and to troubleshoot when faced with obstacles.

Social Disposition

DYN encourages students to be social advocates for better futures by developing their ability to participate in communities of practice, in both the real world and the virtual world. This process includes sharing ideas and project work across different digital media spaces and collaborating with others around topics of shared interest. In this way, they assert their ownership stake in their own lives and in their communities. They develop an awareness of self, their local and national communities, the environment, and the world, and they use digital media to promote positive ideas, equity, and change at a variety of levels.

Combining a critical eye with the fluency of technique and tools that they develop as they construct digital media products, students become more reflective—and therefore more effective—producers of digital media messages. The additional social component of student participation and ownership of their work allows them to become true innovators, working toward better futures for themselves, their families, and their communities.

MODES OF DIGITAL MEDIA COMMUNICATION

Dramatic advances in technology over the past two decades have brought about a significant shift in how we communicate, and we are now witnessing the latest transformation in our shared understanding of what it means to be literate (Partnership for 21st Century Skills 2009). In the lifetime of a high school senior graduating in 2013, the web browser, smart phone, iPod, wireless connectivity, broadband Internet access, texting, Facebook, Twitter, and YouTube entered the mainstream public consciousness. Thanks to the prevalence of Internet access and the portability and affordability of media software and of computing and image-capture devices, the cost and expertise needed to communicate with media artifacts (video, music, simulations, games, etc.) have been drastically reduced. As these tools increasingly permeate our everyday lives, it is conceivable that for a child in elementary school today, success as an adult will demand not only computational, verbal, and textual skills, but also visual, cinematic, procedural, and aural abilities.

As DYN was developed and implemented, two important and interrelated questions emerged: What is the spectrum of artifacts that youth need to be able to produce as digital media citizens today? How can youth adapt their knowledge so that it remains relevant when they enter the workforce? The answers to these questions are based on an understanding of how the definition of literacy is inextricably linked to technological innovations and therefore to changes over time.

DYN adopted the view that digital media literacy can be understood as a constantly evolving collection of literacies defined by five basic modes of digital media communication: verbal, visual, aural, cinematic, and interactive (see table 1.1). The program requires strong traditional literacy skills (i.e., text based) as well as the literacies across multiple modes of communication (e.g., making use of images, text, and tools to transform them into something new and original). Any categorization must be viewed as fluid, with significant overlap between modes. This sort of production also requires students to make use of multiple sources simultaneously (Braasch, Lawless, Goldman, et al. 2009) in order to choose the best components, forms, and messages for their projects. This movement back and forth across a metaphorical bridge between traditional literacies and new literacies is an essential skill for the twenty-first-century learner.

All of these modes of communication have relevance in education. Suppose, for example, a student in a social studies class is asked to create an artifact that represents the impact of a historical figure on today's generation. Although current standards

TABLE 1.1
Basic Modes of Digital Media Communication

Mode	Description
Verbal	The use of written and spoken text in digital media. This mode provides a bridge from traditional print literacy to the multiliteracies required by digital media.
Visual	The use of graphics and images in digital media, including an understanding of the basic elements and principles of visual design.
Aural	The use of music and sound in digital media.
Cinematic	The use of motion in media, including live-action film and animation.
Interactive	The use of interactive experiences in digital media, including the building and designing of technologies such as robotics, videogames, and simulations.

expect all students to be able to complete this assignment by writing a research paper, we as a nation currently have no expectations about a student's ability to create a video, a song, or a visual representation that answers the question. As these ways of sharing ideas become more commonplace, however, our expectations can—and should—shift. For many urban youth, aural, cinematic, and interactive modes provide entry points into interpreting and communicating ideas, building on preexisting interests in music, videos, and videogames.

A student who has fluidity in cinema, for example, can take the results of a research paper and create a short film to communicate in ways not afforded by the text. An eighth grader at Renaissance created a ten-minute movie that visually demonstrates the impact of Josephine Baker on today's female performing artists by means of a video montage that moves across time periods from Josephine Baker to Tina Turner, Janet Jackson, Little Kim, and Beyoncé. A video montage can accomplish in twenty-five seconds what may take multiple pages of descriptive writing to portray. It can also be easily posted on YouTube, potentially reaching a larger audience and inviting feedback from outside the walls of the traditional classroom.

The DYN learning model defines core artifacts that a student needs to be able to create in each mode of communication and articulates the production process. Students can employ different modes of digital media communication: writing, designing, performing, building, and managing. These tasks—which can be taken on by an individual or a group, performed linearly or concurrently, and combined and adapted as warranted—play out in various ways depending on the mode of communication being employed. Table 1.2 outlines these five tasks, including sample roles taken on by people who perform these tasks and sample deliverables that can result from task execution.

TABLE 1.2
Five Tasks of Digital Media Communication

Task	Description	Sample Roles	Sample Artifacts
Writing	Writing tasks can be applied to all modes of digital media communication. Writing tasks across modes of communication differ most obviously in how words are presented to the audience. In the verbal mode, text may be written or spoken. In the visual mode, text is presented typographically and combined with visual elements such as graphics and images to communicate a message. In the musical and cinematic modes, most words are presented aurally to the audience and combined with music and motion. In the virtual mode, words are often presented to the audience both aurally and visually.	writer, editor	song lyrics, documentary voice-over script, blog, game instructions
Designing	Design processes and activities extend across all modes of digital media communication and include the organization and arrangement of elements from text to graphics to ideas. Whereas written communication depends primarily on the meaning of the message, artistic communication depends primarily on the aural or visual effect of the message. Across different modes of digital media communication, design tasks involve creating, gathering feedback, revising, and reconstructing a variety of content to achieve a desired outcome.	artist, layout editor, critic, programmer	blog layout, school newspaper, product packaging, robot

Task	Description	Sample Roles	Sample Artifacts
Performing	Performing tasks requires use of the voice and body to communicate a message to an audience. Performers usually interpret messages created by writers or artists, and some performing tasks may be extemporaneous. An interviewer or reporter may begin with written questions but adapt them based on each response; a host or master of ceremonies may begin with prepared comments but redirect them based on events and audience reaction.	Model, singer, rapper, actor	speech, music video, public-service announcement, podcast
Building	Building tasks are similar to performing tasks in that both primarily involve working with content originally created by others. Whereas performers typically use the voice and body to interpret messages created by writers and artists, builders use a variety of tools to manufacture or manipulate content and plans created by writers, designers, and performers. Across different modes of communication, the tools used in a medium largely define the building roles.	sound engineer, robot constructor, programmer	digital song, robot, web page, database
Managing	Managing tasks involve the coordination of all roles and formats to ensure a digital media artifact is completed and distributed to an audience. Managing roles may appear at first glance to be the easiest to pin down, but in fact they often differ significantly across modes of digital media communication. For example, music producers often step into other roles, especially building roles, whereas movie producers spend most of their time coordinating other roles.	producer, project manager, note taker, distributor	magazine, music CD, website, digital game

INTEGRATED LEARNING SPACES

As we have already discussed, research from Na'ilah Nasir (2002) and others points to the importance of meaningful, experience-driven learning as well as the value of affinity learning spaces (Gee 2004; Jenkins 2009).

The DYN learning model is based on the premise that although some youth (in particular urban youth) are disengaged from traditional school learning, the same youth are engaged and committed to the development of a set of skills in other learning environments. The model draws on research about what makes those other environments work. For the most part, the aim of these initiatives, found in after-school programs, museums, and neighborhood community centers, has been to provide a wide range of young people with safe spaces and regular opportunities to feel comfortable and confident with computers and their applications. The Computer Clubhouse and Fifth Dimension are two examples. Both are international programs originally designed by local community–university partnerships and intended to provide at-risk youth with safe places to hang out after school. Both use mentors to work with youth in technology activities. Rather than focusing on direct technical training or technology as an instructional aid, the Computer Clubhouse allows inner-city or rural youth an open space, adult mentors, and the opportunity to experiment with professional digital media technologies (Center for Children and Technology 2002; Resnick and Rusk 1996). Likewise, Fifth Dimension provides opportunities for young people to participate in learning and social activities, including playing computer and board games and communicating with local and distant Fifth Dimension participants via the Internet (Cole 1996).

Building on these models, DYN provides multiple integrated spaces for youth to learn and use these different modes of communication and to develop digital media literacy across different contexts (at home, in school, after school) supported by an online social learning network (see figure 1.3).

In school, the DYN learning model involves the integration of digital media skills into core classes and mandatory media arts classes to expose all students to digital media literacy and to allow them to see its intrinsic value in their everyday academic pursuits. After-school, interest-driven "pods" allow youth to go into more depth in specific areas as they learn content, share artifacts with others, and find a place of belonging. The online social learning network developed specifically for DYN, Remix World, both extends learning begun during classes and pods and provides new learning opportunities with near continuous access to other members in the affinity space, helping them to create new identities while simultaneously affecting their existing identities within the school community. This extended and enhanced learning environment allows students to participate across different areas of their learning ecology at different levels of participation across time and thus allows for greater social

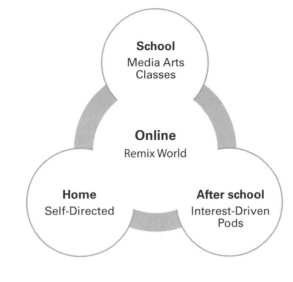

FIGURE 1.3
DYN integrated learning spaces.

interactions with peers and mentors and a more authentic digital media learning environment. More about what happens at home is discussed in later chapters that look at informal interactions across settings. The intentional design of the other aspects of DYN's integrated learning spaces are discussed here in greater detail.

School: Media Arts Classes and Cross-Curricula Projects

DYN offers a developmental sequence of media arts classes for middle school students using curricula created based on best practices and refined through several iterations of development. (More about the content and structure of the three media arts classes is shared in the curriculum section later in this chapter.) In addition to the focused classes, mentors and core curriculum teachers are encouraged to work together to combine mentor talents and new modes of communication with topics in core classes such as science and social studies.

At Renaissance during our three years of research, the media arts classes were mandatory for all students, and were implemented during a weekly 90-minute block. Many cross-curricular opportunities were developed as well. For example, the annual history contest called "Living Museum" became a collaborative venture between the social studies teacher and mentors with expertise in oral histories and digital video production. And a short-term (eight-week) programming design class in which students developed their own game or simulation to teach about global warming was offered in tandem with the sixth-grade environmental science unit.

After School: Interest-Driven Pods

Whereas in-school digital media arts classes ensure that all students have basic literacy across modes of digital media communication, voluntary after-school programs allow students to explore particular themes or media in depth with other students across grades. At Renaissance during our research period, each of the seven pods was implemented as one 2-hour block per week over the course of an academic school year. Table 1.3 describes the pods in more detail.

During- and after-school learning spaces (including the pods and media arts classes) create settings for activities that deepen skills. The DYN learning model offers comparable learning activities within and across learning spaces. In practice, this means that students are provided opportunities to *observe* a mentor editing a video segment, *practice* using the camera to film different shot angles, *critique* their peers' videos, and *improve* by applying what they've learned to their next project. In addition to providing a different type of activity, each learning activity is applied differently in each learning space. This variation affords students additional opportunities to build on their existing knowledge and to take this knowledge a step further.

Online: Remix World

A critical component of the DYN learning model is that youth can engage in DYN at home, at school, and after school. The glue that enables this connected engagement across spaces is the use of an online social learning network. During the first year of the program at Renaissance, DYN staff used various online forums—such as existing social networking and video hosting sites—to showcase student work and solicit feedback. However, the staff quickly felt the need for a dedicated online space for the DYN community to encourage more students to participate in sharing and critique, to keep student work and feedback focused on the DYN experience, and to maintain the participating youth's privacy.

Remix World is DYN's dedicated social learning network and accessible only to DYN youth participants and adult mentors. The networked community of active media producers and consumers is designed to support learning through presentation and critique. Remix World has an interface and functionality similar to popular online communities. Students set up a profile like those on Facebook. As with other social networking sites, members have the ability to identify and view friends and colleagues and can post their ideas, link to existing online media, post their own work, and create groups around similar interests. They may also comment on other members' pages

TABLE 1.3
DYN After-School Pods

Pod	Description	Mode(s)	Possible Roles
Spoken Word	The pod focuses on artistic writing and oral performance of poetry and song lyrics. Students may design online or print publications of poems and lyrics, produce recordings or videos of oral performances, or collaborate with students in other pods.	verbal, textual	author, editor, blogger, poet, host, reporter, interviewer, sound engineer, event coordinator
Graphic Design	All students learn to use basic image-editing software such as Photoshop, and interested students may gain some experience with professional-level design tools such as Illustrator. Students create gallery pieces of visual art, design promotional clothing and products, or create cover art or posters for students in other pods.	visual	copywriter, graphic artist, photographer, product designer, model, web developer, art director
Digital Music	All students learn to use consumer-level music-creation software such as GarageBand, and interested students gain experience with professional-level music production tools. Students learn to apply musical techniques such as sequencing, sound manipulation, sampling, and recording. Students who participate in this pod for a full year compose original beats, write lyrics, score films, and produce collaborative albums and soundtracks.	musical	songwriter, music critic, musician, singer, rapper, engineer, DJ, producer
Digital Video	All students learn to use consumer-level video-editing software such as iMovie, and interested students gain experience with professional-level video production tools. Students learn to apply visual storytelling techniques by constructing relationships among image, sound, and motion. Students collaborate in small production teams to produce short films and documentaries, music videos, commercials, and public-service announcements.	cinematic	scriptwriter, film critic, camera person, actor, editor, producer, director, project coordinator

Pod	Description	Mode(s)	Possible Roles
Digital Queendom	Female students provided with opportunities to develop their critical thinking skills using gender as a focal point for critique. Students examine the messages and ideas behind mass media, how media are used to influence their view of themselves, and how they often change themselves to fit images designed by corporate advertisers. Students also explore digital media journalism by video podcasting a television talk show and publishing an online magazine to communicate ideas on gender and identity.	cinematic, visual, verbal	blogger, scriptwriter, podcaster, video producer, graphic designer, poet
Game Design	All students learn to use basic game design software such as GameStar Mechanic. Interested students gain experience with content creation and design tools in commercial videogames. Students learn to apply basic animation and programming techniques to create engaging and immersive interactive experiences.	procedural, visual	game writer, game critic, game designer, animator, programmer, game developer, game producer, voice actor
Robotics	Students participate in the US FIRST LEGO League robotics competition and gain hands-on experience in engineering and computer programming as they design and build custom robots to accomplish unique challenges.	procedural	programmer, engineer, designer, presenter, builder, manager

and posts, thus supporting the critique of student media work, and can share perspectives and create dialogue through regular blog postings and discussion threads. Students can request and earn virtual currency through online participation, including critiquing, commenting, and sharing their own work. The virtual currency, Remix dollars, can serve as an identity marker through placement on the leader board or a resource for purchasing media products (e.g., USB drives, studio time, color poster prints) to support a student's media development. Remix World leverages the affordances of mainstream social networking sites to increase student engagement and to extend youth and mentor collaborative opportunities.

In the third year of DYN, it was clear that the online space required more specific functionality for the community, including the ability to assess student media project uploads using multidimensional rubrics instead of the original five-star rating system; to highlight quality work via the awarding of virtual currency; to document individual student roles on collaborative projects; and to customize templates for different sections of the site to scaffold desired online interactions, including the development of a modified forum for student debates. A new version of Remix World was built from the bottom up and carefully integrated into DYN's existing activities with an eye toward developing a promising tool for scaffolding media critique. Figure 1.4 highlights the design of the Remix World, depicting a poem uploaded by a student on her Remix World blog. She has requested that the poem be critiqued by a mentor in order to earn remix dollars. The assessment rubric for this type of media submission is in the upper-left-hand corner of the screen.

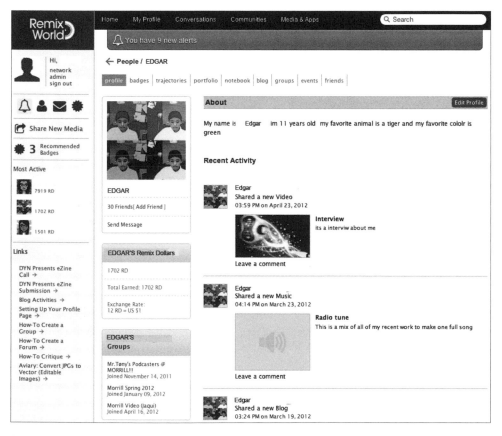

FIGURE 1.4
Screenshot of the Remix World site from 2012.

Remix World serves as a unique space for students to integrate digital work done for traditional classes with digital work created for after-school pods or on their own time or both. It is not uncommon to see a video for a social studies class project alongside an audio tribute about a student's favorite musician next to a graphic poster a student made depicting a family event. In essence, Remix World serves as a media hub where students freely use their developing digital literacies to give snapshots of several aspects of their lives that are normally bracketed off from each other.

SHOWCASING OPPORTUNITIES

Each of the DYN integrated learning spaces incorporates multiple opportunities to showcase work, which allows presentation, review, and critique to happen simultaneously across contexts. Through these showcase opportunities, one students' presentation can demonstrate his or her perspective on an issue through a media artifact or his or her command of knowledge or a set of skills, while simultaneously serving as motivation and inspiration for another to develop skills or try something new. In addition, these opportunities enable mentors to provide feedback that can inform a larger base of students. Examples of structures for showcasing student work in DYN are shared in table 1.4. Some of these opportunities occur once a year (e.g., Living Museum and DYN Showcase) whereas others, such as Remix World, are fluid depending on when students want to put their work on display.

The inclusion of frequent diverse showcase opportunities is essential for building environments that encourage youth to put consistent effort toward their development as digital media citizens.

TABLE 1.4
DYN Structures for Showcasing Student Work

Showcase Structure	Description
Freedom Friday	Weekly event with rotating theme. Most often serves as a space where students are presented a topic and challenged to create media artifacts (individually or collectively in groups) that demonstrate their perspective on the issue. Freedom Fridays are often combined in a series to enable a theme to unfold across several Fridays. Freedom Fridays also serve as a space for students to apply their developing digital literacies toward a socially conscious service project. The audience consists of members of the after-school program.

Showcase Structure	Description
Living Museum	A school-based showcase competition designed to support students' engagement in social studies inquiry through the creation of ten-minute video documentaries that tackle a historical person, place, or question related to a period in time. Winners of the school showcase represent the school at regional competitions as part of the Chicago Metro History Fair, with the potential to advance to the state level. The audience for Living Museum is the entire school, parents, and siblings. Students view Living Museum as a key opportunity to showcase their digital video skills.
Remix World	The best of student work in Remix World is featured on this social network website's homepage. Mentors select the work to feature.
Student of the Month	Mentors select this student based on the student's demonstration of predetermined qualities adapted monthly. Both a media arts and an after-school program student are selected.
DYN Showcase	An annual presentation of the best work created in media arts classes and pods, performed twice: once for fellow students and once for family and friends.
Renaissance Learner	School-wide annual competition inviting eighth-grade students to present themselves and their work to persuade the school community that they embody the Renaissance ideal.
Community opportunities	Mentors and designers work with schoolteachers to find local community competitions and showcase spaces for their students to participate in, working toward these showcases in classes and pods. Examples include the national robotics competition FIRST LEGO League and the citywide Digital History project.

SKILLED MENTORS

DYN believes that the most important component of any affinity space is the shared experience between members that motivates them to put in the effort to developing the skills and knowledge to enhance their identity within the community. As research on after-school program models such as Computer Clubhouse and Fifth Dimension shows, the role of mentors is a critical component for creating an environment where students are learning and sharing with each other. In these models, the mentor's role is frequently to act as a facilitator designed to support users on the learning path that they select. While building on these existing adult mentor models, DYN extends the mentor's role specifically to guide the development of members of the after-school communities. Although DYN is designed to provide students with many learning options and to create an informal learning space, the model calls for mentors to create structures in the classes and pods to support a shared media literacy across all students and to expose students to interests that they might not have explored on their own.

In the DYN model, it is critical that mentors approach all student interactions with a set of tools that they can use both in formal and informal contexts to impact each child. They are experts in their particular fields as artists of engineering, digital media, and expression, and they are encouraged to remain active in their domain-specific communities outside of DYN. In most cases, however, mentors do not come to DYN with formal and informal teaching pedagogy or practices, DYN early on designed and implemented a weekly professional development program for all mentors. The professional development program is set up to support mentors in deepening their technical fluency, portfolio, pedagogical knowledge, and cultural capital. Because DYN mentors are not expected to be proficient in all areas and their expertise varies (e.g., some mentors may have taught previously but may not be proficient with the technology, whereas other mentors will be novice teachers but have expertise with digital media), DYN professional development is designed to cycle repeatedly through different foci, including pedagogical knowledge, cultural capital, and technical fluency. Mentors are constantly called to bring their expertise to the table to support and co-lead professional development when their expertise is relevant to the theme of instruction. In addition, workshops that focus on technical fluency are led and developed by mentors for mentors.

ARTIFACT-DRIVEN CURRICULUM

Through the implementation of the integrated spaces for learning and multiple opportunities for showcasing work, best practices and content have become distilled into the DYN curriculum. The curriculum is influenced by informal learning approaches such as those used for the Computer Clubhouse (Resnick and Rusk 1996), but also by the more structured goal-based scenario articulated by Roger Schank and his colleagues (1994). This approach provides a structure for learning by doing that is engaging and authentic, particularly for urban youth. It focuses learning on "how to" rather than "knowing that." More precisely, the essential components of a goal-based scenario are learning goals, a mission for students to complete, a cover story that frames the mission and motivates students, roles within the cover story, operations or activities involved in completing the mission, resources needed to complete the mission, and situated feedback.

The DYN model grounds students' learning in authentic roles that require them to use germane skills and knowledge to successfully accomplish desirable tasks or "artifacts." Youth work collaboratively to create digital media artifacts, with each individual taking on roles and performing tasks that are essential for completing the larger project (see table 1.2). The concrete goal within this scenario provides a structure for learning that is more engaging and authentic for learners.

At a broader level, DYN employs a curriculum approach that combines the goal-based scenario with specific pathways to digital media literacy. Students are first oriented into a culture of critical thinking about digital media messages and begin to develop critical dispositions. They then move through a common rotation to learn basic techniques involved in the production of different types of media, honing constructive dispositions as producers of digital media artifacts. As a final phase, students apply what they learn in a goal-based scenario. Here, they cultivate social dispositions by learning to take ownership of their work, showcasing their design artifacts, receiving feedback, and participating in a variety of production roles.

Students in DYN have the opportunity to explore numerous genres and media in order to achieve these curricular goals. Table 1.5 revisits the specific types of digital media communications used in DYN and identifies how the DYN curriculum develops student literacy within each.

In sixth grade, the media arts course draws from the goal-based scenario of a record label, and students write and record their own songs. The orientation tier introduces students to five core concepts of media literacy (Thoman and Jolls 2008) and builds background knowledge around musical media. In the rotation tier, all students create a picture podcast on the theme "I Am" by writing a poem, designing a graphic, composing a beat, and taking digital photographs. In the innovation tier, students apply for positions in the record label's four departments: Artists & Repertoire, Creative Services, Music Production, and Video Production and learn the tools and techniques specific to their roles.

The second course, in seventh grade, is designed around the goal-based scenario of a film production company in which students write, perform, and produce a short film adaptation of a work from the literature curriculum. The orientation tier strengthens students' understanding of the five core concepts of media literacy by examining the role of culture, gender, ethnicity, and language in media messages and builds background knowledge around cinematic media. In the rotation tier, all students create a video podcast on the theme "We Are" by conducting an interview, designing titles, composing a beat, and shooting digital video of the interview. In the innovation tier, students apply for positions in the production company's four departments: Creative Development, Film Music, Film Production, and Marketing & Publicity.

The final, eighth-grade course is designed around the goal-based scenario of a concept development studio in which students design, develop, and market a product to help finance an eighth-grade trip. The orientation tier strengthens students' understanding of the five core concepts of media literacy by examining historical, economic, political, and institutional aspects of mass media and builds background knowledge around procedural media. In the rotation tier, all students design a simple product using basic three-dimensional modeling software and techniques. In the innovation tier, they write digital product proposals and form departments within the development studio to design, develop, and market approved products.

TABLE 1.5
Specific Applications of the Modes of Digital Media Communications in the DYN Curriculum

Mode	DYN Application
Verbal	Verbal genres such as journalism, spoken word, and storytelling provide opportunities for students to develop the oral communication skills they can use in other digital media modes.
Visual	Students learn to think and communicate visually through projects that are found in real-world production and distribution, including logos, business cards, and posters.
Aura	DYN leverages the intense intrinsic interest many students have in music, developing a broader understanding of history and the basic properties, elements, and methods used to produce musical media across different genres.
Cinematic	DYN taps into interest in film and video to develop a broader understanding of preproduction, production, and postproduction across genres.
Interactive	Youths' broader understanding of problem solving and computational thinking develops as they explore topics such as robotics and game design in introductory programming environments.

SUMMARY

In the beginning of this chapter we put forth four questions that originally drove the design of the DYN learning model. Strategies for reflecting on these questions are built into the model:

- *What does it mean for youth to be digital media literate?* What it means to be digital media literate is based on existing research as well as in experience in DYN. A digital media citizen possesses a critical, constructive, and social disposition, allowing him or her to consume and produce digital media artifacts across multiple modes of communication. More discussion of this question can be found in chapters 4 through 7.

- *How do we know if youth are digital media literate?* DYN grounds its understanding of youth's digital media literacy in their peers' and mentors' analysis and critique of their produced artifacts, their participation in the online and face-to-face communities, and their ability and desire to use their developing digital literacies outside the boundaries of DYN through in-school class projects and family and community settings. More discussion of this question can be found in chapters 4, 5, and 7.

- *How do we develop mentors and teachers who cultivate youth's digital media literacy?* The development of adult mentors who possess pedagogical knowledge, technical knowledge, and the cultural capital to work with urban youth is often quite difficult and has been a major focus of DYN work. The program provides opportunities similar to those used in effective preservice teacher education programs: educators study and implement proven practices, reflect on their experiences with colleagues, and repeat the cycle of implementation and reflection. This approach enables mentors to develop the pedagogical knowledge and technical skills that are central to the DYN mission. At the same time, mentors do not remove themselves too far from their own digital media communities, which feed their creativity and provide the inspiration that allows them to create artifacts that are meaningful to students. More discussion of this question can be found in chapter 3.

- *How do we motivate youth to intrinsically want to develop digital media literacy?* If youth are going to be motivated to put in the effort to develop their digital media literacies, they must see this goal as desirable, obtainable, and useful. The components of the DYN learning model work together to create such an environment. It is important that youth in DYN after-school programs and Remix World are not segregated by age; a sixth grader who joins DYN instantly sees what is possible by exploring the work of students who have been in the program longer. More discussion of this question can be found in chapter 6.

As we document later in this book, DYN's curriculum model and its intentional design as a collection of affinity spaces have resulted in a dramatic increase in digital media literacy among participants. By providing overlapping affinity spaces—through in-school media arts classes, after-school learning pods, and an online social network—DYN has helped to facilitate students' interactions with cultures of participation. When the model is put into action, we see the emergence of a set of organic practices within the resulting affinity spaces.

The remaining chapters depiction the DYN curriculum model at work. This model addresses the questions of how to teach digital media literacy and to develop a theory of learning through intentionally designed formal and informal learning spaces. The key practices in this model—affinity spaces and goal-based scenarios—not only draw from existing research but also contribute to our understanding by extending these concepts. Subsequent chapters illustrate the centrality of the role of student interests and projects in motivating learning as well as the value of relationship building between and among peers and mentors. As we will see, these relationships are at the core of the DYN learning experience.

2

DOCUMENTING PATHWAYS TO DIGITAL MEDIA PRODUCTION THROUGH LONGITUDINAL AND MULTISETTING RESEARCH METHODS

Brigid Barron, Caitlin K. Martin, and Kimberley Gomez

> When I apply for an engineering job, I will say I have had eleven years with work-
> ing with technology from middle school to college. . . . I remember one of my
> friends asked, "Why do you want eleven years of technology?" I just said, 'Because
> I just need it—I just want it to make a good foundation, so once that foundation is
> finished, then I can start getting a job. Then one day maybe I will make history.

—Calvin (eighth grade), 2009

Whether inside of schools or out in the community, those who organize learning opportunities need to understand how to support idea generation, to nurture learning partnerships, and to provide social and material resources to inspire imaginative work and sustain learning. Novel approaches to assessment are needed that can help document and theorize the social and interest-driven practices these learning spaces are intended to nurture. Three specific use-inspired (Stokes 1997) goals led us to undertake our multiyear study of DYN at Renaissance Academy. First, we intended to support the efforts of other educators who are working to combat inequalities linked to both structural and cultural variables. We felt this goal could best be accomplished by sharing detailed portraits of the designed and emergent learning opportunities in DYN. As a design experiment and hybrid system, it would be difficult if not impossible to replicate DYN in its entirety, but elements can be taken up and adapted, and we believe that this book can serve as an inspirational resource. Second, we hoped that our longitudinal portraits of particular students would help broaden the way educators and researchers conceptualize learning to go beyond a focus on near-term measures of knowledge and to include the emergence and development of interest-driven learning. Although it is easy to recognize highly developed interest, we know less about what it looks like in early stages or the factors that account for its evolution (Hidi and Renninger 2006), making this an especially important focus of our inquiry.

Third, we hoped to provide an account of the ways this intentionally designed creative community promoted new connections among learning opportunities inside and outside of school. When adolescents opt to spend free time building new projects—in the process forming relationships with mentors who can help them learn, seeking out feedback from peers, and joining online learning communities—they advance their capacities to create (Barron 2006). Networked technologies make these kinds of self-sustained learning processes easier, but there is a great deal of room for new design work that more intentionally makes these informal learning opportunities possible and probable, and we hope our research advances this work.

THE DYN LEARNERS

These goals required that we document both the environment and the learners as they matured over time. As shared in chapter 1, the DYN program evolved as new challenges arose and leadership responded (see figure 1.1). At the same time, the student learners were making many choices about how to spend their time over the course of their three years in middle school. These choices in turn influenced their developing expertise and ideas about the future. The grade cohort we followed from sixth through eighth grade from 2006 to 2009 included nineteen girls and thirty-four boys, all of whom were African American. The students' families varied in their economic profiles. Using criteria from the state of Illinois, which classifies children who receive free or reduced-price lunches at school as low income, we found that 73 percent of our sample would be considered economically disadvantaged. It is important to note, however, that free or reduced-price lunch programs are a crude indicator of socioeconomic status. During the period of our study, the parents who chose to enroll their children at Renaissance Academy varied substantially in their educational backgrounds, their jobs, their personal social networks, and the types of material resources they provided for their children, even within the three broad categories of economic profiles as reflected by enrollment in reduced-cost lunch programs (full-price, reduced-price, or no-cost lunch). We know that some students shared small apartments with extended family members and that others lived in homes where they had their own bedrooms. For reasons of personal privacy, we did not collect detailed data on these variables.[1] Of the grade cohort focused on in the study, we followed nine case learners in more detail, and they were selected to represent a range of interests, levels of engagement, and gender and socioeconomic status variation across the broader group. The narrative following chapter 3 offers an introduction to our nine focal case learners—Calvin, Evan, Kiley, Michael, Monica, Maurice, Renee, Ruby, and Zach.[2] Within DYN, each learner came with particular backgrounds and expertise and made particular choices during his or her time in DYN depending on his or her preferences and interests. After three years in DYN, each left with accrued experiences and skills and varying future intentions. In the next section, we share our approach to capturing these dynamics.

APPROACHES TO LONGITUDINAL DOCUMENTATION AND ANALYSIS

Our approach to charting both the environment and the learners was multifaceted. We carried out a longitudinal, multimethod study in order to document the dynamic DYN environment and to describe how learners such as Calvin benefitted from participating in it. In this chapter, we describe in detail our research methods for following a group of learners from sixth through eighth grade and the corresponding development of the DYN environment during that same time. We offer these accounts in the hope that they will be of use to other researchers and educators. We organize this discussion in terms of the nine main strategies we used to carry out the work.

Strategy 1: Team Ethnography

We were fortunate to have funding that allowed for three years of data collection organized by two teams of researchers who could distribute their efforts, share their unique perspectives, and collaborate to analyze data. One team was based in Chicago (University of Illinois at Chicago and University of Chicago), and the other team was based in Palo Alto (Stanford University).[3] Together, the teams included eight graduate students, one research associate, and three university faculty members. All twelve team members have contributed to this book. Although both teams were involved in quantitative and qualitative data collection and analysis (including survey research, interviews, and artifact analysis), each of the two teams also took on primary roles for particular data sets. The Chicago-based team was focused primarily on collecting observational data of mentor and student interactions at school and online and on observing and analyzing the professional development sessions. The Stanford-led team took responsibility for organizing and collecting quantitative data and student learner cases, working with DYN mentors and the Chicago-based team to collect data in pods and other school spaces. Data analysis took place across the three years of the study and for another two years beyond the data-collection period and formal grant. The two-and-a-half-year analysis period was made possible in part by funding from the LIFE Center. Both teams collected and coded field notes, photographs, and video records. We utilized all data records to carry out analyses focused on specific case study students, projects, mentor practices, and other themes. Both teams wrote theoretical memos and engaged in focused mining of the data set for examples of key practices. Specific data-collection methods are described in the remainder of this chapter.

Strategy 2: Observations and Analysis of Pods and Classes

Over the study's three-year period, the research team systematically observed class-rooms, after-school pods, after-school forums, professional development sessions, and online interactions and other related school events such as FIRST LEGO League Robotics competitions, Living Museum presentations, and the Renaissance Learner contest. We documented what we saw by means of field notes, photographs, video and audio recordings, and collections of student artifacts. Members of the Chicago-based team typically observed pod activity for one to two hours per day, three to four days per week. Members of the Stanford team observed pods, forums, and special events approximately three weeks of each academic year, collecting video records and still photographs to document the learning spaces and interactions. In all, the team observed more than 195 hours of the forty-five-minute classes and two-hour after-school sessions. Observations typically focused on: (1) case study student activity; (2) mentor instruction and support for student activities; and (3) pod activity development (e.g., ongoing group projects). Across the three years of observation, members of both research groups regularly conducted formal and informal interviews with student learners and DYN mentors, which served to supplement the analysis of the observation data and to inform new observation foci. The results of this work are found in chapters 3 through 8.

Strategy 3: Documentation and Analysis of Professional Development

We originally expected to observe the mentors engaged in the pod activities and to document their formal and informal guidance of students' development of digital and computational skills. In 2007–2008, however, the DYN leadership team identified the need for a year-long professional development experience for mentors. We decided to document this activity over the course of the school year—from November 2007 to May 2008. The Chicago-based research team members attended the monthly professional development meetings and related mentor meetings. These meetings were audio-recorded and compiled into observational field notes that included transcriptions of interactions, a summary of main topics and themes presented in the meetings, and researcher reflections. The research team created and critiqued analytic memos. The results of this work are presented in chapter 3.

Strategy 4: Documentation and Analysis of Remix World

Two graduate student researchers were given Remix World accounts in order to observe and document site activities. These researchers followed activity on Remix World for about eighteen months (March 2007 to August 2008), aiming to log in to the site at least once every week. Our purpose in tracking mentor and student activity on Remix World was to understand the evolution of student use of this social website and to document instances of students using the site to develop literacy skills. Online observations and documentation, which focused on forum and media posts by both students and mentors—specifically the content, language, and quality of posts—were supplemented with classroom and pod observations. We observed Remix World planning meetings as well as DYN pods and classes that used Remix World. We documented how mentors asked students to use Remix World and if and how mentors encouraged the use of Remix World during classes. During meetings, we documented goals and design decisions about the site. We interviewed six Remix World mentors and students to gain a more comprehensive understanding of the purpose, design, and use of the site. This analysis can be found in chapter 5 and in peer-reviewed publications (Richards and Gomez 2011; Zywica, Richards, and Gomez 2011).

Strategy 5: Collection of Quantitative Metrics of Access, Interests, Expertise, and Experiences over Time

To better understand this particular DYN group's prior experiences, we asked the entire cohort of fifty-three students to complete questionnaires at various points during their time in middle school. Our goal was to capture a broad range of learning outcomes consistent with a range of national and international efforts to define clusters of twenty-first-century competencies (Griffin, McGaw, and Care 2012; National Research Council 2012) that could complement our ethnographic portraits and allow us to chart changes over time and do comparative work with middle school students growing up in other communities. These measures—focused on expertise, social learning dispositions, and creator identities—are described fully in chapter 7. We also collected data on a broad range of other variables, including access to tools at home, parents' contributions to learning, grades, standardized test scores, and free or reduced-cost lunch program participation. Many of the same questions were asked repeatedly to gauge changes over the course of the study and new items were added as the study progressed. We were able to use these data to chart changes for cohort students between the beginning of sixth grade and the end of eighth grade as well as to compare outcomes for students who had become more and less deeply engaged with the pods and mentors. In this book, we analyze this quantitative data set in three ways: (1) we provide an analysis of changes between the sixth grade and eighth grade years for the DYN cohort; (2) we compare outcomes and characteristics of learners who became differentially engaged in production experiences during the middle school years; (3) we compare the DYN students with a group of same-age peers in Silicon Valley, which we describe in more detail in the next section.

Strategy 6: Collecting and Analyzing Comparative Data from Silicon Valley Eighth Graders

In addition to charting growth and variability within the cohort in DYN at Renaissance Academy, we were interested in understanding how their experiences compared to youth in Silicon Valley, whose parents were likely to work in technical fields, but who did not have a laptop program at their school. We recruited a public middle school in 2009 and were able to collect data from approximately 350 students concurrently with the final data collection from DYN at Renaissance (both groups were completing their eighth grade year). In chapter 7, we report our findings with respect to our measures of identity, expertise, and social learning disposition.

Strategy 7: Constructing Technobiographies

After six months of data collection and ongoing analysis and discussion, we identified a subset of students from the focal cohort for in-depth case studies. To start, we looked at the twenty-three students for whom we had survey and interview data from our first wave of data collection in the fall of 2006 and who had participated in at least one pod during their sixth-grade year. This group intentionally included students who varied on key demographics: gender, socioeconomic status (based on school lunch eligibility), home access to a computer, and experience with technology prior to the sixth grade. Although twelve students were identified for this phase of the research, three cases were dropped over the first year due to school attendance issues or because parent permission for individual interviews was misplaced and new forms could not be obtained. Of the remaining nine focal case learners, five were female; five qualified for free or reduced-price lunch; and six began DYN with home access to a computer, a printer, and the Internet.

To understand the processes of learning and identity development in depth, DYN participants were followed closely across their three middle school years. Five types of interviews were adapted or designed for these purposes (see table 2.1) and were based on protocols developed for research in Silicon Valley (Barron, Martin, Takeuchi, et al. 2009). We also collected their digital media work, observed them in pods, and documented how they engaged with technologies across settings—pods, media arts classes, home, and community-based settings—where they spent their time. We interviewed DYN mentors about each of the students and, where possible, interviewed their parents. With numerous in-depth data sources, we can offer very personal accounts of learning. As such, these accounts represent an emic, or "insider's," perspective on learning: from the point of view of the learners themselves as well as from the point of view of some of the adults who support them in their learning. We charted learning histories that go beyond metrics such as numbers of courses taken, focusing instead on the meanings and attributions behind the students' decision making. Our resulting narratives are consistent with a genre that Flis Henwood, Helen Kennedy, and Nod Miller (2001) call "technobiography." The results are narratives that describe how learning activities unfolded across time for particular students (Bruner 1994; Elder 1995; Linde 1993).

TABLE 2.1
Interviews Used in DYN Data Collection

Name	Description	Implementation
Learning Ecologies Interview	This interview was designed to understand learners' history of access to networks and devices, learning opportunities, and interests. A special focus was learning within and across settings and how interests and social relationships were involved. Questions targeted how computers were used at home, at school, with peers, online, and in community-based contexts such as churches, libraries, and community centers. Additional questions queried perspectives on expertise, hobbies, interests, and future plans.	Each interview was conducted in a quiet room and was recorded with an audio recorder and a video camera when possible. The interviews varied from thirty minutes to more than an hour. A diagram depicting different settings was utilized to provide a concrete reference for the place-based questions.
Artifact-Based Interview	This interview was designed to provide a focused look at the projects students were working on and to obtain the learners' accounts of how they learned, the origins and evolution of the projects, and who else was involved as learning partners. Prior to the interviews, possible focal projects were identified for each student from field notes, observations, and prior interviews. These ideas were discussed with the pod leaders for additional projects and/or insights into students' interests, processes, or engagement. The questions were focused primarily on stories of creation and learning, and, when appropriate, we asked students to define terms or share technical knowledge.	Researchers interviewed each student in a private room at school with student work displayed on their laptops. Interviews lasted approximately one hour and were video-recorded with the camera focused on the screen and keyboard to capture the artifacts the interviewee was describing.

Name	Description	Implementation
Mentor/ Teacher Case-Focused Interview	This interview protocol asked mentors and teachers about a particular focal case student. Mentors and teachers were first asked to describe how they knew the student. The remainder of the interview protocol centered around mentors' and teachers' perceptions of the case study student in four areas: as learner, as producer-creator, as collaborator, and as member of the DYN community.	Each mentor or teacher was interviewed about four to five focal students. The student cases for each mentor were chosen beforehand based on pod participation. The interview was audio-recorded.
Parent Interview	This semistructured interview was designed to provide a parental perspective on the student's "learning technology timeline" (i.e., the technobiography). The goal of the parent interview was to obtain a developmental history that would confirm the information provided by the case study learners and allow for a better understanding of parents' perspectives on their children's activities and their role in helping their children learn. We were also interested in understanding parents' own experiences with technology. We began with a request for them to tell the story of their family and technology.	Researchers contacted parents at school events and by phone to set up interviews. Four parents (representing five of the focal case learners) were interviewed. Interviews were audio-recorded and took place either at the interviewee's home or at a neighborhood venue, such as a coffee shop.
Living Museum Interview	This interview focused on student-created documentaries produced for their eighth-grade social studies class. Documentaries focused on history relevant to the local community and had to answer a research question formulated by the students. Interview questions were designed to shed light on how students crafted their questions, what research methods they used, which resources were important to the project (including people who helped), how they collaborated with peers, and how the content took shape.	Students were interviewed about their documentaries, and, when possible, copies of the documentary videos they produced were obtained. Students were interviewed individually, and the interviews were video- and audio-taped.

Strategy 8: Ongoing Analysis, Intermediate Data Representations, and Visualizations of Learning Pathways

Our research strategies yielded an enormous data set. Table 2.2 provides the schedule of data collection across three years. By the end of the study, the research teams had generated more than one thousand pages of interview transcripts representing more than seventy hours of conversations with students and mentors as well as hundreds of field notes and had summarized numerous digital artifacts. In addition, we had collected five waves of quantitative data. The density and cumulative nature of these data required that we develop approaches to understanding it as we went along. Our ongoing analysis was aided by several types of intermediate representations of data. For example, during the sixth-grade year we studied (2006), we began creating written narratives for each case study student. These narratives contained a number of themes that had emerged from earlier case study work carried out by members of the DYN research team, including research conducted in Silicon Valley (Barron 2006, 2010; Barron, Martin, Takeuchi, et al. 2009) and Bermuda (Barron, Martin, Roberts, et al. 2002).

We specifically looked at interest development, social networks, identity, access to resources, and how different activities moved across different spaces—such as school, home, and online. We also added new themes as data analysis progressed, including experience with collaboration, mentor relationships, and participation as a DYN community member. To create these narratives, we drew from interviews with the students, their parents, and DYN mentors as well as from digital project artifacts, survey data, and field notes. We used spreadsheets to track and summarize student projects and their origins, peer and adult collaborators, and use of specific production tools. After every new interview over the three years of data collection and at the end of each school year, we updated these written narratives to track each of the case study learner's developing interactions, activities, and portfolios of work. The Stanford team took responsibility for creating these narratives, and members of the Chicago team provided feedback, posed questions, and identified new sources of data when possible.

We also created timeline representations that mapped students' projects, depicted relations between activities, showed the involvement of peers or adults in the activity, and noted the types of material resources used for learning. These were designed to easily show learning activities over time and in different settings (home, school-day classes, media arts classes, pods). In figure 2.1, we provide an annotated timeline representation for one of our focal case study students, Maurice. These visual representations have been useful for analysis, for communicating with teacher and researcher audiences, and, as noted earlier, for gathering additional data from teachers and mentors. For analysis, they helped us easily see where activities are clustered, when they began, and who was involved. Comparing individual learners' timelines highlighted differences in developmental history, and these differences raised additional questions that we pursued in later analyses.

Visual Learning Pathway Sample: **Maurice**

Time is represented along the x-axis and *learning context* is represented along the y-axis. *Learning events* (activities, classes, projects) are placed into this pathway space. In this example, units of time are marked by school years from pre-K through the end of seventh grade, and the four learning context layers include home, school, an after school program, and other community-based spaces.

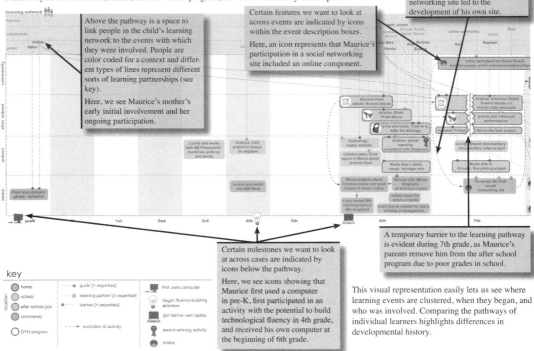

FIGURE 2.1
Annotated representation of one student's learning pathway.

TABLE 2.2
Overall Schedule of Data Collection

	Month	Participants	N
Year 1: 2006–2007			
Survey Measures	October	sixth grade cohort	46
Learning Ecologies Interview	December	sixth grade pod members	22
Artifact-Based Interview	May	case study students	12
Survey Measures	June	sixth grade cohort	49
Year 2: 2007–2008			
Survey Measures	September	seventh grade cohort	46
Parent Interview	January–April	parents of case study students	4
Adult Mentor/Teacher Interview	February	mentors and teachers	8
Artifact-Based Interview	May	case study students	12
Survey Measures	June	seventh grade cohort	50
Year 3: 2008–2009			
Living Museum Interview	March	case study students	12
Learning Ecologies Interview	May	case study students	12
Survey Measures	May	eighth grade cohort	54
Survey Measures	June	California sample	358

FIGURE 2.2
Mentor adding to student technobiographies and resulting map.

Strategy 9: Ongoing Communication with the DYN Leaders and Mentors to Share and Collect Data

DYN leaders made sure that they were learning from the combined California and Chicago research teams' efforts. Regular meetings were held between the entire research team and DYN leadership to share data. The DYN leadership responded to the data with design changes. The research team also recruited the DYN leaders and mentors to help build up the data set for each case study learner and to better understand how they were conceptualizing their work as artist-mentors. For example, during February 2008 all DYN mentors and two Renaissance teachers went to a professional development workshop at Stanford[4] and simultaneously participated in a number of data-collection efforts. We used three primary methods to learn more about the specific case study learners from the perspective of the pod leaders and classroom teachers: one-on-one interviews, collaborative timeline generation, and an online survey. For our meeting with the mentors, we enlarged the middle school section of the case map for each focal case learner and posted those sections on the wall, allowing mentors to correct, edit, and add to these representations (see figure 2.2). This activity served as a learning experience for mentors and enhanced the validity of our data set.

SUMMARY

Since the coining of the phrase *digital divide*, the discourse on information technologies has rapidly shifted from a concern about who has access to those technologies to who will have access to the learning opportunities that will position them to design, create, invent, and use digital networks to enhance their personal lives and social worlds (Castells 1996; New London Group 1996; Reich 2002; Warschauer and Matuchniak 2010). This redefinition helps define an important research agenda that can guide the design of environments and document their generativity (Livingston 2012). Our exploration of DYN had both applied and theoretical goals. From the outset, we intended for this work to be of use not only to DYN leaders, but also to other educators interested in designing new kinds of learning environments. Learning is increasingly recognized as lifelong, life wide, and life deep (Banks, Au, and Ball et al. 2007), and this more complicated view puts the social aspects of learning at the center of a new research agenda. Social processes that underlie learning are relevant to educational designers as there are increasing opportunities to craft personally meaningful configurations of network-enabled resources that can be used by families, teachers, and out-of-school mentors and learning partners who come together in community settings. We also hoped to contribute material that would illuminate the relational processes that help account for interest development and self-sustained learning over time and across settings. As a consequence, our exploration of DYN and its effects on student learning necessitated a multilayered approach to data collection and analysis. No single method could have captured the variety of ways that the students we followed experienced the program and navigated through the development of their capacities as digital media citizens. In this chapter, we have described our approach to the research in terms of nine strategies. Our combination of ethnographic and biographic methods, online analysis of Web 2.0 tools, and quantitative data collection allowed us to capture this richness and to tell the DYN students' stories and mentors' approaches to guiding and inspiring them. The next section of this book includes six chapters that report our findings. We pair four of the chapters with "case narratives," each one focusing on a particular case learner (Calvin, Maurice, Ruby, and Michael), chosen to illustrate how a central theme described in the chapter took form for individual learners. The learning portraits of Calvin, Maurice, Ruby, and Michael show the unique ways that DYN participants' families, friends, prior interests, and future goals came to play a part in how they chose to engage with DYN. We share the ways that the relationships they built with mentors were consequential for their learning and report on the self-created projects and roles that sustained their development within and outside of DYN. Our hope is that these portraits will serve to inspire future designers, mentors, and researchers committed to creating dynamic cross-setting learning spaces for young people and their families.

FINDINGS FROM THE FIELD: CATALYSTS, CHALLENGES, AND
SOURCES OF VARIABILITY

PROFESSIONAL DEVELOPMENT REMIXED: ENGAGING ARTISTS AS MENTORS AND TEACHERS

Kimberly A. Richards, Kimberly Austin, Kimberley Gomez, and Tene Gray

It's late morning at the Renaissance Academy. DYN mentors, leadership, and the professional development facilitator are sitting in the media arts room. The DYN team is facing a large plasma television screen that is mounted high on the wall. On the screen is a PowerPoint slide that reads: "iRemix Education: Professional Learning Community (PLC) group." Outside the media arts room, students are rushing to get to their classes. Locker doors are slamming, and the voices of the students are echoing throughout the room. Inside mentors are preparing to learn.

One of the mentors, Brother Mike, is leading this meeting. He goes to the board and points to a section titled "Agenda" and to the word "Connections." As Brother Mike begins to address the group, the school bell rings loudly. He continues to speak, "I'm wondering how we can reach students. . . . For us to be connected in this work, we have to stand for our students and make that our dedication for the whole year. Take three minutes to yourself to reflect on that student, who you are going to stand for, if students are at the center of our work, then which student are you going to 'ride' with, who are you doing this for?"

—DYN professional development session field notes, 2007

A core principle of DYN is that youth participants are not just students, but rather part of a global community, and it is DYN's responsibility to prepare them to become twenty-first-century learners and digital media citizens. This undertaking is significant, and program leaders recognized that as much as students need support in this type of growth, so too do DYN mentors. Through formal and informal professional development spaces, DYN mentors built professional identities, practices, and tools. Through this structure DYN forged a common language in the DYN community, and the community had shared goals for preparing students to be digital media citizens and practices that supported the achievement of those goals.

In this chapter, we examine closely the launch of DYN's professional development model and the impact it had on DYN mentors. During the first two years of the DYN program at Renaissance Academy, the professional development model rapidly evolved through an intensive, iterative process that used evidence collected from field observations, survey data, and interviews to inform programmatic design. In the second year of research, the structures and goals of the professional development model had stabilized and become more integrated into DYN's organizational system. As we discuss in this chapter, for the majority of mentors, the professional development model executed during the research period provided structures and supports to challenge and develop best practices for teaching and mentoring in DYN's after-school pods and in-school media arts classes. In terms of the organization, however, these new structures, roles, and responsibilities also created tensions and challenges for what it meant to effectively support mentors and develop authentic teaching and learning practices within diverse modes of digital media production and learning environments.

In this chapter, we explain the relationship between the professional development model and mentor practice through a historical and structural analysis of the evolution of the model and mentor practice. First, we describe DYN's early experiences and growth in order to discuss how this expansion propelled the need for DYN mentors to develop more traditional pedagogical practices. Next, we describe the ways in which the DYN professional development model evolved to include structures for collaboration, community, and accountability in an effort to blend the roles of artist, mentor, and teacher. Third, we offer an introduction to a core group of DYN mentors to illustrate how mentors integrated domain knowledge (for example, spoken word, animation, graphic design, music production), artistry, and pedagogical practices into in- and out-of-school learning contexts. Last, we share the tensions and challenges that emerged at the organizational level between the professional development structures and mentor practice.

HISTORICAL FACTORS FOR DEVELOPING PROFESSIONAL MENTORS

In its pilot year, DYN was initially designed to provide a safe, out-of-school space for youth to interact with technology and to work with mentors who possessed high technological fluency. Similar to the Computer Clubhouse (Resnick and Rusk 1996) and Fifth Dimension (Cole 2006) models, Nichole Pinkard and other DYN leaders imagined an informal learning environment in which mentor–student interactions exposed youth to new ideas and provided compelling spaces for youth to develop their interests and technological fluency. Programmatic evaluations of the Computer Clubhouse model revealed the vital link between effective mentor practices and student engagement (Center for Children and Technology 2002), and, in part guided by these findings, mentor development became an essential component within the DYN model.

After this one-year pilot, however, DYN leadership and mentors saw the limitations of a traditional out-of-school model for attracting and retaining students. Preliminary observations of the program suggested that when mentors relied primarily on youth interest to support engagement and retention, they often struggled to attract and sustain participation among those who were novices in digital media production. This challenge was compounded by the fact that, as discussed in earlier chapters, DYN targeted urban youth who had relatively little prior experience with digital media production. Unlike for their Silicon Valley peers (Barron, Walter, Martin, et al. 2010), maintaining urban and rural youths' interest in digital technologies is at times a challenge because students from these communities may lack awareness of the broad scope of productive capabilities that these technologies offer.

DYN began to expand the limits of a traditional out-of-school program first through collaborations with Renaissance Academy around the Living Museum project—an annual, district-wide competition in which students research and present historical events (see chapter 4 for additional detail). As this partnership evolved, Renaissance Academy faculty continued to teach the academic skills necessary to conduct the research, but students, and increasingly school faculty, sought DYN's technical assistance with the creation of multimedia presentations. The Living Museum project and other collaborations increased over a relatively short period. To support and sustain these collaborations, DYN was integrated into Renaissance Academy's formal school day through media arts classes led by DYN mentors (see chapter 1). Unlike the out-of-school space where youth participation was voluntary and classes had approximately five to ten students, the digital media arts classes were mandatory and involved twenty-five to thirty students. This integration into the school day required mentors to adjust instruction with respect to class size and student interest. It also meant that mentors were required to position themselves more as teachers, in contrast to their position in the out-of-school space, where they were primarily viewed as artists and advisers. As a result, mentors needed to develop pedagogical knowledge of how to create lessons and assessments as well as how to deliver lessons and use more formalized classroom-management techniques.

With hindsight, it is clear that two principal factors compelled the formation of a more expansive and institutionalized mentor professional development model within the DYN program: (1) an internal push from the DYN leadership team to create more structured mentor–youth interactions around digital media literacy with the goal of better supporting and retaining student participation and (2) an external pull from Renaissance Academy to translate digital media literacy into the school-day. The resulting combination of push and pull factors required a new type of DYN mentor, one who was charged not only with exposing youth to new ideas and providing them encouragement and compelling work spaces, but also with carrying the added responsibilities of:

- Blending the formal practice of teaching with informal mentoring;
- Creating a digital media literacy curriculum that infused domain knowledge related to digital media into traditional literacies; and
- Creating and adapting rubrics to support critique and understanding of students' digital media work.

EVOLUTION OF DYN PROFESSIONAL DEVELOPMENT STRUCTURES

Led by Tene Gray, a veteran teaching coach, the professional development at DYN reflected some of the best practices in the literature. In particular, DYN's professional development model contained formal and informal learning opportunities such as face-to-face professional development sessions, observations and coaching, and common planning time for teachers to problem solve and collaborate. Table 3.1 provides an overview of DYN's professional development structures during the first and second years of the study (referred to as year 1 and year 2 in the table).[1] These structures included whole-group meetings, retreats, institute days, and common collaboration space called "power hour." Each component was designed to seed the DYN professional development community through opportunities for meaningful, sustained engagement.

DYN mentors were charged with creating and implementing a goal- and interest-driven learning environment for youth across in-school and out-of-school contexts. DYN's professional development goals for mentors aligned with this charge. Specifically, the professional development model included:

- Supports for developing solid instructional practices for teaching digital media literacies.
- Spaces for mentors to work collaboratively, using shared norms, common language, structures, and routines for implementation across all programming.
- Leadership/facilitative roles to empower mentors in their own professional development.

Underlying these expanding goals to guide mentor professional development were four important assumptions. First, the mentors were willing and able to manage the roles of artist, mentor, and teacher. Second, these individuals came to the program with high-level domain knowledge in media, but (likely) insufficient pedagogical knowledge to be effective in a traditional classroom. Third, traditional pedagogical tools for literacy development could be adapted for digital media instruction. And fourth, the lead DYN professional development facilitator had the background in literacy and industrial design to drive the development and implementation of a digital media arts–based curriculum across multiple modes of communication.

TABLE 3.1
Group Collaboration Structures in DYN's Professional Development Model

	Participation Structure	Description
Year 1 (2006–2007)	Whole-group weekly sessions	Six mentors and the facilitator-coach met weekly for two hours to discuss classroom structures, routines, and expectations and to develop lessons and rubrics.
Year 2 (2007–2008)	Whole-group monthly sessions	Six mentors and the facilitator-coach met monthly for three hours to discuss instructional practices and assignments, examine student work, and solve problems.
	Retreat	Six mentors, the program coordinator, the principal investigator, and the facilitator met during a week-long retreat to define and develop twenty-first-century literacies and student learning outcomes.
	Curriculum Institute	Six mentors met for one week, four hours a day, during the summer of 2007 to develop and revise unit plans with a focus on twenty-first-century literacies and student learning outcomes.

These expanded goals and shared understandings enabled DYN to design and deliver a digital media curriculum that spanned after-school pods, in-school media arts classes, and various online spaces. This section reviews the steps the team took in order to reach this point.

Developing Skilled Artists as Mentors and Teachers

The DYN model hinged on its mentors, who as professional artists with diverse expertise could serve as positive role models and guides to help youth access digital tools and build technological fluency. To achieve this goal, DYN mentors needed to possess: proficiency in or commitment to building proficiency in digital technology; technical fluency (knowledge of technology and tools); a personal digital media portfolio (compelling examples of mentor-created work); and cultural capital (relationships with students as well as with relevant professional and local communities). With the expansion of DYN into the school day, a fourth qualification also became necessary: pedagogical knowledge. Thus, DYN's organizational leaders designed a professional development model that helped these skilled mentors evolve so that they could more effectively share their knowledge and skills with students.

In order to foster pedagogical proficiency, DYN expanded its professional development model to include the creation of professional learning communities (Darling-Hammond and McLaughlin 1995; McLaughlin and Talbert 2001). Based on successful professional development theories emerging from research examining traditionally certified K–12 teachers, this approach offered a framework for cultivating shared norms, routines, and practices among mentors, which led to consistent and intentional interactions with students. The guiding principle in the design of the professional learning community was that mentors would become socialized into teaching by becoming a part of a community of learners and practitioners who question, reflect, and view learning as a lifelong task (Cochran-Smith and Lytle 1999).

As DYN's learning community developed, mentors worked with Gray to strike a balance between the experiential, hands-on learning of the pods and the more structured, intentional learning found in the media arts classes. Gray introduced pedagogical concepts and processes to mentors and guided them through the design and implementation of a digital media curriculum. Weekly whole-group meetings supported mentor professional development through discussions and the creation of lesson plans and rubrics. These conversations incorporated the Critical Friends methodology, a framework rooted in cooperative learning that draws on reflection and discussion to promote collaboration and improve teaching practices (Annenberg Institute for School Reform 1994). In the process, mentors developed effective pedagogical practices and learning goals that informed lesson plans and interactions with youth (Gray, Pinkard, Gomez, et al. 2008).

Through regular weekly workshops, mentors were offered key concepts and strategies intended to support their work as teachers. For example, a series of sessions revolved around the use of questioning as an instructional technique. Gray introduced the mentors to Bloom's Taxonomy using an inquiry-based approach (Cecil 1995). Learning objectives were classified under three categories: cognitive, affective, and psychomotor. Within each level of higher-order thinking, Bloom's Taxonomy has been used as the basis for teacher professional development (Bambino 1995), and the mentors learned how it could be applied to their work, as well. Mentors also learned practical classroom tools, such as how to design activities (Calkins 1994) and to create instructional supports for independent student learning. Finally, they were taught how to analyze student work for evidence of learning and understanding using the Critical Friends methodology.

In the second year, mentors' professional development also included opportunities to apply their pedagogical understandings as they created lesson plans and completed reflections on the planning and delivery of those plans. However, as professional digital artists with fluency in expert languages, several mentors found it difficult to scaffold instruction to support the development of expert language among novice learners. Evidence also suggested that in order to most effectively use pedagogical tools such as guided practice and rubrics in the classroom (Gray, Pinkard, Gomez, et al. 2008), mentors needed additional coaching to support their self-reflection about their own practice. In the next section, we describe the redesign of the professional development model in its second year, which was intended to develop instructional approaches and assessment practices appropriate for both out-of-school and in-school contexts.

Instructional Theory of Action

In an effort to incorporate mentor expertise with pedagogical practices into a shared organizational vision, Gray, working with DYN leaders and mentors during the summer before the second year, drafted an instructional theory of action (ITOA). This artifact would serve as a touchstone for the DYN team as they engaged in professional development (Gray, Pinkard, Gomez, et al. 2008). The ITOA's purpose was to highlight the mentors' abilities as artists and teachers and to outline the various steps necessary to prepare their students as twenty-first-century learners.

This first draft of the ITOA was based on existing models that were in development in the University of Chicago's USI partnership schools. Over the course of four meetings, Gray, DYN cofounders Pinkard and Akili Lee, researchers, and mentor Mike Hawkins (referred to as Brother Mike) adapted the ITOA to DYN. The completed first draft was presented to the DYN mentors, who were invited to ask clarifying questions and to share critical feedback. Gray and others used this feedback to revise the ITOA into its final form (see box 3.1).

BOX 3.1
DYN Instructional Theory of Action

Our instructional theory of action states that . . .
If we:
- Develop students media literacy skills while mentors share expertise, analyze teacher practice, and examine student work for understanding, and
- Develop a collaborative, reflective community of students and mentors, and
- Create opportunities for students to become producers of media artifacts while mentors provide consistent, guided feedback, and
- Develop students' ability to critique their work and others' while mentors consistently monitor student understanding, and
- Implement workshop structures to support student learning and student dialogue,
Then:
- Our students will demonstrate deep learning and fluidity in twenty-first-century literacies and become digital media citizens.

DYN's ITOA required not only that mentors develop technical fluency, digital media portfolios, and cultural capital, but also that they be committed to developing their pedagogical knowledge. As such, it informed the goals and practices necessary for DYN mentors to be successful, which in turn informed the design of the professional development structures.

Group Collaboration Structures

As DYN leadership and mentors addressed the need for more school-day focused and intentional interactions with youth, a more sustainable and differentiated mentor professional development plan was being created. The first significant change was a shift from hour-long weekly meetings to monthly whole-group meetings that lasted two to three hours. The shift to longer, whole-group sessions allowed more focused time for DYN personnel to reflect on both their own pedagogical development and youth development of digital media literacies. Moreover, less frequent meetings gave mentors more time to collaborate in order to design lessons and to partner with and support teachers in the school.

A central component of the mentors' professional development was participation in self-reflective practices. These practices were designed to allow mentors to engage critically in their own development and to collaborate with Gray to refine instructional practices (Gray, Pinkard, Gomez, et al. 2008). Whole-group meetings were mandatory for all DYN personnel, and Gray created the agenda and led the meetings—these aspects did not change from the original model. However, a new reflective space called "Opening Moves" was added to the first thirty to forty-five minutes of each meeting. In this space, Gray, or other meeting facilitators, invited mentors to describe how they were connecting to or struggling with some aspect of their own professional development or of their work with DYN youth. The facilitator also shared anonymous, written mentor reflections from previous weeks. The subsequent two hours of the meeting was virtually unchanged from the earlier model and consisted of various activities focused on specific learning goals and outcomes. The team also continued to use the Critical Friends methodology as a tool to support collaboration and to create participation structures that allowed all members to engage actively and jointly in achieving targeted learning goals and outcomes.

Additional group collaboration opportunities—such as retreats and institute days—were also added to the professional development calendar. After the creation of the ITOA, the staff met for a weeklong retreat in Vancouver, British Columbia. Pinkard and Gray wanted the retreat to provide a sheltered opportunity to develop a grounded understanding of the ITOA. At the retreat, the team created an organizational vision of the characteristics and attributes of the "digital media citizen," which, as described in chapter 1, included key literacies across multiple modes of communication. In addition to the summer retreats, three institute days were implemented during the Renaissance Academy's winter break. During these institute days, mentors and the facilitator critiqued unit plans based on student-produced artifacts. These retreats and institute days became an important piece of DYN's professional development model.

The DYN Professional Development Cycle

The DYN leadership determined that a formalized cycle (see figure 3.1) was needed to address diverse mentor professional development needs and to provide structures and spaces for mentors to engage actively in their professional development. The creation of a cycle allowed the facilitator to differentiate supports and guidance for each mentor while at the same time introducing and developing shared programmatic learning goals, pedagogical concepts, and practices that the DYN community would work in collaboration to implement. The learning cycle, which typically lasted four weeks, comprised numerous professional activity spaces that varied in terms of time, levels of participation, roles, norms, attendees, and types of artifacts created. Each cycle began with the *whole-group professional development* meetings, which introduced and reinforced programmatic goals, pedagogical concepts, and practices. The second week included the Mentor Learning Group (MLG) meeting where mentors would lead and participate without the facilitator and DYN leadership. During the third week of the cycle, the facilitator and a designated mentor would meet "one to one" in a *coaching session* to identify individual mentor needs. The facilitator would then identify additional supports to assist in the mentor's pedagogical development. The final week of the cycle typically ended with an MLG meeting.

Overall, each mentor was expected to engage and interact within the formal spaces (whole group, MLG, and coaching sessions), to produce weekly lesson plans, and to create and reflect on individualized action plans with Gray. The model also included less-structured opportunities for development, such as a virtual space within the program's social networking site, Remix World, where mentors could digitally post work, comment, and communicate about events and other relevant information (Pinkard and Austin 2011). Mentors could access this online space at any time of the day and from any location. Likewise, within a face-to-face, in-school space called "Power Hour," mentors could interact with no rules or formal expectations. The space was intentionally designed to be less structured as a way to spark creativity and collaboration among mentors (Gray, Pinkard, Gomez, et al. 2008). Specific aspects of DYN's professional development cycle are discussed in more detail in the remainder of this section.

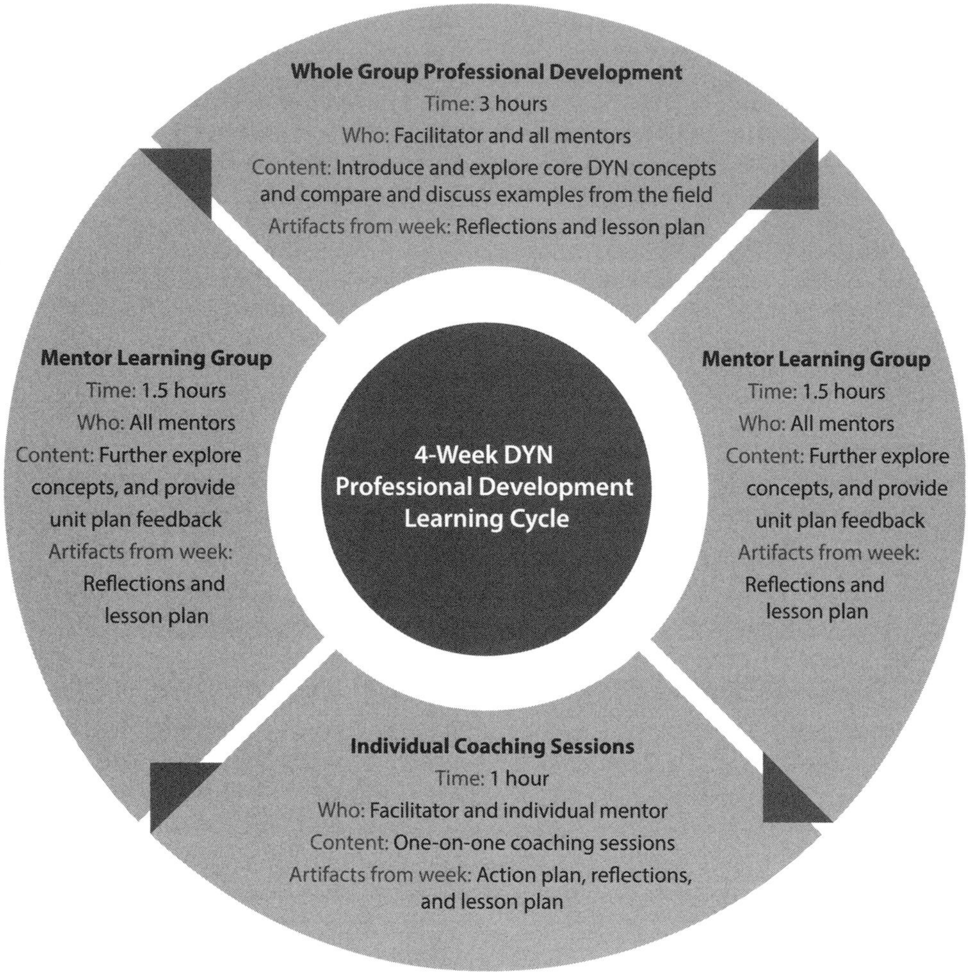

Whole Group Professional Development
Time: 3 hours
Who: Facilitator and all mentors
Content: Introduce and explore core DYN concepts
and compare and discuss examples from the field
Artifacts from week: Reflections and lesson plan

Mentor Learning Group
Time: 1.5 hours
Who: All mentors
Content: Further explore
concepts, and provide
unit plan feedback
Artifacts from week:
Reflections and
lesson plan

**4-Week DYN
Professional Development
Learning Cycle**

Mentor Learning Group
Time: 1.5 hours
Who: All mentors
Content: Further explore
concepts, and provide
unit plan feedback
Artifacts from week:
Reflections and
lesson plan

Individual Coaching Sessions
Time: 1 hour
Who: Facilitator and individual mentor
Content: One-on-one coaching sessions
Artifacts from week: Action plan, reflections,
and lesson plan

FIGURE 3.1
The professional development learning cycle.

Community Development Structures

In an effort to leverage mentor expertise and build a sustainable, adaptable learning community, the DYN staff implemented several formal community development structures (see table 3.2). For example, the MLG was intended to build leadership capacity within the team and to provide the mentors with biweekly support around lesson planning and instructional work. Brother Mike, one of DYN's lead mentors, first served as MLG facilitator until another mentor, Asia Roberson, took over; both mentors had attended Critical Friends facilitator trainings at a local university in order to prepare for this leadership role. Although Gray did not attend the MLG sessions unless invited, she did meet regularly with the two lead mentors to plan the meetings. This mentor-only setting provided a space to hold discussions, build understanding, and critique knowledge presented in the whole-group meetings while also connecting these concepts to lesson plans for and instructional practices with the DYN youth.

TABLE 3.2
Community Development Structures in DYN's Professional Development Model

	Participant Structures	Description
Year 1 (2006–2007)	None	N/A
Year 2 (2007–2008)	Mentor Learning Group (MLG)	Monthly, one-and-a-half-hour sessions led by one mentor that involved revising lesson plans and deepening understanding of content presented in whole-group professional development.
	Power Hour	One hour of informal time, mentors only, three times per week, that involved sharing and discussing work, examples, and experiences as well as planning and designing.
	Skill-Building Workshops	Five days of one-hour sessions led by mentors during the summer of 2007 that provided a space for participants to share knowledge and expertise.

The MLG sessions were patterned after the monthly professional development sessions, but the original structure was "remixed" to better serve the mentors' needs. For example, similar to Opening Moves in the whole-group meetings where mentors were invited to share experiences or struggles in developing their pedagogical knowledge, the MLG space began with a reflective space for mentors to discuss or to represent ("stand for") individual youth. The purpose of these interactions was to ground pedagogical concepts in reality and to motivate the mentors to work toward the development of best practices for the youth of DYN.

Power Hour was created as a less-structured space for encouraging mentor collaboration and creativity. Held three days a week, these mentor-only sessions enabled mentors to grapple with issues they faced in lesson preparation and delivery as well as to share and discuss openly their own work, digital media examples they were excited about bringing into the classrooms, and ideas around their roles as artists in the field and as instructors and mentors to the students. Here, mentors frequently mentored each other—sharing, questioning, and supporting.

A third community structure, Skill-Building Workshops, created a forum for mentors to lead workshops and to share their knowledge and expertise with colleagues. For each workshop, a mentor with a recognized expertise in a given mode, for example videogame design, taught other DYN mentors the knowledge and skills related to creating a videogame. Each workshop culminated with a final project that required the mentors to apply the targeted skill. Practically, these workshops helped build mentors' technical fluency, but with rewards given to the mentor who best demonstrated the workshop's targeted skill, they also helped to foster healthy competition. Students judged their mentors' work, which allowed youth to see mentors act as twenty-first-century learners and to use their developing digital media knowledge and skills to evaluate mentor-produced products. Lastly, the products mentors created later served as examples for various pod- and media arts–related projects, which helped students better envision their own end products.

Accountability Structures

In the first year that the DYN professional development model was implemented, mentors were asked to submit lesson plans and reflections on a weekly basis. At that time, the lesson plans followed a template that Gray had preselected, and the reflections were open-ended, allowing the mentors to reflect on any struggles, successes, or questions. The movement of DYN into the school day, however, required that mentors appropriate standards more aligned to the professional standards for K–12 teachers. To build these standards, several accountability structures were instituted (see table 3.3).

TABLE 3.3
DYN Accountability Structures

	Participant Structures	Description
Year 1 (2006–2007)	Lesson plans	Day-to-day explanation of what content was being taught and how it was being taught
	Open weekly reflections	Weekly written reflections on what was happening in DYN
Year 2 (2007–2008)	Unit plans and lesson plans	Quarterly/daily lessons describing learning outcomes and how they would be met
	Structured weekly reflections	Weekly written reflections that described strengths, challenges, supports, and next steps
	Mentor action plans	Individualized learning plans that described goals, resources, and timelines

In an effort to support mentor agency and expertise in the creation of the curriculum, such as the ITOA, mentors were invited to collaborate on the design of a curricular unit that would in turn inform the redesign of the lesson-plan template. Using the *Understanding by Design* framework (Wiggins and McTighe 2005), the facilitator introduced the guiding principles of evidence, outcomes, and activities as a way to structure the unit plans and to create a common language for talking about unit-plan features.

In the second year of professional development implementation, mentor reflections became more structured. Each week the mentors were asked to reflect on their previous week's classroom experiences and to identify strengths and challenges related to their practice. They were encouraged to consider what supports were needed and what the logical next steps would be. This practice allowed the facilitator to assess mentor development and learning more readily and to provide needed support and scaffolds related to instructional challenges (Gray, Pinkard, Gomez, et al. 2008).

In both years, mentors were still expected to produce weekly lesson plans and reflections, which were then submitted to the facilitator. These documents became artifacts around which the facilitator and mentors could interact and build knowledge related to mentor practice. These artifacts eventually became central to the norms and practices of the DYN professional learning component, clearly illustrating the extent of mentor participation within the professional learning community. These and other documents were developed and stored using online collaborative writing tools—first within an interactive online document or wiki space, second within a list serve or blog space, and then later on a more sophisticated virtual platform called SPACE (Supporting Projects with Authoring, Critique, and Exemplars), a database-backed web application designed to support evidence-based instruction within schools (Shapiro, Nacu, and Pinkard 2010).

Finally, a coaching model was adapted from work used by literacy coaches (Newmann and Wehlage 1995). The adapted model consisted of a series of coaching sessions between one mentor and the facilitator. These coaching sessions included a preconference, an in-class observation, a debriefing following the observation, and formulation of an action plan or next steps. Together the mentor and the coach created individualized action plans, which were used to differentiate professional development for each mentor based on needs identified during the coaching sessions. Each mentor's plan was based on individual strengths and challenges and included the following: (1) goals, (2) the mentor's responsibilities, (3) the coach's responsibilities, (4) necessary materials or resources, and (5) a timeline. The goals consisted of overarching learning goals determined by the facilitator and individual goals set by the mentor, which were related to a specific instructional area or to a strategy that the mentor wanted to learn more about.

UNDERSTANDING MENTOR PEDAGOGICAL KNOWLEDGE DEVELOPMENT

The discussion thus far has described at an abstract level the structures that surrounded the DYN mentors as they combined the roles of artist, mentor, and teacher. In this section, we present a more grounded discussion not only of how mentors managed these roles, but also of how their identities shaped their professional development. To do this, we focus on three mentors—Brother Mike, Asia, and Raphael Nash. Table 3.4 summarizes these mentors' background knowledge and expertise along the dimensions Pinkard and others imagined were necessary to be a DYN mentor. The table also includes this information about the members of the leadership team that included founder Pinkard, cofounder Lee, and professional development facilitator Gray.

These are but three of the thirteen mentors who worked with DYN participants during the time of the study. These three mentors represent a successful navigation of the professional development pathway that Gray and others created. Some mentors, however, encountered challenges along their professional development. Even among those who valued the professional development model, challenges existed. The discussion concludes by describing the common obstacles mentors encountered.

TABLE 3.4
DYN Professional Development Team

	Mentors		

	Brother Mike Hawkins	**Raphael Nash**	**Asia Roberson**
Joined DYN	2005 (pilot year)	2006 (Year 1)	2007 (Year 1)
Technical Fluency	Digital music and publication tools	Video and film production and tools; videogame programming	Digital music and digital video production tools
Digital Media Portfolio	Published poetry, performed on television and in local spoken-word showcases	Directed and edited music videos, short films, and documentaries	Music and television performance artist
Cultural Capital	Lived in the community while working for DYN; former teacher assistant in the public schools; former artist-in-residence in the public schools; hip-hop and spoken-word performer	Lived in the community while working for DYN; mentor in out-of-school digital arts program for youth in grades 6–12; independent film director, editor, and writer	Part-time support staff member at Renaissance Academy prior to joining DYN; mentor working with youth using digital media to address social and emotional issues affecting young women; musician and vocalist in local funk and punk bands

	Design Team		
	 Nichole Pinkard	Akili Lee	Tene Gray
Role	Founder-Mentor	Cofounder-Mentor	Facilitator
Joined DYN	2005 (pilot year)	2005 (pilot year)	2006 (Year 1)
Technical Fluency	Computer programming tools; educational software development and design tools; robotics; videogame design tools and software	Computational programming tools; social media development and web design tools; marketing and graphic design tools; videogame design skills; audio editing; production software and tools	Industrial technology; CAD software, computer programming, instructional design language; iMovie software
Digital Media Portfolio	Designed and developed educational software targeting culturally relevant literacy development (STEP); designed social networking site (Remix World); programmed and designed videogames	Designed and developed websites; designed and developed social networking site (Remix World); programmed computer software; worked as DJ, radio host, and producer	Designed visual graphics for developing writing processes; designed website; created personal movies using iMovie
Cultural Capital	Led efforts to implement one-to-one computing in urban schools; integrated digital media learning opportunities outside of the school day; served on the advisory boards of a charter school and organizations connected with children, learning, play, and technology	Served as associate director of digital media and technology in a local community-based organization; worked as consultant for small businesses and community organizations to leverage digital media; was owner of an events promotion company; had strong networks within artist communities	Former middle school classroom teacher and education doctoral student; professional development facilitator for Chicago public-school teachers; developed and maintained personal relationships with students and their families; coached volleyball in elementary school; tutored students in the foster care system; member of Critical Friends group

DYN Mentor Portraits

Given the diversity of technical fluency, digital media production, and cultural capital among the mentors, it is not surprising that each mentor had a unique professional development experience. The three mentor portraits that follow illustrate these variations. As we compiled field notes and conducted interviews, it became clear that these mentors viewed their work with DYN not as a job, but as a social responsibility to bring state-of-the-art equipment and knowledge to a community that has historically been neglected.

In spite of this common motivation, we also learned that each mentor internalized pedagogical concepts differently. For example, as will be discussed, Brother Mike connected theories of learning and teaching to his practice; Raphael found success using curricular structures and questioning strategies to support project-based learning and critique; Asia found success with goal-based scenarios and inquiry. All three were able to draw on DYN structures to provide the youth with access to digital technology and opportunities to learn digital literacies across multiple domains.

BROTHER MIKE

Once you're on the playing field, you got the tools. You got the access. You got the ability to become this twenty-first-century learner. What are you going to do?

—Brother Mike, 2007

In 2005, Brother Mike was approached by Lee to consider joining DYN. As a working spoken-word artist and performer as well as a former teacher assistant in Chicago's public-school system, Brother Mike saw joining DYN as an opportunity to develop transformative learning opportunities for youth and for himself: "I teach out of an approach of knowledge and love. I feel like [the students] are mine. I think many teachers feel that way." This notion of personal responsibility and growth was not new to Brother Mike, who described the motivating influence that media artists had on him early in his life: "To see the entrepreneur where it was like, 'I don't just rap. I make movies. I'm an actor, I direct videos.'" This cultural renaissance within the African American media community is what inspired Brother Mike and Pinkard to explore the connection between spoken word and hip-hop culture, on the one hand, and the development of a twenty-first-century learner and digital media citizen, on the other. Brother Mike was "first and foremost a poet." He was a well-established spoken-word artist and core participant within the open-mic, spoken-word scene. His affinity and talent for writing were validated during his sophomore year of high school. A teacher whom Brother Mike described as "more mentor than teacher" suggested that Brother Mike write for the school newspaper. This validation from his teacher led to his pursuing writing and poetry. During college, Brother Mike sought out a community of poets. At this time, he met established poets such as Sonia Sanchez and the Last Poets as well as emerging cutting-edge performers such as Malik Yusef and J. Ivy. He was also closely mentored by spoken-word artist Reggie Gibson. Brother Mike related his early interactions with Gibson and the importance that Gibson placed on reading particular books and poetry, including playwright and poet Ntozake Shange, writer and music critic Amiri Baraka, poet Pablo Naruda, and Beat poets such as Jack Kerouac, Charles Bukowski, and Hunter S. Thompson. "Every week before [Gibson's] open mic, I would sit down with him, and he would give me a list of books to read. I would watch his sets, and I would watch what he would do. I found my voice after a while." Brother Mike mentioned how he practiced his writing and that the structure was "self-paced." After college, he organized open-mic performances and stayed active in the local hip-hop community, performing with well-known and highly influential musical artists such as Erykah Badu, Common, Talib Kweli, and the Roots. In Chicago, Brother Mike was a founder of the spoken-word group POETREE (People's Organized Entertainment Teaching Righteous Education Everywhere), regularly served as a master of ceremonies, and performed in various spoken-word performances throughout the city.

In addition to performing and organizing open-mic performances, Brother Mike had work experience in the Chicago public-school system. He worked in a school lunchroom to help support his artistic pursuits, and through his organization of spoken-word and poetry workshops for local schools he was eventually offered part-time work in the classroom as a teacher's aide. A nuanced pedagogical approach that combined mentorship with teaching began to form when Brother Mike was working as a teacher assistant alongside a veteran teacher who, as Brother Mike explained, "put the children and the community at the center" of her pedagogy. These experiences had a great impact on his commitment to building transformative learning experiences for youth. At the same time, he recognized the challenges to real transformation in schooling, noting that he "didn't feel like the student was valued as much as the testing of the student."

These experiences in the public schools and the emphasis on testing made Brother Mike at first hesitant to join DYN. Lee continued to press him to visit Renaissance Academy in person, emphasizing the different model of schooling. His skepticism shifted after he observed the school and understood the design principles behind the program as well as the collaboration and support with the University of Chicago's Urban Education Institute. During his first visit, he saw students creating videos and making recordings using professional tools and studio space. These were practices he was very familiar with through his performance work, but up until then he had equated this type of work with adult professionals who had invested significant expenses. As he framed his reaction, "At that point, it was a no brainer—I was like, 'Where do I sign?'"

Upon reflecting on his experiences working as a mentor in the DYN after-school program, Brother Mike noticed similarities between his own mentorship style and the mentorship style of his mentors. He described his mentor pedagogical development as beginning with those early experiences when he was being mentored by his high school teacher and Gibson: "I'm taking those pieces of those mentors that guided me throughout my life." When spoken-word students approach Brother Mike, he, like his own mentor Gibson, asked the students, "What do you read?"

When Brother Mike began working with DYN, he also modeled for students how to be a learner. Although he was confident in spoken word, writing, and performance, he initially struggled with the technology. When confronting the digital aspect of the DYN program, he described himself as "a technophobe" in the sense that he did not have technological expertise as a creator, though he had always been interested in computers. When he was younger, his mother had signed him up for technology camps at Radio Shack, and he had enjoyed playing videogames, but as he grew up, lack of access and funds in combination with a growing interest in poetry and spoken-word pursuits limited the growth of his technology expertise. When he joined DYN, he was using networked tools such as Gmail and MySpace to promote performances and had noticed the increasing prevalence of digital media in his professional community. His lack of digital expertise motivated him to position himself to the students as both a learner and a teacher. He lived a few blocks from the school, and although he initially worked part-time at Renaissance Academy, he came to the space on his own time to sit in on workshops led by other mentors, spending "hours and hours on

FIGURE 3.2
Brother Mike working with DYN students.

[his] own" learning the technology. And, as he put it, "I made it my business to sit there and learn from the kids and studied digital media through those kids. I learned from those students, and they learned from me." Brother Mike was open with his students about his own learning and saw himself as a model for the youth. "I'm always a blueprint to the students."

When developing his role as a teacher, Brother Mike constantly revisited his lesson plans based on observations of students' interactions and work. In the spoken-word pod, for example, he designed his lessons around the reading and writing of text and media related to student interests. His goal was to "plant seeds" and to promote "cross-pod collaborations" where students would take ideas that began in the spoken-word/radio pod and carry them over into the music and video pods. In each class, students would "start off with a journal, watch some media, and do a journal reflection on it." This structure became more intentional when Brother Mike integrated structures introduced in the DYN professional development. For example, goal-based scenarios became part of his repertoire of pedagogical practices, as did group collaborations that connected students and their work with other mentors and DYN pods.

Partnerships and collaborations between Brother Mike and teachers were also commonplace. Renaissance Academy's "signature projects" became a focal point for this collaboration. The partnership around signature projects started with a series of workshops offered by DYN mentors to help Renaissance Academy students and faculty incorporate digital media literacy and technologies into traditional classroom projects already in existence. For example, DYN team members collaborated with the social studies teacher to develop documentaries as a new format for the annual school-wide history project Living Museum (see chapter 4 for more detail). As Brother Mike explained, these workshops allowed DYN to "ease into the school day."

In summer of 2006, the principal at Renaissance Academy took notice of this collaboration and invited DYN into the school day to teach a media arts class. This opportunity pushed Brother Mike and other mentors to begin to develop an artifact-driven, project-based curriculum. The idea first came to Brother Mike during the DYN summer program in 2006. After engaging with DYN youth around many different projects, he noticed that the "star of the summer" was the record label project, which yielded the highest number of student-produced videos. "Just the involvement [of] those students really inspired what would be the media arts class." The year-long, in-school DYN class was called "iRemix Records" and became a project-based simulation of a record label company.

The goal for "iRemix Records," which was taught during sixth grade as an introductory survey course, was to motivate youth to develop critical literacies and to introduce them to digital tools that could lead to deeper participation in out-of-school DYN pods. The challenge for DYN's effort to increase participation and motivation, according to Brother Mike, lay in how to scale up the curriculum for a school classroom and how to extend and expand the learning into a year-long project. During the course's first year, Brother Mike drew on his professional development experiences and began to apply his pedagogical knowledge to the design of the course. Using a project-based approach, he designed various structures for the class that were connected to authentic practices. For example, he assigned roles—such as sound engineer, reporter, and so on—within the record label, and each role carried a level of responsibility, privilege, and practices.

As Brother Mike developed his pedagogical knowledge, he became a key leader and supporter of DYN's professional development vision. He participated in the creation of the ITOA framework. During this retreat, Brother Mike began to shift into a leadership role as he learned facilitator techniques and the Critical Friends methodology. When recounting these experiences, he repeated his belief in a need for structure and accountability systems that ensure engagement and participation as well as the constant improvement of the DYN program. "We have a culture where it's not cool to be like 'I just ain't doing it.'" Brother Mike describes the professional development program as a "support system. . . . I have a theory of action. I have research to back up what happened in the classroom. I have Tene to say, 'Let's be more explicit about this,' which all transfers back to the student who is the center of all this."

RAPHAEL

Being able to want to for your own benefit, to learn or be able to explore media and then eventually be able to utilize it on your own.

—Raphael, 2007

In this quote, Raphael, a DYN mentor who joined DYN in September 2006, described his sense of the opportunities afforded by DYN for youth motivation, engagement, and skill building. Raphael brought a strong foundation in film theory and the visual arts. His formal education included an undergraduate degree in fine arts (photography and cinema studies), and he was working toward a master's degree in film and media arts. This background provided Raphael with experience learning visual art concepts and practices in a formal instructional setting. While working on his master's thesis, Raphael was a teaching assistant, and for five semesters he led an undergraduate film theory course. In the summer before he joined DYN, he taught film and videogame programming to youth from ten to seventeen years old at a technology-focused summer camp. He was acutely aware of the advantages those campers had, noting that "some had been using computers all their lives."

At DYN, Raphael taught a set of pods and media arts classes related to film production. In spite of his extensive background, however, he faced the challenge of having to translate highly academic and abstract concepts and terminology into a language that was accessible to middle school students. As he explained, the students "are learning film theory and visual art theory, but they still needed a product to show. That's part of the reason why I was interested in this program." A major focus in Raphael's teaching was providing students with skills that were technical and conceptual so that when consuming media, the students would know "the fact that whatever [the youth] are watching on television or Internet, that it was intentionally edited for a purpose, and where students are able to say to themselves, 'Man, this was a whole production. This wasn't just someone with a camera telling people to start talking.' So for them to be able to know that and know that, 'OK, I can rearrange this to how I want and it'll tell this story. As long as I can get the same lines to stop here and start here, I'm good.'"

Raphael's experiences as a university teaching assistant and an out-of-school instructor helped him to develop his own distinct pedagogical style. He focused on creating connections, trust, and rapport with students as a way to build pathways for sharing his knowledge. In describing his ability to relate to the youth participating in DYN, he noted, "Sometimes it's about taking the work that I know, the skill sets, and being able to kind of translate it into a way, making it practical for the [kids]." Raphael cited his eldest sister, a tenured university professor, as a primary influence on his style of teaching: "She had the same kind of approach, still trying to maintain those social connections and being honest . . . in [her] teaching."

When Raphael joined DYN, he had not only a developed pedagogical approach, but also a strong understanding of what students needed to learn about film production and editing. As he engaged in DYN's professional development, he began to develop a structured curriculum, identifying key literacies, concepts, and terminologies that were essential for students to learn in digital video production. In the summer of 2007–2008, he participated in several unit-planning sessions and, using this project-based approach, divided the digital video pod into three main stages: preproduction, production, and postproduction. Within each of these three phases of project development, students were exposed to new concepts, roles, and tools.

As Raphael's students learned about digital video production, they experienced a mix of whole-class, small-group, and one-on-one structures, with a primary focus on small groups. When describing his rationale for this approach, Raphael explained, "It's a very collaborative medium, very collaborative if you want to get [the film] done well." It was important to Raphael that students are able to identify their interests and roles within the film production process, and he formed production teams based on these roles. As he described the students' successful collaborative production of a film titled *The Missing*, he explained that the students "had recognized each other's skills and had no problem doing their role because they knew they could do it well."

FIGURE 3.3
Raphael working with DYN student.

Although Raphael emphasized collaboration, he was also very aware of the value of one-on-one instruction. He referenced a video produced by a student named Calvin (described in greater detail in the case portrait after chapter 4) to explain the process: "Calvin and I planned the video out visually. He knew how to do it visually, and he had the whole narrative down. I worked with him on translating that visually and we did [the narrative] in storyboard form. He performed it and that was it for him. . . . At that point it was his." But when it came time to edit Calvin's video, Calvin was not interested in this process, so Raphael identified an older student who enjoyed editing, and the two students collaborated on this phase of film production. As Raphael noted, "I kind of forced [Calvin], like, 'No, you sit with the editor, and you make sure that she's doing things the way you want them to be; otherwise, she can represent your project wrong.'" These types of partnerships across grade level were commonplace in Raphael's digital video pod, where he often positioned older students as junior mentors.

Because the digital video pod was project centered and highly collaborative, Raphael struggled to engage all students consistently and to maintain participation levels throughout all three stages of video production. He discussed how challenging project-based learning can be for students, noting, "It's very difficult to hold an eleven-year-old's attention and to work towards a project that they can't see yet." A turning point for Raphael's digital video pod occurred when students began to display the videos they had produced on the DYN online social networking site, Remix World. Raphael could show students work that was produced by their peers, and "Just the weight of those projects and the attention that they got, I think that kind of solidified a lot of people's attendance with the [digital video] class."

As Raphael prepared for his second year with DYN, one of his major struggles was how to develop instructional practices that could guide and build understanding and skills in individual students and teams, engaging them as they moved across diverse roles and through all three phases of production. The focus for Raphael in his pedagogical development was how to create independent practice and then integrate it into a collaborative framework. To accomplish these goals, he recalled an activity from art school in which students were asked to express individually a concept by following a common set of rules and using the same raw materials.

With this earlier experience in mind, Raphael designed a project in which all students used the same video footage and worked in pairs to execute a "match cut." He created a scoring rubric that was a modified version of the cinematic rubric that the professional development team had created. He described his rationale for using the rubric in his media arts classes. "After the students finished their first editing exercise, I wanted them to separate and know the two components that they had edited [sound and image] and that these are the two components that we were going to judge [using] a scale, one, two, three, four. So if one's the worst, [and] four's the best, what does [a one or a four] sound [and look] like?"

Raphael used this rubric and scale for students to critique the match cuts. The student-edited footage created in the in-school media arts classes were then used as an instructional tool to teach match cutting in the out-of-school spaces. In the following conversation, recorded in field notes in 2008, Raphael was leading the digital video pod in the out-of-school space, and several students, including Calvin, one of the focal cases shared in this book, were viewing a student-produced video.

> RAPHAEL: We need to figure out which angle.
>
> [Raphael shows the three different angles in the video by playing back each scene.]
>
> CALVIN: Both angles, because you'll see both expressions on the face close up then go to middle shot. . . . Cut right there, then find the one closer to her face Apple t [with a Macintosh computer, students use two function keys to cut and paste], then the middle shot, Apple t, then bam!
>
> [Raphael plays the footage again.]
>
> RAPHAEL: Let's see this from the beginning.
>
> STUDENT: Yeah, that's good.
>
> RAPHAEL: At what moment are they doing the same thing?
>
> ANOTHER STUDENT: Right there! [When the actor says,] "You're not worth a penny to me."
>
> RAPHAEL: Everything we just did is matched cutting.

Rather than simply telling the youth the meaning of a concept, Raphael used questions and student responses to guide understandings. The concept of "matched cutting" was contextualized through the use of mentor–youth interactions around the artifact. Raphael intentionally designed this classroom interaction after thinking in professional development about how certain activities would integrate terminology into classroom dialogue as a way to build digital literacies. "Am I using terminologies consistently, or am I—in my dialog with them—just giving it? Is there a dialog with this terminology among the students? . . . And then in terms of the students, listening to their language."

ASIA

> We are all accountable. . . . If I'm lacking in some sort of digital skill, then somebody needs to come in and help so that we can all have the best functioning group. [Working for DYN] is not an individual thing.
>
> —Asia, 2007

When Asia began working with DYN in March 2007, her artistic background was expansive. Working as a performance artist in television and improvisation theater and as a musician and a singer, she brought extensive knowledge to DYN. While completing a degree in film, she also worked as a film instructor in an out-of-school program for youth from a local housing project. There, she taught a group of young women who, in spite of any interest they may have had in the subject matter, were constantly pulled by other responsibilities at home. As such, attendance was a sacrifice for many of them, and participation was inconsistent. Asia found that she struggled to connect with her students: "The goal was to get them to come every week, just doing [work], just to finish."

It was while Asia worked as a film instructor that she began to develop what would become her vision for the DYN pod titled "digital queendom." She focused on developing social emotional awareness, on creating a healthy language of communication with the young women, and on the use of digital tools as a way to express one's voice creatively. As Asia explained, "[It was] a lot of getting out all the things that [the young women] really didn't have a voice for. How do you channel what you're feeling instead of having verbal confrontations?"

Asia identified herself as a learner who welcomed support from her peers and students. "Before [the professional development sessions], it was like, 'Yeah, I know I'm working with computers, but I don't even know anything about computers.' And they gave me these girls, and I like it, and I want to do better, but I don't know how. I don't know what I'm supposed to be doing." Although Asia possessed strong skills and confidence in film, writing, and critical media theory, she also acknowledged her desire to develop her technical fluency with digital tools and to develop her knowledge within the pods. Brother Mike and other mentors assisted Asia in cultivating her technical expertise through the creation of podcasts and the editing of video using iMovie software.

Asia cotaught a media arts class with Raphael. This partnership was influential in developing her pedagogical style. She explained that when she was teaching the digital video pod, she worked with one group of students on a script, while Raphael had a separate group of students working on a different script. Raphael chose to have his students create their storyboard collaboratively as group, whereas Asia assigned different students to develop different parts of their story. She learned from this process as she saw the outcomes of each approach: "I saw the difference. The way I did it, it was all over the place." Asia equated this outcome with her instructional decision: "Don't break up the group; when you break up the group, you break up the concentration."

During the 2007–2008 year, Asia began to use an inquiry-based approach in her classroom and pod. She included goal-based scenarios and questioning strategies as a way to structure the interactions in her classroom and pod. The following example of Asia's teaching style, recorded in field notes taken from observations of the digital queendom pod in 2008, illustrates her evolving approach to effective practice in her classroom: "Ladies, we are working on a four-week goal. I need a video blog and slogan product and a commercial so that in four weeks you will have [three] products. By the end of the day, you all should have learned these practices. [She is reading from her lesson plan.] I asked you, 'What do you assume about the power of words?' So what we are going to do is look at these slogans." In this interaction, Asia stated the goals and the guiding question, both of which were designed to motivate the production of

FIGURE 3.4
Asia working with DYN student.

digital artifacts. In the research team's interview of her, Asia pointed to the concepts and materials introduced in the whole-group professional development sessions as influencing her pedagogical approach. She explained, "The whole art of inquiry . . . may actually take a life unto itself, and students are doing it on their own. [W]orking with that has given me a tool into how you produce [student-created media artifacts]. [The professional development] also helps in helping you focus in on what it is you want to come out of a class." Asia also incorporated professional development proto- cols and activities by organizing students into dyad structures within her pods, noting, "I usually do dyads. We do that in almost every single [professional development meeting]. I usually put it in the guided practice."

As Asia was developing as a teacher, she was also becoming a leader within the program. In the summer of 2007, Gray, Brother Mike, and Asia attended facilitator trainings, which prepared Asia to take on a leadership role in DYN professional devel- opment. In November 2008, she became the facilitator of the MLG space. She met with Gray to design the agenda and plan the activity structures. Asia treated the MLG space as an opportunity for professional development, appropriating many of the same structures, practices, and norms from the whole-group meetings. "Whatever we did in [professional development] before, we come back [in the MLG] and we support it. . . . We did a protocol, and what I wanted out of that was for mentors to actually take a step back and reflect on what it is that we're doing. Is it working? And how do we know that it is working?"

CHALLENGES AND TENSIONS

Coats of Many Colors

Brother Mike, Raphael, and Asia appreciated the DYN professional development model, yet even these mentors acknowledged that developing a reflective and critical community of learners is challenging, especially when those learners come from many different disciplinary and experiential backgrounds. DYN mentors were also charged with the task of negotiating and adapting to new roles, responsibilities, and participation in activities that for some of them were unfamiliar. Participation in DYN's professional development required mentors to learn new knowledge and skills related to digital media and general pedagogy, to produce artifacts that reflected that learning, and to engage in critical dialogue about those artifacts. This participation also required mentors to produce lesson plans, reflections, and rubrics, which were all indicators of their evolving practice as teachers. However, this negotiation process was challenging for several mentors who had little to no prior experience working as a teacher within formal school environments. Creating weekly artifacts (e.g., reflec- tions and lesson plans) and developing routinized instructional practices and rubrics were especially difficult for these mentors. The initial unfamiliarity with these formal practices consequently limited their access to and participation in the professional development.

Learning How to Listen

In addition, DYN mentors had to be open and willing to learn and participate in critical dialogue and practices where activities and thinking would be problematized and challenged. Critical and reflective practices are challenging for teachers, and so they were for the DYN mentors (Cochran-Smith 2002). Openly receiving critical feedback from peers in the professional development meetings was particularly challenging for some mentors. However, some mentors indicated that critiquing student work as evidence of effective instruction was more agreeable than critiquing personal practice and beliefs about learning and instruction.

Common Language, Common Tools

Another challenge for the DYN professional development team was identifying and assessing student understandings across the disciplines and integrating assessment methods into classroom practice. Building assessment tools at the programmatic level was particularly challenging as mentors and the facilitator struggled to find a common language and practice that spanned the disciplines. For example, when developing rubrics in the whole-group professional development space, the music mentors described evidence of student understanding as nonverbal, embodied performances using instruments and gestures (e.g., head nodding to the beat). This method of assessing understanding was different from assessment in spoken-word courses, which relied on verbal and gestural modes of communication.

These varied disciplinary practices created another major tension around developing assessments and how these assessments would function within the program. Rubrics had at least two functions. One function was to establish a programmatic standard of practice across the after-school, in-school, and online spaces. A second function of assessment was to measure student learning in the specific disciplines. The tension between standardizing and customizing the rubrics was also intensified by the need to recognize artistic thinking within the disciplines. As one mentor, Hondo Lawrence, explained in a professional development meeting, "It just got me thinking about, you know, everything about rubrics. One thing about art, we think about not constraining the creative mind."

SUMMARY

For DYN mentors, students were at the center of the work. As student and school interest increased, so too did the DYN program. The introduction of DYN into the formal school day meant that mentors needed to acquire new skills and pedagogical knowledge. The skilled DYN mentor needed to be a K–12 teacher as well as an out-of-school mentor and artist. In other words, to develop twenty-first-century learners, the mentors needed to develop into twenty-first-century teachers.

It seems fair to say that the mentor professional development program served as a catalyst and a mirror for DYN's development. Mentors were catalyzed to adopt and adapt new knowledge and skills. As an organization, DYN was catalyzed to create organizational structures and resources to leverage mentor expertise, while developing in the mentors the skills that were unique to DYN's needs. Mentors' development, challenges, and successes served as a mirror for self-reflection and as a window into understanding and collaborating with their peers, the professional development facilitator, and the organizational leadership. This "mirroring" allowed those involved to take the reflective turn, iteratively refining the professional development approach and building opportunities for learning.

Developing skilled mentors required the creation of a professional development model that positioned them both as experts with technical fluency, digital media portfolios, and cultural capital and as students learning to adopt and implement pedagogical knowledge. As DYN leadership sought a balance between leveraging expertise and cultivating a community of learners, the professional development program evolved through a process of constant reflection on student work and mentor development. DYN mentors had to be willing to engage in this reflective process in order to identify challenges and areas where they needed support. They were able to learn and employ the most effective pedagogical practices when they engaged in all aspects of DYN professional development, drawing from their past experiences to articulate and plan for where they wanted and needed to go next.

The development of mentors' pedagogical knowledge affected the interactions between them and their students. Unlike earlier models of mentorship in digital media, DYN aimed to be more intentional about the relationship between mentors and students. The impact of this model on student learning and development will be explored in the next three chapters. In chapter 4, we will see how mentors intentionally "seeded" projects to encourage student identities as digital media citizens across multiple social spaces inside and outside the DYN. Before that chapter, however, we present our first case narrative, which introduces the nine focal case learners whom you will hear more about in subsequent chapters.

INTRODUCING THE NINE FOCAL CASE LEARNERS

As discussed in chapter 2, we spent a great deal of time with the students at Renaissance Academy over three years and across in-school and after-school time, with a particular focus on nine case learners. These nine students varied on key demographics: gender, socioeconomic status (based on school lunch status), home access to a computer, and experience with technology prior to sixth grade. We interviewed the nine focal cases five times during their three years of middle school, collected their digital media work, observed them in pods, and documented how they engaged with technologies across settings where they spent their time. To see a broader picture of their lives, we also interviewed DYN mentors about each of the students and, where possible, interviewed their parents. You will hear more about these students in the following chapters through their stories, their projects, and their words. Complete technobiographies that trace learning in more detail over time and settings are shared for four of the nine case study students (Calvin, Maurice, Ruby, and Michael) as case narratives B, C, D, and E between chapters. This first narrative provides summaries of all nine learners, including their pre-DYN experience, access to tools at home, and time in DYN during middle school, focusing on their interests, projects, and future goals. Pod participation is indicated by graphic icons (see the key in figure A.1).

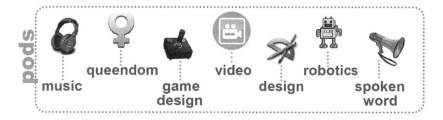

FIGURE A.1
Key to pod graphic icons.

CALVIN GAME DESIGNER, PROGRAMMER

And what really inspires me to make video-games is just videogames in general, like . . . you see all these different videogames, and one day you always wanted to make one.

—Calvin (sixth grade), 2007

6th:	✓	✓		
7th:	✓	✓	✓	
8th:	✓	✓	✓	✓

Described by his teachers as a lovable person, a hard worker, and sometimes a challenged learner, Calvin was an energetic kid ready to come up with many ideas at once. He lived with his parents, two younger brothers, one younger sister, and a female cousin two years older than himself. The family shared one computer with no Internet access and had a game console. Though Calvin reported that both parents had some computer skills, they often asked him or his cousin, Misha, for help using Microsoft Word, doing Internet searches, or troubleshooting basic technology issues. Calvin entered sixth grade with basic Internet research and word-processing skills as well as an interest in videogames. He enjoyed playing games on his game console, his home computer, and online. He was thrilled to receive his school-issued laptop in sixth grade and quickly signed up to participate in the game design pod.

During middle school, Calvin translated his interest in computer games into an avid pursuit of making games. In addition, in the robotics and digital video pods he took on programming roles, script writing, and directing. The interest-driven focus and absence of deadlines or formal assessments in the pods fit with Calvin's working style of applying deep interests to long-term projects. He was frequently found remixing existing games on his own time. His enthusiasm and dedication to his work earned him a reputation in the DYN community as an expert with game-making tools and processes.

At graduation, Calvin was headed to a technology charter high school and excited about a possible future in game design and engineering.

As long as it's interesting, [Calvin] will do it faster than everybody. He will get on it. So his thing for him, it's just being engaged. If he's engaged . . . he don't stop until he's done.

—Hondo (mentor), 2008

EVAN MUSICIAN, DESIGNER, WRITER

BRINGING BLUES AND JAZZ TO BRONZEVILLE
PLAY

I'm a musician, so I wanted to know where the music I made came from, so the audience I was targeting were also other musicians and producers and other people in that area.

—Evan (seventh grade), 2008

6th:	✓		✓ ✓
7th:	✓		✓
8th:	✓		✓

Evan was an only child and lived with his parents. A passionate musician, skater, and designer, he described himself as funny and "weird" in a good way. He came to DYN with a strong interest in technology and reported regularly using the computer and the Internet at home. By the beginning of his sixth-grade year, the family had at least three computers, Internet access, a printer, a digital camera, a game console, and a digital music player.

In middle school, Evan was an active and consistent participant in the digital music pod. He also participated in the design and robotics pods. By the end of eighth grade, he had created projects across a range of media genres, his main areas of focus being digital music, digital video, and graphic design.

Evan, I think, is a little more humble; he will sit there and just work and see how far he can go with his design.

—Hondo (mentor), 2008

Evan had a strong desire to solicit and offer feedback on media projects and ideas within the DYN community. Family members and friends provided important support. Evan was part of a number of productions with friends he had had since elementary school based on their collective interests, including the formation of a rap group and a video production company that they started to film each other skating. In seventh grade, his mother helped him to develop his history fair video documentary by setting up interviews with relevant contacts in the community and signed him up for a screenwriting class after his project did well.

When asked in the eighth grade about what he considered the ideal job, Evan described a possible future that spanned business, engineering, design, art, and music production. He was accepted into a top-tier magnet high school with a focus on academics and college preparation and was planning to attend in the fall.

KILEY POET, PRODUCER, CRITIC

> *I had the attitude where I thought that everything I did was right. . . . I [now] feel like there are people in the world who know way more than me and they can help me a lot.*
>
> —Kiley (eighth grade), 2009

	🎧	♀	👊	📹	✈	🤖	📢
6th:	✓	✓		✓	✓		✓
7th:		✓	✓	✓			
8th:	✓	✓	✓	✓	✓		

Kiley lived with her parents, grandmother, a younger brother, and an older sister. Prior to middle school, the two sisters shared one desktop computer at home, and their parents used a separate one. There was also a printer, a digital camera, game devices, and a digital music player in their home. Kiley developed an interest in media production in the fifth grade when her older sister, Simone, began DYN and showed Kiley programs and projects on her school-issued laptop. When Kiley entered sixth grade, she joined Simone in the DYN pods.

During middle school, Kiley, a popular student, developed a reputation as an outspoken and assertive young woman with the potential to be a leader.

> *There is a culture in [Kiley's] house where women are seen as strong. They're expressive, and that's something that's expected. For [Kiley], the idea of respect is really strong.*
>
> —Brother Mike (mentor), 2007

Her portfolio of work focused on digital music and digital video. Her willingness to take on serious topics was apparent in her projects. In sixth grade, she was a leader in the production of a song that challenged disrespectful images of women in mainstream rap culture. She created a podcast about the Holocaust for a history class and a documentary video about abortion for a local competition.

Kiley cited Asia, the mentor of the digital queendom pod, as a role model who was particularly important to her digital media work and development.

In eighth grade, Kiley followed in Simone's footsteps and shared her technical skills with her younger brother, who would attend Renaissance Academy the following year.

Kiley valued her digital skills but did not think technology was all that important. She planned to be a pediatrician and was set to attend a selective-enrollment high school with a focus on academic achievement and college preparation.

MAURICE ACTIVIST, CREATOR, ORATOR

> *With everything I do, I make things with the intention that other people will see it or hear it or read it . . . it's disappointing when I don't get to share it. If it's particularly good, I'll share it with anyone I can find.*
>
> —Maurice (eighth grade), 2009

	🎧	♀	📷	🎬	✂	🤖	📣
6th:	✓		✓				✓
7th:			✓				✓
8th:	✓		✓				

Maurice liked to play baseball, basketball, and soccer; watch TV; listen to music; dance; and read. He lived with his mother, father, and sister, who is nine years younger. They had at least three computers at home as well as a printer, a scanner, a digital camera, a video camera, and a game console. In sixth grade, Maurice joined DYN with little experience using technology beyond basic Internet surfing, educational games, and clip art. At that time, he described a computer as a "TV that could do a lot of things." Maurice's parents were very involved in his learning in and out of school.

During middle school, Maurice quickly gravitated toward verbally expressive pods and projects. A self-defined inventor, artist, and activist, he was perceived by peers, mentors, and

> *I think, for Maurice, he understands whether [his peers] see him as a leader or not, he's a leader; and he has a responsibility because of that knowledge.*
>
> —Brother Mike (mentor), 2007

teachers as an inspirational member of the DYN community. Maurice's work was often controversial and message driven and illustrated his attempts to situate himself within this social context. For instance, he created documentaries that explored current events and topics such as African Americans in history. He created numerous beats, movies, and websites and was also known for his quirky humor and thoughtful media work. Maurice capitalized on opportunities to share his work and was an active participant on Remix World and in after-school forums. Mentors spoke of him as an advanced and independent learner and highlighted him as an exemplar of the program. By eighth grade, Maurice wanted to become a politician or CEO of a large media distributor to have "true social impact." Upon graduation from Renaissance Academy, he was set to attend a private college preparatory high school with a focus on community and citizenship.

MICHAEL VIDEO EDITOR

I have grown to love the media editing part. So I guess I'm ready to do that. So every time we have to do it, I'm ready, and I'm ecstatic about doing it.

—Michael (eighth grade), 2009

6th:	✓
7th:	
8th:	

Michael had a clear vision of his future career as a pilot before starting middle school. He lived with his parents, an older brother, and a sister, and when he started sixth grade, the family had two computers at home and multiple peripheral devices. Michael reported that he had been using computers since the first grade to play educational games, and his mother reported that he often enjoyed figuring things out and tinkering with computers for the fun of it.

His older brother participated in DYN, and, as a result, Michael and his sister were invited to attend a DYN program at Renaissance Academy the summer before sixth grade. He entered this program with basic knowledge of word processing and the Internet, but

Instead of being the sidekick with the editors now, [Michael] was kind of leading the video team and doing a lot of the editing.

—Brother Mike (mentor), 2007

had not yet created digital media. Despite the early introduction to DYN, Michael participated fully in only one pod in his three years with DYN. His interest in aviation and computer tinkering did not lead to a connection with the DYN program. He did, however, develop media skills during middle school through school projects and community opportunities brokered by his parents. His mother arranged for him to redesign their church's website. During school time and through access to mentors, Michael became knowledgeable about digital video and served as the video editor on a number of school assignments. Through middle school, he was a consistently good student, and his grades were very important to him.

At graduation from Renaissance Academy, his primary ambition was still to be an airline pilot, but he also considered digital video production as a possible career choice. He planned to attend a private college-preparatory high school with a strong academic focus.

MONICA MANAGER, GAME DESIGNER, WRITER

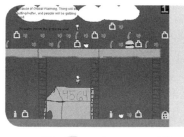

> *I'm not very good at just grabbing things and putting it together. So I usually just have to do an outline first and then start, like, getting examples from other games or other pictures . . . and putting it together.*
>
> —Monica (eighth grade), 2009

6th:	✓	✓
7th:	✓	✓
8th:	✓	

Monica lived with her parents and two brothers. Her parents made sure the children had computers available from an early age. The family had two computers at home when Monica began sixth grade and access to a printer, a digital camera, a video camera, a game console, and a digital music player. Ever since Monica first started playing pinball on her father's laptop computer at age five, she had loved videogames.

She showed interest in digital media, but it was not her exclusive interest, nor did she emphasize it over other pursuits such as reading, writing, playing tennis, and doing community service.

In middle school, she participated in pods and other after-school activities, including basketball and community service. She was meticulous about her work and held very high standards for quality in everything she did. The adults around Monica described her as a leader— helpful, responsible, and very collaborative. She often took on the role of project manager, motivating and supporting her partners.

I think [Monica is] very goal oriented. I mean, she wants to build a portfolio. She wants to build a portfolio of different things of hot quality, though. I think she has pride in that.

—Hondo (mentor), 2007

After winning an award for a videogame she made for a class assignment in sixth grade, Monica was recruited into the game design pod. Through DYN, she created media projects ranging from podcasts to website design, graphics, and digital video. Her mother was very engaged and influential in Monica's learning and arranged for her to design a cover of a CD that her church was selling and for her participation in volunteer work.

At graduation from Renaissance, Monica did not know what career she wanted to have but hoped it would be something she was interested in. She planned to attend a private college-preparatory high school with a focus on math, science, and world languages.

RUBY WRITER, ACTRESS, DESIGNER

> *I feel like I kind of hold myself back sometimes. So I won't do that anymore. . . . I don't want to be afraid to be seen. I want people to see what I can do.*
>
> —Ruby (eighth grade), 2009

6th:	✓						
7th:							
8th:							✓

Ruby remembered first using a computer when she played games as an eight-year-old. In fourth grade, she was part of a group that gave tech support to classrooms at school, and she began using the computer to do research. When she began sixth grade, her family—including herself, her parents, and a younger brother—had one computer at home, but no other equipment. Ruby's grandmother, however, had three computers, and her husband taught Ruby various computer and Internet skills.

Ruby began sixth grade with some technology experience and an avid interest in writing and reading. Ruby's mother, a journalist and poet, was instrumental to Ruby's development as a writer. Throughout middle school, Ruby was diligent with her schoolwork and

Last year [Ruby] wrote a book . . . so she presented this book toward the end of the year. And I was floored by the stories she tells and even some of the poems she wrote.

—Brother Mike (mentor), 2008

with her personal writing, and she deliberately sought opportunities with DYN. Though she could not attend many after-school pods because of difficulties finding a ride home and conflicts with other after-school activities, she appreciated DYN as a venue for learning new skills. In classes and on her own time, Ruby produced an impressive body of creative work, including a self-initiated novel, a book of poetry, and articles and layouts for a youth magazine at her local YMCA. Ruby also produced an award-winning video documentary on African American youth identity and performed her poetry in community venues.

Ruby developed from a self-identified "shy" sixth grader reluctant to share her writing to a confident, aspiring actress who was class valedictorian. At the end of eighth grade, her ideal future was to become an actress, writer, and artist. She planned to attend a private college-preparatory high school with a focus on math, science, and world languages.

RENEE DESIGNER, VIDEOGRAPHER, PRODUCER

I can be very creative. My work can be unique, and when I turn in my work, it's not crappy. It's something that, like, I want everyone else to see.

—Renee (eighth grade), 2009

6th:	✓	✓	✓	✓			
7th:		✓			✓		
8th:	✓	✓			✓		✓

Renee was involved in dance, cheerleading, track, and writing. She was an only child with an extended family close by, her grandparents and cousins being especially present in her life. Renee began middle school without much computer experience beyond basic word processing. She first used a computer at school when she was seven to play simple videogames and read books. She later learned to type in school and began to use computers for Internet research and to write school reports. Her grandmother taught her how to play card games on the computer when she was younger, and her grandfather gave her family a refurbished machine from his office. They kept this computer in Renee's room, where her parents also made use of it. At the beginning of sixth grade,

Some kids will just turn in whatever. But [Renee] . . . when she did a podcast about herself, she didn't have any of the choppy edits. Everything was all clear. It was all connected.

—Asia (mentor), 2008

Renee reported at least three computers at home as well as a printer, a game console, and a digital music player.

During middle school, Renee was a frequent and consistent pod participant across all three years. However, she did not seek out the spotlight; DYN mentors described her as "mellow" and "soft-spoken," but also "articulate," "not a pushover," and "definitely talented."

In sixth grade, although Renee had independently produced a ten-minute movie about her cousins and created a multipage website about her work, mentors were not aware of her growing design interests and talents. Renee kept this early digital production work to herself, but she slowly made it more visible. By the end of her eighth-grade year, her identification as a designer had evolved, and her work was recognized through her frequent participation on Remix World.

At graduation from Renaissance Academy, Renee hoped to become a pediatric surgeon and planned to attend a selective-enrollment, college-preparatory high school.

ZACH BEAT MAKER, DESIGNER, ENTREPRENEUR

> *I mostly get my ideas from the world, just life, experiences. Go to school, somebody talks about something, I think that'll be funny, make a movie about that.*
>
> —Zach (eighth grade), 2009

6th: ✓			✓	✓	✓	✓
7th: ✓				✓	✓	
8th: ✓						

Described as high spirited and ambitious, Zach was very interested in basketball, skateboarding, and music and spent a great deal of time outdoors. He began using computers at age four to play games. Second grade was the first time Zach remembered using a computer in school, mostly to type essays, search the Internet, and do other written work. At the same time, his godbrother introduced him to online computer games. Zach's parents were divorced, and he lived primarily with his father but stayed at his mother's house as well. His three older siblings were out of the house by the time Zach was in middle school. Each house had a computer, and in the two homes collectively Zach also had access to a printer, a scanner, a handheld game player, and a digital music player. Zach's family had a strong influence on his learning and interests. His mother, brother, and sister-in-law, a designer, were especially influential.

In sixth grade, Zach joined a number of pods and first began digital media projects such as programming in the robotics pod and producing music using Garage-Band and ProTools. He was eager to learn new skills and not too shy to ask for special attention and guidance, forming close relationships with several of the DYN mentors.

Zach was a leading member of LTD Entertainment and the Hurricanes, friendship-based rap and film production groups that began during his sixth grade year. By eighth grade, Zach was more often creating projects by himself and with friends than in pods, using available DYN resources such as space, mentors, and equipment.

As Zach headed to high school with Evan at a selective-enrollment magnet school, he was interested in becoming an engineer or a commercial designer.

> *[Zach] is well versed in a lot of different areas. . . . [H]e is kind of a budding Renaissance artist, but he just—he has to at some point make up in his mind that he wants to be great.*
>
> —Hondo (mentor), 2008

STEPPING INTO PRODUCTION: SEEDING CREATIVE PROJECT WORK

Maryanna Rogers, Brigid Barron, Caitlin K. Martin, Amber Levinson, and Jolie Matthews

It's an afternoon in the early spring. Brother Mike and six DYN middle school students are huddled around a small video camera, watching a spoken-word piece performed by pod member Matthew that was filmed moments ago. Brother Mike takes a moment to explain the importance of voice projection and models the benefit of speaking from the diaphragm. Later, at the classroom board, he reviews assignments for the upcoming week. Included are instructions to review the work of some of the major authors represented in the Black arts movement, such as Ntozake Shange, the Lost Poets, Oscar Brown Jr., and Sonia Chavez. This is the spoken-word pod, and students are preparing for an upcoming open-mic night.

—Spoken-word pod researcher observation, 2007

The DYN program integrated a variety of social practices and structures to seed creative projects intentionally. We use the term *seeding* as a metaphor to express the strategic way that the mentors created conditions that encouraged students to take on roles as creative producers. The vignette in the chapter epigraph provides a brief glimpse of the compelling mix of teaching, mentoring, and collaboration characteristic of project work in the DYN after-school pods. Students in Brother Mike's spoken-word pod were preparing for an upcoming open-mic night themed "A Tribute to Our Fallen Heroes." Students nominated a broad range of possible honorees, whom Brother Mike listed on the board, including Rosa Parks, Malcolm X, Frederick Douglass, Betty Shabazz, and Sammy Davis Jr. (see figure 4.1). Integral to the spoken-word pod was the development of students' interest-driven projects, which allowed them to tailor their work to topics of personal interest. In addition, by establishing a link to prominent poets and activists from the past, students had an opportunity to learn about African American history and culture and to make a connection between their own work and work that had come before. A photograph of the session reveals the

FIGURE 4.1
Brainstorming on the white board and students and mentor watching a spoken-word performance, 2006.

close coordination of mentor and students as they sat side by side, watching and jointly critiquing Matthew's performance (see figure 4.1). The technology, the mentor, and the peer interactions at their disposal allowed for rehearsal, immediate feedback, and revision. Across time, the spoken-word pod mentor and the participants alternated between guiding, following, and collaborating as they learned together.

Workspaces and tools that enabled students to build what they envisioned were critical resources. As noted in previous chapters, DYN students had access to professional equipment and software, musical instruments, printers, cameras, and personal laptops as well as to a recording studio and school classroom space, where they could collaborate, work, and perform. However, DYN's program aimed to support students far beyond providing access to tools and spaces. In this chapter, we identify three broad approaches that seeded creative work: *project-based assignments*, *contests*, and *models* of production that connected youth to authentic communities of practice (see box 4.1). Through rich examples of observations across the pods, media arts classes, and within the virtual space of Remix World, we illustrate how these approaches, situated within the DYN program, supported student work and prepared students to adopt *constructive dispositions*. We also introduce the reader to the challenges and concerns that arose as the program aimed to reach these goals during the period we observed DYN at Renaissance Academy.

BOX 4.1
Approaches to Seeding Creative Production

• Project-based assignments
• Contests and competition
• Models and connections to broader communities

PROJECT-BASED ASSIGNMENTS

At DYN, project-based assignments seeded creative production by tapping into students' interests and providing a context to develop meaningful goals. A project-based approach is not new to educational settings, but in practice it does not always succeed in creating an effective learning experience. In this section, we discuss the value of project-based assignments and elaborate on examples from the DYN community at Renaissance from 2006 to 2008, where such assignments became an important way to seed creative production.

As we discussed in the introduction, the evolving workforce and the need for twenty-first-century skills have changed what it means to provide every child with an effective education that prepares them for a full and productive life. It is no longer enough to transmit information with the expectation that students will memorize and store it for future use. Education today must focus on helping students *learn how to learn* so that they can manage the demands of ever-changing information, technologies, jobs, and social conditions. To develop these higher-order skills, students need to take part in complex, meaningful projects that require sustained engagement, collaboration, research, management of resources, and the development of an ambitious performance or product. A growing body of research suggests that students learn more deeply and perform better on complex tasks if they have the opportunity to engage in more authentic learning—projects and activities that require them to employ subject knowledge to solve real-world problems (Barron and Darling-Hammond 2008). Project-based learning involves completing complex tasks that typically result in a real-world product, event, or presentation to an audience.

As discussed in chapter 1, one approach to linking classroom learning to students' individual skills and interests is the use of goal-based scenarios. Focal skills are embedded into a set of tasks or activities around a goal that the learner is likely to find interesting or motivating. The aim of the goal-based scenario approach is to support the Deweyian idea of learning by doing. It is based on the insight that goals are at the heart of human learning and assumes that learners come with interests and that connecting to these interests is critical. In practice, goal-based scenarios often take the form of multimedia learning environments in which students undertake authentic roles. For example, Roger Schank (1994) designed the Broadcast News multimedia environment in which students managed a virtual newscast, developed story lines by accessing and organizing a large resource database, and delivered the news as professionals. Students learned historical facts by organizing and representing available data. (See chapter 1 for more detail about how DYN purposefully used Schank's model of goal-based scenarios). Project-based assignments that incorporate design have several features that make them ideal for developing technical and subject-matter knowledge (Newstetter 2000). For example, design projects support revisions and iterative refinement as students create, assess, and redesign their work. The complexity of the work often dictates the need for collaboration and the appropriation of specific roles for different students, providing them with the opportunity to become experts in a particular area. The DYN model considers experience with complex and meaningful projects the basis for developing *constructive dispositions*, wherein students take an exploratory and iterative approach to their work, engage facilely with tools and media, and see themselves as creators (see chapter 1).

DYN pod activities at Renaissance during the observation period offered opportunities to deepen expertise through a variety of long-term project-based assignments that involved design and original production. In the game design and robotics pods, design projects supported the development of conceptual understanding of programming or engineering concepts. In the spoken-word pod, as illustrated in the vignette at the beginning of this chapter, and also in the radio, digital queendom, and digital music pods, project assignments made links to both popular culture and the historical roots of these art forms. Most DYN project assignments were open enough to link to idiosyncratic student interests and inspired meaningful goals. In the following example, what began as an in-class exercise turned into a longer, self-initiated recording project for a group of girls.

Example from the Field: "Jappin"

In the 2007 sixth-grade in-school media arts class, mentors Brother Mike and Simeon Viltz screened *Merchants of Cool*, a PBS documentary about mainstream media corporations' influence on the stereotyping of young women and men. A heated discussion ensued. According to Brother Mike's written reflection on the class,

> This raised many questions from the ladies especially when the video began to focus on "the Midriff," a marketer's idea of what/who a teenage girl is. Our ladies saw little reflection in "the Midriff" character. Some of the boys in the group made comments during the video and our discussion that made me question how much we actually respect our ladies. I prompted the class with a journal entry, "Respect Our Ladies." We did a share-out shortly after the journal time was finished. I must admit I was looking for the boys' reaction to the piece, and we received some powerful work from many of the boys (even the ones who were throwing disrespect). However, the ladies (who would become the Female Stunnaz) were clearly moving everyone with their words.

The following week Brother Mike instructed the students to transform their journal entries about the documentary and the "Respect Our Ladies" discussion into poems. Kiley, one of the sixth-grade girls who had been vocal in the conversation, wrote a powerful poem. Her classmate Keira was then inspired to write a rap based on the poem. The two girls joined forces with other classmates to form a group they called "The Female Stunnaz." Brother Mike remembered the girls' impassioned reactions to the topic: "The Female Stunnaz . . . [weren't] having it. Like, 'No, we want to be respected. . . .We don't want to balance the images, we want that image erased.' You know, it's like, there's no place for it. And I had never seen, you know, girls run up to the studio or beg to go to the studio. They was ready, like, 'Yo!' You know? And it was really . . . I thought it was ironic 'cause I didn't really know them as being friends, but they all ran up to the studio together."

The girls recorded the song, which they described as "a female uprising," and as one Female Stunna declared, "It's for some men—boys—to let them know that women can become better things." They called the song "Jappin," a term the girls defined as "like you go off on somebody" or "talk back." (See box 4.1 for partial lyrics.) The *Urban Dictionary* similarly defines the term *jappin* as "when another person snaps (or yells) at another" or "getting upset over something that might only be upsetting to you" (2013). A school-day teacher, Darrel Johnson, saw the girls' song in the context of the hip-hop movement: "I love the fact the ladies spoke up because one of the ongoing things in even the professional hip-hop community is the lack of female voices. So I'm glad, you know, that the girls at school are like, 'Oh really? Let me tell you. . . .' You know?" This teacher also noted the additional layer of importance in this work, helping to recognize, cultivate, and maintain female interest and after-school involvement. "Our ladies do seem to be involved, but I will not undercut the importance of them staying involved. . . . I think parents are quicker to pull a young lady from this sort of [program]—'But this is distracting you from something else'—than they might be their sons. Now, I'm not saying that's always the case, but I think it's safe to say that we . . . we still hold gender issues that we don't even see as gender issues."

A closer look at the case of "Jappin" illustrates how some of the structures at DYN seeded this creative production. More precisely, students were invited to take on roles as authors and critics in a process that can be broken down into three distinct yet ultimately connected projects. First, mentors invited students to reflect creatively and exchange ideas by prompting them to respond to a documentary about marketing, the use of stereotyping, and teen culture. It is worth noting that this part of the creative process is a key element of the artistic communities to which the mentors belong. Both Brother Mike and Simeon are rappers and spoken-word poets—practitioners of an art form that carries a tradition of questioning and reversing structures of oppression and discrimination (Smitherman 1997). These artists create by building off of the works of others and adding something new of their own.

Second, in the session that gave rise to "Jappin" and the Female Stunnaz group, Brother Mike fashioned the lesson around the idea of responsibility. In his words, "I think we're very keen about . . . kind of making that link between who's accountable and who is responsible and not to mimic that ourselves." The class had been viewing and discussing widely accepted, negative media stereotypes, encouraging students to be critical consumers of the media to which they are exposed. Although the boys initially declined to question the images they were used to seeing, the girls in the class quickly adopted a position of protest. The girls then went beyond Brother Mike's original goals and responded via the song.

And third, when Kiley wrote her poem, it sparked the energy of her classmates, who crafted "Jappin" and requested the studio space to record it. Through the process of producing the piece, the mentors were present as guides. In a sixth grade interview, Kiley recalled, "That was the first piece [of the song], so [Brother Mike's] like, 'Wow, that's really cool.' So we tried it, and the first part was really shaky; it didn't go through so well. But then the last part, it went through very good, and we started to get very, very popular because everybody wanted to be in the group. They wanted to be co-producers and managers."

Once "Jappin" was produced, its message took on a life of its own in the school community and became "quite the buzz," according to Brother Mike. Via the video

---

BOX 4.2
Partial Lyrics to "Jappin"

You should respect our ladies. . . .
Because they respect YOU!!!
You should respect our women,
Because we put up with you
If there weren't any women . . . HUH?
WHAT WOULD YOU DO?
Everybody think because we be women
That we can't do this . . . can't do that
But I think its about that time
we show 'em
Who we represent
So you betta back off
because we running this.
So you betta back off
because we in the game.
So you betta back off
because we spinning things.
I might be a girl
I might be cute
But you won't be saying nothing
If you playing with my crew

pod, a group of girls including some of the original Female Stunnaz created a music video from the song under the guidance of mentor Raphael. Students chose "Jappin" as their cell phone ring tone, and the song became an embedded symbol in the DYN culture. A year later in a media arts class, when several boys challenged whether women belonged "on the mic," both the mentor and many of the other male students in the class countered this challenge with evidence of the Female Stunnaz and "Jappin."

"Jappin" provided opportunities for seeding creative production beyond its original creators; it became an example through which mentors were able to continue inviting students to question and respond to the issue of gender. According to Brother Mike, the use of digital media for conveyance of these ideas was central: "But I think for them to see the power of what they write, what they record, and the next step making this video, like, I think for [Kiley] and all those students it . . . , again, it just empowered them to own identity in a new, powerful way that just writing a paper about it or discussing it couldn't do. . . . For her to kind of lead that movement—let's go up to the studio and translate it in many different forms. So you had the song, you had the video."

The suggestion to "go up to the studio" illustrates the importance of freely available digital tools that facilitated seeding creative production on many levels. DYN teaching practices relied on students' ubiquitous access to computers, and the combination of workspaces and student laptops made it possible for creators to move quickly from a recording studio to another task, such as video editing, easily. As the creation of "Jappin" shows, the availability of technology and workspaces allowed ideas to be carried across multiple media, inviting more of the school community to experience and participate in the project. Although the technology per se was not the focus of the pedagogy, broad access was vital to students' freedom to create at will.

CONTESTS

Beyond the motivations associated with interests and goals inherent to project-based assignments, DYN students were also incentivized by competition. Across the three years of the study, our team documented a number of both regional and local contests that motivated student work. Within the education literature, there is considerable controversy over the use of competitive structures as a motivational tool. Some laboratory studies have shown that intrinsic motivation—the desire to be involved in an activity for its own sake—can diminish when the activity becomes a means to a reward (Lepper, Sagotsky, and Dafoe, et al. 1982), and individuals may produce less creative work when evaluation or rewards are present (Amabile 1996). However, some contextual factors may mediate the negative effects of extrinsic motivators on intrinsic motivation. First, if a task is connected to one's personal goals or sense of purpose, extrinsic motivators may actually increase intrinsic motivation for the task (Amabile

1998; Amabile, Hadley, and Kramer 2002). Second, the framing and follow-up of contests may affect student motivation. Even when competitions spark excitement and motivation for the project at hand, students who lose competitions may experience decreases in intrinsic motivation for future related work. Orienting participants toward learning goals rather than toward achievement goals and providing positive feedback based on participation rather than competition outcome can mediate the detrimental motivational effects of losing (Czaja and Cummings 2009; Vansteenkiste and Deci 2003). Third, the nature of the competitive task may be associated with the extent to which competitions are motivating for students. E. Paul Torrance (1974) points out the particular benefits of interscholastic competitions that highlight creative output as opposed to contests such as spelling bees, where there is one right answer. Research in real-world settings has demonstrated that competitions are highly motivating for students in such areas as robotics (e.g., Ruíz-del-Solar and Avilés 2004), computer science (e.g., Burguillo 2010), and literacy and writing (e.g., Jocson 2009).

This research suggests a need to differentiate between a simplified performance–reward scenario and authentic competitions that become forums for expression, performance, and sharing. According to our observations, DYN mentors described the locally defined competitions at DYN in terms that went beyond winning and losing. Instead, they spoke about these competitions' energizing and focusing quality as well as about the opportunities they provide for connecting students to the larger community. One mentor, Karla Thomas, voiced these sentiments with respect to the regional contests in which DYN was involved:

> Having a competition is key for them. That's when, ultimately, they perform; when they think that the lights are on, cameras rolling, and somebody's watching. . . . You know, they're great when they get in front of judges or when folks come around . . . or anything like that. They love to perform and put it up there. So I think they like that part of it. Definitely, even as I was organizing this mini-competition, they turned to me, and they were like, "Is this against other schools?" I said, "No, it's just with you." Like aww, you know, they really wanted to get revved up to sort of show their skills. So I think they're enjoying it.

As we observed, competitions can shift both how students see themselves and how others see students. Several of our case study students were pleasantly surprised by their own achievement in competitions, and this experience seemed to reframe their relationship to their work. For instance, winning a game design competition convinced Monica that she might benefit from further developing her skills in this area. A DYN mentor subsequently encouraged her to join the game design pod and arranged for her to meet with a well-known female game designer. Similarly, Evan, who had low expectations for the documentary he submitted to the Living Museum competition, was surprised to receive positive feedback from the panel judges. In this case, which we describe in more detail later in this chapter, the competition helped Evan recognize his own skills, and his mother subsequently enrolled him in after-school screenwriting courses. In the next two subsections, we elaborate on examples of two regional contests that seeded DYN creative work: the FIRST LEGO League robotics competition and the annual history project, Living Museum.

Example from the Field: FIRST LEGO League Robotics Competition

The robotics pod was organized around an external competition, FIRST (For Inspiration and Recognition of Science and Technology). Founded by engineer and inventor Dean Kamen, FIRST was intended to inspire and motivate students to become engaged in science, technology, engineering, and math. Each year teams of students, teachers, and professional engineers respond to the FIRST challenge by designing and building a robot. "To passively sit in a classroom is a nineteenth-century format," Kamen has said. "In this next century, you're going to have to be creative, or you're not going to make it" (*Nanotechnology Now* 2007). Separate challenges are given for three different age groups, providing an entryway for children as young as six. The regional and national competitions are the culmination of six intense weeks during which students, working with mentors, design and build remote-controlled robots that can complete specific tasks and maneuver through a specially designed course.

From 2006 to 2007, Karla, a working mechanical engineer, taught the robotics pod for DYN. With assistance from Brother Mike, Karla ran the pod on Saturdays for two hours and then for longer time periods as the competition neared. As is typical for robotics clubs around the country, the highlight of the year was the city-level robotics competition, held in January.

Working with middle-school-level LEGO kits, Karla was able to give students a tangible introduction to robotics, an experience that allowed them to see the immediate results of their thinking and tinkering (see figure 4.2). For Karla, the cycles of discovery and feedback were key to seeding students' interest and engagement in building.

I think the kids really enjoy [robotics] because they're able to do it for themselves. There's some basics they have to learn about programming, which, because the programming is very easy to catch—it's not like sitting there with tons of code like I learned when I was in high school—it's drop and drag with icons that they designate which motors they're putting on, how much time they're putting it on for. So it was very easy for them to use the program. You impart very little knowledge, but then they get to see it work almost instantly. Instant gratification, I think, is the key thing. They get to be hands-on, and the instant gratification. They get to plan on the computer, they put it together, they download it instantly

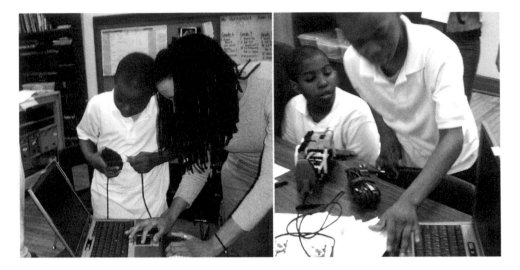

FIGURE 4.2
Robotics pod mentor working with student and students working together on the challenge set out by the FIRST LEGO League competition in 2006.

to a robot, and then they see it do all the things that they just told it to do. So, the biggest thing I have going for me is that, one, they're hands on. I'm not spending a lot of time at the board; I'm not spending a lot of time in presentations or anything like that. They're sort of out there discovering it for themselves.

Preparing for the regional robotics competition was the focal point of the curriculum. The pod members built a test platform that allowed them to try out their prototypes under contest-like conditions. According to Karla, this competition—or any opportunity to show off skills or win—was a centrally motivating factor for students. "So the kids are extremely reactive to—I mean, they are a highly competitive nature. I mean, for some reason cameras are around, or judges are around, or there's something like chocolate at stake or pizza at stake or anything at stake, everybody's at attention, focused, and running around doing what they're supposed to be doing."

To capture the momentum of this competitive spirit, Karla not only prepared the students for the citywide competition but also created mini-competitions within the pod. Like all DYN pods, robotics was "intergenerational," with students from the sixth, seventh, and eighth grades working together at the same level. Karla and Brother Mike set up opportunities for the older students, those with more experience and knowledge of the tools and competitions, to share their advice and expertise. In one such exchange, pod member Montez suggested that team members should "respect people behind you" and "check out your competition . . . shake their hand . . . ask them about their robot."

In addition to requiring that the robots be prepared to complete designated "missions," the competition asks students to create a presentation on a given theme. For example, the theme of the 2006–2007 competition was nanotechnology (see box 4.3). With Karla's guidance and with the skills the students had garnered in other DYN activities, such as Internet searching and poster creation, they researched and prepared science-based talks to accompany their robot demonstrations. The research team observed pod members running multiple simultaneous searches on nanotechnology and collaboratively reading articles posted on *EE Times* (http://www.eetimes.com) as they prepared the research component of the presentation. They manually built their LEGO robots and programmed them using ROBOLAB programming software according to the conditions set by the competition (see figure 4.3).

The robotics pod was also a context in which students applied their learning from other pods, including game design and music. According to Karla, the creative capacities that students developed in other DYN pods led to unique representations of science concepts that helped differentiate the DYN robotics team from competitors. Karla explains how this came into play during the presentation component of the 2005–2006 FIRST LEGO Competition that focused on marine-themed tasks, including cleaning up oil after a shipping spill.

BOX 4.3
2008 DYN Robotics Team Wins Best Research Presentation

It is January 2008, and the DYN Robo Stars have arrived at the regional robotics competition, where they are to compete with sixteen or more other teams. All African American, the DYN team stands out amid the mostly white faces of the other urban and suburban teams. When it is their turn to perform, the DYN students cheer louder and louder as their robots complete all of the missions successfully. In the presentation round, a girl from the DYN team moves the judges with her words about communication and how the team had to overcome their poor communication with one another to finally succeed in their efforts. In the awards ceremony, the DYN students hold their breath as the winner for Best Research Presentation is about to be announced. "Team 3571" barely escapes the announcer's lips before the DYN team members are jumping and cheering, making their way to the front of the room to accept their medals.

I've seen a lot of the other pods coming in to robotics. For instance, for the competition we had to do a presentation on water pollution. . . . [T]hey did have a chart, but they also made a video, a game. . . . A videogame, yes. . . . So it was picture of these little fishies going around, and they were happy, happy. And all of a sudden the camera turned over, and all of a sudden it was black, and the fishes were saying something. You know, they [the students] designed that from what they learned in their videogame pod. And then they created a song. So it might help them learn the words to the song, and then they used what they had learned in digital music to combine that. And that was one of the things that kind of helped them. . . . It kind of set us apart from the other groups.

Karla continually faced group dynamics and collaboration challenges while teaching the pod. At times, older students were impatient with the younger, less experienced ones. In other instances, students had trouble communicating effectively to distribute tasks within a group. Despite these challenges, the students seemed to know that in order to win a competition they had to demonstrate good teamwork. The problem for Karla was that she had to ensure that this productive collaboration happened during weekly pod activities, not just as a facade presented to the judges. "I think the place where we struggle the most is teamwork. You know, it's hard to keep them focused in a group. . . . You know, there are a couple of people who would much rather just work on their own: 'Could I build my own?' I'm like, 'No, that's your team. Go work with them.' So I could say that's where our biggest challenge is. But again, the cameras come on, [and] they are their biggest advocates. They are like buddies, best of friends."

During the 2007–2008 robotics pod, the DYN team won a prize for their presentation of their project and research (described in box 4.3), part of which included a description of how the team worked together.

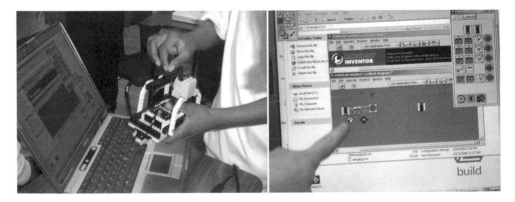

FIGURE 4.3
Students working with LEGO and ROBOLAB programming software, 2006.

Contests motivated student work, and, in the case of collaborative projects such as FIRST, these contests required a level of team commitment that introduced more social challenges. Such intensive team experiences provided an authentic context for students to learn how to manage complex social interactions on their own. Although the DYN program facilitated peer mentorship, there was no explicit instruction on how to handle team dynamics. Rather, the process was learning by doing and learning from peer and mentor modeling. More about the challenges of collaboration at DYN is shared in chapter 8.

Example from the Field: Evan, Bringing Jazz and Blues to Silvertown

As part of social studies class, Renaissance Academy students participated in an annual history contest called "Living Museum." The winners at the school level could move on to compete in regional and nationwide history fairs (see box 4.4). Students presented their local history projects as papers, exhibits, media documentaries, and live performances.

BOX 4.4
Living Museum Project: A Regional Competition

Renaissance Academy students participate in an annual history contest at the school called "Living Museum." Winners at the school level can move on to compete in regional and nationwide history fairs, including the Chicago Metro History Fair. Each year, twenty thousand students and five hundred teachers in two hundred area schools participate in school, regional, state, and national levels of competition. Students spend up to three months working individually or in groups of no more than five creating research projects in local, family, and community history that is in some way connected to their region. Students are encouraged to use primary sources as well as books and the Internet to create their projects. To present their work, students produce papers, exhibits, media documentaries, and live performances. At Renaissance Academy during our three years of research, DYN mentors allowed students to borrow cameras to conduct interviews and helped students plan out and edit their video projects during free periods and after school. Student project topics included Agnes Nestor (a women's labor activist), local radio personalities, abortion, Reverend Jeremiah Wright, and images of women in hip-hop. Several DYN students advanced to the regional level, and a couple of students advanced to the state level.

Although the competition allows entries in various formats, most Renaissance Academy students chose to utilize their emerging expertise in video production to create historical documentaries. One seventh-grade student, Evan, produced a video about the history of jazz and blues entitled *Bringing Jazz and Blues to Silvertown*. The film traces the development of American music from its African roots, integrating the social-historical contexts of slavery, segregation, and contemporary issues of race.

Evan's interest in jazz and blues history stems from his personal identification with music. "I'm a musician, so I wanted to know where the music I make came from, so the audience I was targeting were also other musicians and producers and other people in that area." Evan harnessed resources at home, such as books and videos, to help with his research of the topic. While he and his project partner, Jordan, were watching a music history documentary, they noticed that one of the featured historians was based in their local area. As it turned out, the man was working at a nearby library, and with some effort the boys were able to find him and set up an interview.

Evan and Jordan also worked together in the editing process, applying their knowledge of editing music videos with GarageBand and iMovie. They structured the story first by selecting quotes from their interviews and then by choosing images to match the content of the quotes. When Evan and Jordan had completed a rough cut, Evan's mother provided feedback, which the boys used to refine their edit.

Although the two students were dedicated to their work on the project, Evan was still not sure how the panel of judges would receive the documentary. He remembered, "When I finally got it in, they were watching it at lunch, so I walked past the room where they were watching it, and my teachers called me and gave me . . . I thought that they were going to tell me something that I should have changed, and I wasn't going to do that good, but they called me and gave me a hand shake and told me it was great." Evan and Jordan's video was named best seventh-grade documentary, qualifying the team to move on to the citywide competition. In addition, the project highlighted a talent of Evan's that he and his parents may not have recognized earlier. Following the documentary's success, Evan's mother enrolled him in screenwriting classes.

The Living Museum competition gave students the chance to explore personal interests grounded in their community's history as well as to develop production skills. In the case of *Bringing Jazz and Blues to Silvertown*, creating a documentary gave Evan and Jordan an incentive to enter into their larger community and speak with a professional historian, and it sparked the beginning of Evan's trajectory as a budding filmmaker.

MODELS AND CONNECTIONS TO BROADER COMMUNITIES

In the DYN community, everyone started out at a novice level. Becoming a central participant involved learning the tools and norms of the culture while working toward expert performance. One way we observed this happening was through forms of apprenticeship. Research on communities of practice conceptualizes learning as a matter of becoming a practitioner—a process that goes beyond acquiring knowledge and includes learning to be a community member who understands norms, values, and appropriate ways of contributing (Wenger 1998).

We witnessed DYN supporting students to become community members and practitioners by helping them make connections to other mature communities of practice. DYN engaged students directly with professional artists and media figures in the local community (see box 4.5), including the adults who were the DYN mentors. This engagement allows students to watch, question, and learn from modeled authentic performance and work, an important step toward taking on similar roles and developing constructive dispositions. For example, DYN students participated in city events that brought together musicians from the local area. Here they often conducted interviews with the artists about their work and ideas and in this way build up a library of video interviews (see figure 4.4).

BOX 4.5
Interview with and Encouragement from Doug E. Fresh

At a fund-raiser for a local foundation started by a popular hip-hop artist, DYN students interviewed Doug E. Fresh, who became popular in the 1980s as an early rapper and beat-box artist. Fresh compared the students' work to his own and encouraged them to keep creating. "You're using your energy to do something positive. What you are doing is continuing on with what we started. So I think it's real good. I think it's great. I think it's about being in the mix. See, you gotta do something to make something happen, you know what I mean? . . . Doug E. Fresh sending it out to Digital Youth Network. Keep on grindin' and keep on making it happen. Alright?"

Digital Youth Network's Interview with Twilite Tone   **Digital Youth Network's All-Access Interview with Common**   **DYN Interview with JKwest**

FIGURE 4.4
Screenshots of DYN interviews with Twilite Tone, Common, and JKwest on YouTube, 2008.

From the engineers who directed the robotics and game design pods to the spoken-word artists who led the digital queendom and spoken-word pods to connections with artists outside of the school, students in DYN encountered a range of professionals enacting roles that they were learning to take on themselves. These adults not only shared their work and knowledge with students but also encouraged the students to create and sustain their own good work. For many students, this link to the professional world was a source of inspiration for creativity and took the production process out of the narrow boundaries of a single assignment or class and into the real world.

Example from the Field: "Be a Voice, Not an Echo"

The DYN mentors modeled their skills and professional roles by engaging with students in pods and classes, but they also generated occasions for publicly modeling their own creative work. For instance, during the observation period, as a way to invite students to participate in DYN projects, the mentors pooled their own skills to create videos that they posted on the internal social network site Remix World as well as on public video-sharing sites such as YouTube. One of these invitations was *Be a Voice, Not an Echo*, a video call for school-wide participation in a multiweek poetry slam during the Freedom Friday after-school forum (see chapters 1 and 5 for a definition and discussion of Freedom Friday). The video call showcased mentors performing their own spoken-word pieces and modeled the development of a digital video (see figure 4.5).

FIGURE 4.5
Mentors performing their own spoken word as part of the *Be a Voice, Not an Echo* DYN video invitation.

Though the poetry slam was initiated in the spoken-word pod, the video invitation was designed to be seen by all students in the school and expressly invited the entire student body to participate. In the video, during the space between their spoken-word performances, mentors repeated the invitation to "be a voice, not an echo." A section of a performance piece included in the video reads:

Be a voice not an echo and let go of preconceived notions
Open up to lyrical motion
Get your mind perked
With Digital Youth Network

Part of the closing words of the video, read by Brother Mike, inspired students by calmly suggesting, "This is your chance to leave your voice, your imprint, your mark on the school as top poet. I want everybody to come out." The mentors were inviting students not only to participate in a DYN contest, but also to explore and express their own voices and to participate deeply in the community.

SUMMARY

This chapter describes the ways we observed the mentors strategically seeding creative production within the DYN program and offers findings about how these enacted strategies play out in practice. Through meaningful project-based assignments, contests, and models that connect youth to authentic communities of practice, students acquired skills, developed constructive dispositions, and became practitioners within the DYN community. Long-term, goal-based project work, such as the iRemix record label project in the media arts class (see chapter 3), gave students an opportunity to adopt "expert" roles while working toward ambitious, real-world end products. During these types of projects, students were no longer just students: they became songwriters, beat makers, music producers, graphic designers, and managers. Like the mentors who guided these projects, students critiqued and reappropriated existing work, tackled challenging topics that were intrinsically interesting to them, and contributed to the public dialogue within and beyond the DYN community. As the project example "Jappin" illustrates, students felt free to address controversial issues such as gender identity, and the project-inspired dialogue that lived on within the culture of the program as a representation of both how students saw themselves and how the program supported these explorations.

Across the three years of this study, we documented regional and local contests that motivated student work. Research suggests that, with the right framing and support, contests and competitions can be rewarding and powerful experiences for students. When contests are connected to students' personal goals and framed with a learning orientation, and when students receive positive feedback for their participation (even when they do not "win"), they can be highly motivating and provide opportunities for students to develop interest and to discover unrecognized talents. Moving beyond winning and losing, mentors believed in the energizing and focusing quality of competitions and the opportunities they provide for teamwork and community participation. As we observed during our research, the robotics pod was organized around an external competition, FIRST LEGO League, which provided a specific structure for the students' work in the pod. Working with middle-school-level LEGO kits, students were able to see the immediate results of their work, and they had the opportunity to share their final products with a large community of fellow robotics enthusiasts. In 2008, the DYN team won an award for their research report on nanotechnology. Not only was the award exciting, but the work to prepare for the competition was an incredibly rich learning experience. Team members faced challenges coordinating as a group, which they were forced to overcome in order capitalize on each person's skills and succeed in the competition.

The annual school history fair competition, Living Museum, gave students the opportunity to work individually or in groups to create research projects on local, family, and community history connected to Chicago. Winning at the school level can result in dramatic reconceptualizations of potential talent by parents, teachers, and the students themselves. This was the case for Evan, who was surprised to learn that his documentary on the history of jazz was selected as a winner by the panel of teachers who judged the 2008 Living Museum contest. His family subsequently perceived this award as a sign to further invest in developing Evan's writing skills, and his mother enrolled him in a screenwriting class offered by a nearby community center.

DYN gave students direct access to various artists and media figures who modeled how to be practitioners within authentic communities of practice. Through sharing their own work and, in the case of the mentors, creating new collaborative projects such as the video *Be a Voice, Not an Echo*, these authentic practitioners encouraged students to envision how they might take on expert roles and how their project work related to work created outside of the DYN community. This real-world connection was possible in part because of the social networks that the mentors brought with them. As practicing artists, performers, creators, designers, and engineers, they had contacts in an array of fields who could be invited to participate. All of this, of course, was intentional. The mentors were recruited to DYN on the basis of having their own portfolio of work. Pinkard and the other designers of DYN knew that for young adolescents, mentorship offered by talented artists and engineers was attractive and communicated the possibility of traveling similar pathways.

The kind of learning processes and outcomes that we describe in this chapter are not typically assessed. It is much easier to focus on near-term knowledge gains than it is to develop approaches that chart growth in interest, identity, reputations as learners, collaborative practices, and the diversity of learning resources accessed. However, the latter outcomes are no less important and, indeed, may be even more important to future learning than typically assessed outcomes. As we saw in the example describing Evan's experience during the Living Museum project, being recognized as having a potential talent can set in motion social processes that open up new opportunities for learning. The case narrative that follows this chapter continues to explore these themes, highlighting Calvin's prolific production and the practices that helped to seed his projects. Chapter 5 elaborates on how media production can be a mechanism for self-discovery and the exploration and diversification of one's identity as a potential creator and collaborator—outcomes that we care about deeply but too often leave untracked.

CALVIN: FOCUSING IN ON A FUTURE IN ENGINEERING

> You know how most kids [say] . . . "I am going to join the NBA" or "I am going to join the NFL" or "I am going to join tennis" or sports and everything? With the pods that is from this school, and the laptop, it really shows that there is more to life.
>
> —Calvin (eighth grade), 2009

Calvin was a consistent and enthusiastic participant of DYN across all three years of middle school. Project development was at the heart of his DYN experience, and he created more than twenty digital artifacts in different genres. His work was heavily influenced by the three approaches to seeding creative work discussed in chapter 4. He easily found connections to project-based pod assignments, became motivated to produce through formal contests and even created informal competitions of his own, and used existing designs as models for his work. By the end of eighth grade, Calvin had a clear picture of his accomplishments over the three years of middle school and how these experiences contributed to his plans for becoming an engineer.

PROJECT-BASED ASSIGNMENTS FIT WITH PRIOR INTERESTS

> I like mostly using the laptop a lot, because I be on it like twenty-four/seven . . . Because I like it, because I never had my very own computer where I get to take home, I never had that. That's why I'm so excited.
>
> —Calvin (sixth grade), 2006

Calvin was an avid computer game player from as far back as he could remember. At four years old, he remembered using a computer in preschool to play educational games. The first thing he did on his new school-issued laptop was to find out where to play games and how to play them. He enjoyed adventure and multiplayer games, citing competition, increasing skills or levels, and collecting artifacts within the game as motivating factors.

> Because I was looking through all of the pods, all the pods, and they gave us like a little sample of what you'd be doing in each pod, and when I came to video games . . . I know I like videogames, and I also wanted to make one of my own.
>
> —Calvin (sixth grade), 2006

Calvin's ongoing passion for gaming heavily influenced his media choice and his project work throughout DYN. He participated in the game design and digital video pods in the sixth, seventh, and eighth grades, the robotics pod in seventh and eighth grades, and the digital design pod in eighth grade. Calvin's participation in the robotics pod linked to his interest in building and working with his hands.

Fifteen of his projects were directly related to his pod work; the others he initiated and worked on during his own time, but they were tightly linked to work in the pods. Overall, he created seven movies using cameras, iMovie, and GarageBand; nine games and simulations using three different introductory programming environments (Scratch, GameStar Mechanic, and Stagecast); one robotics project using LEGO Mindstorms; as well as publications and other graphic designs with Comic Life and Photoshop.

Calvin Working on a Scratch Game Project

In a discussion about people who like computers, Calvin introduced the term *gamehead* to refer to someone who enjoys playing computer games. He noted that though some people would call him a gamehead because he spent a great deal of time, including at lunch, playing and making games, he identified himself as someone who also socializes with people, a "game person" rather than a "gamehead." As evidence of his characterization, Calvin taught other students in his game design pod,

> When I critique a videogame at home, somebody might ask me, "Can you help me?" And then I will usually tell them, "Can you send it?" and then I'll try to help them with it.
>
> —Calvin (seventh grade), 2008

showed his work to classmates, and sometimes learned from his peers. He was regularly sought out for help with game design and happily obliged for his peers in class, in pods, and on Remix World.

USING CONTESTS AND MODELS FOR PROJECT INSPIRATION

Contests were frequently an interesting entry point of project work for Calvin; as with his gaming, he enjoyed the challenge. In seventh grade, he was required to create a simulation or game about global warming for his science class, the winner of which would receive an iPod. He reflected that he could have won had he been able to create in the programming environment he used in the sixth-grade game design pod instead of in a new one that he was "not very good at." Despite his own frustrations, he convinced Monica, the ultimate winner of the iPod, to rise to the contest challenge and persist in her efforts. Calvin also participated in the robotics pod that culminated in the citywide FIRST robotics competition and in seventh grade was part of the DYN team that won an award for their group presentation.

Informal interaction with peers in school became important parts of Calvin's learning, and these interactions sometimes included informal competitions that drove his work. When he was in the seventh grade, he encountered Justin, a new talented sixth grader, in the game design pod. Calvin was impressed with Justin's quick learning, and they soon became collaborators, shared resources, and competed with each other through their projects. This mixed-grade relationship continued in this pod through Calvin's eighth-grade year, when Justin shared his online gaming account with Calvin when Calvin's was hacked, and when Calvin cited Justin as the person he went to for help when he had trouble with his game work.

And Calvin [helped me to finish] because he was—I was like, "You know, I'm just tired of this." And Calvin was like, "Don't give up. Because when you don't get the iPod, they'll rub it all in your face." Yeah, he got me up in the spirit of trying to get that iPod.

—Monica (sixth grade), 2007

[Justin] just learned it off the bat. It took me a while to do this. It took him only a couple of days to learn this. I'm like, "How does he know that?". . . Then we usually have a competition trying to see who will be the best.

—Calvin (seventh grade), 2008

Calvin tended to build off of models of work in wider gaming communities, including professional games and the Scratch programming environment online space. He was aware of his ability to hone his ideas by spending extended time viewing the work of others and messing around with it.

He talked about sometimes using the help menu with new programming environments when he was stuck, but the most influential learning tool for him was remixing existing artifacts. He spent significant time finding new ideas from games; he also reused background code from other games, building off of bits and pieces to create his own work. It was in this process of discovery that new ideas seemed to seed for him.

> If I want to make an adventure game, I will pull up like two or three, and then I will both click on adventure, and I'll first play this one and then think about [how] I might take this from this game to make my new adventure game, and that's how I get my inspiration.
>
> —Calvin (seventh grade), 2008

PROJECT SPOTLIGHT: EXERCISE IS GOOD FOR YOU

Over eight weeks, students in the digital video pod developed public-service announcements (PSAs). After watching a short video on the Cartoon Network, seventh-grader Calvin came up with an idea for a PSA about the benefits of exercise for children. He felt that the DYN community knew him as someone who made games and thought they wouldn't be interested in his video work. He was surprised that people not only liked the PSA but wanted to know more about how he did it.

Through this PSA project, Calvin took a stance, promoting the importance of physical activity and health. This project took on a social awareness dimension, which, for Calvin, was a different focus from his gaming and robotics platforms, where design and scripting skills were more central. This example also shows how peers and artist-mentors helped Calvin to complete the project.

Calvin drove the vision for his film, and DYN mentor Raphael helped sequence events and

Text, Screenshots, and Descriptions of *Exercise Is Good for You* PSA Video

Text: Calvin is restless in class.

Calvin is increasingly off task while a neighbor is busy working.

Text: Go outside. NOW!

The teacher sends him outside, where there are a series of shots of him exercising.

Text: And this is why exercise is good for ya!!!

A cut-away shot demonstrates his new strength as he hurls a chair across the yard.

Text: Later that day . . .

Back in the classroom, Calvin works diligently, while neighbor yawns. The teacher returns to the frame.

Text: Very good work, Calvin.

suggested film techniques. After Calvin arranged, shot, and uploaded the raw footage to iMovie, Raphael recruited Janice, a girl one year older than Calvin with more editing experience. As Janice helped edit, Calvin complained of being bored and was heard saying, "Can I reshoot mine? Mine sucks . . . it's stupid." Janice and Raphael worked together to pull Calvin back into the process. Calvin and Janice organized the clips into a narrative sequence, and Janice added transitions and captions.

The completed video was two minutes, fifty seconds long and reminiscent of a silent film, with simple, mimed comedic actions, no audio other than music, and captions to convey story and speech. It also had a series of technical features, such as cutaway shots and repeated clips.

Mentors showcased the video on Remix World and on external sites such as YouTube. Hondo, a new mentor at the time, was shown the video as an example of student work at DYN and recalled being incredibly impressed.

> I just thought that was an exceptional piece. It kind of prepared me for what the potential was for these children. I was like, "Wow, OK, that's what these children are doing."
>
> —Hondo (mentor), 2008

At the end of eighth grade, Calvin cited the video as one of the projects he was most proud of and recounted, "Everybody loved it."

DEVELOPING AN IDENTITY THROUGH DYN PRACTICES AND MENTORS

Calvin had a reputation with both teachers and peers at school as someone who had trouble organizing his schoolwork. One of his teachers described his trouble with traditional literacy and his propensity to conjure a number of ideas that seemed to lack a unifying theme or clear trajectory. Within the DYN program, some of these qualities—namely, his ability to generate numerous ideas—were channeled into his creative work.

Through the use of technology, Calvin had the opportunity to express his ideas through a number of modes of communication. When asked whether

> I honestly don't. I think it gives him another way . . . to express things and to show what he knows that's away from the traditional "read, write, and produce."
>
> —Tracy Lee Edwards (teacher), 2008

Calvin would be as engaged without the technology component, his language arts teacher emphasized the important role the technology played in allowing him to share his ideas.

Once Calvin started a technology project that captured his interest, he was doggedly focused on project details and work whenever he had a free moment in order to create his intended vision. He often stayed after school to work on his projects, even on days that he was not participating in pods.

Calvin's enthusiasm for and dedication to game design, the fit of this interest with DYN project-based game design opportunities, and the repositioning of his talents by mentors to focus on his creativity earned him a reputation in the DYN community as a knowledgeable game designer. Other students often sought him out for help, and mentors featured him in a series of *DYN Behind the Scenes* web videos presenting his games. Within the DYN community and his own mind, Calvin emerged as a programmer and game designer. His creativity and tenacity fit well with these roles. As a programmer, he talked about the long, tedious hours being worth it in order to create a final product he was proud of. Calvin thought his imagination and creativity were traits he brought to game design that helped him in his work. Others, both mentors and fellow students, recognized these qualities in him and appreciated them. Hondo went so far to say, "As an artist, I respect that, the ability to have all these ideas and not lose them in the midst."

The mentors of the digital video and game design pods were especially influential for Calvin's learning. During his sixth-grade year, this role was filled by Raphael and Benjamin Shapiro, who taught him the new software and content ideas but also played the role of audience to his work and monitored his behavior, reminding him not to work on his games too much: "they usually tell me to go home; I be on it too long." During seventh grade,

> [F]or some reason I just enjoy it. I have no problem making an hour-long script. That comes more quicker for me, but the reason why is because when all this boring stuff be put together, it makes this really cool effect.
>
> —Calvin (eighth grade), 2009

> [Calvin has the] ability to think far and long and then at the same time [to] pull all of these ideas back so he can shoot the ideas out simultaneously, any ideas, and then pull them all back and tie them up together and put it down in front of you.
>
> —Hondo (mentor), 2008

Hondo became the game design pod mentor and a primary influence for Calvin. He was appreciative of Calvin's work and his ideas and directly supported Calvin's digital media projects in and out of the game design pod.

Though Calvin developed expertise and was recognized in the community, he rarely took on a leadership role and instead preferred to leave this role to other students and to focus on his own private work. In collaborative work, he tended to follow directions to complete tasks and left decision-making up to other members of his groups. For example, in his eighth-grade Living Museum project, though Calvin had been in the video pod for three years, he did not do any of the editing on the documentary. He instead followed the team leaders' direction. He said, "I am really good at group work. I do whatever they need for me to get finished."

TAKING SKILLS AND INTERESTS FROM DYN TO HOME

Informal interactions at home emerged as important parts of Calvin's learning. At home, his older cousin Misha, a graduate of Renaissance Academy, and his younger brother Covan, who planned to enter Renaissance Academy the year after Calvin graduated, were especially influential. At home, he showed his project work to his family, saying that "the little ones" especially liked to see his games and animations. In addition to audience, Misha was also a teacher for Calvin, offered tech support, and helped him find resources for his projects. She showed him the basics of the Macintosh laptop operating system, such as how to use the built-in camera and how to load images on the computer screensaver, fixed his computer when something was not behaving properly, looked at and critiqued his work, and emailed him certain music that he wanted to add to his games. In turn, Calvin took on this role for Covan. Calvin taught Covan

> When I do a school project, I will usually like the design part, and I will usually go to Hondo to get some feedback on design. When I was doing the We Liberty Jam project, I told him is there any design tips that he could give me, and he said, "You should . . . ," I had a timeline, and they was just straight. He said, "Maybe make it like this," and that's what I did, and then [when] I looked at it, it looked a whole lot better.
>
> —Calvin (seventh grade), 2008

> [When I showed my family my projects,] they said like, "I want to be in middle school too!" Well, my cousin don't really want to be in a middle school because she is at high school, but she said, "It's OK; it's cool," but I know she really likes it. My brother he always wants to go to the middle school since I can do all this cool stuff and he can't.
>
> —Calvin (seventh grade), 2008

everything he knew, from Scratch and videogame creation to Internet searching. Covan also sometimes collaborated with him on project work, doing sound effects that Calvin recorded for his games. At the end of eighth grade, Calvin anticipated his brother's entrance into the DYN community. He worried that he would want to use his brother's DYN laptop and hoped he had been generous enough with his own so that his brother would reciprocate. He also wanted to prepare Covan for his work at DYN, specifically thinking that Covan could take over his role as resident Scratch expert in the game design pod.

CHALLENGES IN ARCHIVING AND SHOWCASING WORK

Despite Calvin's prolific production work, he infrequently presented his work to a wider audience and had trouble saving his project artifacts. His game projects frequently had no clear or definitive end until the project was lost when school servers were reset or his laptop crashed. His video projects seemed to have more of a clear beginning and end, and some, such as *Exercise Is Good for You*, were published online. Saving his work was an ongoing issue through all three years of middle school. Though mentors sometimes posted his work, Calvin rarely did, despite two forums that were readily available to him, Remix World and the Scratch programming environment website. As Calvin admitted at the end of eighth grade, "I produce a lot. I always forget to post it . . . but I do a lot." At that time, most of Calvin's work was on his laptop, but he was not able to keep the machine beyond the end of the academic year and instead spoke of doing all he could on it before he had to return it to the school. As Calvin stated, he often had intentions to work as far as he could on projects and to enjoy the process.

Two of the pods that Calvin was intensely interested in and consistently participated in, robotics

> Yep, I teach my brother all the tricks to it—Apple tab, Apple H, Apple arrow key; I teach him all the tricks and all the software things, all the software updates, so when he gets his, he is going to be prepared for it. . . . And when he comes [to DYN], I can teach him how to use Scratch, so then if he ever go to the pod, he know a lot of stuff about Scratch; he knows how to use it. So there would at least be some type of expert who normally use Scratch will be there.
>
> —Calvin (eighth grade), 2009

> Everything I mostly do is on the [my laptop]. It is going to be kind of difficult leaving it next year—I mean in high school—so I am trying to get at least as far as I can with all my games and all my videos and all my games that I made—at least get as far as I can so when I have to turn it in, I can at least say I had some good times.
>
> —Calvin (eighth grade), 2009

and game design, had a new mentor each year. Though he was definitely recognized for his engaging and prolific work, more consistent mentor relationships might have helped to support him in completing and sharing his work and in taking on more leadership positions. Furthermore, though Calvin was intensely aware of his growing skills and experiences, keeping an actual portfolio of his work might have helped him to share his experiences with others and to map out his growing experiences over the three years of middle school and beyond. Artists, musicians, and writers, often use portfolios to make their own work and process transparent, allowing them to track their development over time, reflecting back on and continuing to contribute to a constantly changing body of work. The practice of having student portfolios was added to the DYN curriculum for these reasons when Calvin was in eighth grade, but this change also presented challenges for DYN, including ownership and management of server space and the technological difficulty of combining different media artifacts into one portfolio presentation.

LOOKING TO THE FUTURE

Using what he knew and what he had done, Calvin hoped to be involved with computers his whole life and planned for a career in the field. He visited a number of different high schools and saw a "really cool robot" they had made out of LEGOs at TECH, a local technical high school, which became his number one choice. When he applied, although he did not submit his actual media artifacts, he did share a résumé that included his involvement with the DYN pods over three years, highlighting his participation in the robotics pod.

At the end of eighth grade, Calvin had been accepted at TECH and planned to enter in the fall. He believed that there was "no media stuff" at TECH,

> What I am looking forward to is more detailed information about robotics—like I seen—they made this really cool robot. It was an R2D2 out of LEGOs—that was really cool. That is what really made me interested.
>
> —Calvin (eighth grade), 2009

Calvin Working in the Robotics Pod

but that he would be able to learn more about engineering, robotics, programming, and math. He was excited about blending the digital media skills he had developed at Renaissance Academy with the new computational skills he would gain from TECH. As Calvin enthusiastically stated in eighth grade, "I will have all these places. I would say that I was in Renaissance Academy for three years and learned a whole bunch about media, about programming, about robotics; then when I went to TECH, I learned about engineering and robotics and computer language and about math. I am learning all this new different kinds of math stuff. When I go to college, I try to get a job doing something that I like to do—robotics and stuff . . . get a job there. That is it."

After TECH, he planned to attend the Illinois Institute of Technology in Chicago and then to apply for an engineering job. Within the engineering field, he spoke of going into robotics or being a programmer or both. He also was still interested in becoming a game designer, producing games for Wii or developing a new gaming platform altogether.

> I have been working with games for three years. I am hoping that maybe someday I will continue making games—so then I can produce games like on the Wii and stuff. Since I was going to be an engineer, I was thinking I would make a really cool game system, like an original one—it is going to be something like Wii, but I hadn't really designed it.
>
> —Calvin (eighth grade), 2009

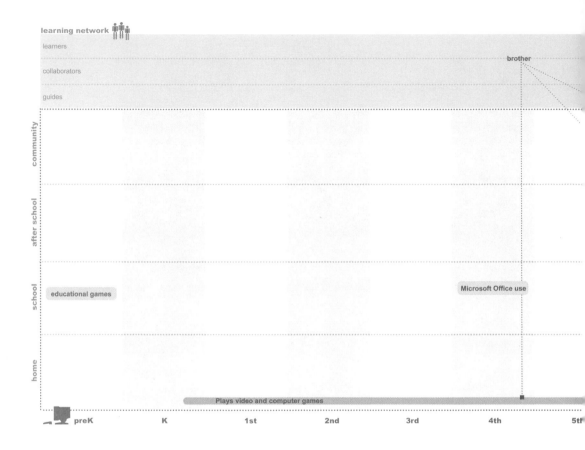

Calvin's participation in digital games began at school and at home and was in fact his first use of computers 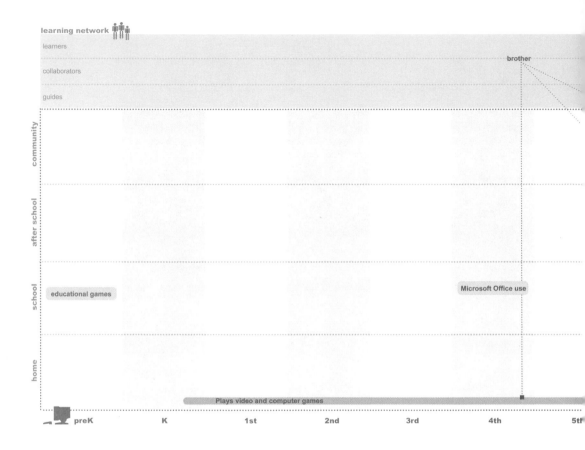. Aside from games, his technology learning pathway was relatively bare until he entered middle school in sixth grade. Once there, his media projects took off at **home**, at school, and after school primarily through **DYN** programs.

Calvin was especially involved in the DYN after-school program. He quickly connected his interest in gaming to the game design pod 👆 and also signed up to participate in the robotics 🤖 and digital video pods 📷, first participating in fluency-building 💡 design activities. He attended all three of these pods each year of middle school, continuing projects and themes across years. He used his school-issued laptop 💻 to continue project themes at **home**, such as his Naruto-themed anime games and

Calvin

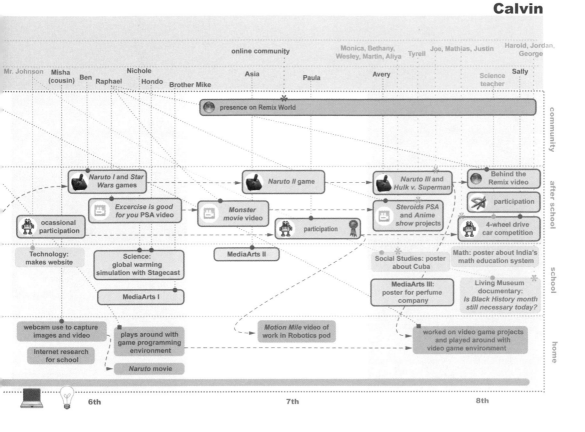

movies. In seventh grade, Calvin was part of the robotics team that won a prize 🏆 for their presentation at a citywide robotics competition. Aside from participation on Remix World, he did not have much activity in the wider **community** context outside of DYN.

Calvin built up a substantial social learning network 👪 during middle school, including **family**, **mentors**, teachers, and peers. In seventh grade, he learned ⠅ more about video production from his older **cousin** Misha, and from fifth through eighth grade he taught ⣰ his younger **brother** what he knew about gaming and game design.

Raphael was a consistent mentor for Calvin, supporting his digital video efforts through all three years of middle school. For the other media genres Calvin was particularly interested in, game design and robotics, the pod mentors changed each year.

"BE A VOICE, NOT AN ECHO": SUPPORTING IDENTITIES AS DIGITAL MEDIA CITIZENS

Amber Levinson, Daniel Stringer, Jolene Zywica, Brigid Barron, Jolie Matthews, Caitlin K. Martin, and Maryanna Rogers

> Between sixth and eighth grade, you hear kids saying that "I'm a music producer and a designer." They'll say two or three things they're really good at . . . but they also develop—and I think this is across the board from middle school and high school—an identity of engagement. It's not just, "I'm a creator," [but] "I'm a critical creator," "I'm a critical thinker." You know, "I don't just create to create; I create with a purpose."
>
> —Brother Mike (mentor), 2010

The intentional seeding of creative production through contests, modeling, and project-based learning opportunities allowed DYN students to develop media production skills as they took on roles as authors, song writers, graphic designers, movie directors, and film editors. These opportunities were foundational experiences in the development of digital media fluency that the DYN leadership imagined. However, DYN's vision of a digital media citizen went beyond the capacity to simply create with digital media and sought rather to help students become critical consumers, constructive producers, and social advocates for better futures. The epigraph quote from Brother Mike reflects the shift that many DYN participants made as they became more deeply engaged in the DYN community, transitioning from casual makers of digital artifacts to creators with a purpose. Developing these deeper values required multiple opportunities to engage in reflection and dialogue in response to original work. Participants needed spaces—formal and informal, online and offline—that provide them with opportunities to inquire about media, to think about its implications, and to consider artifacts that they and their peers have produced and transformed. In such spaces, participants could employ colloquial language, formal school language, and the specialized language (Heath 1983; Gee 2000) of digital literacies as they demonstrated their development as digital media citizens.

Although many programs are successful in providing technology resources to students, only some are able to engage students more meaningfully and change the way they see themselves in relationship to media and their communities. In this chapter, we share our observations of the ways in which DYN achieved this in the period under study by providing opportunities for youth to develop their identities not only as skilled media producers, but also as critical, constructive producers who envisioned applying their newfound capacities to improving conditions for themselves and their communities. To do this, we share examples of the social interactions that mentors and students engaged in, connecting these examples to previous research on learning and identity. We focus on the program's supportive spaces and structures, the ways that mentors invited students to take up learning opportunities on a regular basis, and how individual learners chose to participate as they developed their portfolios of work across the three years of middle school that we studied.

Our exploration of these issues was guided by a perspective that sees one's identity as deeply cultural, socially embedded, dynamic, and linked to learning through practices associated with a particular community (Holland, Lachicotte, Skinner, et al. 1998; Wenger 1998). This notion of practice-linked identity is rooted in the idea that people develop their sense of self in relationship to specific areas of activity such as school, work, sports, and the arts (Herrenkohl and Mertl 2010; Nasir and Hand 2006, 2008) and that practice-linked identities can grow when people have the right types of social, physical, and emotional supports (Nasir and Cooks 2009). Within even the most resource-rich environments, learners must still choose whether to take up the opportunities that are offered, and those who become more deeply connected can then access additional resources such as mentoring or tools. At this juncture, the social processes of supporting new identities in students become particularly important. Physical tools have been provided, courses and activities have been made available, and a curriculum put in place. However, the specific choices and interactions made by instructors—in this case the DYN mentors—play a vital role in determining whether students actively take up the resources offered.

The concept of "positioning," drawn from studies of everyday discourse (Harré and Van Langenhove 1999; Holland and Leander 2004), also helps us to show how mentors engage students as creative producers, critical consumers, and social advocates for a better future. Researchers have coined the term *positioning* to highlight pivotal points where people have opportunities to take on particular roles, stances, or personas, either through everyday interactions or representations communicated through media (Holland and Leander 2004; Nasir and Saxe 2003). At these junctures, individuals may accept, reject, or negotiate particular roles. Although the concept of positioning has been used to illustrate ways that young people are positioned in undesirable or inferior roles (e.g., Tzou, Scalone, and Bell 2010; Wortham 2004), it has also been used to show how students are positioned in positive ways. For example, Indigo

Esmonde (2009) found that students were positioned in a variety of roles, including "expert" and "facilitator," when working on math problems in groups. Na'ilah Nasir and Jamal Cooks (2009) also show how young athletes use available resources to position themselves as experts in their practice.

For example, for beginning hurdlers in track and field, specific resources—including physical practice space, interactions with a coach and teammates, and the goals and credos of the sport—are instrumental in helping to form identity. Becoming a hurdler requires, for instance, mastering material resources, including the track, uniforms, spikes, and hurdles. Regular practices led by the coach offer a context for communicating expectations, goals, and what it means to use these artifacts correctly. Practices and meets provide the opportunity to build relationships that sustain engagement through difficult challenges and help to solidify connections to the sport. In addition, becoming associated with a specialization such as hurdling means more focused coaching, which then deepens athletes' expertise and identification with the sport. Explicit communication that positions students as future athletes (e.g., "you are going to be a hurdler") bolsters the connection between a novice athlete and the track practice, particularly when he or she encounters challenges in mastering a specific skill.

This practice-linked identity framework helped us identify novel forms of positioning consistent with DYN's goals of supporting students' dispositions as critical, constructive producers and social advocates. Across the examples we provide in this chapter, we highlight the explicit positioning of students as individuals with something to offer the local and global community and see that intentional positioning is a powerful strategy for nurturing their identities as digital media citizens. We illustrate how mentors invited students to take on roles that reflected and contributed to their developing knowledge and skill, and identify five forms of positioning we observed (see box 5.1).

DYN leadership provided regular forums and an online social network to allow for serious dialogue. These spaces to showcase work offered multiple opportunities to position students as valuable contributors within and outside the local community. A junior mentors program allowed older learners to take on additional responsibility as leaders and to participate in outside projects that facilitated their growth as digital media creators. This program and its students identified future pathways for DYN participants as they moved on to high school, college, and professional careers. Below we share examples from each of these settings.

REGULAR FORUMS: FREEDOM FRIDAYS

One of the features of DYN that aims to support learner identities is Freedom Friday, a regular Friday after-school session designed to explore DYN-related topics and provide

BOX 5.1
Forms of Positioning

Identifying future pathways	Connecting present activity to a possible future activity (e.g., marking career fields where a more diverse workforce is needed and suggesting immediate engagement, as in making games to prepare for contributing to the field of game design)
Reframing contributions	Reframing a personal style to highlight benefits rather than deficits (e.g., reframing a tendency to be unfocused as a tendency to be creative)
Recognizing expertise through roles	Asking members to speak at forums, participate in committees, or lead workshops (e.g., introducing teachers to social networking)
Inviting social analysis	Presenting examples and asking for reflection and critique (e.g., of stereotypical representations portrayed in the media)
Recruiting bystanders	Offering personal invitations to take part in opportunities, (e.g., inviting individual girls to participate in game design)

a showcase space for all students in the school. As we will discuss in this section, Freedom Fridays provided important opportunities for mentors to position students in different ways—by recognizing student expertise through roles and inviting social analysis (see box 5.1).

At Freedom Fridays food is often provided, and the venue can become a social opportunity for students, parents, and teachers. During our observations, the sessions varied in their format (see box 5.2). Some Freedom Fridays were held in an open-mic style; others focused on spoken-word performances. There were discussion-based events that fostered dialogue around themes such as gender discrimination and voting, often incorporating media clips or film screenings, and some sessions included working time for creating artifacts inspired by the day's topic. Mentors promoted these events through videos and posters (see figures 5.1 and 5.2) and encouraged all students at Renaissance Academy to attend as many Freedom Fridays as they could— recruiting "bystanders" into more active participation. Between twenty-five and thirty-nine students were present at the sample of Freedom Fridays we observed.

BOX 5.2
Freedom Friday Formats

Open-mic sessions	All students and mentors are invited to share their original work through performance.
Summits	Organized discussions are planned to give students opportunities to debate topics of relevance to them, such as gun control, gender stereotypes, bullying, and school violence. Summits often include a film screening to inspire the conversation.
Working sessions	Specific topics or production techniques are introduced and students create projects on the spot.
Special projects	Current events such as the presidential election are used as an opportunity to generate ideas for media projects.

Mentors used Freedom Fridays in a range of ways to allow students to showcase their development. Participants at different grade levels and involved in a variety of after-school pods attended and shared work with one another and with audiences from the broader community (family members, guests, etc.). Mentors also used Freedom Fridays to open up deeper discussions with students around themes and values, encouraging them to think about the content of their projects separately from the technological tools and techniques they were mastering. Sometimes these forums allowed for mentors to reframe a student's contributions, first perceived as annoying or too academic, as insightful, as Brother Mike described in relation to one of our case study students, Maurice. Mentor Simeon spoke of Freedom Friday as an opportunity to reinforce teachings that he initiated with students in classes and pods. For example, he saw it as an opportunity to encourage students to critically reflect on the messages of certain mainstream hip-hop artists, positioning them as social analysts. Describing how he spoke to the students about the meaning of hip-hop lyrics and critically reflecting on their messages, Simeon referred to the role of Freedom Fridays as a "barrage of reinforcements" for the concepts he shared with students: "They may never hear that concept again, and they may forget. It'll be like, 'OK. Yeah. Mr. Simeon said something about it, but, hey, I'm loving this new 50 Cent [track], and I don't care.' Where at least the Freedom Friday space, that reinforces it, and it allows them to continue that, and I think it's really giving it some impact on their lives and just empowers them."

Simeon echoed Brother Mike, quoted at the beginning of the chapter, stressing the mentors' intentional cultivation of students' critical abilities as well as their technical skills. It was not enough for students simply to produce media in quantity or to mimic media they were familiar with. Rather, mentors emphasized the ideas behind projects and encouraged students to question—not imitate—dominant media messages. By initiating this kind of dialogue and by inviting attendees to offer commentary and perspectives, mentors both invited students to perform social analysis and recognized their expertise through their roles in discussion and media production.

During the time we observed, mentors also utilized the Freedom Friday space to follow up on these important discussions with guided production sessions, where students worked on new projects based on the topics at hand. For instance, one Freedom Friday that took on a creative production workshop format was entitled "Black History 365," based on a slogan and logo created by Hondo, another mentor (see figure 5.1). The idea was sparked by African American History Month, with the idea of celebrating African American history and culture all 365 days of the year. In this way, students were positioned as social analysts to provide critique not only verbally in discussions, but also creatively through their work, remixing and reimagining messages based on the ideas expressed in the forum.

FIGURE 5.1
Freedom Friday flyer.

As Brother Mike introduced the session, he asked students to create work based on what black history meant to them, reminding them that they were "part of black history right now." He also highlighted the importance of exploring different media, seeking help from the mentors who had the most insight in given fields, and distributing work via as many channels as possible. He encouraged students to "push [their] work out," suggesting various publishing venues, such as Vocalo, a Chicago-based online public media service that allows listeners to create their own blog spaces and share podcasts and other types of broadcasts. The production session was also a chance for students to obtain feedback and guidance from any of the mentors, regardless of whether they had pod activities with those particular instructors.

Other Freedom Fridays we observed were "summits," where the entire school community was invited to watch films or clips on a relevant topic and to participate in a panel discussion made up of students and guests. At these Freedom Fridays, the mentors invited students to comment on the topic of the day, while also integrating views from recent documentaries or from parents, teachers, and other community members. Rather than inviting a panel made up entirely of experts from the outside, mentors developed the practice of designating students who had particular interest in or knowledge of an issue to participate as panelists in a discussion, recognizing the expertise of those students as an important resource for the entire group. For example, in a summit entitled "Does Hip-Hop Hate Our Women?" a student who had produced media about images of women was one of the invited panelists. Conversations that developed during Freedom Fridays continued through the use of Remix World and through original productions centered on the focal theme.

The mentors used the Freedom Friday space to encourage student growth in all three areas: developing students as critical consumers (through media critique and discussion), creative producers (of their own media artifacts), and social advocates for a better future (through production of media around socially significant themes). In the next two examples, we detail episodes that reveal the specific ways that Freedom Fridays contribute to students' learning in DYN: "Stop the Violence," a Freedom Friday summit, and "Remix the Vote," which involved students in the issues raised during the 2008 election campaigns.

Example from the Field: "Stop the Violence"

In the fall of 2007, DYN mentors and students had explored the issue of violence in schools both in person and online using Remix World. Building on those discussions, mentors organized a Freedom Friday summit the following semester entitled "Stop the Violence" and focused on the theme of shootings on school and college campuses (figure 5.2). To inspire discussion, mentors showed video clips, including an excerpt from Michael Moore's *Bowling for Columbine* and news stories about attacks on college campuses.

FIGURE 5.2
Flyer for "Stop the Violence" summit.

Leading up to the summit, mentors invited reflection on specific ideas about the sources of violence, positioning students as both knowledgeable and welcome participants in the summit. The mentors posted a new discussion topic on Remix World prior to the event, which had the heading "WHEN IS IT GOING TO STOP!?!?!?!??!?!" The post aimed to solicit student answers and included five questions: (1) Do we need guns in America? (2) Why do you think this movie was made? (3) What do we do to stop shootings in the schools? (4) Are the guns the problem or the people who use/abuse them? (5) What can you do to stop the violence? Students responded question by question, expressing a variety of viewpoints on the issues.

At the start of the summit, Brother Mike announced the theme and showed the video clips from *Bowling for Columbine* and the news to the twenty-five students, five mentors, and one teacher in attendance. Brother Mike then explained that a live discussion would be held where everyone was expected to contribute: "We're about to have a quick talk, and I expect everyone to kind of contribute. . . . [T]he first question is: Is it . . . the guns that are the problem or the people who are behind them?" In this way, rather than offering outside opinions or information on the topic, Brother Mike first invited students to provide their own social analysis, again communicating his belief that they had important perspectives to contribute. By suggesting these polarized choices for answering the question, the mentors sparked conversation among students, who then explored the problem from multiple viewpoints. The following excerpts are from 2008 field notes from this Freedom Friday summit.

JUSTIN: I think it's the people pulling the trigger . . . the reason that it's happening is their anger.

THOMAS: It's the people . . . because a gun is an inanimate object. It has to have a person . . . the gun does not do anything.

KEIRA: I agree with Thomas, and I also think it's the people causing the people to pull the trigger; [the shooter at Northern Illinois University] did that because he was under a lot of pressure.

Others brought up the responsibility of the media, considering that some prevalent images may have inspired violent acts. One student, Jerome, argued: "I think it's the thing that motivates you . . . the big thing with Columbine was Marilyn Manson. . . . [P]eople are motivated if they hear violence and all these things . . . they're going to go out and find a gun."

Students built on this idea and, with probing from Brother Mike, discussed the role of violence in music, movies, and videogames.

CALVIN: I say it's the videogames because . . . because on video games, I saw a video it had a lot of killing. People kept shooting at each other. . . .

THOMAS: I think it has to do with the music and the videos . . . and games and stuff and that influences a lot of African Americans and makes them want to go out an be in a gang and shoot somebody. . . .

These comments met with critique from some of the other students, who felt that individual agency and choice should not be discounted—even with media influence, perpetrators of these violent acts still have a choice to act the way they do. DYN mentor Hondo steered the question toward some students whom he knew to be avid players of violent videogames—recognizing them and positioning them to speak as experts on the topic. These students, however, did not feel they were influenced by what they called "fake" or "animated" fighting in the games.

After the students debated for some time, Brother Mike invited them to move to the online space, Remix World, and share their answers there in written form, inviting them to critique and renegotiate the ideas and images discussed at the summit. Students were also encouraged to create media artifacts, such as posters or podcasts, that were inspired by the discussion and post them on Remix World as well.

Students posted a variety of responses. For example, a group of female students— including Renee, one of our case learners—worked together to create a rap entitled "Stop the Violence." The song did not address violence in schools specifically, referring instead to violence "in the 'hood," where (per the song lyrics) "most African Americans, less Caucasians" are killed. The students used their composition to send the message that "we need to stop the violence to build a community." The mentors later posted this work on Vocalo. An excerpt from the song appears in box 5.3.

BOX 5.3
Partial Lyrics to "Stop the Violence"

It doesn't feel good to be a murder capital
Without walking down the street
and somebody capping you
They ain't even slapping you
They got guns, you can't even run, can't even run
When a bullet hits your body
Violence in the shot, is at a high velocity
High velocity
Is at a high
Velocity
So stop the violence for me

This summit is an example of how mentors identified a relevant theme and leveraged the Freedom Friday space to invite students to perform social analysis, all in a way that positioned students as experts and creative voices who could concretely express their ideas on real issues. The mentors shared provocative media examples and questions, facilitated discussion, and invited students to respond with creative work. Rather than emphasizing a particular medium or technical skill, mentors used this opportunity to open up dialogue around a powerful theme and create a springboard for creative work that incorporated social critique. In these ways, mentors encouraged students to practice creating with a message and to develop points of view that they could express in their productions.

Example from the Field: "Remix the Vote"

The "Remix the Vote" project is an example of how DYN mentors used the Freedom Friday space to help students build their critical skills while creating media based on current events. They offered students a broad topic to focus on: the 2008 presidential elections. The mentors then guided students to find relevant, specific issues within that broader theme that appealed to their individual interests. There was an explicit focus within the "Remix the Vote" project on the use of digital media to gain knowledge, construct messages, and spread ideas.

"Remix the Vote" was modeled after the project "Vote or Die," which a group of celebrities developed to increase awareness about voting among young people. Mentors created a modified, DYN version of the project to encourage students to cast a critical lens on a variety of social issues, produce media related to their topics of choice, and inform parents and community members about pertinent local issues. Through "Remix the Vote," students drew on civics knowledge gathered in school and knowledge about their local community to create digital media in a way that cast new light on a recent pop-culture initiative. Brother Mike recounted:

> Remix the Vote? . . . Well, the idea was to kind of empower not only youth to be educated about voting and the process. . . . My inspiration came from Puff Daddy's little campaign "Vote or Die" . . . and continued it from there, and obviously it became an election year. And trying to find ways to get our students to find some empowerment among themselves because they are obviously going to be future voters—get the platform laid out to them.

As a part of the project, students used their laptops and the skills they had learned through DYN to create media pieces—including digital videos, posters, and comic book layouts—all meant to promote awareness of social issues. One set of students created a piece that provided information about global warming. Another group recorded a mock talk show that offered commentary on a variety of social issues. In the process of creating media that spoke to their issues, students enhanced their skills with technology and engaged in reflective processes that exercised their abilities to effectively communicate with audiences through digital media. This mastery of the technical and literary aspects of making a statement is at the core of many notions of digital media literacy.

Through this creative process, students were invited to see themselves in new ways and to reframe certain ideas (see box 5.1). Mentors encouraged them to view civic engagement in a new light by making a connection to what celebrities were doing at the time. In this project, students were positioned to see themselves as potential change agents of the present and future, part of a broader category of young activists. Brother Mike explicitly stated: "One of my things I initially told them was any important movement in this country has been started by—anywhere in the world— has been started by youth, whether it be Soweto, whether it be Tiananmen Square, whether it be in the sixties, the civil rights. Those are all students."

The mentors positioned students as empowered community members and challenged them to see the impact of this in-school activity as not confined to within school walls. Through "Remix the Vote," students could see their skills as relevant to something beyond their grades; they were learning to have an impact on their own communities and futures.

SOCIAL LEARNING NETWORK: REMIX WORLD

In the previous examples, we have alluded to some ways that Remix World, DYN's private social network site, became an important way for students to continue discussions and share work online. Remix World was designed to provide an in- and out-of-school space where mentors could continue supporting students' growth as critical consumers, constructive producers, and social advocates (see figure 5.3). Social networking sites more generally can be transformative environments for youth and are considered integral to the promotion of identity development (Greenhow, Robelia, and Hughes 2009; Ito, Baumer, Bittanti, et al. 2010). The DYN site was intended to facilitate access to media resources through mentor and student postings, provide a context for encouraging participation (see box 5.4), and provide access to mentors. Indeed, as we learned, Remix World served as a key venue for DYN students to showcase original and remixed work; receive feedback from peers and mentors; share ideas, design process, and media; and discuss topics of interest. The name "Remix World" is

---

BOX 5.4

Calling All Game Designers

[S]o you all need to start posting up your games [on Remix World], then you all are gonna be cool. . . . [A]ctually someone saw one of your games. Akili posted it, and Brian wanted to . . . he was like "how do I start playing games?"
—Dr. Pinkard (mentor), game design pod, 2008

Here, the game design pod mentor pointed out that students' videogames posted on Remix World generated inquiries about how they could be played. This demonstrates how Remix World and the content on the site have the potential to influence other users and their desire to explore digital media and potentially new identities. It also provides insight on how Remix World positions students—both by recognizing the game design students as designers and media creators in the eyes of the DYN community, and by recruiting students into DYN activities.

Calling All DYN Gamers: The Game Design Community Needs You!

Only 2% of game developers are African American while African Americans are increasingly increasing the money and resources they spend on playing games. Please read this blog to hear from some of the few African Americans in the game industry. I believe that in the next 10 years I will be reading about some of you.

What do you think of the conversation in the blog regarding Resident Evil 5? Is the trailer racist? If so why? If not why not?

About This Discussion

Started Apr 14 2008 by:

Nichole Pinkard
View Discussions »
⊕ Add as friend

Tag

Category: General
Tags: game, careers, design

In this post, Nichole Pinkard, in the role of the game design mentor, recruited bystanders (see forms of positioning in box 5.1). She used the pod to encourage participation on the site and also used the site to encourage participation in the pod. A call for participation she posted on Remix World spoke specifically to the African American student audience and positioned them to participate actively as game designers, framing this participation in terms of their possible futures in the field and noting the underrepresentation of African Americans currently. She also positioned students as social analysts when she asked them to provide and justify their view on whether a particular gaming ad is racist.

a reference to the idea of "remixing," or appropriating existing ideas and images to create a new and different message.

Remix World was originally conceived as an extension of DYN's in-school and after-school programming. As we show in the field examples, mentors used the site to enhance lessons, address the challenges of limited face-to-face time with students, archive and track students' progress, and negotiate levels of student engagement in activities. Mentors actively encouraged students to join Remix World; set up personal profiles; comment on media, artifacts, and designs; and post original work. Remix World was widely used in the school; during the 2007–2008 school year, the site had 252 registered users. By the end of eighth grade, 93 percent of eighth graders reported having their own personal Remix World profile pages. There were 524 individual discussion topics and 3,863 discussion or profile comments. The site consisted of 1,965 photos, 222 blog entries, 355 videos, and 424 song tracks, suggesting that it was used as a hub for sharing ideas and media within DYN. Logs of student participation on the site showed that students signed in to Remix World during, before, and after school and used it to connect with each other on a regular basis. Of the field notes from 159 unique classes, pods, and events that we observed, 89 (56 percent) contained references to Remix World (Zywica, Richards, and Gomez 2011).

Remix World had many features of informal social networking sites such as Facebook, but it also had a strong emphasis on privacy (all members had to be approved by the site codesigner or by DYN mentors) and moderation by site designers and mentors. The site also relied on scaffolding that extended and deepened its power as a learning space. The result was what we refer to as a "scaffolded social learning network" (Riel 2005; Riel and Harasim 1994). Mentors "scaffolded" by guiding students informally and through intentionally structured interactions to develop their skills as critical consumers. Rather than always modeling standard English, mentors often used a vernacular that students could relate to, which placed more of an emphasis on engagement and discussion than on formal writing skills. Of importance was the fact that mentors posted their own original creations, critiqued each other's work, and contributed to discussions—all in order to model how to use Remix World and to scaffold participation on the site. Also significant was the fact that teachers and parents were not allowed on the site, a rule established to help develop a student-driven space.

Our data show a rich variety of activities that developed on Remix World during the time of our field research. Analysis of the content on the site and the results of a short questionnaire administered to students revealed that students used Remix World for many different purposes, ranging from the basic—creating profiles, chatting and sending messages to friends, sharing favorite songs and videos—to the more advanced. In keeping with DYN's goals, students used Remix World to share photos and media; view, critique, and respond to other students' media and posts; submit homework; and post journal or blog entries (Zywica, Richards, and Gomez 2011).

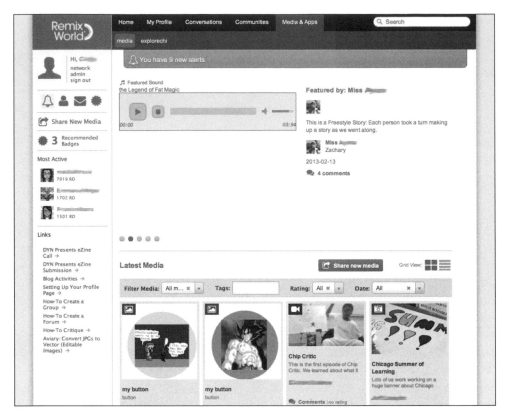

FIGURE 5.3
Screenshot of the Remix World site from 2012.

The examples in the next two subsections illustrate some of the types of interactions that emerged on Remix World, allowing mentors to leverage this space to develop and support learner identities as creative producers, critical consumers, and social advocates for better futures. The first example highlights the value of student profile pages and online discussions and demonstrates how mentors helped scaffold these discussions to facilitate more meaningful engagement in Remix World. The second example describes how Remix World became a space to showcase students' creative processes and outcomes.

Example from the Field: Student Blogs and Discussion Threads

Two of the students' primary activities on Remix World were posting blog entries and participating in discussions. These dialogues often revolved around posting and critiquing media, posing challenging questions about social issues or in response to popular media, and continuing discussions from classes and after-school pods. In May 2007, after Remix World had been live for a few months, many discussion topics had been posted, but there were relatively few comments under each one. One student introduced herself on her blog and encouraged students to be social activists.

<heart>!!I have arrived!!<heart>

Hey wats up,[1] This is belinda. I am new to REmix World. Just so i'm clear, i am in deed revolutionary..ya digg!! What i plan to do is connect with people, and touch bases with other students from other schools, and basically share my ideas and thoughts. Myabe chnged the views of how others think, becuase again "i am indeed revolutionary"!!! So K.I.T. An leave your comments on how you plan to change the world as we know it!!

In this initial phase of Remix World, many similar posts and threads existed on the site. Many of the students expressed their goals and dreams for changing the world, and some used the site to share their own poems and writings. As mentors began asking students to post their assignments for classes and to create their own blogs on Remix World, the site saw a considerable increase in activity. For example, in 2007 students were asked to write their own "I Have a Dream" remix. Renee, then in seventh grade, posted hers on her Remix World blog space:

I have a dream that drugs will go away. Nobody will killing people for no reason at all. I have a dream that all races will get to know each other more. Black and whites won't be talking about each other so much. I have a dream that more African American children will get to collage. More children will take their education seriously. I have a dream that minstrel shows will go away. No stereotypes will go on about black people. I have a dream that children will stop doing whatever they see on T.V that is violent. Ads on T.V.'s will stop persuading Young adults to drink, start drugs, and doing other bad thing like robbing someone, killing someone, and joining the game or becoming a thug. I have a dream. . . .

This personal post from Renee can be directly tied to a number of current topics in her DYN community. At the time of this post, minstrel shows were being discussed in her social studies class, and related student projects were being created in the after-school pods. Stereotyping of African Americans and women were topics in her digital queendom pod and, as we discussed earlier, violence in the media was the focus of a number of Freedom Friday events. On Remix World, Renee was able to continue her thoughts and conversations about these important and complex topics.

For many of these early posts, there were few or no responses from other students. However, as the site developed, mentors introduced more scaffolding and integrated the site more into activities. Much of this scaffolding happened through classroom conversations and through the mentors' modeling of participation by posting on Remix World themselves and commenting on student posts. In this way, they endeavored to create more networked and thoughtful discussions and postings on Remix World rather than the one-post threads described earlier or the simple updates to profiles.

For example, Brother Mike posted the trailer for the Hip-Hop Project, an arts-based education organization in New York City that offers multimedia tools and opportunities for youth to find a voice through the development of their own hip-hop expression. In a Remix World discussion thread, Brother Mike posed the question, "If you had the WHOLE WORLD READING . . . WHAT WOULD YOU SAY???" Several responses to this question were posted. One female student wrote, "If i had the whole world reading i would educate then conversate on the views of the world that dont know, understand, or want to understand. if i had the whole world reading educate the woman that you are not just female you are wise, strong, sexy, finer than wine, you know what u are woman and thats all the explanation u need."

In this example, Brother Mike scaffolded the interaction by providing a video and an open-ended question for students to respond to. At the same time, he encouraged students to craft their responses as though they "had the WHOLE WORLD READING" and to consider the stance they wanted to project to outside audiences rather than the private response they knew would be viewed only by a community of known instructors and peers—yet another example of how DYN positioned students as social analysts and contributors with a voice.

Recall that DYN students were encouraged to become social advocates for better futures. Issues of race and social justice were frequently discussed at Renaissance Academy, and they were important to the community and to mentors. As indicated in the example from Renee, Remix World soon became a powerful space for exploring these issues. In other instances, mentors provided feedback on student posts they found interesting or thoughtful and encouraged other students to respond to their peers' ideas.

In one case, a student posted a discussion thread about the "N word." In May 2007, Belinda posted a provocative and arguably plaintive set of comments about how African Americans are regarded in the United States. She began her claim suggesting that African Americans have been "brought down," "embarrassed," and "bamboozled" by society. She argued that this state of affairs has resulted in "embarrassment" and an embracing of the negative images. Belinda offered evidence of the multiple monikers applied to African Americans including *black*, *colored*, and the "N-word." She ended her post by suggesting that African Americans "fight back" against the negative views, making a plea to other Remix World participants for "feedback please!!"

Akili Lee and Brother Mike were the first to respond to Belinda. They recognized her thoughtful contribution on the site but also shared their views in response, helping to redefine her argument and offering ways to reframe the issue (see box 5.1). Akili praised her comments and posed a question: "excellent point Mzzzzz George. . . . I think the real question connected to this is why do we let other people define us?" In his response, Brother Mike referred to Belinda as a "Queen" and argued that "we" (African Americans) must see "ourselves" as "Kings and Queens." Further positioning Belinda and her peers as empowered persons who could use media creation in the future as a way to change stereotypes, Brother Mike commented, "I depend on you and the DYN family to be the seed to Remix the language . . . Remix the minds . . . Remix the hoods . . . Remix the World.—Keep Fighting/Writing."

Students also provided feedback to Belinda in the discussion forum. In their responses, Belinda's peers praised her comments and her passion: "I am awed at the intensity of your word however it is true"; "who knew that everybody has a little powerful words in them"; and "it sounds that you have worked hard on defining the meaning of 'Black.'" Belinda thanked respondents for their comments and wrote back, "i've been wanting 2 say this but never had place where my voice cud b heard, but no[w] i see what power they have done in return."

We see clearly through this example how Remix World became a very personal space for some students to express themselves and to develop their identities as socially aware media consumers and producers. Remix World offered a safe environment where students could openly and naturally discuss challenging and personal topics with their peers and mentors. We suggest that spaces such as Remix World are essential for developing the twenty-first-century student. On a daily basis, children and teenagers are exposed to images that, if left unexamined, can be confusing and misleading. For DYN participants, issues that emerged in contemporary media and were brought into classes and pods by mentors or students could be followed up online, whether serendipitously or deliberately. Remix World became a part of the mentors' routines, and they encouraged students to incorporate it as part of their own routines. They thus enabled another forum for students to voice their ideas and opinions while strengthening and exploring their emerging identities as digital media creators online. Even while students were free to contribute in the forms that they wished, the mentors also participated and continued to position students, inviting them and challenging them to critique and create.

Example from the Field: *Behind the Remix*

Behind the Remix was a series of videos posted on Remix World in 2008 in which students gave detailed "behind-the-scenes" accounts of how and why they created their projects. The videos highlighted student work in a variety of genres, including poetry, music, video, and design. Each episode focused on a particular piece (or series of pieces) and its process and prominently featured a student creator or creative team. Mentors collaborated with students, working behind the camera and as interviewers.

The various episodes highlighted examples of commendable student work and provided a point of collective reflection for DYN students. It was a venue for developing artists to showcase their work and their views of that work as they explicitly reflected on the creative process and for peers to observe each other as they took on these identities. By emulating the "behind-the-scenes" format used by major film studios, musicians, and other media producers, mentors positioned students by recognizing them as experienced or expert creators with a history of work to share.

The value of *Behind the Remix* for students was not only in the creation of these videos, but also in the way mentors demonstrated genuine enthusiasm for the students' work during episodes, providing encouraging and constructive feedback. For instance, during an interview with the sixth-grade student group ABC, the mentor compliments the young women on a rap song they had recently created. He suggests that the song itself was high quality and gives positive feedback on the way they integrated African proverbs, which they had been studying in class. In response, the students exhibit confidence that seemed to be bolstered by their mentor's encouraging tone.

Sometimes these invitations helped to reframe the reputations of students from disorganized to creative. For example, another *Behind the Remix* interview features Calvin and several peers talking about how their digital videogame, which they had created using the program Scratch, was still under construction (see figure 5.4). In the video, Calvin, who was sometimes characterized as disorganized by his peers, stands in front of an audience of students next to a screen projecting his laptop display. He explains the characters and the basic game play and, when prompted by the mentor, shows how the game actions are related to the script he has developed: "Here is the script. Scripts [*sic*] is how the game is supposed to play out. Like this is how the moves are." Calvin opens the Scratch window, showing both the on-screen game play and the code. He steps through actions in his game, explaining the highlighted Scratch code frame by frame. In the video, he answers questions from the audience. The mentor behind the camera also elicits answers about the team's ideas for the game, including what type of background they plan to implement. At the end of the segment, each team member stands up and briefly describes his or her role in the project. The mentor compliments Calvin on his graphics and specific functionality in the game. In this case, there is an implicit endorsement of this work as an example for future video games and of Calvin as a strong game creator. In this way, the *Behind the Remix* interviews became a space where students could feel comfortable discussing the contributions of their work to the DYN community and position themselves further as legitimate artists.

FIGURE 5.4
Video still of Calvin presenting his videogame designs on *Behind the Remix*.

Behind the Remix episodes were opportunities for the showcased individuals to reflect on their own identities as creators in response to the ways that their work had progressed over time. All students who participated in an episode were prompted to think about the various influences on their work and the different stages through which their work had progressed. In this process of reflection, they were invited to consider the ways that their work had changed as well as how they, as crafters of the work, had also changed. Reproducing the DYN program's strong emphasis on understanding work within a historical frame of reference, *Behind the Remix* also positioned students to consider themselves in relationship to historical figures and their work in relation to well-established genres. By comparing a group's hip-hop track or videogame to the work of established artists and designers, mentors positioned students to decide whether they identified with, rejected, or wanted in some way to rethink and redo those artists' style or message.

JUNIOR MENTORS PROGRAM

In addition to regular forums such as Freedom Fridays and the online space provided through Remix World, DYN also offered pathways for advanced students to further their skills as they served as role models for younger students. During the research period at Renaissance Academy, one such pathway was the Junior Mentors Program. The junior mentors were high school students who, after graduating from Renaissance Academy, continued learning and developing as "digital creators" while they helped the adult DYN mentors teach and guide younger students. Junior mentors had not only demonstrated impressive media skills while in middle school but also "exemplified a certain sense of leadership and seriousness to the work to which other students should aspire," according to Brother Mike. This "seriousness" was demonstrated by a high level of commitment to their craft and strong technical abilities.

Junior mentors at Renaissance Academy were paid for their efforts, serving as teachers' assistants in the after-school program, managing classes, and working in the front office. They were also given side projects, such as putting together "demo videos" or working on film crews for people or organizations that wanted to involve youth in their projects. They built deeper relationships with the DYN mentors, who held weekly professional development sessions with them to focus on skills both specific to and outside of their media of choice. Raphael, a Junior Mentors Program coordinator and a DYN mentor, commented:

We selected [junior mentors] because they were the standout students, the model DYN students. . . . One of the biggest reasons why it was me who was chosen to . . . start work on this project was because my focus was film, and two of the three original junior mentors, you know, film was their thing, film was their focus. So, you know, it was more so about me giving them more advanced things to do, to kind of maintain their skill set, to kind of develop their skill set throughout high school.

Brother Mike further remarked:

I can remember one story in particular, a student named David who was a seventh grader when Tony was in . . . eighth grade. . . . Tony moved into high school, and I remember [David] specifically saying that he wanted to take Tony's spot. So for us that kind of gave us a window into how students were seeing each other, that they saw very clearly that this group of students were getting a lot of outside work; they were being commissioned for a lot of things; the teachers saw them as leaders; the [mentors] would often ask them to do certain cool projects.

Opportunities like the Junior Mentors Program were beneficial in multiple ways. Mentors positioned students on pathways to deepen their media practice, to become mentors for younger students, and to earn money for quality work. The selected students were perceived as leaders within their community and built relationships with the younger students accordingly, learning how to teach and guide as they were taught and guided. Younger students had slightly older peers who were in their position not long ago and could be looked up to as models for what they might become. Thus, although junior mentors took on leadership positions, they continued to be learners, advancing to higher levels of creative practice. At Renaissance during our research period, the Junior Mentors Program was a valuable transition stage for students: junior mentors shifted from thinking of themselves as "students who do media" to identifying as artists. Though still growing, they had knowledge to impart to others and professional skills to showcase and utilize in the broader, professional artist community. This transition is illustrated in the summer film *Division 201*.

Example from the Field: *Division 201*

Division 201 is a collaborative film made in the summer of 2008. It demonstrates one way that student work continued to be supported and guided even after students moved on to high school (in this case, both middle and high school students were involved). The film was produced thanks to a partnership between DYN and the Chicago branch of the Independent Feature Project (IFP), a group of nonprofit organizations that assists independent filmmakers. Together, representatives from IFP, DYN mentor Rafael, and seven high school students—five of whom were at the time or would go on to become junior mentors—worked to develop a short film from pre- to postproduction. Raphael saw the project as a way for some of the older, more advanced students to work with professionals in the film industry and to gain the experience necessary to prepare them for college-level film and media programs as well as internships in the industry. IFP worked with different high schools and students, and, according to Raphael, the group "kind of educated them to be producers, directors, writers, the full gambit, so it was a good opportunity for us to put kids in a position they hadn't, hadn't been able to do with us. Most of the stuff they, students, had done with us at that time . . . were independent projects. There was some group work when it came to film, but it wasn't something that was big and had a budget, and we went and hired actors and really treated it like it was a film project."

The summer project was intended to help students understand the various roles involved in filmmaking (for example, what skill sets were required of an assistant editor versus those required of a producer or casting director) and to allow them to experience the collaborative process—even though each individual had a role with specific duties, he or she still had to work with the others to achieve a single, larger goal. The project was also meant to show students that with time and effort they, too, could produce results like what they saw on television or online and that such professional work was, as Raphael said, "within your grasp as long as you organize it and produce it the right way."

During the early sessions of June 2008, students, along with adults from DYN and IFP, brainstormed ideas and assigned roles. Students wrote script treatments for approximately fifteen stories. The list was whittled down to six treatments, and full scripts were written for those ideas. The students voted for their favorite; the chosen script was written by Tony, one of the junior mentors, who based the plot on his own experiences. The story concerned racial divisions within a school and how a class with a diverse makeup remained segregated until a new foreign student forced them to confront their prejudices and segregation. The young filmmakers debated the vision for their film, character names, where the foreign character should be from, scene effectiveness, necessary props, and set locations (see figure 5.5). Because one of the project's aims was to expose students to the professional community, there were "break-out" sessions with visiting industry professionals, who met with individual students to go into more depth about their assigned roles. Students also had to deal with real-life conflict when one of the team members quit the project, which, as Raphael pointed out, also happens in the industry. However, they were able to find a replacement who eagerly stepped into the role.

In postproduction, seventh- and eighth-grade students joined the project and were assigned to various teams to produce the soundtrack, design, or press for the film. *Division 201* was included in youth film festivals in Atlanta, Georgia, and Evanston, Illinois. It was also screened in Chicago at Columbia College and at an independent theater. The students who had collaborated in creating the film used it as part of their portfolios for college admissions and scholarships.

Division 201 provided an opportunity for students to be constructive producers and identified future pathways for them. During the process, students met industry professionals who would serve as important resources and expand their knowledge of filmmaking. As the students decided upon characters or worked out set locations and camera angles, they not only developed practical skills but also had to think about how each of these elements contributed to the overall vision of the story they wanted

FIGURE 5.5
Screenshot from *Division 201*.

to tell. The subject of the film—racial division—and the ways the students sought to convey their message to the audience reflected DYN's social advocate disposition. In the end, this project exposed junior mentors to professional filmmakers and digital film work processes and provided an important collaborative opportunity for all DYN participants. The middle school students learned from and worked with the junior mentors, and they were offered a concrete example of how their learning and interest in DYN could be sustained and nurtured in the future.

SUMMARY

As Na'ilah Nasir argues, identities are shaped over time by everyday interactions:

> [M]icro-interactions in learning moments come to shape broader trajectories of learning and identity. This is a critical point to understand for teachers and others who work with young people because it means that the bulk of what students will take from learning environments is the accumulation of multiple small-scale interactions where students are given access to learning or not, where their identities as learners are afforded or constrained. (2011, 131–132)

At the same time, we recognize that students' understandings of their rights and obligations with respect to the production and critique of media, the value of particular skill sets, and their potential as serious contributors to community life are dynamic processes rather than static aspects of their identities.

In this chapter, we have reviewed several ways in which the Digital Youth Network supported emerging creator identities in students, positioning them on a day-to-day level as critical media producers and consumers as well as social advocates for themselves and their communities. The program activities we have described provided an important structure for the development of DYN participants as digital media producers and exposed them to core values that the program aimed to foster. These specific spaces, where all students had the opportunity to participate, were dedicated to nurturing students' identities as digital media citizens.

Forums for showcasing student work were especially important in this process. The Freedom Friday activities provided students a space to share their finished projects, receive feedback, and view others' work. These same activities also allowed mentors to invite students to discuss significant themes pertinent to their lives and current events and give rise to socially relevant media projects. The *Behind the Remix* series, for example, used online video to transcend the limits of a live event and allowed all members of the school community to access examples of student projects. Although each *Behind the Remix* episode or Freedom Friday session focused on a particular issue, genre, or process, each was also a part of a larger DYN practice of modeling creative identities and helping students position themselves in relationship to these identities. Students with a diverse range of interests and skills—from game design to video production to poetry—were showcased as exemplars. As students were encouraged to respond to their peers' work, the showcasing and feedback process allowed them to organize their own sense of what a model creator is and to understand their DYN participation in relationship to those models.

Also vital to supporting creator identities was the initiation of dialogue around important issues that can inspire students' creative work. The Freedom Friday summit on school violence offered mentors a chance to deepen discussion around a topic with a larger group of students, regardless of which grade or pods they were in. Likewise, "Remix the Vote" brought relevant issues to the forefront and positioned students as change makers through media production practices. The online space Remix World provided an additional venue where students and mentors could expand conversations, share work and ideas more broadly, and affirm developing identities.

Features such as the Junior Mentors Program allowed adult mentors to identify future pathways for younger students. Although the mentors themselves provided models of mature artists, junior mentors exemplified young people close to middle school age who were building on their DYN experience to progress in their practice and work toward professional level activities.

Beyond the activities themselves, DYN mentors engaged in individual and group interactions that positioned students as sources of knowledge and expertise within the community and beyond. Within Freedom Friday forums, students were intentionally positioned as experts and sources of knowledge on relevant topics. News and other pieces of popular media were presented not as information to be memorized, but as portrayals that could be appropriated, rejected, or reconsidered depending on students' own points of view. In interviews, mentors expressed their vision of students as strong voices and initiators of social change, and this vision in turn shaped their interactions with students. In the *Behind the Remix* series, the format itself was envisioned to position students as experienced producers with important work to share. However, equally important was the way that mentors followed through with the positioning process in their interactions with students during the episodes, as in the example of the mentor's encouragement and feedback on the ABC track. In this way, positioning students as digital media citizens and nurturing these emerging identities happened on two levels—the level of program design and the level of specific discussions and interactions.

Finally, it is important to highlight the interplay between supporting identities as digital media citizens in other aspects of adolescents' developing identities as young women, young men, and, specifically in the case of Renaissance Academy's student body, young African Americans. The DYN program created a space in which racial and gender identity was explored. Categories of identity, Nasir argues, are made available by society and "filtered" for youth in important ways by the institutions and settings they attend (2011, 142). Through DYN, mentors brought into question many of the negatively stereotyped African American identities made available to students through mainstream media. At the same time, many of the mentors themselves provided role models as African American artists, designers, engineers, educators, and activists. Through programs such as the Junior Mentors Program and the *Behind the Remix* series, the mentors also set up advanced students as models. By representing these pathways within the program as well as calling on students to question identities often projected in the media, the DYN mentors offered students a means to confirm and strengthen their identities as both digital media citizens *and* young African American men and women.

In chapter 4, we traced the ways in which mentors invite students to become producers, as in the *Be a Voice, Not an Echo* video. In this chapter, we have illustrated the ways in which DYN guides students beyond this initial point of departure, helping them to develop their own unique voices and positioning them to apply their new expertise as media producers in constructive ways. These practices are further explored in the case narrative following this chapter, in which we share more about Maurice's development as a digital media citizen.

MAURICE: CREATING FOR SOCIAL CHANGE

But the main purpose [of my website] is to give teens a way to talk about and express their feelings about things you might not find in normal conversations. Like politics, the economy . . . things like that. And so that's the goal of [my social networking website] We Shift.

—Maurice (eighth grade), 2009

In the three years in which we collected data, Maurice was an active and vocal participant in the DYN community, eager to analyze media messages and use his skills to mobilize change, but also playful and humorous in his choice of content. Mentors described him as an innovator and a passionate, committed learner. His regular contributions to pod and class conversations did not always go over well with his peers, and mentors actively worked to reframe them as important and cool rather than as overbearing or nerdy. This reframing was consequential for Maurice and his peers alike. Although he developed strong skills in digital media production, his deeper interest was in the content he produced. Maurice made frequent use of the forum spaces at DYN—including Freedom Friday and Remix World—to showcase the work he produced for pods and classes as well as his own self-motivated projects. As we illustrate in the case portrait here, opportunities to share work and take on new roles within the community were important to Maurice's development as a creator, particularly given the social and political messages he hoped to communicate to others in the school and beyond.

DEVELOPING CAPACITY AS A CONSTRUCTIVE PRODUCER

> With the pods, it's more experiencing it yourself; in school, before you have a chance to experience something, they're explaining it to YOU.
>
> —Maurice (seventh grade), 2008

Maurice described pods as venues for pursuing "what *you* want to do," which made projects engaging and interesting for him. In this way, he contrasted the pods to his school classes, where, even when projects were flexible in some ways, students had less freedom of choice.

Maurice attended numerous pods across his middle school years. In sixth and seventh grades, he took the spoken-word, digital music, and radio pods, and in eighth grade he was in the digital music and digital video pods. In the sixth grade, he often attended Freedom Friday forums, and his projects were regularly in the DYN community's eye.

> I think just him kind of exploring what his computer was and what it could do, like, "Oh man, I can make a movie." I think once he realized those skills, he owns them. And then watching what he did in school from the iRemix class to spoken word last year to [the] radio show. . . . It's just amazing to watch a young person cover so many different mediums and do fairly well in all of them.
>
> —Brother Mike (mentor), 2008

In addition to his school and pod projects, Maurice learned on his own time. He became adept at seeking out help and locating the resources necessary to build what he envisioned, and he taught himself new software programs through exploration and trial and error. For instance, he made his first movie, *Great Leaders*, as a way to teach himself how to use iMovie HD. The topic was inspired by a discussion on minstrel shows at school, and he was further compelled to create the project by his desire to learn iMovie.

Maurice found inspiration and support at home for his media projects. He shared "good projects" with his parents, and several members of his extended family were involved in his digital media creations. Maurice took opportunities to teach his family how to use the technologies. For instance, he taught his aunt and cousin how to create digital music, and he occasionally sat with his three-year-old sister and supported her when she played online games. In addition, several of his self-initiated movie projects were biographies inspired by his home life, including an autobiography called *A Kid Named Mo* and a story about his cousin and aunt called *Harvest Life*. On one occasion, both Maurice and his uncle screened movies they had made for the entire family in an impromptu, friendly competition.

Maurice enjoyed showing his work to friends and family, and he seemed to have his audience in mind when he created. As he developed skills and gained experience, he began adopting a more iterative approach to his media creation. He sought feedback more often and stayed open to the evolution of his projects, driven by a desire to make the best final product. For instance, while working on his eighth-grade Living Museum documentary, Maurice watched several documentaries that gave him new ideas for how he could integrate facts, introduce his topic, and communicate content without being explicit. As a result, he edited and revised his documentary a number of times.

Despite Maurice's being very self-driven, several mentors were instrumental to his learning as they took on the roles of teacher, collaborator, audience, and critic. For instance, when Maurice was in the sixth grade, Pierre Tchetgen, who was a mentor for two of the pods Maurice attended, acted as Maurice's technology "tutor," informally helping him with projects during the after-school homework hour. Maurice oftentimes learned the basics of a production activity at DYN and then took off on his own, deepening his skills independently.

LEARNING TO CREATE AS A SOCIAL ADVOCATE AND CRITICAL THINKER

Several of Maurice's projects showcased him within his local community. For instance, when students

So when I went over to my dad's side of the family [for Thanksgiving], I showed them my movie, and, um, they gave a lot of input, too. . . . They were asking me really a lot about the theme and what it was mainly about and some of the—I put a lot of words in there, like *peace* and, you know, something—a lot of theme words, and they were asking me why I put those in there and did they mean anything particularly.

—Maurice (sixth grade), 2006

I showed him [Maurice] how to use [the] Pages application that I like, and he just picked it up really quickly, and I really didn't go over how to lay out with him, but he understood kind of what needed to go where and was able to teach that to some other students in the class. . . . He was able to kind of be that student teacher for me in that situation.

—Brother Mike (mentor), 2008

Screenshot from *American Rebel* by Maurice

were asked to create a video about an American rebel, Maurice chose to highlight himself and his work within the school community to advocate for the reinstatement of middle school recess. The project was screened at a Freedom Friday and posted on Remix World. Maurice thought he might use the video in the future if he ran for a class president "or something like that."

Several of his other projects situated Maurice within a larger sociohistorical-cultural context. Compared to some of his peers, Maurice had a sophisticated understanding of the big ideas the DYN program introduced, such as critical historical and social perspectives on media messages, and he often chose intellectually challenging topics for his projects. For instance, he created two documentaries that explored current events relevant to African Americans in history, including a documentary on Reverend Jeremiah Wright, focusing on his role as a creative and spiritual leader in Trinity Church before the controversy that arose during the Obama presidential campaign in 2008.

In seventh grade, Maurice began a social networking site to engage peers in political and social discourse. He viewed himself as an "inventor" and a "student activist." He explained that he was an inventor when he "put what [he] was thinking about into motion." "I was personally discovering new stuff that I had never known about," he said. "I never knew how to make a social network, I never knew what all these different words meant, and I was discovering this for myself." Maurice saw himself as an "activist" because his purpose in making the site "was a way of social activism to get people to stand up to what they believed in to talk about it, to discuss it, and to come together." In eighth grade, Maurice started a website to collect student and parent comments and ideas about school practices, and he used Google analytics to track participation in the site.

PROJECT SPOTLIGHT: WE SHIFT

In the spring of seventh grade, Maurice began We Shift, an online social networking space for youth to discuss what he called "twenty-first-century" issues. Maurice's goal in creating the website was to initiate a shift in young people's current mindset. He was convinced that the only way to create change was to "change the way people think."

According to Maurice, his website was completely self-initiated, and he worked on this project only in his free time. He had learned about the platform Ning from the first incarnation of Remix World and from an older student he met at camp who had used it to create his own site. Maurice viewed his We Shift endeavor as a serious enterprise—he set up business meetings and even created letterhead.

Maurice designed the website using a template from ning.com, which did not offer quite the flexibility he was accustomed to having after creating a website using Apple's iWeb in the sixth grade. Nonetheless, he learned several important facets of creating websites. He said that creating this website taught him about domains. He described what a domain is by using an analogy: "it's like owning property online." He discovered this meaning by investigating the topic on the Internet, and he said that this experience changed his approach to web design in that he read things more closely now.

Maurice planned to continue to attract new members to We Shift (at the time of the interview, June 2008, there were forty-two members), which was the part of creating the site that he seemed to enjoy most. He said that he was excited every time he got a new member. With respect to future plans for We Shift, Maurice hoped to develop it into an online and offline "organization" for twenty-first-century thinking. The website index page described the venture.

Text and Screenshot from We Shift by Maurice

Welcome to We Shift. The purpose of this network is to educate the young mind and to nurture the future. We want to change how people think in order to open their mind into a twenty-first century Enlightenment era. At We Shift we understand how important it is to educate the people. We are the facilitators of today's insightful intellectuals and tomorrow's leaders. We change from a realm of old thought to one of new thought. We redefine the twenty-first century.

POSITIONING MAURICE AS A TEACHER AND INNOVATIVE CONTRIBUTOR

Maurice frequently mentored and taught other students in pods or classes when mentors requested his assistance as a peer tutor. Thus, in a sense, he and these mentors became collaborators: when he mastered a concept or tool, they asked him to help other students. They also saw his perspective as useful in class discussions because he served as a bridge between the mentor perspective and the student perspective. Maurice often had ideas about music and video critique that were similar to those of the mentors, and he was able to persuade students to listen to these new perspectives and ideas. He occasionally volunteered to help peers with their various projects. For example, he described helping several peers with video editing and storyboarding.

Recognizing his expertise and teaching skills and aware of his We Shift website, a DYN researcher nominated Maurice to lead a professional development workshop for preservice teachers during the summer before he was in the eighth grade. Maurice was invited to play a formal role as educator. The goal of the session was to help teachers understand how social networks could be used to enhance the teaching of traditional academic content. After introducing himself as "CEO of We Shift," Maurice presented his social network, fielded questions from teachers, and worked one on one with teachers to build their own simple sites. This was an important leadership and teaching opportunity for Maurice, solidifying his commitment to educating others about technology.

LOOKING AHEAD TO THE FUTURE

By the end of eighth grade, Maurice's commitment to learning and technology and his ability to take advantage of new opportunities were clear. He claimed that he used to suffer from boredom. After having developed skills in technology, however, he began to recognize what he could accomplish if he dedicated enough time and effort. Maurice was then continually engaged in multiple technology-based projects and emerged as a creative producer in the DYN program.

In his eighth-grade interview, Maurice expressed interest in becoming a CEO of a large media distributor, such as Viacom or Time Warner, because he believed that they control what people see and hear, which means they are capable of true social impact. He demonstrated confidence and a strong sense of identity as a social activist and critical consumer throughout his time in the DYN program. An email exchange with a researcher, when Maurice was in the ninth grade, demonstrated that this confidence continued to show in his high school activities and projects. He took on leadership as class president and as a nonvoting student member of the Board of Trustees at the competitive, private, college preparatory high school he attended. He continued sharing his technological skills as cohead of the technology committee, which helped students work with technology, and he advocated for spaces for students, such as a laptop-charging center. Maurice's skills as learner, teacher, leader, social activist, and media citizen were evident throughout middle school, and he appeared to maintain these skills as he transitioned to high school.

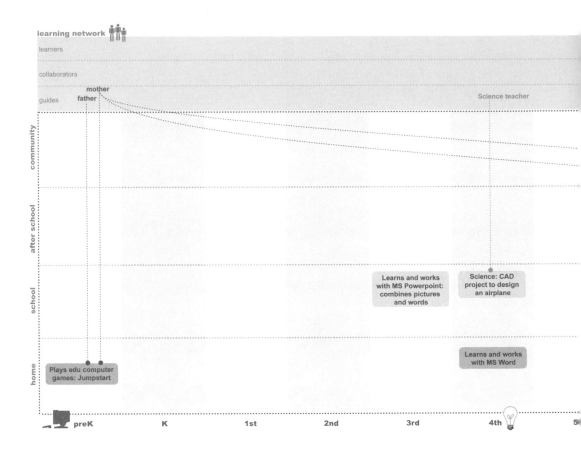

Maurice's learning pathway exhibits work across all four contexts—**home**, school, after school, and **community**—as well as the presence of an extensive social learning network 👫.

His use of a computer started early 🖥 in his playing of educational games at **home** with his **parents**. During elementary school, he learned basic productivity tools such as PowerPoint (school) and Word (**home**), and in fourth grade he first used the computer for a fluency-building 💡 design activity, when he designed an airplane using CAD in science class.

In sixth grade, he got his own laptop 💻 and joined multiple DYN pods, and we see a burst of activity at school and after school. His projects were guided by **mentors** and teachers, and he often collaborated with peers to create movies, music, and websites. Transferring skills and ideas, he began independent activities at **home**—for example, continuing his African American history video projects.

Maurice

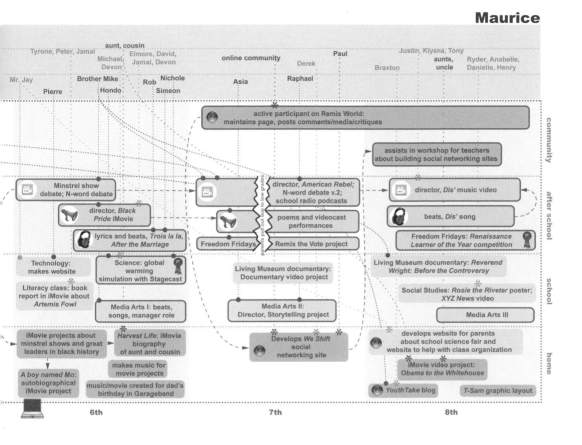

In seventh grade, Maurice became active on Remix World, moving his work into the **community** context. Online communities 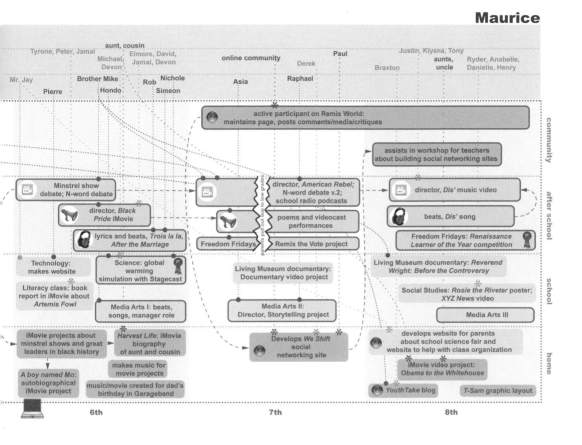 and resources became integral to many of his projects. Despite a temporary break 〰 in pod attendance—his parents took him out of the pods due to poor grades—Maurice developed projects in **pods** and **classes** and shared work online 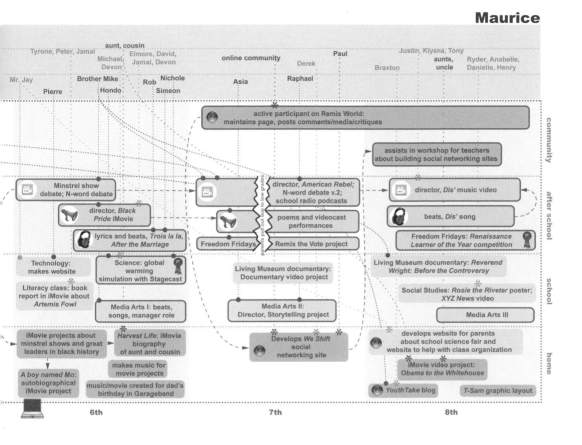 and during **Freedom Friday** forums. On his own time, he developed an online social network, We Shift, which led to an invitation to help at a preservice workshop for teachers. His technology learning network 👪 included early and ongoing **family** presence, peers and **mentors** he connected with during middle school, and, increasingly, partners he met in the wider **community**. Maurice's work was twice recognized by formal awards 🎖, including the **DYN** Renaissance Learner of the Year in 2009.

APPROPRIATING THE PROCESS: CREATIVE PRODUCTION WITHIN INFORMAL INTERACTIONS AND ACROSS SETTINGS

Brigid Barron, Véronique Mertl, and Caitlin K. Martin

> I like to record myself playing and even singing sometimes along with it so I can critique what I'm doing. And I like to create projects, like movies sometimes, like on YouTube. So . . . I just like to play around with it even if we don't have projects.
>
> —Ruby (eighth grade), 2009

Interests are powerful catalysts of learning. Personally engaging topics focus our attention, lead us to persist despite challenges, and often generate new questions we want to pursue (Hidi and Renninger 2006). Under the right conditions, interest-driven learning can lead to consequential decisions to seek out new topic-related resources. Enrolling in classes, finding peers with expertise, searching for online resources, and exploring playfully are all choices that set in motion new opportunities to learn. Over longer periods of time, these less-formal pursuits may coalesce and come to play a role in life choices and prospects. Given the powerful nature of interest-driven learning, understanding the conditions that support it is critical and our three-year study offers an opportunity to contribute to this agenda.

Earlier chapters described the mentor practices and material resources that seeded creative work within pods and media arts classes, nurturing students' capacities to become constructive producers, critical consumers, and social advocates for better futures. In this chapter, we turn to a discussion of the less intentional but, nevertheless, very powerful learning processes that emerge as students deepen their interests and commitments to developing their growing competencies. In our study, we were interested in whether seeds for imaginative work would take root and whether learners would take ownership of—or, in the language of Russian philosopher Mikhail Bakhtin (Wertsch 1998), *appropriate*—the content and practices associated with their DYN projects (John-Steiner 2000; Rogoff 2003). In particular, we sought to determine whether DYN learners would take up these practices in new settings within their broader learning ecologies (Barron 2006; J. Brown 2000) and what resources were important in enabling them to do so.

The framework guiding this set of analyses conceptualizes a child's learning ecology as the totality of settings within and across virtual and physical spaces that provide opportunities for learning. In this framing, learners are recognized as active in creating opportunities for themselves, and boundaries between settings are seen as varyingly permeable. Interest-driven activities in particular are likely to be observed across life settings given time, freedom, and resources to learn. This ecological view foregrounds the possibility that opportunities will diversify and grow over time as well as the possibility that they narrow or falter depending on social, temporal, and material resources (Azevedo 2012; Barron 2006). With these ideas in mind, we designed our research to track whether DYN students would begin to develop their own projects, set their own goals for learning, find resources that supported their expertise development, build relationships that advanced their agendas, and be recognized by others for their expertise, whether in school or out. These outcomes are in fact the ones that most educators would be delighted to see, but they are difficult to document without qualitative longitudinal research methods that can track the evolution of activities and relationships over time.

In the remainder of this chapter, we describe our findings in terms of three types of self-sustaining processes that, although not planned by the DYN leadership, were consequential for learning and for students' identities as creators, collaborators, teachers, and learners. These processes are summarized in table 6.1 and include (1) *creating* personal projects and pursuits outside of pod or class time; (2) *recruiting* support from mentors or other adult guides; and (3) *sharing* DYN-earned expertise with others through teaching or consulting. We elaborate on the significance of these three emergent processes and consider each of our case study participants in relation to them. Although these processes are not independent of one another, it is still useful to consider them separately. Doing so helps us see subtle variations in learners' experiences, sets the stage for recognizing the potential to intentionally design more opportunities for productive learning processes to emerge, and provides ideas for novel metrics of the success of informal and formal learning environments.

CREATION OF PERSONAL PROJECTS AND PURSUITS THAT SUSTAIN LEARNING

Figure 6.1 illustrates learner-initiated moves in relation to the DYN teaching practices. As described in chapters 4 and 5, the DYN leadership intentionally seeded creative work and engaged learners as social, constructive, and critical makers and users of new media. Mentors generated opportunities for students to look closely at the social and political dimensions of their worlds. They invited thoughtful reflection on and

TABLE 6.1
Self-Sustaining Practices and Processes

Creating new personal projects outside of DYN, alone or with others	These interest-driven efforts were not linked explicitly to pods or classroom assignments. They were started when there was free time, and were of varying levels of complexity, duration, and collaborative engagement. The content was linked to long-standing hobbies or could be inspired by recent experiences. For some friendship ensembles, personal digital media projects became focal activities that in turn strengthened and elaborated their group identities to emphasize their collective creative capacity.
Recruiting support from mentors, teachers, and parents	Recruitment involved active attempts to get help with a new technique or software tool or to get feedback on projects. Learners who more actively demonstrated their interests and intentions to learn positioned themselves to recruit support in the form of advice and other resources. In turn, adults' perceptions of DYN participants were shaped by the frequency or absence of these gestures for recognition, attention, and support.
Sharing expertise with family and community, by invitation or self-initiated	Knowledge of how to use hardware and software, design skills, and troubleshooting expertise were shared with parents, siblings, and peers. Parents and mentors connected DYN members with community-based opportunities to assist others with projects or to engage in more organized teaching opportunities.

critique of media messages, the envisioning of alternative perspectives, and the embodiment of these perspectives in a wide range of digital artifacts. Challenges to design original games, graphics, films, beats, lyrics, and poetry encouraged the development of new projects. Contests and connections to practicing filmmakers, poets, musicians, game designers, and engineers also served to inspire production. *Behind the Scenes* interviews, forums, and online spaces provided additional ways to showcase and celebrate their work.

During the three-year period of our study, we found that although DYN participants rapidly took up formally presented challenges to create work, they also pursued their own personally relevant projects. Because each young creator brought his or her own set of concerns, hobbies, preferences, social networks, and constraints to DYN,

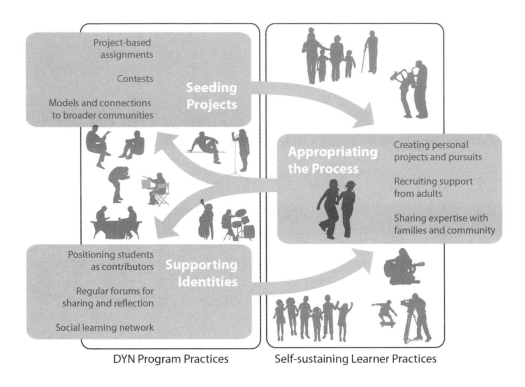

FIGURE 6.1
Relationship between DYN practices and self-sustaining learner practices.

each developed unique collaborations, mentoring relationships, and favored genres of production. In so doing, they created a variety of pathways leading to different profiles of expertise.

The development of unique pathways was made possible through the program's multilayered design. Although the media arts classes were required, the after-school DYN affinity pods were open spaces by design. This flexibility allowed students to choose partners to work with and projects to take on and allowed mentors to develop a wide range of informal teaching practices tailored to the students in their charge. Interactions were often fluid and unplanned, building off of common interests or adapting to particular opportunities. Access to laptops and a suite of software that was designed for creating original media was also critical because they made possible spontaneous project work whenever time allowed. Outside of pod or media arts time, individuals and collaborative groups were able to continue to create and explore topics, genres of production, modes of expression, and learning resources.

The generation of personal projects is a significant marker of consequential learning. It signals a willingness to exert agency, to conceive of new aims, and to pursue learning for oneself (Green 1995). When a new project is started by choice, the learner has a chance to experience the feelings associated with initiating, planning, and pursuing a path of his or her own making. And, importantly, personal projects that involve digital production often provide the impetus for new opportunities to learn as designers seek to create what they have imagined and invariably need additional resources and guides (Barron 2006).

Inspirations for Personal Projects

By the end of eighth grade, each of our nine case study learners described technologically focused personal projects that were not linked explicitly to pod or class assignments. Ideas for these personal projects came from multiple sources. Zach, for example, reported: "I mostly get my ideas from the world, just life, experiences. Go to school, somebody talks about something, I think, 'That'll be funny,' [and I] make a movie about that." Monica took on a project that involved taking apart a solar panel because she was interested in learning about its inner workings and wanted to build one for herself. This interest was prompted by problems managing her own electronics: "My battery always dies with everything. So I'm trying to get something where I don't have to run to an outlet every time." Monica reported that in this pursuit she was not receiving help from anyone she personally knew but instead primarily was using books and the Internet to help her find information.

Some of our case study students created multiple projects that allowed them to reflect on their own identities, the identities of leaders they looked up to, and their future plans for civic and community engagement. For example, Maurice developed one movie project based on his own life, another based on the personal histories of family members, and a third focused on African American leaders. Ruby, a committed writer, explored themes of fitting in socially and an emerging sense of leadership. In one of the poems she submitted for the Renaissance Learner contest, she paired visual images with reflections on her desire to effect positive change in the future: "I am the future. Fearless, unique, talented, unknown, reckless, eager to change my world. Eager to change my world."

Other personal projects reflected themes related to learners' possible adult selves but clearly had deep roots in interests established before their sixth-grade year. For example, Michael's love of aviation took center stage in his discussions about how he used technology on his own time. He made clear during the research interviews that he had long been set on becoming a pilot, and his motivation to engage with this topic came from an imagined future self (Cross and Markus 1991). Michael participated in a forum and photo-sharing website focused on airplanes, Airline.net; he apparently spent a fair amount of time using his computer to find images and information about airplanes online, and his Remix World page was decorated with aviation imagery. He also reported how his mother's affiliation with the airline industry gave him access to semiprofessional-grade flight-simulation software. Although this long-standing interest in aviation remained focal for him, Michael also developed new interests during middle school. For example, he reported that a female peer's simulation science project motivated him to try to do his own project with Scratch, the programming and game-making environment used at DYN. Like many other students we talked to, he reported that some projects he started were motivated by boredom, such as a four-minute movie he made while visiting a relative in the hospital. Other digital projects of his were tied to long-term goals such as seeking funding for a youth-oriented ambassador's program. He used the Internet to find sponsors, created and posted a website about his hoped-for journey, and wrote to companies to secure support.

When learners' prior interests were a good fit with mentor expertise or pod offerings or both, we found that they were often intensified and elaborated through DYN. Evan, a prolific creator of beats, attributed his commitment to developing this skill to a long-standing family focus on music. In his three years of participation in the DYN digital music pod, Evan reported producing between sixty and eighty unique beats. Simeon, the digital music pod mentor, taught Evan how to create music using Garage-Band and the sampling and sequencing machine Music Production Center. Evan went on to use these technologies to create pieces on his own time, and he routinely sought out information online about ways to improve his practice. In particular, he used the video-sharing website YouTube as his main source of video tutorials; he subscribed to a YouTube channel with helpful videos about using the Music Production Center. Evan observed, "I can learn better by seeing something than by trying to read it." He also communicated with people online to get advice and noted that he routinely received responses within a few days. He was continually inspired by artists he came across online: "I see a lot of artist MySpace pages, and I check out what they do and what they did and things like that. . . . I get a lot of ideas." In seventh grade, besides learning to create beats and continuing to make music, Evan found himself analyzing songs using concepts learned in the music pod and contrasting newer and older styles: "I've noticed that in a lot of songs played nowadays, they usually have a kick, a snare, and then a hi-hat. Back then, they'd just have a kick and the snare and a hi-hat here and there, but now in songs they have kicks, snares, and hi-hats everywhere."

Calvin, who became known for his skills as a game creator, came to DYN with a passion for playing games and was therefore thrilled to be involved in the game design pod. Through his participation, a persistent interest in developing games emerged, and he became a local expert with Scratch. Moreover, real or imagined competition motivated Calvin and his mates as they worked on their latest characters and game narratives. At times, Calvin imagined his own competitive context as he worked or played alone, claiming that this vision energized him: "To me, it is like a contest because that is how I do well, is by pretending it is a contest when it really isn't."

Personal Projects in Collaboration with Peers or Family

Case study learners frequently reported projects where they worked with or gained inspiration from peers or family members. Renee first thought of creating a personal website when she saw one that a classmate had built. She was further encouraged in the course of a media critique session in the sixth grade: "Brother Mike said instead of going to everybody else's websites and stuff, you can create your own, create your own comments that people will want to read, and videos and games."

One Friday afternoon when Renee was bored, she decided to try out the iWeb application that came bundled on her school laptop. With encouragement from Brother Mike, she learned the application on her own. Later that year in the publishing and design pod, the pod mentor, Pierre, gave her a few more tips on using this app. In this project, Renee created "a blog of myself and my life," and her website had "pictures pasted, like from the Disney World trip I went to, pictures of me, my family, my pets I had in the past or have now." It included a video of a friend dancing and singing, and another video of her five- and six-year-old cousins dancing so that "they would know about what timing is like doing ballet, hip-hop dancing, singing." The home video she produced also showcased her cousins reciting the alphabet.

Kiley (one of the leads of the "Jappin" project described in chapter 4) similarly took the initiative to carry out at least four independent projects that involved family members. These projects included animated scenes created with her older sister, a "picture photo with me and my sister and my family," and an iWeb page about her family. She also created an iWeb page with her friends.

In some cases, personal projects started by one student became collaborative as a leader realized the student could use some help. For example, in the spring of his seventh-grade year, Maurice began a social networking website, We Shift (see case narrative C for more detail on this extended effort). His goal in creating the website was to initiate a shift in the current mindset of young people; he crafted an online space for youth to discuss what he called "twenty-first-century" issues. He started the project on a day that he had "nothing else to do" and no plans for the entire day. Maurice said that he created this project alone, but he also reported two "administrators" for the site: DYN students Michael and Devon. Michael was the first administrator, the "Dean of Admissions," a position he acquired after Maurice asked him to recruit three to five members. In another business-minded decision, Maurice appointed Devon, a ninth grader and DYN alumnus, as administrator after Devon offered to bring members of his own website over to WeShift.com. Like many collaborative ventures we learned about, this one had its troubles, and Michael ultimately left the group because he believed his position was being taken over by other group members.

Maurice drew on other learning resources as well. He originally created We Shift through a social networking server, Ning. At camp during the summer after seventh grade, Maurice met Andre, a student from a different school who was willing to teach him the computer programming language HTML. Maurice reported that he was learning this language so that We Shift would eventually have its own domain and not be affiliated with or controlled by the Ning server. He was seen carrying around a thick paperback book about HTML and XML.

We also noted friendship groups whose members worked closely together over extended periods of time and formed collective identities as creative collaborators or competitors. As we noted, Calvin enjoyed friendly competitions and in seventh grade reported that informal game-making sessions sparked ideas: "How I come up with the idea? Well, because we having a competition where—like a friendly competition who will make the best videogame. It's me, Jordan—it's—like Jordan and Harrison, they're working together, and I'm working by myself. And we're trying to see who can make the best videogame."

Collaborative ventures with peers were often challenging and proved to be important learning opportunities for DYN participants. Difficulties in generating a common vision or in coordinating efforts, maintaining joint attention, and recruiting the participation of all collaborators were typical. Although these challenges led many learners to be wary of joint efforts, the fact that most had multiple experiences with different configurations of partners gave them opportunities to reflect on the processes that worked and those that did not. They were also able to begin to identify ventures that felt more positive, and these ventures often included projects that required complementary skills and alignment of efforts.

Several students noted how working with friends, particularly on graded projects, was risky. Despite this view, we found evidence that for some friendship ensembles, personal digital media projects became focal activities that in turn strengthened and elaborated their group identities as mates to emphasize their collective creative capacity not only in school, but out of school as well. For example, in her seventh-grade publishing and design pod, Renee and best friend Tashi formed a production company that, in a way, served to formalize the duo's frequent partnerships on their at-home and pod projects. They named themselves "Twilight Zone Productions" so that "people they will remember us: 'Okay, they're unique, they do stuff that's crazy-good.'" Whereas this duo worked together mostly at school, other groups did much of their collective work outside of school or pod time. Given the importance of supporting youth's developing repertoires of collaborative practices (Mercier, Tyson, Mertl, et al. 2008), coupled with the common challenges we observed, we return to this topic in chapter 8 and highlight the need for continued effort to design resources that scaffold joint efforts. For now, we provide a detailed example of another informal and successful friendship-based collaboration between Evan and Zach.

Example from the Field: Legends 'til Death

Two of our case study students, Evan and Zach, were members of an informal group called "LTD Entertainment" (LTD stood for "Legends 'til Death"). The friendships were born when the original members began roller-skating together at an early age. During their sixth-grade year, when some began to acquire video skills (Evan and Zach among them), they began making videos of themselves skating and added music to the background. In middle school, they began to create other projects unrelated to skating, particularly videos that they would post on YouTube or on their group's MySpace page. Many of their projects were spontaneous. For example, one evening at Zach's house they stayed up until after midnight making a fictional short film. Evan participated as cameraman and editor and did some of the directing as well. They used their laptop cameras to record, and the acting was improvised. As Evan reported when he was in the eighth grade, "We just decided to make a movie. We just randomly got up and said, 'Let's make a movie. What is it going to be about?' We found a topic, and then after it was just improv from the actors to the cameras. We said, 'Let's shoot it this way' and 'You do that that way' and 'You say this' as we progressed."

There is some evidence that competition was important in inspiring the group's creative work. One of their movies, *Revenge*, which Zach counted among his group's best, was made in part to outdo their rival group (composed of other DYN students in the same grade), Group 5 Entertainment. Within pods, competition between the Hurricanes (which overlapped with the LTD group) and the group that created the song "Jappin" (see chapter 4 for more detail) was sparked when it became clear that "Jappin" was becoming a popular piece among students and mentors. These frequent references to competition need to be put in the context of the local and global professional norms and practices among artists that influence DYN practices. For example, local hip-hop artists establish "beat battles" as a way to generate enthusiasm. DYN mentor Simeon described this trend:

It is healthy competition. That's something that has gotten kind of big. A lot of people in Chicago would—musicians would come together, and they would have these—they are really beat showcases, but they would frame it as beat battles . . . and that is where you would play a beat, somebody else would play a beat, and the crowd and judges would decide which beat they think is better. Well, that's all kind of relative. I mean people have different tastes, but the whole purpose is to generate a level of enthusiasm.

At the end of their eighth grade year, the LTD members were working on another movie with support from DYN mentor Erica, even though the project was not specifically linked to a pod or class. Zach wanted to keep the content a surprise: "It's action, romantic, comedy. We're just putting everything in it. Just to make one big movie of every category."

RECRUITING SUPPORT FROM ADULTS

As the examples shared in the previous section suggest, learning to create within DYN was typically a deeply social process, connected to and emergent from ongoing stable relationships. However, the extent to which any stable relationship offers the potential for learning depends on many factors, including partners' types of interests and forms of expertise, the interactional practices that develop, and the partners' intentions with respect to their own and others' learning and development (Barron 2003; John-Steiner 1999). So beyond the development of personal projects carried out alone or with peers or siblings, a second type of emergent learning opportunity stems from learners' interactions with various adults. This type of learning is more likely when learners make their personal work and commitment to learning visible to the adults they interact with or when those adults actively encourage less-visible DYN students to share their work with others.

Our research indicated that students vary in how energetically they work to recruit the attention of adults in ways that support their learning. Some actively promoted their projects, whereas others kept them under the radar or only chose to share their work with a small circle of trusted parents, teachers, or mentors. Similarly, some students were deeply persistent when they want to learn a new technique or software tool, whereas others requested help quietly or not at all. In turn, adults' perceptions of DYN participants were shaped by the frequency or absence of these gestures for recognition. Learners who more actively demonstrated their interests and intentions to learn positioned themselves to recruit support in the form of advice and other resources.

Across our nine case study students, we found multiple examples of ways that parents and mentors supported learning. We also found links between adult expertise and the types of support provided as well as variability in parent and mentor recognition of independent project work and nascent interests. Here we provide examples of what we observed with respect to students sharing projects with their families and mentors. We also discuss the use of media project portfolios as a means for students to demonstrate their competence to adults not familiar with their histories of media production, especially in the context of applying to high school.

Soliciting Feedback and Help from Parents

Empirical work reveals a complex portrait of computer use in the home that suggests it is highly influenced by the specific family context and mediated by parent interests, knowledge, and values (Kerawalla and Crook 2002; Livingstone 2002). Disparities in family-based expertise and resources have been well documented (Warschauer and Matuchniak 2010). In one comparative study of the use of computers at home, researchers found that parent involvement was rare, with 72 percent of parents feeling that their children would not like it if they were present during computer use and many feeling that their children were quite competent and did not need their help (Kerawalla and Crook 2002). However, other research suggests that parents may play key roles in their children's technology learning and that these roles do not always require specific technical knowledge.

In a study carried out in Silicon Valley, parents played a variety of roles that were fundamental for the advancement of learners' production activity (Barron, Martin, Takeuchi, et al. 2009). Some of these roles did not require the parent to have greater technical expertise than the child. For example, parents could collaborate, learn from their children, broker outside learning opportunities, provide nontechnical support, or employ their children as technical helpers around the house. These types of engagement—though not dependent on technical expertise—helped their children learn. When parents did have technical expertise, they could also teach their children more directly through explanations or demonstrations. We used this analytic scheme to consider how DYN parents supported their teens and to deepen our framework.

The parents of our DYN case study students also engaged with their children around projects the children brought home, enabled by the laptops that traveled with them to and from school. Consistent with the learner/audience and nontechnical consultant roles we found in Silicon Valley, six of our nine case students (Zach, Maurice, Ruby, Evan, Michael, and Monica) gave multiple examples of how their parents had inspired and encouraged them to continue to develop their technical and expressive expertise. These positioning interactions were frequently future oriented and went beyond the content of the specific project; parents were driven by the goal of helping their children become socially, emotionally, and personally mature. For example, when Zach learned new skills at school, such as how to make beats using GarageBand, he shared his creations with his parents, giving them an opportunity to provide feedback and encouragement. Zach's mother noted that Zach could lose interest in endeavors when he felt he was not leading or excelling in the way he would like, and she acted as a nontechnical consultant by helping him to increase his patience and perseverance with encouragement and framing challenges as events to be expected. Zach's mother included his friends and LTD members in activities—such as creating "vision boards"—that were designed to help them envision their futures.

Zach, actively seeking adults' opinions, said that he "like[s] showing things to people" and that their feedback affected his work. He saw the value of critical feedback from his older brother, who was in his late twenties, as well as from teachers and mentors, depending on their area of expertise, "[b]ecause [without feedback] I would just say that it is good, all my work I say is good. . . . I like it even if it's horrible. I can't do that, so I have to, you know, have their input. If they say that it is horrible and I say it is good, I know that there is something wrong with me in my taste or design."

Evan also found his parents' feedback and suggestions to be important. In fact, he gauged the amount he had learned—in the DYN pods, for example—by the amount of new knowledge and number of projects that he brought home and shared with his parents. Evan's mother actively encouraged him to share his skills with friends and relatives; for example, she told him that he was good with iTunes playlists, and he followed her suggestion to make CD mixes to give to friends as gifts. When Evan won the Living Museum contest (see chapter 4 for a description of the Living Museum contest) for his history of jazz documentary, his mother consequently signed him up for a script-writing class in a local community center, an example of brokering a new related opportunity for him to learn. For more detail on this, see the section "Example from the Field: Evan, Bringing Jazz and Blues to Silvertown" in chapter 4.

Michael's mother reported that she often didn't have the time, expertise, or patience to teach any of her children technical skills directly, though she noted that Michael often watched her work and would immediately try out what he learned in his own projects. Additionally, she brokered a significant learning opportunity for him when she perceived that he needed to learn more about Internet security—she had him do research on privacy laws and investigate what might happen if a family member's identity were compromised.

Monica sought feedback from both her parents, though in different ways. Her parents' expertise played a role in how they supported her efforts. For example, she said that her father provided gentle feedback for her ideas and projects, whereas her mother dependably provided in-depth critiques on the topics that Monica brought to her. Monica emphasized her mother's creativity—her mother was a painter and a photographer and often gave feedback on the visual dimensions of Monica's projects.

Expertise also played a role in the type of help that Ruby got from her mother, whose experience as a journalist positioned her to be able to comment on and encourage Ruby's writing. Her mother also worked at the YMCA and helped produce the magazine that Ruby worked on, so she was able initially to teach Ruby the layout and design tools the group used, providing both explanations and demonstrations. Interestingly, Ruby actively engaged her mother in her writing projects but did not share other DYN projects, such as her game and simulation work.

Maurice showed his movies to his parents and extended family and reported that they not only gave him feedback but also asked him questions about his choice of images and text. Maurice's mother was one of the few parents who sat in on pods, and Brother Mike reported, "She would always be there and have a word afterwards." She wanted to know what they were teaching him and kept a close eye on how his deepening interest in media might be competing for his homework time (see case narrative C for a full account). She was also attentive to the themes of African American identity in his media work and attributed this emphasis at least in part to family values: "Because we're very conscious about who we are as people, that seems to come out a lot in his work." Maurice's mother was the first one to teach him word processing and continued to help him format and edit his written work because, according to Maurice, "she is the 'literacy scholar'" in the family.

Tacitly or explicitly soliciting feedback is an important move on the part of a learner, but those adults targeted for sharing need to have the time and confidence to be responsive for the effort to pay off. In spite of the students' enthusiasm, some of their parents did not show a great deal of interest in their children's digital production work. Other parents explicitly said that they did not see it as their role to intrude on their children's activities, but rather to provide materially for them and be there as a resource in the event of emergencies. Some parents who did take the time to hear about their children's work still felt a lack of technical expertise that caused them to shy away from offering their perspectives. Both of Renee's parents, for example, had been an audience for some of her digital project work, and when she shared her website with them, they asked her to explain how she made it, impressed that it looked like a professional site. Finally, mentors reported that some parents indicated little interest when their children showed them the games they had been working on. However, the majority of case study students gave examples of sharing their work with their parents, leading to feedback, encouragement, or access to resources that would further their efforts. Several of the parents of our case study learners benefited from their children's expertise—for example, when the children taught their parents what they were learning or served as general computing consultants at home. We provide detailed examples of parents as learners later in the chapter when we discuss how DYN students shared their expertise with others. We also offer quantitative data about parent roles and expertise at DYN in chapter 7.

Building Relationships with Mentors

The struggles that mentors felt in their hybrid teaching and mentoring role did not necessarily come across strongly to the DYN members. Most of our nine case study students described mentors as unique teaching and learning partners within their broader learning network of parents, teachers, and tutors. They were described as "friends," as teaching "side by side," as "fun," "laid back," "cool," and "challenging." Some mentors ended up leaving DYN because they were less willing to take on some of the expectations for documenting their teaching plans or because their experience with DYN was not working for other reasons. Several students noted how much they had learned from those who left, and some chose not to participate in particular pods because a favorite mentor was no longer teaching. The research literature on mentoring confirms the importance of stability for effective mentoring to occur (Rhodes and Lowe 2008). We return to this topic in chapters 8 and 9 when we consider challenges and opportunities for future work.

In spite of some turnover, the DYN mentors were a largely stable group during the period we observed, which allowed learners to develop trusting relationships with them. However, we did find variability in the quality and quantity of interactions between mentors and our nine case study students. And as the quantitative data we describe in chapter 7 reveal, not all students rated mentors as an important learning resource, though we found less of a range among our nine case learners. Four of the nine (Ruby, Calvin, Renee, and Monica) rated the mentors as "extremely important" to their learning about technology. Another four (Michael, Kiley, Zach, and Maurice) rated mentors as "very important," and one student (Evan) rated them as "somewhat important."

The amount of attention mentors gave to learners depended on a number of factors. Our conversations with the mentors suggested that their relationships with DYN learners were constantly negotiated. As Brother Mike noted, "I teach everybody, but my mentorship needs to be earned." Part of earning mentorship was showing up regularly and participating in DYN activities, although as the case narrative following this chapter and highlighting Ruby's relationship with Brother Mike illustrates, where the learner's drive was sufficient, even showing up was not always strictly necessary. Rather, demonstrating a level of commitment to learning was key.

During our case study students' seventh-grade year, the research team had the opportunity to gather data from mentors on how they perceived they had interacted with these students. We created an inventory of roles based on our California research, which included teaching, collaborating, learning, employing or assigning responsibility, providing resources, and brokering connections. Based on mentor input, we added two more categories ("being an audience for their work" and "providing examples") and asked each mentor to indicate which of these roles he or she had played for each student. The results reflected what we saw in the qualitative data. That is, the breadth of roles and the number of mentors playing these roles varied for individual DYN students. For ease of communication, we have created one score that reflects the depth of mentor attention as represented by the total number of roles played by all mentors (roles across mentors) and a second score that represents the number of roles mentors played for each case study student among the nine roles we asked about (breadth of role types). These data are presented in table 6.2.

TABLE 6.2
Roles across Mentors and Breadth of Role Types for Each Case Study Student

	Roles across Mentors*	Breadth of Role Types**
Boys		
Zach	37	9
Maurice	35	9
Calvin	29	8
Michael	17	5
Girls		
Renee	27	7
Monica	27	7
Kiley	25	7
Ruby	22	6

* Total roles played by all mentors.

** Number of roles played out of the nine roles we asked about.

Note: We do not have this data for Evan, who was added as a case study student after this data collection effort.

One factor that differentiated our DYN case learners from each other was how aggressively they sought the mentors' attention. Mentors described Zach, who had the highest mentor attention score, as "thirsty for learning," especially when it came to technical skills. They reported that he needed to feel he was doing something new and original and described him as persistent and relentless when he established a learning goal. "Zach wants to learn," mentor Rob Price-Guma told us, "like he wants to learn, and he is going to beg you for it. Like [he will] call you and just [say] 'I want to learn this' and 'Mr. Rob come here, I want to learn this, let's do this, come here, come here, right now, can we go do this? I want to go do this right now.'"

Mentor Hondo also noted that Zach made an effort to create work that would "look and feel unique and fresh." Importantly, he also noted that Zach worked toward this goal at least in part by building on what he learned from all the mentors: "Yeah, he's gotten with all the mentors, so like I can't say that there is one mentor that's worked very closely with Zach. I feel like he's pulled from every pod and has gained valuable insight from each mentor. I can definitely say—he is probably one of the few students that I can say that for. Maurice would be another one that was able to pull from a lot of the pods, but Zach, he was relentless as far as just, you know, his desire is there."

Evan was also assertive in requesting demonstrations and explanations from mentors. Simeon, the pod mentor for digital music, taught Evan how to use GarageBand and the Music Production Center. Evan went on to use those technologies to create pieces on his own time as well. During the summer that he spent in the DYN summer program (between sixth and seventh grade), he had the opportunity to create a musical score. Though he did not finish the score, he did receive feedback and praise from Simeon during the process.

Maurice, who was generally perceived as a leader among DYN participants, had a mentor score of 35, just below Zach's. His submission to the Renaissance Learner contest in eighth grade (see box 6.1) won him the Renaissance Learner award, and by this time the DYN community already held him (along with Zach) in high esteem. Many of the projects he submitted were supported by mentors (see the timeline representation in case narrative C).

As we found for parents, individual mentors' expertise was consequential for making connections with particular students. Michael's interests in aviation, for example, did not match the interests or expertise of most of the mentors, and we did not find examples of them supporting this interest. Although Michael did develop a love of video editing and reported learning from video pod leader Raphael, in general the mentors were surprised that Michael did not engage more in the DYN community given that he was enthusiastic about technology and used it to advance his own interests and hobbies (see case narrative E).

The visibility of learners' interests varied, too. In some cases, the research team uncovered projects that the mentors were unaware of. For example, Renee did not share her website project with any of the mentors, and they were surprised to learn about it from the research team. She did report sharing her work with her family and enjoyed being the home expert when it came to computing, so her tendency to keep her work to herself was not generalized, and over time she became increasingly visible and willing to share publically.

We also saw evidence of mentors intentionally soliciting participation by attending to interests and potential talent, most clearly during the period when the DYN leadership became concerned about the flagging interest of girls in DYN's activities. For example, Dr. Pinkard encouraged Monica to work on game designs, and she subsequently sought out Dr. Pinkard via email with questions about Stagecast, the software she used to program her videogame *Global Meltdown*. And, as documented in chapter 5, we also observed explicit recruitment of participation when mentors explained the facts about the underrepresentation of females or African Americans in particular fields, such as digital game design. This positioning strategy (Holland and Leander 2004) was particularly powerful when it allowed students to hear directly from adults who had pursued those careers, despite being in the minority. Mentors were also important in brokering access to studio time and making sure that conditions were

BOX 6.1
The Renaissance Learner Contest

Mentors introduced the concept of the Renaissance Learner in 2008 as a way for students to think about their emerging roles as digital artists. Building on the concept of the Renaissance artist—described by Brother Mike as "somebody like a Michelangelo, who can do almost anything"—the idea of the Renaissance Learner also incorporated an orientation toward social consciousness and global thinking. In discussions with students, mentors described different historical contexts that produced multitalented people, such as Florence, Italy, during the European Renaissance or more modern-day equivalents such as the Harlem Renaissance. They encouraged students to see DYN as a similar context for Renaissance-style learning and to see themselves as developing artists within the context of digital media citizenship and as part of a broader twenty-first-century cultural movement.

The Renaissance Learner contest was announced to students as a competition in their eighth-grade year to identify a leader and model participant in the DYN community. The students were asked to submit a portfolio of their work. They took their mentors' words to heart and grounded their contest entries in their understandings of historical settings and time periods where creative work flourished, renewing communities in the process. But they also incorporated their forward-looking digital media citizen dispositions (involving critical consumption, constructive production, and social advocacy for better futures), with an emphasis on contemporary tools and community empowerment. Both sets of powerful ideas were reflected in students' projects and their claims to the title of Renaissance Learner. Some submissions were playful demonstrations of technical and dramatic skills, whereas others were powerful expressions of students' growing identities as agents of change. But it was also clear how many of the DYN students understood that being a Renaissance Learner also meant adopting a positive stance toward the future and using media artifacts to articulate personal or political issues of concern.

Two of our case study students—Ruby and Maurice—chose to submit exemplars of their work. Ruby's submission to the Renaissance Learner contest consisted of two spoken-word pieces—a recording of her performing an original piece accompanied by a series of images that complemented and amplified her metaphors, together with another typed submission, also an original poem. Maurice's portfolio was the most extensive of those submitted to the contest. He presented three videos that incorporated his own spoken-word pieces, a dramatic reading, and a music beat he had created. In his first video piece, he defined what it meant to be a Renaissance Learner and described how this definition matched his own identity. He explained that the term *renaissance* means "rebirth," and that he had tried to "rebirth many things in [his] life," including raising consciousness. Following this introduction, he performed a skit with three characters, all played by him, who sit around a table discussing (in various dialects) why Maurice should be selected as "the Renaissance Kid." His other two videos were from his work in DYN pods and school-day projects, including a documentary on Reverend Jeremiah Wright and a light-hearted hazing of the seventh graders. Maurice was the ultimate winner of the 2009 contest.

right for recording. For example, Kiley reported that mentor Raphael was key in helping the Female Stunnaz to record their song "Jappin." She noted: "He helped us record, and he made sure it was together in the studio and made sure it was quiet."

The relationship between Ruby and Brother Mike provides an excellent example of the power of a mentoring relationship that worked, despite the fact that Ruby was often unable to attend pods. Ruby described the power of having a mentor who created a trusting space for sharing ideas and feelings and who expressed confidence in pod-members' capacity to create: "Brother Mike makes us feel like we can do anything, and whatever ideas or feelings we have we can share while we're there." In the case narrative that follows this chapter, we describe how Ruby was able to solicit and harvest Brother Mike's expertise and how this relationship was consequential for Ruby.

SHARING EXPERTISE THROUGH TEACHING AND CONSULTING

A third type of learning opportunity that emerged involved using media-production expertise to help others at home, in the community, and in school. Sometimes a DYN student was excited to share his or her knowledge and initiated the relationship. On other occasions, parents, teachers, or peers requested assistance or brokered opportunities for a DYN student to help with a project. In either case, these teaching or consulting roles were consequential because they marked growing expertise and the capacity to help others (Mercier, Barron, and O'Connor 2006). More narrowly, providing explanations to peers can help clarify and elaborate one's knowledge, resulting in benefits to the explainer as well as to the listener (Webb 1989). In fact, some recent pedagogical approaches take explicit advantage of this phenomenon (Schwartz 2003). Our case study research indicated that each learner had the chance to share his or her expertise and that many had relationships in which they were both teachers and learners. In the next subsection, we describe ways that they shared with their families at home, worked as consultants in the community, and supported teachers and peers at school.

Family- and Peer-Based Opportunities to Share Knowledge

As we observed, sharing media production competencies and technical prowess more generally with family members was common among our case study students. Many of them became technical troubleshooters and assistants to their parents. Both of Evan's parents, for example, used computers for work—his mother was an accountant who used primarily Word and Excel, and his father had a moving business and used online resources for marketing and developing his website. His father also used the computer for billing and for submitting reports. Nevertheless, Evan described his parents as "not used to new technology" because they are from an older generation. He described helping them when they had a problem with the computer or needed to learn something new. He also helped set up and fix problems with other household electronics, such as the home entertainment system. Zach likewise reported teaching his mother and father. Renee also supported her parents, in particular her father, who used computers for basic tasks at home such as information searches, purchasing airline tickets, and playing card games. Renee reported assisting her dad with online tasks, such as car shopping on the Internet.

Younger relatives benefited from DYN students' expertise as well. Zach taught his three-year-old nephew how to enter and use Noggin (Nickelodeon's website for pre-schoolers), play videogames, and create slide shows and videos by himself. He looked forward to teaching his eight-month-old nephew: "I can't wait to show him to use the computer." Calvin was determined that his role as the local Scratch expert be transferred to his younger brother. Because of his laptop, he was able to share his knowledge of game making (see Calvin's full technobiography in case narrative B). Kiley collaborated with, taught, and learned from her older sister, who was one of the junior mentors at DYN, and acknowledged that her sister contributed to her learning about and using technology for projects: "Well, what the mentors taught her, she taught me. . . . She taught me how to use Keynote. She taught me how to edit, how to use GarageBand." Kiley suggested that the teaching was reciprocal, though: "I showed her how to use the character palette. I showed her how to—I think it was a blog on MySpace. I showed her a lot of stuff." Continuing the tradition of early preparation for DYN, Kiley had also taken on responsibility for teaching her younger brother (who was to go to Renaissance the year Kiley entered high school) how to use different programs on her laptop. Specifically, she said that she helped him learn how to edit using videos she made, and she helped him learn Scratch programming. Maurice taught his aunt and cousin how to create digital music and he occasionally sat with his three-year-old sister when she played online games.

Some of our case study students were called upon within pods or school classes to help their peers. For example, Monica was constantly being recruited to help classmates with their game design projects. She said that she was someone that other students came to as an "authority" on gaming. At school, Kiley helped sixth graders learn about Comic Life and video editing. In sixth grade, Michael was also recruited to be part of the school's "tech team": "I'm teaching, well, not really teaching, but most of the times when there's something wrong with their computers, they always come up to me, and they expect me to know the answers."

Calvin reported teaching his peers Scratch. In fact, he claimed that the other two Scratch users in the school had benefited from his expertise, though he also noted that one of them seemed to be surpassing him on some features. Brother Mike showed

Maurice some of the features of Pages, a user-friendly page-layout program, and then asked him to help other students learn it, giving him a role as a teaching assistant.

Consulting with the Broader Community

Other DYN students were recruited by adults to lead projects based on their recognized expertise. For example, playing a brokering role, Monica's mother arranged for her to design the CD cover for a recording of her church pastor's service. This arrangement was consistent with her conviction that her children weren't going to develop into well-rounded individuals from their school experiences alone. On a later occasion, Monica worked on a new design for her church's service program. Most interesting about Monica's discussion of creating this document was that the project was not externally commissioned—she noted that "the program they have is not that attractive," and she decided that she had the skills to address the need for a new one.

Michael was also drawn into helping out at church. His mother's knowledge of his computer skills led her to arrange a job for him working on his church's website during his seventh-grade year. To update and construct various church web pages, Michael used an online website editor that the church provided. This job gave him a chance to transfer some of his existing web-development skills, gained primarily through work with iWeb, to a new platform. He met with the church's pastor to discuss the site's design, which gave him an opportunity to develop skills in communicating his personal vision and collaborating with adults. He did seem challenged, however, by the need to merge his vision for the website's design with the pastor's view. At one point, Michael expressed frustration at having to cede ultimate authority over the design to the pastor, although he also described some methods that he developed to persuade him, including walking him through his own design process and "giving a positive no" during disagreements.

Others learners helped peers who did not attend Renaissance Academy. For example, Ruby helped students from other schools working in the City Year Young Heroes program, who were charged with creating PSAs to encourage the public to clean up neighborhoods or reduce pollution. Though the group had access to a computer lab that included editing tools, few knew how to use them, and Ruby was able to show the group what to do. Finally, although it was fairly routine for mentors to learn with and from students, students were occasionally asked to take on formal roles as educators, as indicated in the next example.

Example from the Field: Maurice's Workshop on Social Networking Sites

Recognizing Maurice's expertise and potential as a teacher, a DYN researcher nominated him the summer after he completed the seventh grade to co-lead a professional development workshop for teachers on the creation of social networking sites and the potential learning opportunities within them. Maurice agreed to help with the workshop and showcased his own site, We Shift, to exemplify what students like about social networking and to demonstrate how these sites can be used to build community and share ideas. To thank him, the program gave Maurice an iPod shuffle, an unexpected gift that he learned about only after he completed the workshop.

During the session, Maurice presented his networking site, fielded questions, and worked one on one with teachers to build their own simple sites. He introduced himself as "CEO of We Shift." He came prepared with a YouTube video that gave background on the Internet and the development of social networking sites as well as his own video on the goal of *his* social networking site. With We Shift open on every teacher's computer, Maurice explained how to communicate on social networking sites and how to create both public spaces (e.g., forums, main pages, personal profile pages) and private spaces (e.g., personal messages to specific members) within the sites.

Maurice's commitment to technology and educating others was clear. In email exchanges about the event, he wrote that he would love to help educate people about one of his favorite pastimes. During the workshop, he appeared confident in fielding questions and explaining concepts. Teachers seemed pleased and inspired as well. After the workshop, one teacher commented, "You are on point, bro!" and gave him a high five. Maurice reported to the cofacilitator that he had never considered talking to teachers previously, but he realized that they have a lot of influence on kids, so he was very excited about the workshop. The teacher development workshop was an important learning, leadership, and teaching opportunity for Maurice.

Referencing Digital Media Expertise to Gain Entry to Desired Schools

In addition to recruiting the attention of parents and mentors, some DYN participants also chose to share their digital media skills with adults they had never met, using them specifically as a resource to gain entry into selective public or private high schools. We think this choice is significant because it was a purposeful and strategic move that potentially affected these students' opportunities to learn in the future. It is also significant because not all DYN students chose to do this in the period under study; in fact, most DYN students at Renaissance Academy did not submit media with their application materials and it is therefore important to understand why they did not.

Six of our nine case study students reported that they either referenced their media skills or offered examples of their work in their high school applications or interviews. Zach was one of them. In eighth grade, he saw his future career in technology, engineering, design, or a related field: "Building cars, building laptops, software. . . . That's what I want to do with computers, you know. Probably design, too. . . . To design cartoons or something like that, design posters, design commercials for like any other business, like Adidas or something like that."

Zach thought his technology skills helped him get into the college prep high school that he ultimately attended. The application process did not provide a way to submit a media portfolio, but Zach said he referenced his projects and websites in his written application. He explained that achievement in high school was important to him because of his goal to get into a good college and win a scholarship in order to avoid placing a heavy financial burden on his father. Monica similarly joined the gaming pod with high school admissions in mind, and in her application to a private school she submitted two of the games she had created. She was successful in gaining admittance but, unfortunately, was unable to attend due to an inadequate scholarship offer. Ruby also reported using her media work for schools that allowed for it—though she believed that the academically selective schools based their decisions solely on grades and standardized test scores. In eighth grade, Calvin reported that he wrote about his experience at DYN: "I wrote about it. I say I have been working with technology for three years from sixth through eighth grade. I have been on the robotics team for two years, and I am pretty good at it."

Maurice also referenced his media skills in his application: "Well, when I was handing out my resume, it was not an electronic copy, but I did mention some of the things that I did with media." And in eighth grade Evan was able to reference his media skills in response to interview questions posed by the college prep school he aimed to get into: "They asked me a couple of questions when I went there for an interview a month or two ago. . . .[T]hey asked me did I have any talent, and I said, 'I can direct and edit and shoot movies; I'm a music producer, and I am good at a lot of digital media.'"

Not all of our case study students reported showcasing their media products, though. For example, Michael, who was admitted to a boarding school about forty miles from his home, said that he should have described his new media experiences but did not. Kylie and Renee also reported that they did not include any media with their applications, though we were not able to determine whether they wrote about their experiences.

SUMMARY

In this chapter, we have shared an analysis of how our case study learners contributed to their own learning as they deepened their interests and commitments to developing their growing competencies as media producers. Through qualitative longitudinal data, we documented how these DYN students drew on the ideas and practices associated with pods and media arts classes but went beyond them to develop their own projects, set their own goals for learning, find resources that supported their expertise development, and build relationships that advanced their agendas. We shared findings about three main learning processes that were made possible by DYN but not explicitly planned for: (1) developing personal projects and pursuits outside of pod or class time; (2) recruiting support from mentors or other adult guides; and (3) sharing expertise with others through teaching or consulting.

Our analyses indicate that students varied in the themes they explored in their work and in the tools that they employed. Some gravitated toward projects that reflected a commitment to being both critical viewers and social advocates, whereas others focused more on developing particular capacities as flexible, constructive producers. But central to all of these students' stories were the webs of learning partnerships that they created with friends, family, and community members. Friendship groups became stable sites of creative collaborative production, both within school and at home; the laptops provided by Renaissance Academy made it possible to share projects and skills with siblings, parents, neighbors, and community organizations. Sharing work and interests, in turn, led to opportunities for feedback and new ideas for revisions or future projects, opportunities to share expertise, and sometimes new invitations to consult, teach, or collaborate. We found that students varied in their strategies for recruiting support from adults, but that they all benefited when they did earn attention and sustained mentorship from the adults around them. This finding leads to an important direction for research; we need to more deeply conceptualize and study variation in the forms of interpersonal interaction that are important for learning in less-structured settings.

The ubiquity of interest-driven learning pursuits emerges as an important finding from these case studies. A high level of interest can have a payoff for learning in the form of increased attention, promotion of self-regulation, generation of curiosity questions, diversity of learning strategies, and goal setting (Hidi and Renninger 2006). Pursuing skill development on one's own time through purposeful and playful exploration signals deepening of engagement. Seemingly small choices—for example, deciding to read a book about HTML to better customize a website or deciding to use an empty afternoon to make a new movie—represent learners' efforts to sustain their learning and thus can become consequential for the development in their expertise over the long term. Future research should be organized to document these short-term learning activities in detail. Understanding the conditions that are associated with them and their evolution over time may be critical to developing theoretical accounts of how stable personal interests emerge (Renninger and Hidi 2011).

Variability in the form and content of these pursuits was also striking in the students we observed. In conceptualizing the choice to engage in interest driven activities, we agree with Flávio Azevedo (2012), who argues for the utility of a multidimensional analysis of sustained engagement. Choosing to work on projects in spare moments can mark an investment in developing ideas, skills, and a particular identity or the simple enjoyment of the process of creating or connecting with others who share an interest. Azevedo's (2012) longitudinal case studies of adult hobbyists describe both a multiplicity of preferences that were important drivers of continued activity and conditions that made engagement possible. Rather than think of sustained engagement as being driven by any one facet of activity or the topic per se, he argues that multiple lines of practice and sets of preferences can coexist and alternate in their prominence over time. This characterization suggests that designers and educators should attend to the configurations of factors that might be motivating and attempt to create conditions that allow for many of them to flourish simultaneously.

Evidence of the cumulative power of DYN case study learners' project experiences was visible in their plans for the future and their reflections on their experiences. Immersion in project work also contributed to their sense of themselves as current and future designers, builders, writers, and creators. Several of our case study learners referred to themselves as creative and able to come up with new ideas easily; many spoke about their future selves in relation to what they had experienced during their time with DYN, and several referenced their skills in their applications to public and private high schools.

In closing, as research and design teams work intentionally to create networked hybrid informal learning environments, it is crucial that they have in mind a broad set of interpersonal and participatory arrangements that motivate engagement, specific desired outcomes, possible metrics of change, and strategies for measuring growth over time. We typically do not consider the emergence of self-sustaining learning processes as indicators of the vitality of an educational program. They are hard to define precisely and are not easily measured, and they don't map onto existing standards. Nevertheless, they are consistent with broader national goals for increasing the country's collective capacity for innovation (President's Council of Advisers on Science and Technology 2010; Pellegrino and Hilton 2012), and we believe that future work can begin to design systems that capture relevant metrics such as sustained project work, the collection of learning resources, and growth in personal social networks that provide access to technical, social, cultural, and other forms of capital. Beyond expertise and skill, these interest-driven pursuits may engage processes that support emotional resiliency, providing a route to social resources that help one cope with stressful social or academic circumstances (Rutter 2000). The four case portraits interspersed throughout the book share in more detail how designed and emergent opportunities together led to significant growth in learners' skills, identities, and digital media portfolios. In the case narrative that follows this chapter, we share more about Ruby and how her own self-sustaining practices emerged during her time at Renaissance Academy.

RUBY: STEPPING INTO THE SPOTLIGHT

I used to feel like I have to impress everyone else. It wasn't really based on impressing me. But now I feel like, um, as long as I'm impressed with what I'm doing, then I have to be doing something right. Like, um, I've started realizing that I'm not happy with the way things are now I guess. I don't like kind of sinking into the background. I've never been someone who wanted to fit in with the crowd. I've always wanted to stand out in some sort of way. But I've just realized that I have the potential to be what I want to be, so it's time to start being it, I guess.

—Ruby (eighth grade), 2009

Ruby's development reflects the three types of self-sustaining processes discussed in chapter 6. She created her own personal projects and pursuits in sixth grade, recruited adult support, and sought assignments from mentors when she had difficulty attending pods in seventh grade. She ultimately chose to overcome her shyness and share her work and expertise with others in eighth grade. Ruby learned the importance of cultivating and exposing her voice and talents, and that change emerged from within herself as well as through the support of DYN, her family, and the broader school network.

Unfortunately again, because that's such a rambunctious class, she kind of got swept under, being a quiet kid who just wants to get their work done. If I could say there is a weakness, I would say I don't think she has the confidence she really deserves because she does great work. She is very sweet and very likable. But shy, timid, like sometimes she speaks so low, it's almost a whisper.

—Asia (mentor), 2008

CREATING PERSONAL PROJECTS AND RECRUITING ADULT SUPPORT

Ruby's interest in games had inspired her to join the video games pod in sixth grade, but she had also developed an interest in writing. She self-initiated a project compiling her poetry, short stories, and drawings into a book. She brought the compilation to school and showed it to mentor Brother Mike, who was impressed by the originality and breadth of her work. The respect was mutual. Ruby felt that Brother Mike's encouragement and laid-back style made for an open environment where ideas and feelings were welcomed. She asked him for help in creating a digital edition of her collection, and she also built a website that showcased the poetry she and friends wrote. Brother Mike suggested she take the spoken-word pod the following year.

Ruby unfortunately was unable to attend any pods in seventh grade due to trouble finding a ride home in the afternoon, but she created her own learning avenues by seeking emailed assignments from mentors Brother Mike and Asia for the spoken-word and digital queendom pods. This initiative on Ruby's part reflected her commitment to learn and enhance her craft. When the mentors forgot, she reminded them. She continued to pursue writing and posted her poetry on the DYN social network site, Remix World, for feedback. The Remix site was an important space for her given that she was unable to participate in the pods during her seventh-grade year. Brother Mike also met with her to provide constructive criticism on her work and to encourage her use of the recording studio to record her spoken-word performances. He felt she was shy and underconfident and wanted to find ways to let her talent shine. Ruby repeatedly talked of how Brother Mike was one of a few trusted friends with whom she was comfortable sharing her work, though she felt all the mentors were excellent listeners and helpers, playing

> Last year she wrote a book. And this is something that she wrote out on paper and made all types of pictures, and she wanted to transfer it . . . she wanted to do her own book. So she presented this book toward the end of the year. And I was floored by the stories that she tells and even [by] some of the poems she wrote.
>
> —Brother Mike (mentor), 2008

> They call them mentors, but they don't really act like teachers or parents, which is, I think, what kind of makes them cool because usually it's like, I don't know, they're like the cool older parents, I guess, I don't know. They're fun, but they don't just let you slack off either. And the students actually respect them, even more than they might older people. So it's just easier to talk to them because they always seem like they listen, even if it's not just about DYN or whatever. They seem like you can still talk to them, and they'll help a lot. It's like they can understand everything that you tell them.
>
> —Ruby (eighth grade), 2009

a role that neither teachers nor parents could. Ruby thought that students were "more relaxed and themselves" around the mentors.

Ruby's writing developed in other ways and settings too. Inspired by a dream, she began her first novel about a family and the challenges they faced. It remained a work in progress throughout middle school. The standards she had for her work constantly evolved as she, an avid reader, grew inspired by the different published authors she admired. She participated in online fan discussions of novels, reflecting on storylines, structures, and the age and personalities of the authors she read. Her mother, a journalist, editor, and professional beautician, was another inspiration and offered her support as a friendly critic. Ruby hoped that someday her work would be published and lead to financial resources that she could share with her family. When possible, she brought her personal writing projects to school. In seventh grade, she adapted her novel into a script and PowerPoint storyboard project for an assignment in the media arts class, which focused on digital storytelling.

In the eighth grade, Ruby was able to attend the spoken-word pod, and she enjoyed reading and evaluating professional poets such as Langston Hughes as well as sharing her original poetry.

COLLABORATION CHALLENGES: THE "RIGHT PEOPLE" AND WORKING ALONE

Across her middle school years, Ruby had many opportunities to collaborate with others, but her experiences often left her wanting to work alone. Early on she explained that she didn't want her grades to be reliant upon her peers, many of whom she saw as unfocused and immature.

On one occasion, she sought extra credit in the digital storytelling media arts class because the "rambunctious" class had negatively impacted her grade. She completed an additional media project alone on

> Like some of the projects work out where I have to work with other people, like you pick the right people, like some people they—most people pick their friends, and they end up getting bad grades. But I pick, like, people that do well, even if they're not my friends.
>
> —Ruby (seventh grade), 2008

I think my teachers, they say it's one of my problems 'cause I really like working by myself. Like they'll say, "Why don't you work with somebody else?" or the students even say like, "You don't have to do that much work." But I don't mind working and doing extra work because then I don't have to rely on other people for my grade because, like, if they do something wrong, then we all go down, and I don't like that.

—Ruby (seventh grade), 2008

Elite Portrait of Barack Obama by Ruby

We decided to name [the business] that [Elite Portraits]. Make it sound kind of professional, I guess, but we draw different people. We have a few artists in our group. I draw some things, and other people control, like, sales, but we had a contest where we had to create videos, like commercials, and my group won. So we get like a seventy-dollar investment from Akili, so we're working on that.

—Ruby (eighth grade), 2009

Hurricane Katrina. This focus on grades often led her to take on the major responsibility in many collaborative projects and to choose projects that allowed her to do her part on her own.

Working alone meant that Ruby could ensure the final product was "solid." She was also concerned that her own interests would be incorporated into the work. She liked to "put [her] own creativity into it." When asked to reflect on group work in pods as opposed to school, she observed that it was actually easier to collaborate in pods. She attributed this ease to the greater interest and agency students felt in pods, that they wanted to be there and got to share their own perspectives rather than simply learn assigned material.

One of Ruby's later group projects in her eighth-grade media arts class, an entrepreneurial business model called "Elite Portraits," was successful, and her views on collaboration became more nuanced. For Elite Portraits, she joined with six other students whom she did not know well to create a business idea, and she was surprised and pleased by the results.

PROJECT SPOTLIGHT: ELITE PORTRAITS

In eighth grade, DYN co-founder Akili led a project on entrepreneurship for the media arts class. Brother Mike also came in for a few sessions to provide feedback on the video-based commercials and to share tips on how to make them "intriguing." Students had to create promotional videos, posters, and a survey. Ruby was surprised her team worked so well together. The groups were assigned and she said she would have never chosen the partners she ended up with. Elite Portraits was a business that involved creating original drawings for purchase. The plan won the class competition and received seventy dollars to invest in the business. The six team members worked together in class because they had ample time during the ninety-minute media arts block for the collaborative project work. They also met at lunch and after school to continue working. They showed signs of following through with starting their business; for instance, they got permission from the principal to sell products at school. The project involved several applications: iMovie, Quicktime, and GarageBand. Ruby's theory on why Elite Portraits worked well was that her group members were so different. She noted that they took on different roles. She was one of the artists who would be responsible for creating the drawings. Others focused on tasks such as generating sales and creating promotional materials. Although during interviews Ruby expressed resistance to working in groups, this project gave her an experience in productive group work. Her expanding view of collaboration included the insight that it is sometimes best to choose partners for their complementary skills and focus rather than for friendship's sake.

When you have people who are all the same, I think it's just less creative, it's less special. We all have the same idea, so it's not really anything different, I guess. And I think we have different people. You can put all those different ideas together to make one great idea.

—Ruby (eighth grade), 2009

SHARING EXPERTISE THROUGH TEACHING AND CONSULTING

Ruby became involved in other community programs that gave her opportunities to share what she had learned at DYN. She participated in City Year, an after-school opportunity at Renaissance run by AmeriCorps that places college-age adults in schools to offer academic support, encouragement, and community and school improvements. In one part of this program, Young Heroes, students were charged with creating PSAs that would encourage the public to clean up neighborhoods or reduce pollution. The group had access to a computer lab that included editing tools, but few knew how to use the tools, allowing Ruby to show the group what to do.

Ruby also taught her younger brother how to make beats and record his music. Like other DYN students with an older sibling, Ruby's brother would start his sixth-grade year with considerable media creation skills and familiarity with what the laptops

I do a program called "Young Heroes." And we do volunteer work. But sometimes they'll do like videos to help promote it, or we do like different projects to try to keep people aware about global warming and cleaning up our community, and sometimes they do them on computers, but some of the peers there, they don't know how to use, like, different software that we [at Renaissance Academy] know how to use, so I'll help them with it.

—Ruby (eighth grade), 2009

and pods offer. She also gave her mother tips on Photoshop and Quark, though her mother had been the one originally to show her these tools. Ruby's care for the development of others was not limited to technology. For friends who had less parental support, she went out of her way to help them develop portfolios that would enhance their applications to local high schools.

STEPPING INTO THE SPOTLIGHT

In the sixth and seventh grades, Ruby created many projects in school, after school, and at home but was more likely to share her work with family than with peers. Near the end of middle school, however, she decided to make a change within, grow in confidence, and seek out ways to be more vocal and recognized.

During seventh grade, when she was unable to attend pods, Ruby held a paid internship at *Urban Teen/Urban Girl Magazine*, part of a journalism program run by After School Matters, a nonprofit organization that offers Chicago teens learning opportunities through a network of public and private partnerships throughout the city. The *Urban Teen/Urban Girl Magazine* opportunity operated through a local YMCA. Ruby joined the team as a writer and graphic layout artist. Her mother, who worked as an editor for the magazine, brokered the opportunity. By writing book reviews and opinion pieces, she was able to share her perspective and love of good writing with a broader audience. She reported learning from and enjoying her work with the teen staff of the YMCA magazine projects. She said that they didn't "goof off" as often as her Renaissance Academy peers. Her theory was that they were either simply more mature or that they didn't know each other as well. The teenage staff at the magazine seemed to take their jobs fairly seriously, and Ruby viewed that attitude as a prerequisite to good work: "You just have to be serious about your work or the stories won't turn out that well." They

> I just want to be more open. And I feel like I can do things pretty well, but I feel like I kind of hold myself back sometimes. So I won't do that anymore, and I know that I want to be an actress when I grow up, and actresses I know are, like, not afraid to be seen. And I don't want to be afraid to be seen. I want people to see what I can do.
>
> —Ruby (eighth grade), 2009

were paid a stipend for their participation, and their roles were clearly defined with the labels *editor, associate editor*, and so on. Her staff peers at *Urban Teen/Urban Girl* magazine insisted that she model for a photo shoot because they knew she was too shy to do it otherwise, which led to an increased awareness and interest in being publically visible. By eighth grade, she had decided to create a place for herself in DYN before leaving for high school.

Mentors had helped Ruby cultivate and present her work online. She had modeled and expressed herself at the YMCA. Then she began to explore performance. For example, at the request of the Renaissance principal, Ruby read one of her poems at the opening of the new school building at the end of her seventh-grade year. This reading led to an invitation from the president of the University of Chicago, who happened to be in the audience, to read the poem again at a church on Martin Luther King Jr. Day. The poem was originally about President Barack Obama, but in general it was about "a change that [she feels] is finally coming."

Ruby also expanded her creative repertoire through music, drawing, photography, and acting. Her family could not afford guitar or piano lessons, so she learned to play through YouTube where other teens posted videos of hand placement and chord changes. Ruby also recorded herself so that she could play back her performance for purposes of critique. This practice was observed in the eighth-grade spoken-word pod, where she found it useful for improving her work. To pursue her interest in acting, she tracked down "how to" guides on showing emotion, and she studied actors whom she admired. She contacted her former performing arts teacher to find other ways to learn. She also built a website to showcase her drawings and began posting YouTube videos of her musical performances.

When asked what she had learned about herself in the previous couple of years, Ruby said that she

> I just started doing things I know I normally wouldn't. Like we had this opening ceremony, and they asked me to recite a poem. If I was in sixth or seventh grade, [I would have been] like, "No. I don't want to be center of attention," but I decided to do it, and [it] actually worked out pretty well. But I guess I decided that I want to be remembered like after I'm gone, I guess, and I want to be seen.
>
> —Ruby (eighth grade), 2009

> I guess I just fit into our [DYN] model— "lead yourself, lead your school, lead your world." I would say I'm kind of a leader. I do try to embody what I feel is right, what a good student is, and [what] a real good person [is] overall.
>
> —Ruby (eighth grade), 2009

"I am..." by Ruby

I am the future. Fearless, unique, talented, unknown, reckless, eager to change my world. Eager to change my world.
I am the Sun. Solo, unaware, never ending, hidden behind the clouds, afraid to break through.
I am the city. Creative, ignorant, torn, yearning for a real place to belong.
I am the pieces to the puzzle. Complete but not complete. Fixed but broken.
I am the transformation. It was started by my ancestors decades ago, but I am nowhere near finished. Their ending is my beginning.
I am my neighborhood. My thoughts are my community's tree branches. My heart beat the steady swing of the waves.
I am the truth. Timid, resolved, untold, tarnished, held, and I am ready to be exposed to the world. To relinquish my secrets.
I am light. Loose, invisible but seen, fulfilled, easy. And, I am finally ready to start living.
I am the Renaissance. Tall and strong like a tree. I am undefined. Calm and collected like water.
I am ready.

Excerpt from "That Girl" by Ruby

When you look at me, what do you see? You see that girl who doesn't know what to do or what to be. . . . That girl just wants to fit in, but that girl doesn't want to pretend to be something she's not just for you.

had learned to work toward her own standards—to "impress [herself]"—and had made strides toward being more public with her creative work.

Ruby's growing sense of self can be seen in her Renaissance Learner contest submission (see chapter 6 for a description of this competition). Although she was unable to attend the judging of the contest, she did submit a portfolio. Her primary submission was a digitally recorded original poem set to a series of images chosen to amplify the powerful metaphors she used to share dimensions of herself. The slide-show video with voiceover was powerful. She performed strongly, her voice confident, her words accompanied with images of the stars and the moon. Images of President Barack Obama and Martin Luther King Jr. were the backdrop to the end of her poem. Her voice rang out as she performed the piece. She built the poem from the "I am . . . " assignment created by Brother Mike as a scaffold to support not only poetry writing, but also reflection on identity. The technology in her submission took a backseat to her original writing, which captured so well the story she shared with us of becoming more visible of late and her thoughtful reflections on her past and present and on her readiness to embrace and shape her future.

The second piece, read by artist-mentor Brother Mike, was entitled "That Girl" and was about negotiating how to manage true identity under various peer pressures.

When Ruby's presentation ended, the DYN artist-mentors sitting at the edge of the room quietly commented that they were impressed. Brother Mike prompted everyone to applaud: "Give it up for Ruby, y'all!" These powerful expressions of Ruby's voice were particularly of note given mentors' early impressions of her as shy, quiet, and underconfident, an observer rather than a participant, and preferring to avoid the public spotlight.

LOOKING TO THE FUTURE

Ruby was admitted to one of the academically selective high schools she applied to and planned to attend it in the fall. Her plans for the future included developing her acting skills and continuing to write. She was still eager to learn more about computing. She realized that she was "spoiled" by DYN and was not sure that her high school would offer anything that she would want to take. She saw herself continuing to do projects such as making games on her own time. She was still interested in learning more. In fact, at the end of eighth grade she wanted to know how to build a computer, to see the chips, and to understand what they do and how the screen worked. Despite all of her media production experience, she still saw computers as "out of this world." She had mentioned this interest early on in her sixth-grade interview as well, and it suggests an area of possible expansion for the DYN program.

When asked how she might "remix" DYN, she focused on the need to communicate to students the rarity of the opportunity they were being given. She felt that a few of her peers took the opportunity for granted.

Ruby's career plans were still in flux, as was appropriate for her age. She was interested in an acting career and the overall goal of attending college. She also talked about the possibility of a career in medicine, and on her end-of-the-year survey she wrote that her ideal job was to become an "actor/writer/artist."

For Ruby, focus and commitment to the work were strong values. Initially a quiet girl who shunned public notice, she nevertheless took active steps to change her ways by first taking the initiative to show Brother Mike her private work. Had Ruby kept her writing to herself, she may not have ever garnered the attention that appeared to be critical to the development of her public voice. Other quiet students who preferred to keep their work somewhat under the radar were also at risk of being overlooked as serious DYN producers.

I've always wanted to know how to build [a computer]. I guess it's not actually something that you actually do on the computer. But I want to know how you make everything run. It just seems so, like, out of this world to me, I guess . . . I don't know. I've just always wondered how they can . . . how the screen works, and I've seen little pieces of what they do, but I'm sure it takes a lot. And I want to see all the little chips and everything they put in there.

—Ruby (eighth grade), 2009

I think I would just try to, um, find a way to make the students realize how important it [participation in DYN] is. I think they take it for granted sometimes. . . . I don't think they understand that we're, like, one of the only schools that can actually do this.

—Ruby (eighth grade), 2009

Right now [I want to be] an actress, I think. But I still want to go to college because school's important to me. I'm trying to find a way to do that. It's just kind of story writing with me. I like to be someone else, I guess. To, like, get away from my own world sometimes. . . . I would like to pretend I'm other people—other characters—and experience other lifestyles, I guess.

. . . At one point I was thinking about being a doctor because I think your career should be something important. And I feel like there's really nothing more important than if I can save someone else's life.

—Ruby (eighth grade), 2009

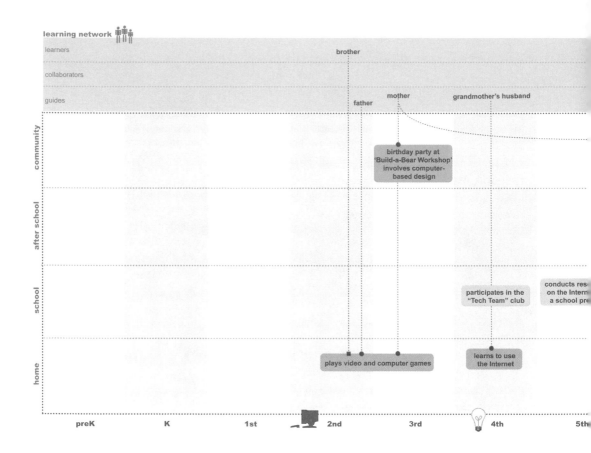

Ruby's learning pathway shows a cluster of events during school through **DYN** programs and other classes from fourth grade through graduation that branched out to other settings by the end of eighth grade, including self-initiated projects at **home**, and connections to related digital design work in the wider **community**.

Ruby's computer use began in second grade 🖥 with her playing educational games at **home** with her **family**. In fourth grade, she began to use computers in school for more activities that had the potential to build technological fluency 💡, such as being a member of her school's tech team and offering tech support to teachers and classrooms. In sixth grade at Renaissance Academy, Ruby received her laptop 💻 and participated in the game design pod 👆 for half of the year. Her growing technology knowledge from school and **DYN** enabled her to plan for a digital version of her writing projects at **home**, and she enlisted the help of **Brother Mike**, who continued to

Ruby

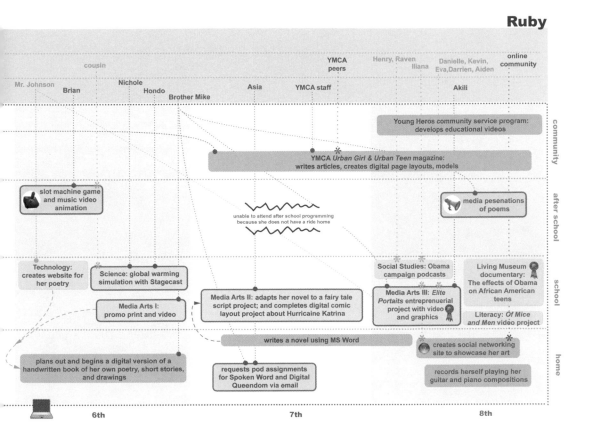

support her out-of-school efforts throughout middle school. In seventh grade, Ruby was not able to attend any pods ⌇⌇ because she did not have a way to get home in the evening. However, she brought the after-school program home by requesting pod assignments from DYN mentors. She also became active in her local YMCA's magazine for girls, working with adults and peers in the wider community.

By eighth grade, Ruby was active across all four contexts—at school, after school, at home, and in the community—creating a number of projects in school and learning from ⋮ and collaborating with ✳ members of her social network 👪 at each setting. That year, she produced videos for a community-service program, won an award 🏆 for her Living Museum documentary, and used the spoken-word pod 📣 to share her poetry.

PATTERNS OF ENGAGEMENT: HOW DEPTH OF EXPERIENCE MATTERS

Caitlin K. Martin, Brigid Barron, Jolie Matthews, and Daniel Stringer

> [T]hat [project] actually got me to express myself a lot more [and] taught me new things—Photoshop, Quark, how to edit photos. . . . I didn't understand how they edit photos, and what I [saw] in magazines, but now I do. And it also helped me become a better writer and gave me more confidence.
>
> —Ruby (eighth grade), 2009

Throughout this book, portraits and vignettes have illustrated how DYN youth took up opportunities to design, build, and express themselves with digital media and in doing so developed new expertise, learning partnerships, and ideas for their future. Although these narratives provide powerful examples of emergent skills and capabilities connected to interests and digital citizenship, we needed measures that allowed us to speak more broadly about the sample as a whole and to contrast this DYN cohort with students in other communities. Although national and international efforts have been made to define specific competencies necessary for productive citizenry in the twenty-first century (Binkley, Erstad, Herman, et al. 2012; National Research Council 2012; Partnership for 21st Century Skills 2009), and general agreement has been reached as to their increasing importance (Levy and Murnane 2004), there are no widely accepted ways to operationalize or measure these competencies, so developing such measures has been called out as an important research direction (National Research Council 2012). Similarly, although there is agreement that the digital divide is multidimensional (Armenta, Serrano, Cabrera, et al. 2012; Hargittai 2011), there is no agreed upon set of metrics that reflect access to tools and learning opportunities. In this chapter, we share our own efforts to develop a set of measures and a framework for analysis to complement our rich qualitative work with quantitative data. The chapter is organized around three questions related to how DYN has supported the development of important twenty-first-century competencies and two other equally critical factors—equity and opportunity. For each question, we use a unique analytic approach.

1. *Did students at Renaissance grow in technical expertise after three years of DYN participation?* We look at overall changes in production experiences and self-reported indicators of expertise for the cohort of Renaissance Academy students we studied from the beginning of sixth grade (October 2006) to the end of eighth grade (May 2009). Given the DYN focus on supporting digital production, we expected that the majority of those students studied would increase their technical expertise, independent of gender or differences in family income levels.

2. *Did deeper engagement with digital media production relate to higher measures of technical expertise and other twenty-first-century competencies?* Empirical evidence from our own past work and the work of others suggests that participation in high-quality, production-oriented technology activities can strengthen both cognitive and noncognitive competencies. For instance, projects that involve the production of a personally meaningful artifact can drive persistence and the setting of learning goals as youth designers work to create what they imagine (Barron 2006). A survey of middle school students in Silicon Valley found that those who reported more experience with sustained media production also had higher levels of confidence in their technical skills and were more likely to share their expertise with friends and family (Barron, Martin, and Roberts 2007; Barron, Walter, Martin, et al. 2010). Identity development and confidence in different roles of production have also been documented in more qualitative studies of online participation and digital media production (Goldman, Booker, and McDermott 2008; Kafai, Peppler and Chapmen 2009; Ito, Baumer, Bittanti, et al. 2010). To address this question, we compare two groups of Renaissance Academy students, those with more and those with less evidence of sustained engagement with digital production activities. Based on these earlier works, we anticipated that those students who engaged in repeated production, going deeper into their particular design and creation activities, would exhibit higher levels of twenty-first-century competencies, such as sharing knowledge with others, being civically engaged online, and exhibiting confidence with tools of production and in their creative ability.

3. *How did students at Renaissance compare to students in Silicon Valley at the end of middle school?* DYN was intentionally designed to address the well-documented findings that students with higher socioeconomic status are using technology in more differentiated, generative, and sustained ways as a result of access to learning opportunities at home (Attewell and Winston 2003; Barron, Walter, Martin, et al. 2010; DeBell and Chapman 2006) and at school (Margolis, Estrella, Goode, et al. 2008; Purcell, Heaps, Buchanan, et al. 2013; Warschauer 2003, 2006; Warschauer and Matuchniak 2010). To illustrate how graduating Renaissance students

compared to students from a community with higher overall socioeconomic status and with more parents working in technical fields, we provide data from a study of eighth graders in California's Silicon Valley (June 2009). We hypothesized that the consistent and pervasive DYN programming at Renaissance would ensure that twenty-first-century competencies for students there would look similar to the competencies of students from a community with a high concentration of technology companies and associated expertise.

METRICS OF LEARNING, ENGAGEMENT, AND ACCESS

To answer these questions, we captured metrics of students' technological learning ecologies (access to tools, activities, and relationships that offered opportunities to learn) and a broad range of experiences, skills, and attitudes consistent with existing definitions of twenty-first-century competencies. The Partnership for 21st Century Skills (2004, 2009) argued that student success in college and beyond is dependent on four broad and transferable skills: critical thinking, communication, collaboration, and creativity. As acceptance of and focus on these forms of deeper learning have grown, definitions have expanded to better understand and articulate what they mean for education around the world. For example, international education officials, including the US secretary of education, and representatives from Cisco, Intel, and Microsoft organized the Assessment and Teaching of 21st Century Skills project to expand global efforts in this area. Their definition of twenty-first-century competencies includes four strands: ways of thinking (creativity, critical thinking, and learning to learn), ways of working (communication and collaboration), tools for working (informational and technological literacy), and living in the world (citizenship, life and career, and personal and social responsibility) (Binkley, Erstad, Herman, et al. 2012). In another effort, public and private foundations invested in the future of education charged the National Research Council to review and synthesize existing research on twenty-first-century learning, which resulted in the council's 2012 report *Education for Life and Work: Developing Transferable Knowledge and Skills in the 21st Century*. This report defines three types of competencies. Cognitive competencies involve thinking and reasoning processes and strategies, including problem-solving skills, specific content knowledge, and creative ability. Intrapersonal competencies refer to individual self-management and ways of working, including intellectual openness, conscientious work ethic, and positive self-evaluation. Interpersonal competencies are those that involve the individual sharing knowledge and working with others, such as leadership and collaboration.

Although these frameworks organize skills, abilities, and attitudes a bit differently from each other, they share a similar focus on both cognitive and noncognitive outcomes and pay attention to individual skills and attitudes as well as to social orientations. Taking these frameworks into account, and being mindful of the model of the digital media citizen that is at the heart of the DYN program, we developed a conceptual framework to look at and better understand DYN students. Our framework is organized into four clusters: technological learning ecologies, technical expertise, identity as a creator, and social learning dispositions.

We adapted measures we had used in previous studies (Barron, Martin, and Roberts 2006; Barron, Walter, Martin, et al. 2010), created new measures, and borrowed existing measures used and validated by others in the field (Bandura 1997; Hargittai 2005; Kahne, Lee, and Feezell 2011). As shared earlier in the book, the term *learning ecology* refers to what learning opportunities and resources youth have access to and are using at home, at school, and at other places in the community and how they choose to participate in those opportunities (Barron 2004, 2006). Survey measures in this cluster asked students about technological tools at home, who they learned from, where they learned about technology, ways that their parents supported their learning, and who valued their knowledge. *Technical expertise* was assessed with a set of items reflecting both experience and expertise, and in this chapter we use the terms *experience* and *expertise* somewhat interchangeably. We did not have skill or knowledge-based behavioral measures but rather relied on student self-report data. Measures in this cluster include reports of the frequency of experience with different media production activities, self-reported expertise with various tools of digital production, and self-reported understanding of a set of Internet terms, which is a validated measure of Internet proficiency (Hargittai 2005). The cluster of items we call "*identity as a creator*" looks at students' confidence in generating new ideas and sense of self as a creator as well as at their views regarding possible futures with technology-related practices, classes, and careers. The cluster of items we refer to as "*social learning orientation*" explores students' relationships with others around learning, including their feelings of efficacy working in a team, the extent to which they share their knowledge with friends and family, their connections to broader communities, and metrics of online civic engagement. Table 7.1 describes the four clusters and individual measures in more detail.[1]

TABLE 7.1
Overview of Measures Used to Look at Student Competencies

Clusters	Measures
Learning ecology. These items measure how and where students are learning about computers and technology, including access to tools and expertise at home and sources of learning about technology at home and school.	• Sources of learning about technology (people and settings) • Valuing of student's technology learning by people at home and at school • Number of computers and other technology tools at home • Parent use of technology at work • Learning support roles played by parents
Technical expertise. This set of items includes self-reported skills, confidence, and experiences with contemporary tools, the Internet, and creative production activities. These measures are reflective of the DYN constructive and critical dispositions, including the ability to apply various tools, techniques, and understandings to the development of a portfolio of work.	• Breadth and depth of production experiences • Proxy of Internet proficiency • Confidence with tools of production (expert tools index)
Identity as a creator. This set of items looks at students' beliefs about themselves and their capacities as well as at their perceptions of possible futures. It relates to the DYN constructive disposition, specifically seeing oneself as a creator and seeking out new opportunities for learning.	• Creative self-efficacy • Future plans for classes and careers • Future plans to create media for social change • Use of technology for personal expression • Commitment to sharing quality work online
Social learning orientation. This cluster of items explores students' relationships with others around learning—including collaborating with, teaching, and learning from others—as well as their civic orientation and connection to online communities. The DYN social and critical dispositions are represented in this cluster, specifically sharing work and ideas, creating with responsibility for social change, and spreading knowledge.	• Online practices of sharing work and ideas • Online civic participation • Participation in online communities • Teaching others about technology • Collaboration self-efficacy

DID STUDENTS AT RENAISSANCE GROW IN TECHNICAL EXPERTISE AFTER THREE YEARS OF DYN PARTICIPATION?

Across the three years of middle school, all of the students in our focal cohort at Renaissance Academy participated in DYN media arts classes and projects that took place jointly between core courses and DYN (for example, the Living Museum project in social studies and the global warming simulation in science). Most students participated in at least one voluntary after-school pod (85 percent) and reported having a Remix World profile page (93 percent). We were interested to see how these common opportunities translated into indicators of expertise. As we predicted, on average, from sixth to eighth grade the entire cohort of students we studied significantly increased their technical expertise (see the summary of results in box 7.1).

BOX 7.1

Changes in Technical Expertise of DYN Students from Sixth to Eighth Grade: Summary of Findings at a Glance

- Overall, students increased their technological expertise from sixth to eighth grade, including breadth and depth of production experiences, confidence with tools, and Internet proficiency.

- There were no differences associated with gender or family income in growth of technological expertise.

- Boys were more likely to have gone into more depth with computational production activities.

One way we assessed expertise was to track experience with digital production activities. We asked students to report their experience with twelve types of activities (see table 7.2), a measure we have used in previous research (Barron 2004; Barron, Martin, and Roberts 2006; Barron, Walter, Martin, et al. 2010). The activities focused on were likely to involve some aspect of design, personal expression, computational thinking, or all three. The different activities utilize multiple modes of communication; for example, *building a website* would include visual layout and graphics as well as verbal written communication and perhaps interaction in the form of a Javascript popup window or a Flash animation. Activities were presented as descriptions of possible products, such as "Created a piece of art using an application" and "Created your own newsgroup, blog, or discussion site on the Internet." Students were asked to indicate the number of times they had participated in each activity from a four-option choice: never, once or twice, three to six times, and more than six times. On average, the cohort evidenced marked growth in experiences across all twelve activities listed over the three years of middle school (see table 7.2).

TABLE 7.2
Students' Reported Participation in an Activity at Least Once, from Beginning of Sixth Grade to End of Eighth Grade

I have made a . . .	Sixth Grade (%)	Eighth Grade (%)
Video	28	98
Publication	38	93
Music	45	90
Art	38	90
Game	0	85
Newsgroup/blog	28	75
Website	20	75
Animation	18	75
Simulation	15	70
Robot	18	65
Database	32	45
Computer program	10	38

To get a sense of the range of media artifacts students had produced, we counted the number of activities each student participated in at least once. This count served as the measure of students' breadth of experience. Breadth of production experience was low for all students at the beginning of sixth grade and increased significantly by the end of middle school, and there was no evidence of differences in breadth as a function of family income level[2] (see figure 7.1) or student gender.[3]

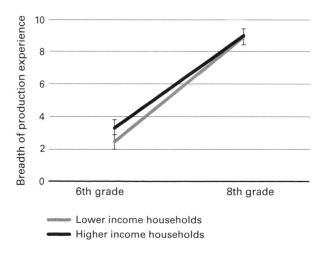

FIGURE 7.1
Number of digital production activities students had ever participated in at the beginning of sixth grade and by the end of eighth grade by household income groups.

In addition to the breadth of experiences, we were also interested in depth—how many of these experiences students had engaged in repeatedly. In order to assess depth of production experiences at Renaissance Academy, we looked at the number of activities each student had participated in more than six times. Similar to the breadth of production, the average depth of production was low for both groups (those with more and those with less evidence of sustained engagement with digital production activities) at the beginning of sixth grade and significantly increased over the three years of middle school, and again there were no significant differences between boys and girls or between students of higher or lower family income levels.[4]

To see if these robust gains held for boys and girls across types of production, we grouped the twelve digital activities into three genres—publication, expressive, and computational (see box 7.2)—and looked at which genres students repeatedly engaged in (meaning they had participated in at least one activity from that genre more than six times). The genre classification system we use here is only one way to group the activities, and most activities could theoretically span multiple categories. We based the classifications on our knowledge of the specific assignments and project instruction for DYN at Renaissance Academy.

Computational activities are arguably the least familiar among young people (Barron 2004) and yet are considered by some researchers to be the most important for building the digital literacy skills needed for future productive work in all types of media (Grover and Pea 2013; Wing 2006, 2011). Although boys and girls similarly increased their depth of production experiences overall, one gender difference became apparent as students chose what to engage in repeatedly. At the end of eighth grade, differences between boys' and girls' depth of experience with publication (69 and 45 percent, respectively) and expressive (44 and 61 percent, respectively) production were not statistically significant. However, the difference between boys' and girls' experience with computational activities was statistically significant, meaning it was unlikely to have occurred by chance.[5] More than twice as many boys (50 percent

---

BOX 7.2
Genres of Production Activities

Publication	Expressive	Computational
Website	Music	Game creation
Newsgroup or blog	Movies	Animation
Newsletter	Art	Database
		Simulation
		Robotics
		Computer programming

compared to 22 percent of girls) had gone into depth with at least one computational activity. This finding reflects a persistent national trend of gender disparities in fields such as computer science that can be seen at all levels of education and professional employment (DuBow 2011; Margolis and Fischer 2003) and points to the "experience gap" that has been articulated as one reason for such disparities. More about the challenge of engaging girls in computational experiences and the affirmative steps DYN has used to address gender issues is described in chapter 8.

In addition to production experiences, we looked at change over time for two other measures of technical expertise. To assess student knowledge of and confidence with digital media production, we created a measure of self-rated expertise with digital media software tools (see the expert tools index, box 7.3). On average, Renaissance students significantly increased their confidence in using production tools from sixth

---

BOX 7.3
Expert Tools Index

Software	Developer	Type of Authoring	Sample Product
Comic Life	Apple	Graphic page layout	Comic book
Dreamweaver	Adobe	Web pages	Website
Flash	Adobe	Interactive applications for the Web and digital devices	Animation
FruityLoops	Image-Line	Digital audio workstation	Audio track
GarageBand	Apple	Digital audio workstation	Podcast
Illustrator	Adobe	Vector-based graphics editing	Graphic logo
iMovie	Apple	Video editing	Digital movie
Photoshop	Adobe	Raster-based graphics editing	Digitally manipulated photo
Scratch	MIT	Programming environment	Interactive game

Note: The expert tools index was created using students' self-rated knowledge of nine digital media production tools. Students rated their experience with each tool, choosing from five options: "I don't know what this is"; "I have no experience, but I have heard of it"; "I've played around with it"; "I have used it to make something"; and "I am an expert and can teach someone how to use it." Students received one point for each tool they rated themselves "expert" with, for a possible total of nine.

BOX 7.4
Proxy of Internet Proficiency

To look at online search skill across large samples, Eszter Hargittai (2005; Hargittai and Hsieh 2012) developed and validated a survey-based proxy measure of Internet proficiency. The proxy was determined to measure both effectiveness (percentage of tasks completed successfully) and efficiency (amount of time spent on tasks) more accurately than users' self-perceived ratings of their skills or the time they spent online.

Note: The Internet proxy score was created by taking an average of students' total ratings of understanding fifteen Internet terms on a scale from 1 (no understanding) to 5 (full understanding).

PDF	tabbed browsing	podcasting
advanced search	spyware	cache
preference settings	firewall	malware
tagging	wiki	phishing
weblog	JPG	RSS

---

to eighth grade, and this was true for both boys and girls and for students from families with both higher and lower home incomes.[6] We also investigated student Internet proficiency using a validated proxy measure (Hargittai 2005; Hargittai and Hsieh 2012) (see box 7.4). Similar to the other expertise measures, the average proxy score increased significantly from sixth to eighth grade for the entire cohort, with no evidence of differences by student gender or family income level.[7]

DID DEEPER ENGAGEMENT WITH DIGITAL MEDIA PRODUCTION LINK TO GREATER TECHNICAL EXPERTISE AND OTHER TWENTY-FIRST-CENTURY LEARNING COMPETENCIES?

The learner portraits of Calvin, Maurice, Ruby, and Michael highlight how even within the DYN community where all students are offered similar opportunities, there was variability in regards to interest, participation, and experience with digital media. For some, DYN projects and pods led to self-directed learning and digital hobbies pursued on their own time. For others, digital media work was limited to required school projects and classes. Although the average depth of production score for the cohort significantly increased over the three years of middle school, there was much variability within the group at the end of eighth grade, with scores ranging from 0 to 8 out of a possible 12. Our earlier research suggested that greater depth is connected to effects in areas such as confidence, the sharing of new knowledge with family and friends, and future technology career considerations (Barron 2006; Barron, Walter,

Martin, et al. 2010). In this chapter, we use the depth score as an indicator of engagement in digital production activities—evidence of persistence in the practice of creating digital media. Given the results of our earlier research, we were interested in whether greater engagement with digital production activities at Renaissance would be associated with twenty-first-century competencies such as technical expertise, identity as a creator, and social learning orientation. In order to compare students with evidence of higher and lower engagement, we employed the same technique from our previous work, using a median split to divide the cohort into two groups: those with lower engagement scores and those with higher engagement scores (see figure 7.2). The engagement scores and specific production activities of our nine case learners are described in box 7.5.

The demographics of both groups were similar. In both groups of students, gender and family income levels were representative of the entire sample, and there were no significant differences in school assessments or standardized test scores at any grade.

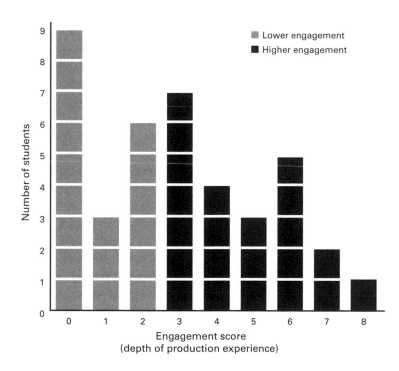

FIGURE 7.2
Distribution of engagement scores at the end of eighth grade for the forty students for whom we had both sixth- and eighth-grade survey data.

The students who did not report depth of production with any activity (an engagement score of zero) reveal a subset of the lower-engagement group that is important to understand and is discussed later in the chapter. As we predicted, the students in the higher-engagement group were more likely to have higher scores in all three clusters: technical expertise, identity as a creator, and social learning orientation (see summary of results in box 7.6).

BOX 7.5
Case Learner Engagement

Two of our case learners, Michael and Evan, fall into the lower-engagement group, engaging in 0 and 2 activities out of 12. The other seven students fall into the higher-engagement group. Ruby, Calvin, and Zach are on the lower end of the higher-engagement group, with engagement scores of 3 and 4. The other four cases are on the high end of the scale, Monica, Renee, Maurice, and Kiley, showing sustained experience with 5 or more production activities.

Name	Score	Group	Repeated Production Activities		
			Expressive	Publication	Computational
Michael	0	Lower			
Evan	2	Lower	art, music		
Ruby	3	Higher	art, video	newsletter	
Calvin	4	Higher	art		animation, games, robotics
Zach	4	Higher	art, music, video		simulation
Monica	5	Higher	art, video	blog, website, newsletter	
Renee	5	Higher	art, video	blog, website	game
Maurice	6	Higher	music, video	blog, website, newsletter	database
Kiley	8	Higher	art, music, video	blog, website, newsletter	database, game

BOX 7.6
Engagement Group Comparison: Findings at a Glance

- Enrollment in voluntary after-school pods was similar for students with higher and lower engagement in the DYN program, but higher-engagement students were more likely to think DYN sources were important to their learning about technology and to perceive people at school as caring about their growing knowledge in that area.

- Higher-engagement students developed greater technical expertise, including confidence with tools and Internet proficiency.

- Higher-engagement students were more likely to identify themselves as a creator, including considering themselves creative, considering technology tools a means of self-expression, caring about the quality of work they posted, and envisioning themselves creating media for social change in the future. Both engagement groups, however, had similar predictions about possible technology-related careers and the likelihood of taking more classes in technology.

- Higher-engagement students had a greater social learning orientation, as indicated by their teaching others, their confidence in their collaborative skills, and their perception of the Internet as a place where they can explore interests and identities. They were not significantly more likely to share work, ideas, and information online.

- The least-engaged students were the least likely to report technical expertise, endorse an identity as a creator, or have a social learning orientation.

Learning Ecologies

> Dr. Pinkard, she was a big help 'cause I would send her emails and ask her questions and see how she liked my game. And she gave me critiques back and said what I need to do to change it around and everything.
>
> —Monica (sixth grade), 2007

Given the critical influences of available learning opportunities and a learner's own role in creating those opportunities (Barron 2006), we first share what we know about the students' technological learning ecology. We first look at the degree of participation in DYN voluntary experiences and at sources of learning at school and home for the students who were more and less engaged, as reflected by their depth of experience at the end of middle school. Results revealed significant differences in how they interacted with DYN, with the highly engaged group evidencing stronger connections to the program.

Both the lower-engagement group and the higher-engagement group participated in an average of four pods over the three years of middle school, and more than 90 percent of both groups had profile pages on Remix World. Though this number indicates what students signed up for, it does not provide a complete picture of engagement in the DYN programming because week-to-week pod attendance and the degree of actual online participation varied. Where the two groups differed was in their perception of the importance of DYN mentors and after-school pods for their learning and in their perceptions of how parents, peers, and teachers in the community valued their developing technical expertise. Both groups considered school-related resources to be more influential than their parents to their learning about computers and technology. Although those with higher engagement were more likely than the less-engaged students to report learning from all sources, only two learning sources were significantly different for the two groups—after-school pods and DYN mentors (figure 7.3).

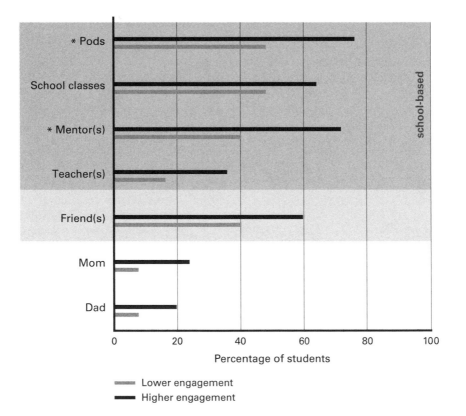

FIGURE 7.3
Percentage of students who considered different people and settings important to their learning about technology, by engagement group. Statistical significance is indicated by asterisks.

With respect to the social value of their computing knowledge, highly engaged students were more inclined than less-engaged students to believe that adults at school (68 percent compared to 44 percent), friends (50 percent compared to 16 percent), and parents (52 percent compared to 24 percent) placed value on their growing computer knowledge. These differences were significant[8] for beliefs about friends and adults at school, suggesting stronger social ties with the DYN community and friendship groups who similarly value learning about technology for those students who were more engaged in production. Our case portraits and vignettes are consistent with these quantitative findings and help explain how depth of interest, commitment to the crafts in which mentors specialized, and pursuit of help shaped the relational patterns within and outside of pods.

Technical Expertise

We're good at everything. Editing, making movies, music. We just know how to do everything, I guess. We've been through everything.

—Zach (eighth grade), 2009

Deeper engagement was linked to several measures of technical expertise, including more technology experiences across media genres, higher confidence in working with technology tools, and greater Internet proficiency.

For all three genres of production activities, there was little report of depth of production (participation in a production activity more than six times) at the beginning of sixth grade, but by the end of eighth grade the two groups significantly differentiated themselves in terms of computational (11 percent of the lower engaged compared to 66 percent of the higher engaged),[9] publication (26 compared to 76 percent),[10] and expressive (32 compared to 95 percent)[11] pursuits.

To look at student knowledge of and confidence with digital media production, we compared the two groups in terms of their self-rated expertise with digital media software tools (see the expert tools index, box 7.3). Whereas all students started out with little or no self-reported expertise with production tools at the beginning of sixth grade, the two groups became differentiated over the three years of middle school (see figure 7.4).[12]

Similarly, although the average Internet proficiency proxy (see box 7.4) for both engagement groups looked alike at the beginning of sixth grade, this was not the case at eighth grade (see figure 7.5). These results suggest that the higher-engagement group increased their effective and efficient use of the Internet throughout middle school by a significantly greater amount.[13]

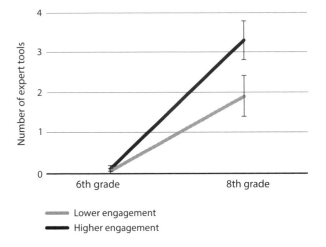

FIGURE 7.4
Expert tools index (see box 7.3) at sixth and eighth grade,
by engagement group.

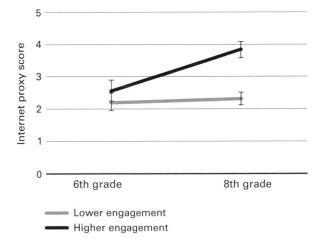

FIGURE 7.5
Internet proxy scores (see box 7.4) at sixth and eighth grade,
by engagement group.

Evidence of Identity as a Creator

> The reason why I made this website is because I wanted to change how people think. And I wanted to open up people's minds into a twenty-first-century era. And I wanted to have, like, a community online where people could discuss ideas.

> —Maurice (seventh grade), 2008

Higher engagement was related to higher levels of students' self-identification as creative, their monitoring of the quality of the productive work they shared with others, and their ideas about creating specific kinds of media in the future.

The majority of students, regardless of whether they were classified as having lower or higher engagement, planned to take more technology classes in the future (see table 7.3). Roughly one-third of each group also could envision themselves as having a highly technology-dependent job, such as programming, graphic design, or network consulting. Based on these measures, it appears that the two groups were quite similar in their outlook on future pursuits, indicating that the majority of the students at Renaissance Academy valued what they had learned and considered pursuing it further once their time in the DYN environment had come to an end. However, differences between the groups were evident when they thought about their future participation in civic-related digital media pursuits. Students in the higher-engagement group were ten times more likely than students in the lower-engagement group to envision themselves creating media to effect social change in the future.

TABLE 7.3
Students Reporting Possible Futures, by Engagement Group

I can see myself . . .	Lower (%)	Higher (%)	p
Taking more technology classes	64	60	
Becoming a programmer, graphic designer, or network consultant	32	40	
Creating media for social change	4	44	**

Note: This table represents students who indicated 4 or 5 on a 5-point Likert scale from 1 (definitely no) to 5 (definitely yes). Statistically significant differences between engagement groups noted by ** ($p < .01$).

As indicated in the preceding chapters, creativity, civic engagement, and participation in the design process to elicit the best work possible were particularly encouraged and supported within the DYN pods and media arts classes. In many cases, the after-school pod mentors were not only teachers in school-day classes, but also professionals in the creative arts, regularly sharing and modeling practices, artifacts, and ideas with the students at Renaissance. More specialized future predictions may reflect students' affinity with the DYN program's ideas, goals, and people. This idea that there was a link between student engagement in DYN and their sense of fit with the program tenets is further supported by the fact that students in the higher-engagement group were significantly more likely to consider themselves to be creative[14] than students in the lower-engagement group (91 percent compared to 65 percent).[15] The former were also significantly more likely to feel that technology allowed them to express themselves in ways that they would otherwise not have been able to (56 compared to 29 percent).[16] Given their affinity with creative pursuits and the use of technology, it is perhaps not surprising that the higher-engaged students were significantly more likely to be selective of the quality of work they posted online, with 67 percent agreeing that they made sure the work they posted online was "really good" compared to 17 percent of the lower-engagement group.[17]

Evidence of Social Learning Orientation

> Well, I usually share—like sometimes my brother will come in, and I will show him what I be working on, or I'll just tell him at home. I teach my brother how to go on Scratch and make video games sometimes.
>
> —Calvin (sixth grade), 2006

As discussed in previous chapters, Remix World encourages students to "mess around" as they update profile pages or share new music, to engage in discussion around topics of importance and interest to the local community, and to post, review, and critique digital media projects. Active participation in online social networks offers young people multiple opportunities to circulate knowledge, learn from others, and develop their expertise (Ito, Baumer, Bittanti, et al. 2010; Jenkins 2009). Joseph Kahne, Nam-Jin Lee, and Jessica Feezell (2011) designed survey measures to assess the impact of media literacy education and found that after participation in such programs young people's participation in online civic and political life increased. We asked students about the frequency of their social networking activities, and we used some of Kahne, Lee, and Feezell's items to ask about civic practices online (see table 7.4).

TABLE 7.4
Students Reporting Online Practices at Least Once a Week, by Engagement Group

I use the Internet at least once per week to . . .	Lower (%)	Higher (%)
Update my profile page	54	72
Share media I have created	46	60
Get or share information about political and social issues	33	48
Receive feedback on my work	32	44
Start discussions about topics I am interested in	24	40
Critique the work of others	32	36
Create and share media with a political or social message	25	24

Note: This table represents students who indicated 5 (once a week) or higher on an 8-point scale from 1 (never) to 8 (several times a day).

Although Internet-use comparisons are not statistically different, the persistent trend across items in conjunction with the statistically significant difference of posting good work suggest that the higher-engagement group was establishing a more active and invested online presence. They were slightly more inclined to get involved and more invested when they did, perhaps reflecting a sense of care in presenting and upholding their digital media identities within the DYN online environment. The idea that the higher-engaged students were more connected to an online community is supported by the fact that they were significantly more likely than the lower-engaged group to feel that the Internet allowed exploration of their interests and parts of their identity that they were not able to explore with family and offline friends (68 percent compared to 21 percent).[18]

In addition to online social orientation, we were also interested in face-to-face interactions and general practices of teaching and collaborating with others. Teaching another person has been shown to have the potential to be a learning experience not only for the learner, but also for the teacher as he or she figures out how to articulate and demonstrate knowledge and skills (Bargh and Schul 1980). As learners become teachers, they not only develop stronger identities as computer users (Mercier, Barron, and O'Conner 2006) but also share new knowledge throughout their home, school, and community contexts. By the eighth grade, those students in the higher-engagement group were more likely to share their growing technological knowledge with others. From a list of seven different types of relations (mother, father, sister, brother, grandparents, other relatives, and friends), the higher-engagement group reported having an average of 3.7 different types of learning partnerships, whereas students with lower-engagement scores reported 2.6 types.[19] Some students reported that they were both teaching and learning from friends. This bidirectional learning was true for 46 percent of the higher-engagement group, but only for 9 percent of the lower-engagement group,[20] consistent with the idea that the relationships of the more highly engaged included collaboration around their digital hobbies. Future ideas about teaching also fit this pattern. Students in the higher-engagement group were more likely to envision becoming a computer teacher (28 percent) than those in the lower-engagement group (4 percent).[21]

Although the majority of both groups believed in their ability to work pretty well in a group, fewer reported an ability to do this well or very well, and the difference between groups was marginally significant[22] (20 percent of the lower-engagement group and 44 percent of higher-engagement group). The ethnographic work at DYN indicated variability in students' collaborative experiences as they worked together in formal and informal groups over the three years of middle school. These frequent experiences in pods and classes may have translated into efficacy. The challenge of collaboration at DYN is discussed in more detail in chapter 8.

A Closer Look at the Least Engaged

The contrasts between engagement groups at Renaissance Academy tell us something about the different ways that students experienced DYN. Deeper, sustained engagement was correlated with distinct benefits. Students who were less engaged received fewer of these benefits. But what about those students at the far end of the lower-engaged spectrum—the 23 percent of the cohort that went through middle school without evidencing depth of production in any activity? These nine students were similar to their peers in terms of their family incomes, gender distribution, grades and standardized test scores, and rates of pod participation. They were not without experience in digital media technologies: these students participated at least once in an average of six different activities, and seven of the nine reported repeated experience (doing something three to six times) for at least one activity. However, their experiences were still markedly different from their higher-engagement group counterparts. We felt it was important to understand why.

Where they differed most noticeably was with respect to their connections to the DYN community. Whereas the identities of students in the higher-engagement group were closely tied to participating in friendship groups, learning from mentors, and sharing work and knowledge, both online and in person, these connections were much weaker for the least engaged. It becomes clear, then, that simply participating in the program was not enough. In order to obtain strong technology learning outcomes, students also had to develop a sense of place and relational ties for themselves within the DYN community.

Researchers use the term *belongingness* to speak to the human need for meaningful, social interaction (Baumeister and Leary 1995; Goodenow 1993; Van Galen 1996). Proponents of belongingness research show that perceived belongingness or feeling a "part of" a community through regular, quality social contact that encompasses caring or concerned interactions is fundamental to engagement (Baumeister and Leary 1995; Noddings 1992; Osterman 2000) and the development of positive self-esteem (Humphrey 2004) and has implications for dropout rates, academic achievement, and career trajectories (Birch and Ladd 1996; Booker 2004; Furrer and Skinner 2003; Pianta and Steinberg 1992; Wentzel 1997).

Some students found a sense of belonging through a perceived match between their individual identity and the DYN program. Examples include Maurice flexing his predilection for public social activism and Calvin linking his gaming interests and creative personality to an avid pursuit of game creation. Other students developed an affinity with the DYN program through social interactions, including forming new relationships with mentors or participating in DYN programming with preexisting friendship groups. We saw this in the cases of Zach producing media with the Hurricanes and Ruby repeatedly seeking out help and support from Brother Mike.

Since belonging is a perception, although a child may appear to receive support from teachers and peers, it is her feeling of this support that makes for a sense of belonging or not. The least-engaged students did not evidence a personal connection to DYN programming or people. They were the least likely to consider themselves creative and to value technological knowledge, and they reported fewer plans to pursue technology-related jobs in the future. Not one of the least-engaged students envisioned making media for social change in their future. The least-engaged students reported infrequently working on their personal social networking pages and did not attend much to the quality of the work they posted online—only 8 percent said they made sure the work they posted on Remix World was of good quality.

These students also did not have strong social affiliations with and within DYN. They were the least likely to feel that parents, friends, and adults at school were important to their technological learning and to perceive those people as caring about their knowledge of computers. The middle school years often coincide with a stage of social development where children depend heavily on their social groups and place high importance on companionship and belonging with friends. Whereas creating, competing, and critiquing among friends amplified some students' engagement, others' engagement may have been diminished because they felt their friends were not interested. It is possible that preexisting interests or friendship groups did not easily fit within the DYN model, and these students remained engaged in other outside activities or pursuits.

There is some evidence to support the idea that the least engaged were involved in other activities. After-school programming at Renaissance Academy was not limited to DYN. Sports, including basketball and drill team, were popular, and the City Year service-learning program offered a mentor alternative, placing local college students at Renaissance to support homework, academic choices, and high school applications. One of the least-engaged students, case learner Michael, made choices about his time that left little room for other pursuits. He had a focus on core academics with an eye toward a competitive traditional private high school, had a passion for aviation that was not picked up on within DYN, and was involved in outside learning opportunities that his parents often brokered. Another student in the least-engaged group was consistently active in pods multiple days after school each of the three years, but field note data indicates that she was on the periphery of production in pods. Field notes often describe her chatting with friends in the hallway between the DYN rooms, perhaps part of cliques that were engaged in activities, interests, and experiences that were not focused on digital media.

HOW DID THE DYN COHORT COMPARE TO STUDENTS IN SILICON VALLEY AT THE END OF MIDDLE SCHOOL?

In this final section, we pull back from variations within Renaissance Academy students to look at the cohort as a whole as they graduated from middle school, providing comparison data from a group of eighth graders in a technologically immersed and higher socioeconomic community in California (Palm Middle School, see box 7.7). When the same criteria were used to measure engagement in digital media at Palm, the impact of the DYN program by the end of eighth grade is apparent. Only 25 percent of students at Palm were classified as having higher engagement with digital media (at least three activities experienced more than six times) compared to 52 percent of the studied cohort at Renaissance Academy. Overall, DYN students evidenced more indicators of technical expertise and social learning orientation than their counterparts in Silicon Valley (see the summary of results in box 7.8).

BOX 7.7
School Comparison

Renaissance Academy (DYN)	Palm Middle School
Public charter middle school	Public middle school
150 students	1,320 students
Urban	Suburban
100% African American	75% Asian American, 20% Caucasian
Economically diverse (66% eligible for subsidized lunch)	Economically homogeneous (2% eligible for subsidized lunch)
Few parents in tech industry jobs	Many parents in tech industry
Internet at home: 84%	Internet at home: 100%
Sample size = 50 eighth graders	Sample size = 358 eighth graders

Note: Although Palm Middle School was located within a hub of technological innovation, the school did not have a technology focus. Palm's core class descriptions (language arts, math, physical fitness, science, and social studies) did not mention technology, and only one elective had a computer focus—using professional layout and graphic design software to create publications. Two after-school clubs were focused on technology: programming and Internet mapping.

BOX 7.8
School Comparisons: Summary of Findings at a Glance

- Students at Palm had more resources at home and were more likely to learn about technology there from their parents. DYN students were more likely to learn from sources at school and to believe that their technological knowledge was valued by the school community, including teachers and friends.
- Parents of students at Palm played more roles to support their child's learning about technology, especially those that required expertise. At both schools, the number of roles parents played was correlated with their use of technology at work.
- DYN students had higher breadth and depth of production experiences and more confidence with technology tools, whereas students at Palm exhibited higher Internet proficiency.
- DYN students were more likely to consider taking technology classes in the future and were more likely to see themselves as pursuing a future as an entrepreneur, engineer, or artist/designer.
- Although students at Palm learned from more types of people about technology, DYN students taught more types of people what they knew and were more likely to share media work and political ideas online.

Learning Ecologies

The major distinction between the two learning communities was that for Renaissance students school was the primary source of learning about computers and technology, whereas for the Palm students this learning happened outside the classroom, frequently at home. When asked to indicate places and people important for their technological learning, the two samples of students differed significantly across every item (figure 7.6), with Palm students learning from parents and Renaissance students learning through school-based opportunities and people.[23] At home, Palm students had more access to people and tools to support their technological learning. Eighty-five percent of Palm students reported that a parent worked in the field of technology, indicating some level of technological knowledge and expertise, compared to 21 percent of Renaissance students.[24] Palm students also reported having more than

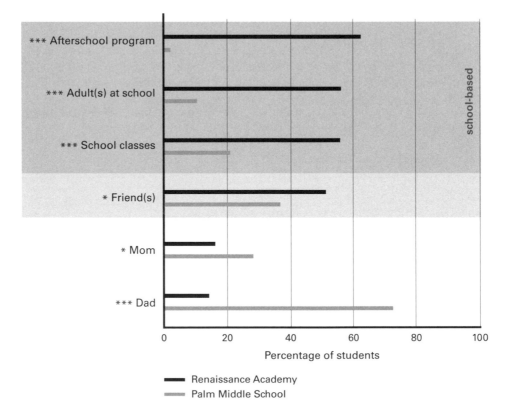

FIGURE 7.6
Percentage of students who considered different people and settings important to their learning about technology, by school. Statistical significance is indicated by asterisks.

twice as many technology tools in their home (based on a count of computers, print-ers, scanners, digital cameras, video cameras, gaming devices, music players, and other handheld devices) than students at Renaissance.[25]

For DYN students, the obvious learning sources were DYN staff and opportunities. Further suggesting the strength of this school-based technology community, students at Renaissance were significantly more likely than those at Palm to feel that friends (33 percent versus 19 percent)[26] and adults at school (56 percent versus 27 percent)[27] considered their knowledge about computers important. Our research does not indi-cate a lack of interest on the part of Renaissance parents—their level of valuing tech-nology knowledge was in fact almost identical to that of Palm parents. Thirty-eight percent of Renaissance students believed that their knowing about computers was important to their parents, compared with 37 percent of Palm students.

To find out more about home learning partnerships, specifically parent involve-ment at Renaissance and Palm, we created a survey measure based on our previous work on roles played by parents to support their children's technology learning (Barron, Martin, Takeuchi, et al. 2009) (see table 7.5 for a summary of the parent roles). On average, parents played significantly more roles (number of roles played by mother or father for a possible total of eight) in California (5.2 roles) than at Renais-sance Academy (3.6 roles).[28]

Consistent with results from our earlier work, parents' technology expertise made a difference, and Palm parents were more likely to have expertise. Students across both schools whose parents worked with computers occasionally[29] or primarily[30] in their job reported significantly more roles played by parents than students whose par-ents did not use computers in their work (figure 7.7), and this pattern played out simi-larly at both schools.[31] However, as reported earlier, students at Renaissance were less likely to have parents who worked with computers. And as indicated in figure 7.7, the children at Renaissance whose parents' jobs did not include a technology component reported on average their parents playing the fewest roles in their technology learn-ing, perhaps pointing to the fact that even people in Silicon Valley who are not directly involved with technology have a basic level of skill and knowledge due to their social connections and surroundings. The fact that parents from Renaissance who were not in technology-oriented jobs played the fewest parent-support roles for their children could also be a result not of parent expertise but rather of a higher per-centage of single-parent households or other situations where there is less time for parents to sit down with their children around technology learning, but we do not have the data to confirm this hypothesis.

The breakdown of the specific roles illustrate further differences between the schools, with those roles that require some technological expertise being significantly more likely to be played by parents at Palm, such as teaching, modeling, and collabo-rating (see table 7.5).

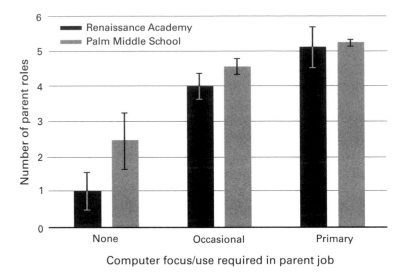

FIGURE 7.7
Number of parent roles (mom or dad) played by parents according to their computer-usage at work, by school.

Eighty-four percent of Renaissance students and 82 percent of Palm students also reported teaching their parents, indicating that the flow of knowledge often occurred in both directions. At Renaissance, 42 percent of parents were described as learners but not teachers, whereas this was true for only 6 percent of parents of students in Silicon Valley.[32] Fifteen percent of Palm students reported learning from their parents but not reciprocating, but this was true for none of the students at Renaissance.[33] At Renaissance, all students who reported that their parents taught them also reported teaching their parents.

Evidence of Technical Expertise

Students at Renaissance had significantly higher breadth[34] and depth[35] of production activities than the students at Palm. Renaissance students were somewhat more likely than Palm students to show evidence of depth in each of the three media production genres (see box 7.2), and this difference was significant for the genre of expressive production[36] (see figure 7.8), reflecting the video, graphic design, and digital music themes of pods and media arts classes as well as mentor expertise. Renaissance students also evidenced significantly higher confidence in their expertise with digital media production tools[37] (see the expert tools index, box 7.3).

TABLE 7.5
Students Reporting Roles Played by at Least One Parent, by School

Role	Description	Renaissance (%)	Palm (%)	p
Teacher	Taught me how to do something on the computer (such as how to type, how to create a Web page, etc.).	40	93	***
Modeler	Let me watch how they do something (such as turn on the computer, set up the printer), which I eventually learned how to do from observing them.	46	81	***
Provider	Has things (such as technology books, equipment, software) at the house that I use.	60	72	
Financier	Bought me things to support my computer activities and learning (such as hardware, software, books, courses).	58	72	*
Nontechnical consultant	Gave me advice on nontechnical issues that have helped me with my technology activities.	34	61	***
Collaborator	Worked with me on a technology or computer-related project (such as building a robot together, working on a Flash tutorial together, etc.).	34	59	**
Broker	Looked for technology-related activities for me to do and/or signed me up for them (such as classes, clubs, camps, etc.).	56	54	
Employer	Paid me to do something technical or on the computer for her or him.	34	23	

Note: Statistically significant differences between schools noted by * (p < .05), ** (p < .01), and *** (p < .001).

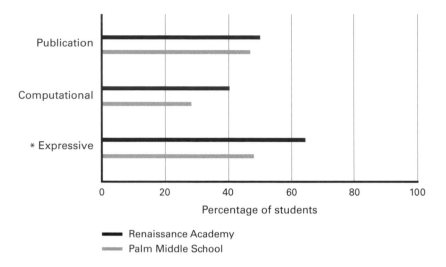

FIGURE 7.8
Percentage of students with in-depth genre production experience, by school. Statistical significance is indicated by asterisks.

Despite the higher production experience and tool confidence levels at Renaissance, the students in California had marginally higher proxies of Internet proficiency[38] (see box 7.4). Palm's position in the Silicon Valley, an environment dense with technology companies with a majority of parents working in them, perhaps ensured that all students—even those less engaged with production activities—were familiar with and savvy about current online terms and practices.

Evidence of Identity as a Creator

Overall, Renaissance students were significantly more likely than Palm students to consider continuing their technological learning through classes (62 percent compared to 26 percent).[39] When the two groups are compared according to their imagined possibility of taking on technology-related jobs in the future (graphic designer, programmer, or network specialist), the groups looked similar. Thirty-six percent of Renaissance students said they could imagine this to be true compared with 30 percent of Palm students. However, DYN was not designed to steer students to a focus on a technology career by the end of eighth grade. Instead, it was intended that all students graduate with a breadth of skills in and knowledge of technology, as well as multiple opportunities to explore different media, tools, roles, and content through the production of digital media. At the end of our focal cohort's eighth-grade year, we asked about a wider range of job clusters and found that Renaissance students were more likely to see themselves taking on more varied careers in the future compared to their counterparts at Palm (see table 7.6). The Renaissance Academy students were significantly more likely to consider traditional jobs such as joining the police force or becoming a firefighter. They also were more likely to consider entrepreneurial ventures, such as starting their own business, and specialized pursuits, such as in the arts and engineering.

None of the other measures used to look at student identity as a creator was shown to be significantly different between the two groups except for their commitment to sharing quality work online. Palm students were more likely to say that they made sure the work they posted online was really good (58 percent) than Renaissance students (43 percent).[40] It is possible that some of this difference can be attributed to the informal context of Remix World, which offered Renaissance students a comfortable space where they could share their work in various stages of production. Because they had access to an internal DYN online network, they may have been less involved in online activities open to the world, whereas Palm students may have felt higher pressure to post good work to an online community beyond the boundaries of familiar face-to-face settings.

TABLE 7.6
Students Agreeing with Statements about Future Plans, by School

I can see myself becoming an/a . . .	Renaissance (%)	Palm (%)	p
Entrepreneur (start own business)	67	34	***
Artist/Designer (graphic designer, artist)	47	27	**
Engineer (programmer, game designer, network specialist)	42	29	*
Medical provider (nurse, doctor)	29	32	
Police officer or firefighter	22	3	***
Educator (teacher)	20	14	
Scientist	18	22	
Journalist	12	11	
Politician	12	6	

Note: This table represents students who indicated 4 or 5 on a 5-point Likert scale from 1 (definitely no) to 5 (definitely yes). Statistically significant differences between schools noted by * ($p < .05$), ** ($p < .01$), and *** ($p < .001$).

Evidence of Social Orientation

Students in Silicon Valley were significantly more likely to report self-efficacy in their collaborative ability. Thirty-two percent of Renaissance students and 57 percent of students at Palm reported they were able to work well or very well in a group.[41] Despite the fact that students at Palm had higher collaborative self-efficacy and reported that they learned about computers and technology from significantly more people outside of school,[42] students at Renaissance more actively shared their knowledge with others. They taught more people in their community about computers and technology[43] and were more likely to be interested in teaching others in the future. At Renaissance, 16 percent of students thought it likely they would become computer teachers, whereas only 2 percent of students at Palm saw this occupation as a possibility.[44] DYN students may have had more teaching opportunities open to them because the culture within DYN specifically encouraged students to share their knowledge and because the local school community, including parents and siblings, were less likely to have existing expertise.

Renaissance students were more likely to share not only their knowledge, but also their work and information. They were more than twice as likely to share their media productions online (53 percent compared to 22 percent of Palm students)[45] and to share and create media with a political message (25 percent compared to 10 percent).[46] They were almost twice as likely as students at Palm to use the Internet to get and share information and media about political topics (41 percent compared to 25 percent).[47] This evidence suggests that the mentors, projects, and practices inspired a class of students to take on this role of sharing knowledge to new generations of learners and that the knowledge flow was intergenerational in that they brought their knowledge home to parents, grandparents, siblings, and cousins. This finding has especially important implications for communities where technological expertise is not the norm, helping to counter the "Matthew effect," introduced in the introduction, wherein the technologically rich get richer and the poor get poorer.

The findings around technological experience and expertise, identification as a creator (including ideas for their future), and social orientations—especially the teaching of others and the sharing of work and ideas—suggest that graduating Renaissance students were as ready, if not more so, than students at Palm to continue their pursuit of technology and media learning and engagement in high school and beyond. This result is especially encouraging given the very different socioeconomic profiles of the two samples of students.

SUMMARY

On average, the students at Renaissance Academy increased their learning about and experience with digital media production from sixth through eighth grade, but some students developed deeper engagement with production activities. At the end of eighth grade, this deeper engagement was associated with a broad range of learning metrics, including technological expertise, identity as a creator, and social learning orientation—all outcomes that are central to DYN's goal of developing digital media citizens. Students who were more fully engaged gained greater expertise with production tools, became more familiar with technical vocabulary, engaged more frequently in online networking and social justice activities, shared knowledge with friends and family, had higher creative self-efficacy, and had more technology-focused ideas for the future. The most-engaged students valued learning, shared ideas and expertise, and actively participated in a community of learning and expression. The least-engaged students developed identities as digital media citizens to a lesser degree. It is possible that certain types of media production and use during the middle school years led to skill development and identification with certain media niches. As students progressed, those who saw themselves as video editors, game designers, or music makers were better able to find their place within DYN programming. Those students who had not deeply engaged or developed a mature skill set after their first or second year at Renaissance may have felt less attached to DYN (and to the media production it promoted) or more attached to other pursuits or both. Technology was the tool for DYN, but in many instances it was the ideas, interests, projects, and people that truly drove learning and the pursuit of knowledge. Our data reflect the importance of fostering all aspects of the DYN learning community and its tenets of sharing ideas, developing meaningful work, and promoting multiple opportunities for learning and teaching.

Our findings also indicate that DYN, in the period studied, was successful in providing youth with opportunities for learning regardless of gender and socioeconomic status within Renaissance Academy and in comparison to a school where students had grown up with greater access to technology-related learning opportunities, including parents in the field, home technology access, and community knowledge. At the end of eighth grade, a higher proportion of students at Renaissance Academy evidenced some higher measures of twenty-first-century competencies than students at our comparison school. The DYN students were more engaged with digital media production and had higher confidence with contemporary tools of production. Although students from Palm Middle School had larger networks of people from whom they learned, Renaissance Academy students were more likely to teach others what they knew about technology and to share media and information related to civic and social causes that were important to them. This focus on community reflects some of the important foci of the DYN program at Renaissance Academy. It also points to the potential for movement of DYN's impact out of the school and into other spaces, such as children's homes, local neighborhoods, and virtual communities. Without DYN programming, these student surveys would have probably looked very different. DYN was an essential resource for the development of important twenty-first-century competencies including their technical expertise, their identity as a creator, and their orientation toward social learning.

We believe this work represents an important contribution to a broader goal of creating measures that can reflect learning outcomes of experiences designed to ensure that all youth have similar opportunities to develop twenty-first-century competencies. However, the findings reported here must be interpreted with an understanding of the limitations of our approach. First, results are reliant primarily on self-report data. Individual students' answers may at times be inaccurate due to anything from misremembering their learning histories to being in a certain mood on the day they completed the survey. Offering pre- and postsurveys—at the beginning of sixth grade and the end of eighth grade—allowed us to see positive change in student confidence and perceived expertise, suggesting that students were not simply over- or underestimating their own knowledge, but reflecting self-perception of growth over time. A second issue is that our data are correlational; we cannot warrant causal inferences about the links we observed between experiences, learning ecologies, and documented indicators of technological expertise, identity as a creator, and social learning orientations. This is especially true for those measures for which we do not have before and after comparisons (those items we did not ask at pretest but added in later). However, the portraits of experience and sustained engagement with production activities provided overall a consistent pattern of differential participation and repeat findings evident in previous work, and our case portraits help to validate the quantitative measures. A third limitation is the possibility of an age effect—that students are doing and knowing more over time simply as a result of growing up. We addressed this limitation by looking at variability within the engagement groups at Renaissance for both sixth and eighth grade and by using Palm as a comparison sample to illuminate differences across students of similar age. Despite these limitations, we believe the results shared in this chapter are important to framing and understanding the qualitative portraits that are included in this book. We also believe that the effort to develop reliable ways to measure cognitive and noncognitive outcomes is critical to the successful design and support of programs created to foster twenty-first-century competencies.

Renaissance Academy students reported that their learning and experiences were largely due to school-based opportunities. This response is a clear indication that the DYN program provided these children—who typically came from homes where parents had limited technical expertise—not only with experiences and opportunities, but with mentors, teachers, and peers who could fulfill a range of important roles that fostered their development as digital media citizens. In short, we believe there is sufficient evidence to support the claim that in areas where there are fewer tools at home, there are higher levels of socioeconomic stress, and parents do not have high levels of technical experience, in-school and after-school programs can offer significant learning opportunities that make a difference.

MICHAEL: NAVIGATING INDIVIDUAL PURSUITS

I really, like, I always liked airplanes. And when I first joined iRemix, I didn't know how to change [the background]. Maurice had put a comment on my page . . . he said to change this to something about airplanes. So I don't know how to do it, so he stepped me through it, walked me through it, and so then that is how I got the airplanes [on my profile page].

—Michael (eighth grade), 2009

Of the nine case learners, Michael was the least outwardly involved with the DYN program, including fewer connections with adult mentors and less after-school pod participation. He was highly motivated to perform well in school but demonstrated a pragmatism and reserve with regard to his DYN participation. It was not that he was not interested in technology, but he was conscious of his time both in and out of school, weighing the choices and opportunities available to him. He engaged in a DYN summer program prior to middle school and participated in the robotics pod in sixth grade and part of the video pod in seventh. He frequently used technology tools to pursue his interests and advocate for himself. In seventh grade, he used his computing skills to raise money from local corporations to sponsor his participation in a junior ambassadors travel program. He researched the companies, wrote professional letters requesting support, and created a personal website that potential funders could visit. Overall, he created five digital videos and three websites during middle school, but he did not repeat any one digital production activity more than six times, which locates him in the less-engaged group overall (see chapter 7). Michael's longtime focal interest in aviation, attention to core academics, and experiences outside of school fostered by his family called for his time and offered him multiple directions for learning during the three years of middle school.

A PASSION FOR AVIATION

Michael's interests in aviation, travel, and technology tools linked to these subjects appear as constant themes throughout his interviews in middle school. His mother's longtime work for the airline industry introduced him to the field, and he had long envisioned himself becoming a professional pilot. With his grandmother's encouragement, he attended a flight-training camp in Denver during the summer after seventh grade, where he first used flight simulators. After that he regularly used Microsoft Flight Simulation game software on his home computer and at his grandmother's house. On his own laptop he reported frequently using the Internet to look up pictures of and information about airplanes. Although Michael was not often found on Remix World, he spent "a couple minutes every day" on Airliners.net, an online community of more than two hundred thousand members that includes a photo database, discussion forums where pilots and crew document their flights, a chat room, and an aircraft history and information section. He was introduced to the site when he noticed many of the photographs he found through Google Image originated there. Though he did not contribute to Airliners.net, he had a profile page and enjoyed

> He's very serious about pretty much all of his schoolwork, so if I give him a grade that he does not agree with, he's very concerned about it. He is very responsive [to feedback] because he wants the better grade.
>
> —Ms. Lee Edwards (teacher), 2008

> You have missions [in Microsoft Flight Simulator], and it teaches you how to fly step by step. Then you can make your own; like you can put in your own airports and fly their route. Or you can go online multiplayer and have other people, like actually you can work as an airport traffic controller. You can get hired for a job, but it is like a virtual airlines.
>
> —Michael (eighth grade), 2009

reading trip reports posted by other members comparing differences between airlines and services.

LEARNING FROM SOCIAL NETWORKS AT HOME

Michael lived with his parents, sister, and older brother, Thomas. His parents were very involved with their children's learning, placing particular emphasis on academics, work ethic, and participation in community service. The children were expected to bring home consistently high grades in school and volunteered at a local outpatient center for Alzheimer's patients, and instead of a weekly allowance they were paid for their work at their father's maintenance company.

> It's like [my parents say,] "Make sure you get them grades." They don't care [if I participate in after-school pods]. "Do what you gotta do. If you get them 4's and skills, then fine." They want me to do good. They want me to be a good student.
>
> —Michael (eighth grade), 2009

There is evidence that Michael learned about technology and engaged in technology-related activities with his family, and as his time in middle school progressed, media production activities in the required media arts classes sometimes prompted further learning at home.

Michael's mother remembered that he used to observe her searching the Internet and making graphs and PowerPoint presentations on the computer for her work in sales and then would use the techniques in his own projects. Michael's parents sometimes bought him the technical tools he requested, including a video camera for Christmas in fifth grade. In addition to modeling computer use and financing technology tools, his parents also served as brokers for his growing knowledge, as when his mother, after hearing that Michael had created a website at school, arranged a job for him to work with the family pastor to design and develop a website for their church.

> So I got paid for it. My mom, she knew that the DYN thing—that we were doing a lot with it. And she saw that we were learning a lot of things because we would show her some of the stuff. So she thought of this thing for me to do the website. You know, the church was upcoming. It was just a new church, so they started a website. . . . They gave me the words; I just made the template, really.
>
> —Michael (eighth grade), 2009

Michael's older brother, Thomas, was a DYN participant at Renaissance Academy and helped Michael to refine his skills in digital video. Michael first learned video editing during the DYN summer program before he entered middle school, something he

I first learned from DYN. That's when [Thomas] saw me doing stuff. He then started teaching me. . . . Editing is the main thing he knows. So I know now.

—Michael (seventh grade), 2008

was recruited for because Thomas was attending. He seemed to adopt video editing skills, as he put it, "by watching by example," in interactions with his older brother. Thomas also showed Michael how to make video mash-ups using a video-downloading program, and his video documentaries served as an example for Michael's eighth-grade Living Museum video work.

OPPORTUNITIES AND CHOICES AT SCHOOL

At Renaissance, Michael first signed up for the robotics pod in sixth grade but did not attend the last few sessions or the final citywide competition. In seventh grade, he took advantage of two after-school opportunities with a video-editing component. He initially signed up for the DYN digital video pod, then switched to non-DYN City Year, which involved digital video project work that he believed to have less theory and critique and more hands-on editing, combined with a community-service component. The digital video pod often required students to watch examples and write out critiques or their ideas and visions for project work before actually working with cameras or digital editing software. Around the time Michael left the pod, one activity was for the group to listen to a popular song posted online and then write five to seven sentences describing their idea of what the song would look like as a music video, a commercial, or a scene from a movie. Michael switched back to the digital video pod, however, when City Year added a requirement of three hours each Saturday, free time that he was not willing to give up. He ultimately stopped attending both of these after-school programs well before the end of the year. Nevertheless, he continued to find small opportunities to exercise and build his video-editing skills. Michael took on editing roles in school projects such as the Living Museum social studies video documentary and the media arts class digital yearbook project.

The video pod was more about editing and interpreting videos. City Year, that video thing, was more different. It was about acting and editing, which I love editing, and filmmaking. So I did that, and I got to do the community-service aspect of it.

—Michael (eighth grade), 2009

I've grown to love the media-editing part of [DYN]. So I guess I'm ready to do that. So every time we have to do it, I'm ready, and I'm ecstatic about doing it.

—Michael (eighth grade), 2009

Despite his relative lack of pod participation, Michael was able to learn from the mentors, in particular Brother Mike, who taught him how to use a number of programs, including GarageBand and iMovie. Brother Mike also introduced him to SketchUp, freely distributed three-dimensional-modeling software, in downtime during media arts classes. Michael had enjoyed modeling on the computer since he had used CAD to create a three-dimensional rendering of his imagined ideal airplane for a fourth-grade science project. SketchUp sparked Michael's enthusiasm, and he began creating architectural diagrams of houses in his free time. He viewed mentors as people who "teach me things," but the nature and depth of his learning relationship with them were not as visible as those of other students.

He's just been one of those kind [of kids] that disappear from DYN in terms of after school or interpersonal interaction with him.

—Brother Mike (mentor), 2008

PROJECT SPOTLIGHT: HURRICANE KATRINA COMIC

Hurricane Katrina Project

For his seventh-grade digital storytelling class, Michael created two visual layouts about the aftermath of Hurricane Katrina. The assignment was to create a sequence using Comic Life that captured both the "psychology and the physiology" of an event. Both strips featured graphic imagery from New Orleans shortly after the city's posthurricane flooding. Michael used this project as a means of creatively expressing what he imagined to be the tragedy and chaos that arose after the hurricane hit New Orleans, "really trying to show what happened." In the first layout, the perspective is on the ground with the victims, the central figure being a man on his roof looking out over his property and wondering, "What happened?" Surrounding him are different scenes that Michael organized around the theme of loss: "I thought of what they had all lost. Some people had lost value items, and some people lost lives." The images include "a woman that is scrambling for pieces she probably really wanted, a dead body floating in the water, dirty water," and "a little girl inside the Superdome looking like she is wondering what next." In the second layout, one large image shows a person on an aircraft removed from the destruction on the ground far below, wondering, "Where am I going to start?" while the voices of the unseen below cry out for help: "Mommy, I am hungry; I am drowning; Jesus Help." Here, Michael utilized his aviation perspective, creating this scene from the point of view of a rescue worker on a helicopter, someone Michael referred to as a "savior": "The man in the helicopter was the person that everybody hoped to look for that they really couldn't find. So . . . the man in the helicopter, he was like their savior, you know, trying to save them." Michael worked on his own and used Comic Life, Google, and *Wikipedia* to complete the project. In describing the affordances of Comic Life relevant to this assignment, he talked about its ability to manipulate images easily and to structure text around those images. He did not consult other students or mentors, nor did he solicit feedback on his work.

RETICENT COLLABORATOR

> [I would rather work by myself because] then you know that it's done in a way that you think is the best and that it's the way that you want it to be.
>
> —Michael (eighth grade), 2009

Michael expressed a strong preference for working alone on self-initiated projects and was selective when choosing group members for mandatory collaborative projects. His preference for independent work seemed to stem from his desire to control the outcome of his project, in terms of both the quality of the work and his final grade, which was very important to him. When Michael was required to collaborate, he chose to work with a group of his friends because they all knew each other well enough to know how they worked and what their standards for that work were, ensuring that they would complete a good project. According to Michael, the dynamic that existed between the group members was what made the project a successful collaborative experience.

Although Michael preferred to work alone, he believed group work was necessary for large media projects due within a certain timeframe: "There is no option because you can't do a project like [that] by yourself."

During his work developing the church website, Michael was challenged by the need to merge his vision for the design with that of the pastor's. He was frustrated at having to cede design decisions, and through the project work he developed methods of persuasion, including walking the pastor through his own design process and "giving a positive no" during disagreements.

PERIPHERAL PARTICIPATION IN DYN

Michael was both complimentary and critical of the DYN program. He appreciated the opportunity to participate in the DYN learning community. However, he was notably absent from performance spaces such as Remix World and Freedom Fridays and evidenced diminishing pod participation over the three years of middle school.

He expressed frustration with the extensive outlined requirements to procure Remix dollars on Remix World, believing that it was too much work for the prize payoffs. He also indicated frustration about what he perceived as occasional digital excess at Renaissance Academy. Reflecting on the eighth-grade media arts class production of the digital yearbook, for which he did video editing, he stated, "I understand it's a technology school, but I don't like everything being so technical and logical. You can't sign a CD. Come on."

Yet Michael paid homage to the creative energy within the DYN environment and said that he would not change anything if given the opportunity: "It's a good program. I don't want to critique such a good program. It's a really good program. I know it took a lot of work to get to where it's at." This mixed view

I used to, like, at one time [go on Remix World]. When they introduced Remix Store, that's when I like, "Oh, I'll get this and this and this!" And then I got disinterested in it because I was like, "You know? I can't do this." Because it was, like, all these things to get Remix dollars. But I was like, "I'm not going to keep doing all this just to get this." That's too much work. So Remix World, it is a cool site.

—Michael (eighth grade), 2009

[I would rather participate in] DYN [than the normal school day], of course. It's so much fun. You get to do many more things, and it's more interesting.

—Michael (eighth grade), 2009

of DYN as having both strengths and weaknesses, paired with his various activities outside of school, from travel to work to time spent with his family and his desire for time to himself, seems to have driven his measured participation in the program during middle school. Even so, it is clear that Michael developed his production portfolio, specifically around digital video editing and website creation, and expanded his skillset and knowledge of contemporary design tools during his three years of middle school.

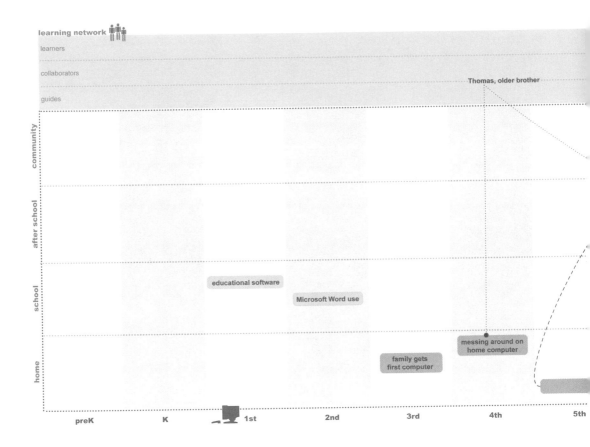

Michael's pathway shows technology learning across all four contexts—**home**, school, after school, and **community**—but his participation was measured and spread out in a way that left time for other pursuits.

He first used a computer 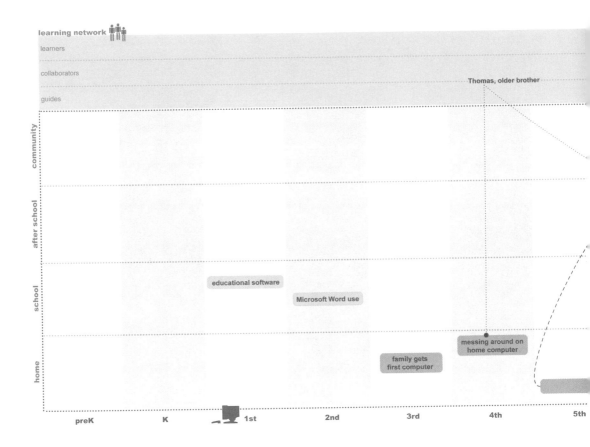 at school in first grade, and early school activities in the elementary grades included using Microsoft Word and educational software. After his family got their first home computer when he was in the third grade, he began to play around with it in collaboration with his older **brother**, Thomas. He also began to use Microsoft Flight Simulator at **home**.

The summer before Michael entered the sixth grade, he was invited to join the **DYN** summer program, where he delved into introductory video production. In the sixth grade, he got his own laptop, and his participation in learning activities and opportunities in school and after school is apparent, along with an increase in

Michael

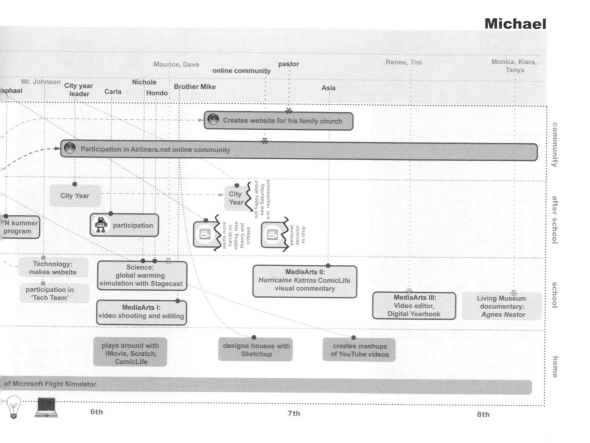

learning partners 👪 On his own, he found and joined an online **community** 🌐 focused on aviation.

In seventh grade, Michael attended the digital video pod 🖥 but did not continue in it for the full year. He also worked with ✳ the family **pastor** to create a website for his new **church**, an opportunity that his **mother** brokered. He learned 🔵 about video mash-up techniques from his **brother** and about SketchUp from **Brother Mike**, and he used this new knowledge to do some design projects on his own time. In eighth grade, Michael was no longer participating in after-school pods but produced multiple collaborative video projects for his in-school **DYN** classes and remained involved with his aviation-related pursuits, including the online aviation-interested community and the flight-simulation game.

8

CHALLENGES AND OPPORTUNITIES OF DEVELOPING DIGITAL MEDIA CITIZENS

Kimberly Austin, Kimberley Gomez, and Kimberly A. Richards

> Working towards a project that they can't see yet, that isn't done, that isn't "hands on," so to say . . . it's hard trying to keep them [focused]. Like, I say, "OK, we got to do all this planning." [And they respond,] "Planning? What do we got to plan for? I just want to do it. Get the camera out."

—Raphael (mentor), 2007

Nichole Pinkard founded the Digital Youth Network on the premise that the limited engagement of minority and low-income youth in digital media affinity spaces was not the result of disinterest or fleeting curiosity. As we have seen, she correctly reasoned that access to the tools of digital media and learning opportunities would increase their engagement in digital media. Although access to tools and learning opportunities are critical components of the model, Pinkard and other DYN leaders also recognized that youth needed intentional learning spaces to become digital media citizens. To this end, Pinkard and others devised and implemented an instructional theory of action that meaningfully brought together access to tools and learning opportunities.

The previous chapters have documented how the DYN theory of action was enacted and have described some of the outcomes for student learning. These chapters and the case study portraits have also hinted at some of the challenges that the DYN team encountered. Of central importance, we described how mentors were required to juggle multiple roles. Consider Brother Mike, who taught both school-day media arts classes and afterschool pods, led the Freedom Friday forums, supported students' online engagement, and collaborated with colleagues to design DYN's curriculum and assessment tools. We have also illustrated the necessity of employing multiple strategies for engaging students in DYN activities and sustaining that participation. These strategies supported, for example, Calvin, who over the course of the study became a prolific producer. Yet, Calvin could have, perhaps, broadened his modes of media production, developed a larger portfolio of work, and showcased his projects to a larger audience by strengthening his project management skills. We have highlighted students such as Ruby and Maurice, who were known as change-oriented students within the community who used digital media to share their voice, but they were cautious about collaborating with peers. Throughout all these challenges, DYN participants and staff often encountered a school and local community that asked the important question of how digital media would serve them in school and in life.

Pinkard and her DYN colleagues anticipated many of these challenges and thought intentionally about how to resolve them. The DYN team did not solve these issues in isolation. The research team offered interim data and analysis to better understand these challenges, and Renaissance Academy educators collaborated with the DYN team to enact solutions. These collaborations enabled the DYN team to monitor, respond to, and manage challenges. Some of these challenges were resolved, but others remained open-ended at the time we concluded our study.

This chapter examines three challenges in more detail. Our discussion opens with an unanticipated obstacle related to blending the tripartite roles of artist, mentor, and teacher. Next, we reflect on the challenges related to encouraging youth participation and production. This discussion focuses on how DYN staff managed student production, encouraged collaboration, and fostered participation among girls. Finally, we explore the challenge of representing DYN's value-added to the broader school audience and local community. These discussions point to several lessons learned and considerations for practitioners and researchers interested in developing digital media citizens. We turn to both in the conclusion of this chapter.

COMBINING THE ROLES OF ARTIST, MENTOR, AND TEACHER

Much of DYN's innovative model is rooted in its multiple, intentionally planned, and overlapping learning spaces led by mentors who combine their artistic expertise with the instructional techniques of traditionally trained teachers. But, as suggested by the title *mentor*, the DYN model views the relationships that these artist-teachers build with students as essential drivers of youth participation and continued learning. As indicated in the previous chapters, the combination of these knowledge domains has helped to animate the DYN model. Specifically, it has led to the "seeding" of production through authentic experiences (chapter 4), the creation of formal and informal learning spaces that support deep engagement with digital media (chapter 5), and the public acknowledgment of students' emergent expertise to encourage more independent production (chapter 6).

At the same time, the leverage DYN gained from reimagining the role of the mentor presented two challenges in the period studied. First, mentors had to participate in a model of professional development that introduced them to teacher techniques. In sharp contrast with artists' more personal and autonomous work practices, DYN mentors were expected to use a set of shared practices and reflect on their use of those practices with peers (chapter 3). In doing so, the DYN professional development model introduced a layer of feedback and accountability that was foreign to many of the mentors. Second, mentors had to balance the informal collaborative relationships frequently seen in mentoring with the ties associated with teacher-student relationships, which are typically marked by greater social distance. In this first section, we examine the role-based challenges DYN mentors encountered and efforts to resolve them.

Introducing Artists to the DYN Professional Development Model

The professional development model created by Tene Gray is characteristic of educational research on professional learning communities (Kruse, Louis, and Bryk 1994; Darling-Hammond and McLaughlin 1995; McLaughlin and Talbert 2001). In chapter 3, we described professional learning communities as contexts in which teachers—in this case mentors—are encouraged to improve their practice by extending their pedagogical knowledge and skills as well as use a shared language, norms, and routines to discuss and reflect on practice. This structure for improving instructional practice is designed to weaken the norm of individualism that exists in teaching in order to improve teaching and learning (Kruse, Louis, and Bryk 1994).

Within the context of DYN, the professional learning community format provided a space for DYN mentors to develop some of the practices typical of teachers, including learning about and reflecting on instructional and behavior management techniques. In interviews, most mentors said they found the professional development model helpful and supportive. For instance, in a 2008 interview DYN mentor Asia explained, "The [professional development] helps a lot. . . . I like [the professional development meetings] a lot better than the last year, [which] felt more abstract. . . . This year it's like really focused on certain techniques and developing the technique."

Other mentors echoed similar sentiments, pointing specifically to several of the professional development techniques, including questioning and goal-based scenarios, as well as activities centered on planning lessons and developing a year-long scope and sequence as helpful.

In addition to learning specific instructional techniques and strategies, the DYN professional development model helped mentors reflect on their practice to support improvement. Gray, in the role of an instructional coach, observed mentors and debriefed those observations with them, identifying strengths and areas of growth. She also facilitated group analyses of student work, which provided an alternative lens for mentors to see their practice. In an interview, Gray recalled the effect this analysis had for DYN mentor Raphael. She explained that DYN mentors and leaders met to discuss a documentary that students in his pod had created about the quality of school cafeteria food. She said, "We actually looked at this piece of work, and we tried to score it. We sat around the table. Well, what would you give this for voice? . . . We had some conversation around that." Later that academic year, Gray said, the same group of student documentarians created a short film, which DYN staff also analyzed. Gray said the difference between the videos was remarkable. "It was a huge difference in terms of quality of the film, quality of the shooting, the thinking that went into the creation, so being very intentional about the music they [the students] were using to create a certain mood, about the lighting that would capture—you could see the difference in how the kids thought about this project and what they were trying to get across."

Gray attributed the improvement in work quality to Raphael's instructional growth, particularly in his realization that structure is important. Raphael agreed. He explained that the reflections and analysis from the professional development sessions helped him realize the importance of chunking learning into student-friendly pieces. "One of my goals now that I'm slowly fulfilling, though, is to give them [students] something different that has a lot of limits. They may feel like they're making a movie, but they're really just learning how to do one thing. Like with the eighth graders or seventh graders, having them all work from one project that we shot that's only six total shots. . . . Everyone's doing it, all working toward the same goal, and it's very limited." The structure created by limiting the task, Raphael observed, helped to keep students focused and gave a sense of accomplishment that motivated them to move on to the next task.

Despite its benefits, mentors also acknowledged that the DYN professional development model was time and labor-intensive work, requiring dialogue and reflection. A discussion at one professional development session illustrates this point. Here, Gray was facilitating a group evaluation of student work. In traditional school settings, though fairly uncommon as a practice, group evaluations involve the use of standards to assess student performance and increasingly to understand teachers' practice. Because such standards are not as developed or established with respect to digital media, these conversations at DYN also involved creating a shared understanding of the qualities that compose exemplary, proficient, and emergent work. The excerpt captures one conversation analyzing work from Raphael's digital storytelling media arts class in which students used footage provided by Raphael to create a PSA about street safety. This excerpt opens with Gray urging the mentors to articulate why the particular PSA they were reviewing should be considered exemplary.

> GRAY: . . . What are the features that make it exemplary and make it accomplished?
>
> ASIA: It had a clear beginning, middle, and end. . . . I felt like he [the student] had intent. . . . He told a really clear story. Instead of using [the existing] dialogue, he used very clear dialogue.

GRAY: He was very clear [about] what?

ASIA: His intent [of] how he wanted the story [to go].

SIMEON: I [was] wondering if we should use intent.

. . .

RAPHAEL: You could use intent. It was still up to them to use the story. . . . There were other students who had a totally different message. . . . Intent is the message because at the end some [PSAs] were like be careful coming home. . . .

GRAY: What could he have done to make this go over there [to exemplary]?

(DYN professional development session field notes, 2008)

The opening and closing questions Gray posed highlights how she pushed mentors' thinking. She asked Asia to justify and clarify her evaluation of the video as exemplary. This nudging led the group to decide that intent should be a component of the rubric language. Raphael, however, questioned this conclusion, noting that students were permitted to select their own intent and, as a result, each video had its own message. Gray ultimately returned to her original question of what defines an exemplary piece. Through conversations like this one, mentors achieved greater clarity not only in evaluating student work, but also in understanding their own instructional practices.

Such conversations were not infrequent. To the contrary, they occurred weekly if not daily as mentors participated in various professional development activities (chapter 3). It is perhaps unsurprising that the demands presented by the professional development model contributed to mentors' perception that professional development was time and labor intensive. This model did not suit all mentors. During our three-year study, some mentors stayed with DYN for the duration of the research period, but others remained on staff for less than year. For instance, Asia was the third mentor to lead the digital queendom pod in one academic year, and a different mentor was at the helm of the game design and robotics pods each year during the study period. A vacancy in the publishing pod remained for most of the study. Other professional commitments and pod-relevant expertise did affect mentors' decision to leave, but even for those committed to the professional development cycle, the work remained challenging.

Gray was cognizant of these challenges. She made iterative refinements to the professional development model to better align its activities with the learning needs and preferences of mentors. Most notably, in the second year of the program, she encouraged mentors to take greater ownership of their professional development by inviting Brother Mike and Asia to lead some of the sessions.

The professional development expectations were also clarified in the recruitment and hiring process. In a 2007 informal interview, Pinkard commented that in order to offer DYN programming in more than one school, she needed full-time mentors who could create lesson plans, scope and sequence maps, and rubrics, and she started to communicate these responsibilities to new hires. Pinkard, however, did not lose sight of the fact that her team was "smart enough and talented enough that they could go get a job someplace else." As a result, she knew that it was important for her and other DYN leaders to create a space for mentors to feel successful.

Establishing Authority as Teachers and Encouraging Autonomy as Mentors

In combining the roles of teacher and mentor, DYN merged two approaches for interacting with students. The teacher interacts with students as a knowledge authority. The teacher interprets, and in some cases defines, learning goals, selects strategies and tools for instruction, and evaluates students' academic and behavioral performance. In sum, the teacher is, at least historically, the classroom authority (Hurn 1985; Pace and Hemmings 2007; Waller 1932). Mentors, in contrast, work more collaboratively with students. Especially in informal learning environments, the student, or protégé, has the autonomy to set learning goals and select instructional strategies and tools. Reciprocity rather than hierarchy characterizes the tie between mentors and students.

During the period studied, DYN mentors regularly negotiated the role of teacher and mentor within a single instructional period. Media arts classes and pods typically opened and closed with practices familiar to direct, formal instruction. At these moments, DYN mentors acted in the role of teacher. This was most pronounced during the media arts classes, which of all the DYN learning spaces most resembled a traditional classroom. In the media arts classes, mentors set learning goals and selected projects that all students would complete. In the pods, by contrast, mentors established learning goals that were more open to student interpretation. Nonetheless, both settings were framed by teacher-directed objectives and outcomes.

Unlike traditional classroom settings, however, independent work within the pods and, to a lesser extent, in the media arts classes required students to make decisions about products, gather resources, act out scenes, practice lyrics, and undertake other collaborative efforts with peers. These activities often involved getting up, moving around the room, and even leaving the room to record in the studio or hallway. During this time, although mentors monitored students' practice, students were often working at different stages of a project cycle, and the content of these projects typically varied. In a very real sense, negotiating the mentor-teacher role involved tremendous flexibility in supporting multiple projects that were simultaneously under development. This meant that DYN mentors not only had to deliver content as well as monitor and adjust learning, but also offer technical, structural, content, and creative advice that was project-specific.

In the time that we observed DYN, students were often not aware of the role shifts their mentors enacted. Because students tended to be product oriented rather than process oriented, students were at times reluctant to accept direct instruction from mentors about how to create a videogame or movie. Field notes document slow starts to media arts classes and pods in which students arrived late, played videogames, or surfed the Internet. Mentors had to be comfortable asserting their authority at the start of lessons. As an illustration, Brother Mike opened one media arts class by explicitly calling for students to behave in a manner more consistent with traditional schooling. Brother Mike: "I'm impressed with the videos so far, the songs, beats— [stops unexpectedly]. People, sit up. You want me to respect you. That's what you ladies [extends hand over to the Female Stunnaz] are hollerin' about in your song. Respect comes as a package" (Media arts class field notes, 2007).

After asserting this authority, however, mentors typically minimized their position as the teacher during independent practice in order to support greater student autonomy. Mentors had to explicitly manage this shift, too, as students were at times reluctant to accept greater responsibility for their learning. Periods of independent practice were more ambiguous in comparison with traditional classrooms. Students had to make decisions about the creative direction of products, divide labor to ensure project completion, gather resources, and even settle disputes. Attempts to shirk these responsibilities were so common that Brother Mike used the slogan "Do for Self" to respond to questions and problems that students could resolve without his assistance. He also looked for opportunities to praise students who showed initiative. In the closing of one media arts class, Brother Mike acknowledged the productivity of one student whose partner was absent, saying: "Even today when Isaiah wasn't here . . . Earl got with a group and was like, 'What you doin'?' . . . and [he] became a part of the project. . . . They were able to work together and produce something—actually, three different things. You gotta commend them for that" (Media arts class field notes, 2007).

Motivating students is a common struggle in traditional and non-traditional educational contexts and this was also the case for mentors. DYN mentors faced a unique challenge in motivating student learning and production while also shifting between teacher–student and mentor–protégé relationships.

ENCOURAGING YOUTH PRODUCTION AND PARTICIPATION

Mentors seeded opportunities for production and remained available as resources to students pursuing their own interests. This motivated students but did not always encourage project completion, as students started more projects than they finished. One source of students' limited persistence came from a reluctance to engage in the planning process, which Raphael describes in the opening quote to this chapter. In other instances, it resulted from poor organizational skills (see Calvin's case profile after chapter 4). Moreover, the challenges inherent in any collaboration presented additional barriers for students. Creative disagreements, differences in working style, and personal disputes interrupted and even dismantled the production process. In this section, we examine these roadblocks on the path to developing digital media citizens and conclude with a closer look at girls' participation as a unique and important case.

Motivating Youth Interest in Productive Processes

Mentors reported that most students were often reluctant to follow the production cycle, especially the planning phase. Preproduction activities such as creating storyboards for videogames, animations, and movies, drafting lyrics and poems, and sketching designs—let alone gathering feedback to revise initial plans—felt too much like school for some students and conflicted with their existing ideas about how artists create. DYN mentor Rob observed this reluctance among new members to his digital music pod: "Some of the newer ones are having a difficult time with it because [they say,] 'I want to make a beat.' I'm like, 'No. You've got to learn this first.' . . . A couple of them are having a hard time with it. Others are getting frustrated, but they are still trying, like Amari and Sienna, they're learning. They really want to learn."

Solutions to this challenge came in a variety of forms. DYN mentors Raphael and Rob, for instance, insisted that students draft plans and then follow through with those plans. Asia took another approach and transformed each session into a goal-based scenario and awarded points for meeting weekly goals, which resulted in a prize for the highest earner.

Although the tactics mentors used to resolve the issue of persistence varied, a general consensus existed that student production was propelled through showcasing completed student work and inviting students to discuss the production process (see chapter 5). A powerful example of such showcasing occurred during one Freedom Friday when Raphael invited the students who created *Mean Boyz*, a popular film trilogy based on the action buddy genre, to participate on a panel discussion. Before the viewing, a panel of the film's participants discussed the production process.

RAPHAEL: . . . [I want each cast member to] talk about your involvement with this as far as the creation . . .

JEFFREY: I kind of thought it would be good to be make a *Mean Boyz 3*. I hooked up with Devon, and he said . . . he was going to write a script . . . we wrote a storyboard. . . .

STEPHEN: . . . Different people came up with the names. . . . I was watching a Sketchers commercial. That's how I came up with the name "Cool Breeze" [the name of one of the main characters in *Mean Boyz*].

. . .

RAPHAEL: Talk about your involvement, Lawrence.

. . .

LAWRENCE: I helped with the script and some of the props.

RAPHAEL: Did you do any of the camera work?

[Lawrence confirmed that he did.]

(Freedom Friday field notes, 2008)

Because Raphael directed the students to share their roles in the film production process, other Renaissance Academy students learned about script writing, casting, prop and scene selection, and filming. Mentors also used *Behind the Remix* to encourage students to document their experiences and provide a behind-the-scenes look at production. *Behind the Remix* productions were often viewed during Freedom Friday forums and posted online.

Collaboration as a Barrier to Youth Production

Mean Boyz is also illustrative of collaboration and cross-grade partnership, which was rare. The production was led by an eighth-grade student and involved other eighth graders as well as seventh- and sixth-grade students. During the panel discussion about *Mean Boyz*, one audience member mocked Lawrence, a sixth grader on the production team. Although Raphael discouraged this line of comments, it was eighth-grade student Devon who effectively ended the teasing:

EDDIE [to Lawrence]: Why were you the oddest one?

RAPHAEL: That sounds like a judgment one.

RICK: Because he is small.

[Other comments from the audience.]

DEVON: While y'all putting Lawrence down, he had one of the most important parts of the movie. Without him we couldn't watch a first, second, or third one.

(Freedom Friday field notes, 2008)

Devon, an eighth grader who was largely responsible for the concept of *Mean Boyz*, publicly recognized Lawrence's contributions as key, which subsequently silenced other negative commentary.

Collaboration, however, also presented DYN mentors with routine challenges. For youth and adults alike, collaboration creates opportunities for discord. The next excerpt underscores the challenges involved in collaboration. In this excerpt, Maurice and his group were creating several TV shows for the digital video pod. The group listed the order for the TV shows on the dry erase board:

MAURICE: The first segment will be "Pimp My Locker."

[James wrote on the board in bubble letters.]

MAURICE: Not so artistic . . . it'll take too long.

NATE: Will you be quiet?

. . .

MAURICE: We're not done . . . you have to write a dash.

JAMES: What? . . . Where?

NATE: A line.

JAMES: I know, but where do I put it?

MAURICE: The dash? [Under the title.] The host will be me.

NATE: No, you're not doing it.

RAPHAEL: I've heard nothing but bickering. . . .You know what I'm going to do. I'm going to assign roles.

(Digital video pod field notes, 2007)

Small disagreements even about issues such as how to write out plans on a board could disrupt groups. Other forms of conflict, however, were more contentious. Disagreement between members of the Female Stunnaz (see chapter 4) led to the group's break-up. A friendly rival to this group was the Hurricanes, an all-male group involving Zach, which also experienced in-group fighting. When possible, mentors intervened and attempted to build bridges, but the sore feelings left from disagreements and the initial trust required to even consider collaboration caused Ruby, Monica, Maurice, and others to shy away from working with peers.

These larger disputes typically involved the artistic direction of a project or the division of labor. Such decisions mattered to students because the final product determined their grades, their esteem within the community, or both. Following the Living

Museum project, Zach, who worked with a group of five to produce a documentary, acknowledged the risks involved in collaboration. In comparing the documentary to writing a research paper, which was also an option, Zach said: "I think the documentary is harder because we all had our moments where we all just broke down. . . . [I]n the documentary, you gotta put your whole grade into somebody else's hand. Like, I had to take some of the documentary home, so they had their whole grade in my hand. . . . [W]e all had our break-down moments, but in the end it was a good documentary."

In realizing that these decisions could be contentious, especially when grades were involved, Zach decided to work with the same group for Living Museum in the coming year. He said, "We're definitely doing the same group in eighth grade. . . . We learned our lessons. We know what not to do and what to do."

Interviews with the entire case study cohort confirmed that although students found collaborative experiences challenging, these experiences also allowed students to reflect on what it takes to work well together (Martin and Barron 2009). When prompted to consider how to make collaboration work, students articulated both person-based and process-based strategies for increasing the odds of success. Person-based strategies reflected their choice of collaborative partners. Some students expressed caution about working with friends or peers they believed would not work hard, had poor organizational skills, or lacked the ability to handle stress well. Students' person-based strategies sometimes reflected consideration about team member configurations—for example, recruiting team members based on a range of talents or avoiding too many headstrong people in a single group. Process-based strategies, in contrast, reflected a growing recognition of the importance of designing conditions for success. These conditions included attending to the collaborative process, being aware of the need for perspective, the importance of establishing a shared vision, and appreciation for tools that could help coordinate team efforts. Given that collaboration is challenging even for adults, these students' ability to reflect on how to make collaborations work is impressive.

Survey data from the end of the studied cohort's seventh-grade year confirm mixed opinions about the benefits of collaboration. Nearly half of all students surveyed valued collaboration for its ability to help one learn (45 percent) and felt it was more fun than working alone (49 percent). More than half believed that it increased the quality of projects (59 percent). At the end of cohort's eighth-grade year, some students indicated that they preferred to work alone (22 percent), but nearly twice as many (43 percent) indicated a preference for working with others. The remaining 35 percent were neutral. Given the prevalence of challenges, particularly when students were asked to collaborate on school projects that were graded, this variability is not surprising.

Engaging All Youth in Digital Media: Girls' Participation in DYN

Informed by accounts in the research literature, DYN leadership anticipated an initial interest-based disparity between boys and girls in signing up for after-school digital media pods. In response, a pod initially called "girls in technology" was offered specifically to engage girls. The overall results of the three-year study suggest success in this area. Survey data show 82 percent of boys and 90 percent of girls participating in at least one pod over three years, with girls actually participating in more pods (an average of 4.7 over the three years studied) than boys (an average of 3.4 over the three years). Though the participation numbers for girls are encouraging, these numbers do not necessarily reflect sustained participation or actual engagement, as suggested in chapter 7. Indeed, the challenges faced by DYN were more complex, including how to sustain engagement and encourage girls' participation in computational modes of communication and creating a space in all the pods for female voices.

Pinkard imagined the girls in technology pod as a launch pad for participation in other DYN activities. Asia, who took over the leadership of this girls-only pod during the 2006–2007 academic year, recalled that her first group of girls was less interested in technology than the students participating in pods with a more substantive digital media focus. The pod also had an image problem. Unlike the clear genre and project outcomes for the digital video or digital music pods, the purpose of the girls in technology pod was not immediately evident to students. So during the summer between the 2006–2007 and 2007–2008 academic years, girls in technology was retooled as "digital queendom." The title, which reflects a community practice of referring to girls and women as "queens," aligned more with other pod names and better reflected DYN's push to develop students' social dispositions. Participation in digital queendom became more stable, and DYN started to see an increase in the presence of girls participating in other pods. For example, Renee, who had dabbled in a number of pods without sustaining participation over time, continued her participation in digital queendom and became a frequent participant in the graphic design pod. Digital queendom and seeding practices used to encourage general participation in DYN (chapter 4) reflected a concerted effort to encourage and increase girls' engagement in the program. In fact, girls' participation increased each year, countering the usual pattern of boys' participation for the most part (see table 8.1).

TABLE 8.1
Pod Participation by Gender and Grade Level

	Sixth Grade	Seventh Grade	Eighth Grade
Girls	68% (M = 1.5 pods)	58% (M = 1.4 pods)	74% (M = 1.9 pods)
Boys	62% (M = 1.5 pods)	50% (M = 1 pod)	53% (M = 0.9 pods)

Although some digital media arts pods, such as digital music, were consistently more popular with boys during the studied cohort's sixth- and seventh-grade years, certain successes, such as the popularity of the song "Jappin" by the Female Stunnaz (chapter 4), provided models of production by girls in other genres. Other digital media arts pods, such as digital video, were more popular with girls.

One important inequity in participation, however, was girls' engagement in opportunities to develop computational literacy. The robotics and game design pods dealt primarily with this mode, using LEGO logo programming to design and build robots and different introductory programming environments to build multilevel interactive simulations, respectively. One source of this challenge was related to differences in boys' and girls' interests. In a survey taken at the beginning of the seventh-grade year, significantly fewer girls reported interest in the robotics, game design, and digital music pods (see figure 8.1).

Limited participation by girls in these pods may also be related to pod mentorship. DYN leadership struggled to recruit and sustain mentors qualified to lead the robotics and game design pods. Due to mentor schedules, the robotics pod had an additional complication of being offered only on Saturdays and of going only from September through December, ending with the FIRST LEGO competition (chapter 4). A similar scheduling conflict may have also affected girls' participation in the game design pod. During our focal cohort's sixth-grade year, game design was offered on the same day and time as girls in technology. Although program leaders adjusted the daily offering of pods so that these two pods did not conflict in the second year, participation by girls in the game design pod remained low.

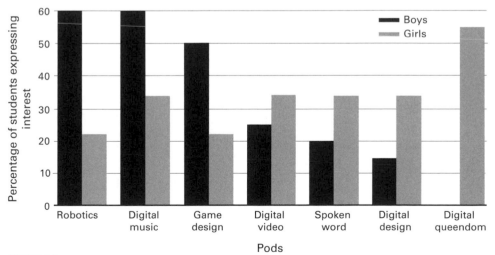

FIGURE 8.1
Percentage of Renaissance Academy students in the focal cohort interested in each of the eight pods at the beginning of seventh grade, by gender.

An interactional component also affected the participation of girls. During the first two years of observation, the game design pod was predominately populated by sixth-grade boys. In its first year, only three girls participated. The dominance of boys and the resulting predominant interests and learning styles discouraged girls from engaging more deeply with game design through the pod.

For the most part, boys were interested in creating first-person fighter games. In contrast, girls produced games that revolved around family and romantic relationships. There were also differences of behavior between genders. The group of boys attending the video design pod during the first year of the study were invested in game design but were often off task during independent work periods, which was distracting to the girls, as illustrated in Ruby's case portrait (following chapter 6). Renee experienced a similar frustration, as indicated in this field note excerpt from 2007:

> Calvin [was] on a website called "Lukira," looking for sprites. Timothy and Earl were fighting. They kept arguing, running around the room, and pretending to [physically] fight. They both ended up on the floor at some point. . . .
>
> Renee was editing a cheerleader sprite she was adding to her game.
>
> Michael and Timothy were fighting—similar to how Timothy and Earl did earlier. Renee said the boys "are so violent and crazy." She said that is why she didn't come last week. [The roughhousing continued], and Renee shouted, "They're driving me insane!"
>
> (Game design pod field notes, 2007)

Girls' limited initial interest in videogames, together with different pod behaviors between boys and girls and rotating, predominately male mentors failed to sustain participation in the game design pod among girls at Renaissance Academy.

As mentioned in chapter 7, this problem is not unique to DYN. Gender differences exist at all levels of participation in the area of computing (Camp 1997). Even when opportunities for learning are equal, girls often report a lack of interest that discourages them from pursuing computational subjects (American Association of University Women 2000; Margolis and Fischer 2003). Research has identified confounding variables, including prior experience, that make understanding gender differences in interest and participation more complex (Barron 2004; Busch 1995). To ensure that girls would have the opportunity to engage in computational opportunities, DYN was determined to ensure that all Renaissance Academy students had some prior experience. In the context of the program, the issue was approached through purposeful mentorship and in-school projects, including one designed and implemented by the founder of DYN.

Pinkard was a well-known and well-respected figure in the Renaissance Academy community and in the field of computer science. As an African American, female computer scientist, Pinkard was in an advantageous position to encourage girls' participation in activities related to computational literacy. In the spring of 2007, Pinkard implemented an eight-week game/simulation course during regular school hours. The course was required of all students in the focal cohort, at this time sixth graders. Pinkard hoped that through this course she could provide an opportunity for girls to experience success with programming in an inviting environment and thus provide another point of entry into the world of game design.

The project was linked to the students' science instruction. At the end of sixth grade, Renaissance Academy students used the program Stagecast to create a simulation or game that taught the user about the effects of global warming. Games were assessed according to demonstration of the scientific content, technical merit, and use of creative problem solving. All projects were posted online and were judged by adults associated with the DYN community and students at the school. The student with the best game won an iPod. Monica was named the winner (see box 8.1). A similar project occurred when the studied cohort was in the eighth grade: students used the popular game *The Sims* to create communities with social, economic, and political systems that responded to real-world social problems.

Using the formal school space, Pinkard and others were able to interact with more female students, challenging them to engage seriously with gaming as a medium and motivating them to evolve as producers. Pinkard recruited a small group of girls to participate, taught the game design pod along with the assistance of mentors, and

---

BOX 8.1
Monica and Game Design

Since learning to play pinball on her father's laptop at age five, Monica loved videogames. As a middle school student, she particularly enjoyed simulations such as *The Sims 2*, so she was excited to create her own. Whereas some students based their projects on the framework of existing games, mentor Hondo remembered that Monica "was like, 'I'm going to make my own game, forget whatever game that was created before. I'm going to design it the way I want it to look, and I'm going to explain it the way I want to explain it.' She didn't copy anything."

Monica explained that watching people litter in her neighborhood inspired her game. Players' actions mirror what they should be doing in their daily lives, such as recycling and reusing materials. However, the game accelerates and magnifies the impact that mindless living can have on climate change, so that players can more directly see the connection between the two phenomena.

To learn the Stagecast game-programming software, Monica frequently emailed for help from Pinkard, who provided technical instruction, critique, and feedback on how to improve the project. Monica was more concerned about failing than winning the prize. Despite the challenges of finishing a complex project and difficulties working with a partner whom she felt had trouble staying focused, her team was awarded best project. Monica was recruited for and participated in the game design pod in seventh and eighth grades.

built relationships with girls through the aforementioned science unit, during pods, and on Remix World. By the eighth grade, the proportion of males and females who participated in the game design pod was equal at 21 percent for both boys and girls.

Though the game design pod was successful in recruiting and retaining girls to participate, upon graduation girls still lagged behind their male counterparts in their experiences with computational activities (see chapter 7 for more detail). As DYN focused its efforts to increase participation among girls, an unsettling and unexpected trend emerged. During the research period, participation in DYN pods declined among boys across each of the three years. The ongoing story of DYN's work to engage all students in digital media learning opportunities and sustain that engagement is continued in chapter 9.

ARTICULATING DIGITAL MEDIA LITERACY'S VALUE-ADDED TO SCHOOL AND LOCAL COMMUNITIES

Maurice, Ruby, and the Female Stunnaz, among others, produced websites, poems, and songs with messages related to social change. Renaissance Academy leaders and teachers as well as the students' families valued these messages, but the connections between these messages, the media, and traditional learning and life outcomes were not always obvious. In fact, dips in grades or behavioral infractions among those who participated in DYN often resulted in the loss of the privilege to attend pods and workshops, suggesting that some families saw DYN as removed from learning.

DYN leaders, however, saw digital media as a body of knowledge and skills that also complemented traditional learning, and they worked to make these same connections for school leaders and families. First, DYN created a set of media arts classes that not only connected with learning in other content areas but also provided a new vehicle for students to demonstrate knowledge. Second, DYN encouraged students to create portfolios of their work to supplement applications to high school and college and used rubrics to translate the learning documented in these pieces.

Creating a Connection between Digital Media and Traditional Academic Content

Bridging digital media and traditional academic content was yet another challenge that Pinkard anticipated. Although access to computers and the Internet in schools has dramatically increased since 2000, with nearly 68 percent of schools in the United States having access to the Internet, this use is typically nonacademic and in some cases decidedly unacademic, with students using the Internet to cheat (Hitlin and Rainie 2005). Digital media are less often used for learning, especially for more cognitively demanding activities such as creating a simulation of the effects of global warming, producing a documentary on gender inequity in music, or performing a song based on Elie Wiesel's *Night*, which tells the story of a teenager's survival in a Nazi death camp—all of which are products that Renaissance Academy students, more specifically DYN participants, created.

The first step in building this bridge between digital media and academic content was to work closely with Renaissance Academy faculty. Over several years, Pinkard had developed positive relationships with school leaders. They offered Pinkard an opportunity to bring DYN into the school day academic program. She leveraged the value-added of digital media and its tools by creating the introductory media arts class. This course provided uniform access to the basic skills of digital media production.

The second year of the digital media arts sequence provided students with a more refined set of production skills that focused on storytelling and video production, designed to support the successful completion of documentaries for the Living Museum competition, which was quickly becoming a signature school project. In doing so, the seventh-grade digital storytelling media arts course served as a critical bond that linked learning in DYN with traditional academic content. Moreover, this course fostered collaboration between DYN mentors and Renaissance Academy teachers to combine digital media tools and literacy with traditional literacy.

Beyond preparation for Living Museum, the class incorporated literature that students encountered in their English language arts units. The conversations supporting the integration of these texts revealed the overlap between the traditional literacy skills needed to write a paper and the digital literacy skills needed to produce, for example, a documentary. For students, this integration provided another point of access to engage the text. Through the production of PSAs, movie trailers, and short films based on *The Outsiders*, *Monster*, and other books, Renaissance Academy students and faculty discovered new representations of learning. The use of the same texts, in contrast with the diversity of projects created in the DYN pods, provided DYN staff with greater insight into teaching and learning. In particular, the digital media format provided an alternative assessment to measure student learning, especially for students who struggled to express their thoughts in writing. The integration similarly provided a new point of view for the DYN team as they designed programming relevant to traditional academics.

Helping Educators Assess Digital Media Products

Even if school members invited students to use digital media tools to demonstrate knowledge, educators needed a way to assess that learning. A major challenge for DYN leadership was the creation of various assessment tools and an assessment system that could authentically measure student work across multiple modes of communication to demonstrate learning. The DYN team worked to create rubrics to assess student work and develop portfolios to share this work with a broader audience.

The function of rubrics is twofold. First, rubrics provide a more standardized measure of student work. Such use acts as a summative assessment, which would accompany student portfolios to describe student learning. A second function is to provide interim data of student learning. Mentors or any educator can use rubrics as an informal assessment to measure students' progress toward achieving year-long academic goals. In this light, the interim use of rubrics provides a lens with which the mentor can adjust instruction.

In order to serve as a reliable measurement tool, rubrics require a degree of expertise to identify evidence of student learning that meets the requirements outlined in the rubrics and, when used as a formative assessment, to determine the appropriate instructional next steps to advance student learning. Although there was some evidence that mentors at Renaissance Academy used grading scales informed by the rubrics in the media arts classes and pods (see the portrait of Raphael in chapter 3), mentors generally did not use the rubrics as tools to inform their instructional practice and support student learning.

This lack of instructional uptake by the majority of mentors suggests that assessment design and implementation require advanced pedagogical knowledge and pedagogical content knowledge. Not surprisingly, the DYN professional development model was unable to build this kind of conceptual knowledge in its first three years, particularly for mentors with little to no pedagogical background. Subsequent professional development sessions aimed to increase this knowledge to better support the use of rubrics.

As planned, rubrics would accompany portfolios, which would track student learning over time. Portfolios, and the authentic assessments often stored in them, support a more holistic evaluation of student learning over time (Haney 1985; Messick 1994). Educational portfolios contain products—digital or otherwise—that provide evidence of student learning related to a specific set of objectives. In using portfolios, DYN mentors and leaders aimed to equip students with a powerful presentation of their digital media literacy that could be shared with families, schools, and employers.

Furthermore, DYN saw portfolios as a tool for career and educational advancement. These portfolios would not only present a student's digital media literacy but also serve as a vehicle for conveying that literacy to others after the student graduated from Renaissance Academy. DYN co-founder Akili Lee discussed the potential impact of portfolios: "We can put that something in front of the parent and say, 'This student . . . he's been doing this design stuff for three years. He's done his own shoot; he's done posters and marketing materials for everyone. Here is a portfolio of what your son has done with this in the last three years. . . . This is how he's taking to music. This is how he's taken to robotics.'"

Lee added that the portfolio is not about simply showcasing the work but instead is about serving as a centerpiece for conversations regarding the student's future. For example, as we saw with Calvin, experiences in robotics or game design can translate into an interest in an engineering career. A more complete portfolio would have enabled Calvin and his teachers to identify strengths and areas of growth related to his computational literacy. Alternatively, the portfolio could also help students realize career goals by examining trends in the digital media strengths highlighted by the portfolio.

In the short term, such portfolios were useful in high school placement. After the program's second year, a handful of Renaissance Academy students used digital media products as supplemental materials in their applications to attend one of Chicago's selective-enrollment high schools. By the time the cohort under study entered high school, more students were doing the same.

At a programmatic level, however, DYN was unable, during the period studied, to implement uniform systems to help all students select the best pieces of work to include in a portfolio. This dilemma was related to two previously discussed challenges. First, the challenges DYN faced concerning students' project completion meant that students may not have had a piece that reflected a specific mode. Students and mentors also struggled to track completed work across the various DYN spaces (i.e., media arts classes, pods, and online) over the three-year period, so even if students completed a project there was not a reliable mechanism for tracking this work. Second, portfolio use was limited by the challenge of creating rubrics and implementing practices for compiling exemplary student work across multiple modes of communication so that the portfolio reflected both depth and breadth of digital media literacy. This organizational problem is one that is typical of portfolios, whether they are paper or electronic.

SUMMARY

This chapter highlighted the reoccurring challenges that the DYN team encountered in transforming DYN participants into digital media citizens in the program's early years. Some of these challenges, such as encouraging participation by girls and articulating the value of digital media to traditional educators and families, were anticipated based on prior research. Pinkard and other DYN leaders designed the space to respond to these anticipated challenges. Still other challenges, such as enacting the hybrid mentor role and supporting students' project completion, were not anticipated. Although unexpected, the DYN team mobilized to address these issues. DYN's intentional and iterative design has revealed several lessons that point to considerations for future learning opportunities and research.

Lessons Learned and Future Directions

Although at times difficult, DYN's professional development model helped to blend the roles of artist, mentor, and teacher. In executing the DYN model, mentors struggled to enact their new hybrid mentor-artist-teacher role. In the program's early years, two mentors taught each DYN pod. The paired or group approach alleviated some of the strain mentors felt in managing student production and participation as they grew accustomed to their roles. Later, as mentors gained greater proficiency with all modes of production and learned to manage student behavior more effectively, DYN moved to a single-instructor model. As happens for most beginning teachers, DYN mentors gained confidence in teaching and expanded their toolkit for engaging and managing students. This experience suggests that professional development structures and practices designed for traditional teachers can successfully be extended to nontraditional educators who work in hybrid and even informal learning spaces.

For researchers, the use of traditional teaching models for professional development creates opportunities to examine adult learning. Specifically, Gray relied on a model for professionalization that was developed for teachers, yet DYN mentors had not and were not attending formal education classes. Chapter 3 discussed the range of mentoring styles that emerged from this approach; the analysis here can serve as a foundation for future studies that compare these learning outcomes with the outcomes for traditionally trained teachers.

Engaging girls' participation in digital media is a well-documented challenge that has roots in the disproportionally low participation of girls in math and science. As in earlier research, we found this limited participation at Renaissance Academy was largely a reflection of existing differences in interests and exposure to digital media. But, critically, we also found that interactions in the pods served as a disincentive to continued participation. Media arts classes and DYN's presence in traditional subjects such as science, English language arts, and history were structural interventions that provided girls with greater exposure to digital media, especially computational literacy. DYN programming that targeted topics of greater interest to girls and reflected the local culture encouraged deeper engagement among girls. The goal for subsequent design work is to continue this cyclical process of engaging and reengaging girls in digital media.

The experiences documented in this chapter do point to the need for additional research on the microinteractions that support or inhibit participation by girls in digital media. Despite mentor efforts to recruit girls and to acknowledge their work, the existing social networks among the boys and their dominance in particular pods—for instance, game design—seemed to dissuade girls from more in-depth engagement. Rather than problematizing girls' interest in reaction to limited participation, researchers should perhaps turn to examining boys' intentional and unintentional exclusionary tactics that dissuade girls from participation. Such research, rather than supporting the need for girls in technology programs, might instead point to opportunities for gender discussions involving both boys and girls.

This chapter and previous ones have illustrated how the tools of digital media and digital media literacy can be leveraged in traditional education settings. To become truly relevant to traditional schools, DYN worked closely with Renaissance Academy school leaders and teachers to redesign projects such as Living Museum. This work also involved creating portfolios that not only aligned digital media artifacts with standards but also served as a format for communicating students' digital media literacy.

When Pinkard and the DYN leadership team began this work, few such efforts were being made; however, schools are increasingly integrating technology into their cultures. Both charter and traditional public schools offer learning opportunities that move beyond basic programming. This integration is also beginning to occur in other learning spaces, such as libraries and museums. Such integration may prove the most effective path for creating a dialogue around the meaningful inclusion of digital media literacy for all students. Pinkard and her colleagues have already started to innovate along these lines. Chapter 11 takes a longer view of DYN and describes its expansion in multiple schools and spaces.

As other programs look to expand digital media literacy opportunities for minority and low-income youth as well as for other groups, the solutions DYN found to its ongoing challenges provide several valuable lessons. At the same time, these experiences also point to the need for additional research. The next two chapters summarize design suggestions based on lessons learned and articulate the specific theoretical implications of this work.

III

LOOKING AHEAD: IMPLICATIONS FOR DESIGN
AND RESEARCH

9

CREATIVE LEARNING ECOLOGIES BY DESIGN: INSIGHTS FROM THE DIGITAL YOUTH NETWORK

Brigid Barron, Caitlin K. Martin, Kimberley Gomez, Nichole Pinkard, and Kimberly Austin

There is a persistent need for environments that allow *all* young people to access quality learning opportunities that can nurture their capacities to use digital tools for learning. Innovative approaches are necessary, especially those that capitalize on the potential of hybrid designs that include physical spaces that nurture sustained face-to-face relationships and digital spaces that support engagement across setting and time. In this chapter, we offer suggestions for those interested in embarking on such a project. Our insights are based on what we learned from our collective design, implementation, and study of DYN. These suggestions are not meant to be prescriptive but are offered in the spirit of supporting the essential work of envisioning possibilities for systemic design. We cluster these suggestions into three key sections: learning spaces and practices, community building, and supporting infrastructure.

LEARNING SPACES AND PRACTICES

1   Provide Access to Tools and Spaces Needed for Production

Physical learning spaces can be flexibly arranged to facilitate digital media production, and virtual spaces can be designed to further support production and to complement and extend face-to-face interactions. At Renaissance during our research period, the DYN recording studios and dedicated media classrooms created the material infrastructure for production. Used for both creation and performance during and after school, these spaces were designed to encourage youth to create a portfolio of media artifacts and share their talents and perspectives with the local community through their work. Continual access to laptops loaded with digital production tools was critical to facilitating creative work. The flexibility of the student laptop made fluid movement between school spaces possible, supporting creators whose projects crossed media. Students used their laptops alongside tools found in DYN spaces, such as digital cameras, professional media-creation and editing software, robotics kits, and musical instruments. DYN's social learning network, Remix World, provided a virtual learning space that further supported the flexibility of the DYN learning space—an online environment explicitly for members of the DYN community where youth could continue conversations started in pods or class, share new ideas, and get feedback on their work. Access to a personal laptop and an online community enabled students to bring work and ideas easily into and out from other spaces where they spent their time, such as home. Personal projects sometimes began when students had free time or were bored or when family members or peers came up with ideas. Access to tools at these unscheduled moments allowed students to generate ideas outside the physical DYN space and later build on them back in the DYN studio spaces that offered additional tools and people who could provide support.

2   Connect Youth to Inspirations for Production and Interest-Related Resources

Tools and spaces for production are essential, but perhaps even more important are the activities, practices, and ideas that can inspire the generation of projects. DYN used multiple approaches to seed creative production in the three-year study period, including interest-driven project-based assignments, competitions, special projects, role models, and forums to generate ideas and showcase work. These opportunities offered students the chance to create a portfolio of projects across multiple media genres, exhibit their emerging roles and talents, collaborate and connect with peers, and develop a social learning network.

Project-based assignments were designed to tap into students' interests and to provide a structure for them to set goals for their own work. In media arts classes, multiweek projects were designed to simulate real-world production activity and to allow students to take on a variety of production roles. For example, during the record label project, team members adopted specific roles as songwriters, beat makers, music producers, graphic designers, and managers, with the end goal of producing their own record label, complete with a logo, album cover, signature song, and video. Other projects were less planned, emerging instead from pod or classroom discussions. In these cases, mentors encouraged students to take on topics that were intrinsically interesting to them and to create media projects to contribute to the public dialogue within and beyond the DYN community. As the "Jappin" project illustrates, students felt free to address controversial issues such as gender equity, and the project-inspired conversation lived on within the program's culture as a representation of both how students see themselves and how the program supports these explorations. Yet other approaches to seeding production were one-time affairs that came about through unique opportunities, such as the film *Division 201* resulting from a summertime collaboration between DYN and a local film company (see chapter 5).

Both regional and DYN-initiated contests and public forums energized student work. Importantly, DYN mentors framed contests in terms that went beyond winning and losing. Instead, they invited students to participate in order to express their views, become recognized, "up their game" by enhancing their skills and knowledge, and be a part of a larger group of students involved in similar work. DYN leadership organized and ran open forums such as Freedom Fridays and contests such as poetry slams, the Renaissance Learner contest, and the environmental science game design competition. Regional contests organized by non-DYN communities—such as the FIRST LEGO League and the Chicago Metro History Fair—provided important design constraints and connections to broader communities. In addition to prompting creative production work, these opportunities resulted in other valuable outcomes. Preparing to compete or present projects encouraged students to consult with other Renaissance students across different grades, benefiting both the advice givers and the advice receivers. Mentors across pods saw that students enjoyed having an audience to whom they might showcase their skills. Public performances and contest successes validated talents that may not have been previously recognized either by the youth themselves or by their peers, families, or teachers and provided mentors a way to publicly present students as valuable contributors. Such contests and performance spaces also provided opportunities to reflect on collaborative practices because team dynamics were often challenging, and the high-stakes nature of the performances motivated reflection on these episodes.

3   Offer Multiple Opportunities for Members of the Community to Form Learning Partnerships

Sustained social relationships with peers and mentors are essential for learning. Though designers of informal learning environments implicitly build in opportunities for mentoring and collaboration, the development of explicit intentional strategies across a variety of learning spaces can be powerful for generating deeper and broader learning networks for youth. During the period studied, DYN purposefully offered multiple integrated spaces for learning that provided similar opportunities for production but that had different implications for community attendance and interaction. Activity across the multiple spaces worked to help students develop stronger relationships with mentors, peers, and members of the larger DYN community both in and out of the school environment.

The school-day classes offered grade-level collaboration and a basic level of instruction for all students. After-school pods, meanwhile, were a chance for students across different grades with different levels of experience and DYN status to collaborate with and learn from each other. Mentors were able to take a less formal approach due to the pods' longer block of time and freedom from school-day constraints such as grades and lesson plans. Freedom Friday sessions were a time for the wider community to get together in the same physical space. Some sessions were held in an open-mic style, whereas others were focused on producing work or were organized as workshops or summits, focusing discussion on particular topics. Mentors promoted these events through videos or posters; students, mentors, teachers, and parents were invited to attend. Having this broader group in one space allowed students to see their peers' productive capacities, which could spark new ideas. Freedom Fridays also allowed students to share completed or nearly completed work with the community to receive feedback. The DYN online social learning space, Remix World, open only to the mentors and students at Renaissance, enabled mentors to transcend their limited face-to-face time with students and continue to support students' growth as social advocates, critical consumers, and constructive producers. This virtual space was especially important for students who could not attend after-school forums or pods due to transportation issues, family needs, or competing activities. It was most often used to start and continue discussions, invite production of media around topics of discussion, share media artifacts, and give and receive feedback and design tips.

4   Watch for and Disrupt Patterns That Favor One Group of Learners over Another

Patterns of interaction that contribute to inequity can arise despite intentions to eliminate them. As noted, the research team observed that despite proactive steps to recruit female mentors and to develop content and spaces specifically of interest and relevant to girls, gender dynamics were evident in the DYN context. During the early years of the DYN program, boys tended to dominate spaces and tools, and some pods seemed to cater more to typical boys' interests, leading some female students to feel frustrated. Upon noticing this issue, members of the DYN leadership team were able to develop fresh strategies to foster the interest of female students and sustain spaces that were more equitable. Rather than expecting that these dynamics can be designed away once and for all, educators should anticipate them, recognize when they occur, and come up with strategies—such as personal recruitment, intervention workshops, and the monitoring of spaces and interactions—to ensure that group dynamics do not become dominated by any subgroup. In addition, adult mentors and educators need support to develop expertise for understanding when and how to do this in the context of everyday interactions to ensure that educators are deliberately and fairly representing students they serve. The repeated, explicit, and intentional positioning of *all* youth learners as potential contributors can be a powerful way to address this issue.

COMMUNITY

5   Bring Together Diverse Adult Role Models and Make Connections to Broader Communities

Organizations that work across traditional boundaries can offer youth connections to inspiring role models and practices. In the case of DYN, at the core of individual students' engagement in production activities and their development as digital citizens was inclusion in the DYN community. We have evidence that students became increasingly socially connected with adult mentors, peers, and members of the wider digital media and arts community in Chicago. Through this community participation, they established new connections with ideas, people, and opportunities and identified new potential futures.

Mentors were recruited for DYN based on their personal portfolios of work, their connections to the local community, and their likelihood of being compelling role models for the students. From the engineers who led the robotics and game design pods to the artists who led the spoken-word, radio, and digital queendom pods, students encountered a range of professionals enacting the roles they were learning to take on. Mentors performed and showcased their own work as a way to inspire student work. These professionals came to DYN with connections to authentic communities of practice and were able to use these relationships to bring in outside artists and media figures, thereby broadening the DYN social network. Intentional practices can be incorporated that strengthen and highlight these connections for youth. Through DYN, students were given the chance to interview these artists about their work and their motivations, and these interviews were frequently videotaped and put on Remix World, becoming an accessible resource for the entire community. The visiting artists not only shared their work and knowledge but also encouraged students to create and contribute, thus offering inspiration and visions of possible pathways outside of the normal pod or media arts spaces. In addition, student peers collaborated, shared, and competed, and older students and junior mentors helped to illuminate pathways and roles for the younger students. Over the three years of the study, we saw students continue to develop additional cultural capital outside the walls of the school, sharing their knowledge, media projects, and ideas online, in their homes, and in local community centers.

6   Provide Ongoing Learning Opportunities for Mentors and Leaders

Educators need regular opportunities to learn and collaborate. In chapter 3, we described how DYN's leadership team learned from and extended the role that mentors played in other after-school and out-of-school digital technology programs (e.g.,

Fifth Dimension, Computer Clubhouse). In these earlier efforts, mentors exposed youth to new ideas and provided compelling spaces for them to further develop their own interests and technological fluency. With this approach in mind and with an awareness that programmatic evaluations of the Computer Clubhouse model revealed the vital link between effective mentor practices and student engagement (Center for Children and Technology 2002), the DYN leadership team decided to create a solid focus on mentor development. However, the DYN model differed from these earlier presentations of mentor roles in three fundamental assumptions: (1) mentors should retain and continue to develop their artistic skills, (2) mentors should expand their technological skills to be maximally supportive of DYN students' twenty-first-century digital skills development, and (3) mentors should develop sound instructional practices that they can apply across in-school and after-school settings. In addition, mentors were expected to be positive role models and share their cultural and social capital with DYN youth.

These assumptions made for an ambitious and innovative view of mentors that was challenging to implement. To support mentors who could scaffold twenty-first-century youth in a hybrid-learning context, the team drew guidance and inspiration from several conceptual and organizational frames described in the research and practice literature. Key among these frames was membership in a learning community. Mentors were introduced to teaching by becoming part of a community of learners and practitioners who were expected to question, engage in self-reflection, and view learning as a lifelong task. As a practice for developing teaching skills, self-reflection was an essential component of this socialization effort. Although mentors were accustomed to self-reflection in their artistry, most had little, if any, experience with teaching or with taking a reflective turn on their own pedagogical practices.

Artists typically have experience with being critiqued and with engaging in critique as well as in providing support for new artistic approaches and techniques. In the context of DYN, mentors were encouraged to learn not only to critique but also to question the "why," "how," and "what next" of young participants' creative and productive efforts. This type of questioning supported the construction of revised and new instructional plans.

Another important component of the DYN professional development approach was to build mentors' pedagogical knowledge and skills for formal learning contexts while simultaneously creating settings in which they could share their artistic skills, technical fluency, and cultural capital with the students. In addition, it was important to provide a space for all the mentors, but especially for those with little prior digital technology experiences, to create and showcase their new media portfolios. The DYN team determined that the task at hand for mentor development was to foster a common language around teaching and learning in an environment that emphasized creativity, production, and critical approaches rather than passive learning and media consumption.

Undergirding this new approach to developing mentors was an instructional theory of action, represented through sustained formal and informal professional development sessions, observations, and coaching. Mentors also worked with the DYN facilitator to engage in collaborative planning, during which they participated in instructional problem solving and developed their common language for talking about teaching, learning, and mentoring. The instructional theory of action was driven by the aim to create a student-centered, goal- and interest-driven learning environment in which all children could create and develop twenty-first-century skills.

This instructional approach had at least two important outcomes for the DYN mentors in the three-year study period. First, they made a commitment to developing pedagogical knowledge. They learned how to question and guide students, organize instructional contexts, and plan and execute instruction. Second, mentors deepened their content knowledge related to digital media, which included developing fluency in the use of digital tools and online spaces, creating new media portfolios, and sharing their cultural capital with peers and DYN youth. Mentors' emergent pedagogical knowledge allowed them to become guides who opened new creative and technical doors for DYN youth. They learned to recognize, access, and use the affordances of digital and Web 2.0 tools (such as Remix World) as they built technological fluency.

7   Support and Document the Important Informal Roles Played by Adult Mentors

Mentorship is a complicated process, and there are often opportunities to expand the forms of learning partnership that go under this broad term. Looking for and calling out these various opportunities can help mentors share their talents and can help both mentors and program design teams highlight approaches that may be identified as especially effective in a particular learning environment but that may not have been explicitly articulated. Renaissance Academy students reported that their technology learning and experiences were due largely to people connected to DYN, including mentors, teachers, and peers, rather than to family members. Mentors were not just teachers and role models, but also strategic members of the DYN community who calibrated the learning environment. Their roles were varied, and new roles for them emerged as they developed their own practice and encountered different situations in different contexts and across time. Informal practices were key. One informal practice often used at DYN was positive positioning, when mentors publicly framed students through a certain lens. Mentors positioned entire groups of students as critical participants by presenting compelling, controversial, and relevant material to them, such as videos and news stories around issues of race and the 2008 election, and then inviting students to respond, listening seriously to what they had to say, and providing feedback. Mentors also positioned individual students—both to themselves and to their classmates—as leaders, critics, and social advocates by showcasing these students' work, highlighting their ideas during discussions, and reframing negative stereotypes as positive assets. Mentors saw it as their responsibility not only to encourage participation, but also to challenge learners to be imaginative, reflective, and positive and to show leadership. At the same time, they also acknowledged that deep mentorship had to be earned and that those students who were the most serious about their craft garnered the most attention.

8   Establish Ways for Families to Be Involved

Constantly changing technologies offer rich opportunities for bidirectional teaching and learning relationships within families. Specific spaces for and practices to support families' participation can encourage knowledge sharing in both directions. As documented in this book, parents and siblings were important partners who contributed to the learning of DYN members by encouraging them, learning from them, working on projects with them, teaching them, being an audience for their projects and performances, and suggesting new opportunities. For parents in both Chicago and Silicon Valley in the research period, the number of different roles they played to support their child's learning was related to their own technological expertise. Although computing skills may make it easier for parents to participate in their child's learning in this area, we believe that all parents can facilitate learning by taking on roles that do not require expert knowledge, such as collaborating with their children; finding new opportunities for them to learn, such as workshops at the local library; and learning from them. Siblings, grandparents, and extended family members can also be recruited as these types of learning partners. As we saw in this study and in earlier work, some parents were concerned about the possibility that digital media would distract their child from traditional academic spheres and so limited their child's participation in DYN. It would be useful to develop innovative ways to engage families in sharing how they support their children's learning, including strategies for support without having content expertise and ways to address concerns about possible negative outcomes of computer use. Throughout the school year, Renaissance Academy and DYN used public performance spaces and events such as Freedom Fridays and school-based competitions to engage families, inviting relatives to attend and in some cases to participate. School vacations and summertime may be particularly productive times to provide learning opportunities for youth that can also engage families, although it is essential to recognize and address the financial, time, and transportation constraints that many families face. DYN was able to implement a summer workshop camp for Renaissance students and a summer video-editing program for high school students in collaboration with a local film company, and though these programs were challenging to maintain, they were generative and popular.

INFRASTRUCTURE

9 Plan for How to Archive Digital Work over Time

Access to laptops does not guarantee stable records of student work, yet records of digital projects can be an important resource to communicate organizational goals and promise. At DYN, students' digital portfolios were not always well preserved as a result of a variety of common challenges to consistent data organization and maintenance. Student files were sometimes unfinished and forgotten, completed but not archived, or simply lost over the summer months. Annual updates to laptops and servers, the unfortunate loss of hard drives, mentor turnover, students' use of a wide variety of media formats, and an evolving online platform posed challenges to the creation of enduring portfolios of work for DYN participants. Educators and scholars have a vested interest in maintaining an accurate record of project development, and students can potentially take this work and build on it after their graduation or completion of a program. Well-documented archives of teacher and learner development and experience are invaluable to both the learner and the program, and as new structures of assessment and merit—for example, badge systems—are developed, sound and stable ways of keeping track of digital work across time are critical.

10 Collaborate with Leaders across Settings and Plan for Cycles of Revision

Collaborative programs that span multiple sites or organizations must incorporate various strategies that encourage and make possible reflection and change. It is impossible to understand DYN's success without acknowledging the role of Renaissance Academy's leadership and management structures and its vision for technology and learning. The DYN model was implemented on top of previous educational interventions at Renaissance, allowing DYN to design new learning opportunities within an existing supportive framework. The supports already in place included an autonomous and flexible learning environment, a robust and inclusive technology infrastructure, and a face-to-face community of learners. We summarize these supports in table 9.1. We do not wish to imply that these elements must exist before an intervention is designed or introduced, but their advantages are important to consider. What was critical to the DYN's success was that its team continuously worked with the school leadership to share information and resources and to revise the program and the collaboration so that it best fit the needs of both organizations. As DYN has expanded its programming to new learning contexts, including virtual spaces, libraries, and traditional public schools, existing supports have not always been in place. A sample of new contexts for scaling up DYN and the corresponding design considerations and questions are shared in chapter 11.

TABLE 9.1
Social and Technical Infrastructure Supporting DYN

Autonomous and Flexible Learning Environment

As a charter school, Renaissance Academy was able to make independent decisions about curriculum content, time spent on different subjects, and staffing in ways that many traditional public schools cannot. The charter school was also innovative, as exemplified by the implementation of DYN programming not only during after-school time, but also within the traditional school day; the blending of digital arts with the core curriculum; and the hiring of professional media artists as classroom teachers without the traditional prerequisite teaching certifications. These decisions resulted in a number of important synergies that strengthened the DYN program at the school. Teachers and DYN mentors worked together to look for opportunities for collaboration and to identify ways to link subject matter and tools across classes and in and out of the school day. These risk-taking innovations resulted in youth who saw digital media not just as an after-school hobby, but rather as a professional skill related to and used for different practices across multiple contexts.

Robust Technology Infrastructure

As discussed, the existing one-to-one laptop program at Renaissance ensured that each child, regardless of income, had his or her own laptop to use at school and at home. The school also had a robust wireless network, a school-based technical support team, and a networked online system, FirstClass, for teachers to post assignments, notes, and grades; to track student progress; and to allow students to ask questions, post work, and track their own progress. These elements resulted in a sound technology infrastructure, teachers and staff who were knowledgeable about technology, and a shared understanding that technology was important and useful in learning environments. This type of support and buy-in is essential. Support can and should exist beyond school walls—if possible at the state policy level.

Face-to-Face Community with Shared Interests and Values

The DYN program was able to build upon an existing social network at Renaissance Academy. A vibrant community of learners, educators, and families from the South Side of Chicago had been involved in the middle school and its feeder elementary school for years. Preexisting student friendship groups as well as established relationships and methods of communication among Renaissance Academy teachers, staff, and parents made for a community of trust and shared values around students' development and learning. The existence of this community made new DYN opportunities—including after-school and online learning contexts—easier to introduce because they were simply new tools and spaces that could be blended with relationships and learning goals that had already been established over time.

11   Invite Research and Incorporate It as Part of the Iterative Process

Research and practice can be complementary and synergistic. The research team was a vital part of DYN's infrastructure. Drawn from three universities, the researchers consisted of professors, senior researchers, and graduate students in the fields of learning, educational technology, and sociology. As outlined in chapter 2, their work included participant observations of after-school pods, school classes, and Freedom Fridays; interviews of students, teachers, and parents; and the collection of student media arts projects and Remix World posts. Assembling these various elements allowed the research teams to develop an informed perspective on the DYN program and Renaissance Academy and offered the DYN community time for reflection and an opportunity to share their ideas more broadly. During the interview process, researchers asked interviewees (such as students and mentors) questions that forced them to articulate their ideas and reflect on their learning process and surroundings. The interviews not only captured information that was valuable in and of itself but also elicited participants' introspection on the program with questions such as "What am I producing?" "What have I learned from this program?" and "What will I take away from it?" Mentors joined the research teams in presenting DYN at education conferences and collaborated with researchers in a workshop where they contributed to the portraits of case learners. The process of preparation, presentation, and response led to a probing and critical eye on DYN that then fed the program itself.

The researchers essentially had two roles. They represented an outside perspective when observing and listening to the challenges and successes for mentors, students, teachers, and administrators and then became insiders as they became an integral part of the community that contributed ideas. This *dual* role plays an important part in making a program so fruitful and has the potential to be implemented in other settings. Such a model would take into account the different realities and structures of the program in question. As with DYN, collaborations can include university professors and researchers in related fields or a board of educators and members from the surrounding community who would first act as outside observers and then become a part of the team that would think through a program's design. Perhaps more practical, a team in which administrators, teachers, and mentors adopt the iterative design process might be formed internally. No matter which combinations are utilized, our experience with collaborative iterative design points to the need to implement it in other settings.

SUMMARY

In this chapter, we shared insights for the design of learning environments based on the implementation and research of DYN at Renaissance Academy, focusing specifically on the collection of opportunities around spaces, people, practices, and inspiring ideas that propel interest-driven student learning. We argue that it is the overlap, diversity, and redundancy of learning opportunities that best support youth participation and learning related to digital media. Our three-year study investigated the iterative design and implementation of integrated spaces that support youth transformation into digital media citizens and in doing so revealed new avenues for design, practice, and policy. For designers of educational spaces, our documentation of DYN practices will, we hope, provide inspiration for the creation of novel spaces for learning and thoughtful rationale for making design decisions and asking important questions. For policymakers and funders, the evidence of student learning that this study of DYN has yielded provides strong support for the expansion of funds to extend these learning opportunities for more youth and for the research that will lead to more generalized understandings (see box 9.1). The pursuit of these recommendations will help ensure that the lessons learned from DYN will contribute to the learning environments that follow.

BOX 9.1
Suggestions for Funding Organizations and Policymakers

- Support systemic, ecological designs that bridge informal and formal learning during schooltime, after school, and in summer hours, particularly in communities that have traditionally been underserved. These designs should include plans for novel forms of collaboration between mentors, teachers, and administrators to generate ideas about the possibilities for school-day and after-school synergies. Fund research to study these innovations and their implementation in enough depth to contribute to theory and practice.
- Develop and support programs of work that conceptualize and design novel forms of professional development for mentors and other informal learning instructors. Create models that allow educators to develop pedagogical knowledge and skill training while also extending their artistic and creative activities and partnerships.
- Fund the development of research tools that support documentation of children's development across learning ecologies. These tools should be designed to chart rarely measured outcomes, such as the teaching of family members and peers, future plans and possible selves, choices to take on new learning ventures, collaborative experiences, and reflections on those experiences. They should also facilitate the maintenance of a record of student projects, making digital portfolio development routine.

10

ADVANCING RESEARCH ON THE DYNAMICS OF INTEREST-DRIVEN LEARNING

Brigid Barron

The empirical effort reported in this book was designed to contribute to both theory and practice, a *use-inspired* genre of basic research notably referred to as "Pasteur's quadrant" (Stokes 1997). Use-inspired basic research is usefully distinguished from research that is driven by practical goals alone or that is a quest for basic scientific understanding only. The urgent practical need to understand how to create dynamic learning ecologies that prepare all youth to capitalize on new learning opportunities offered by digital and networked technologies is clear. There is an equally important case to be made for building a fundamental understanding of how and when these tools are being used to catalyze learning across time and setting. Increasingly, learning is recognized as deeply social and the empowered use of digital technologies is linked to being connected to communities that can informally share technical expertise and learning practices. This more complicated view of learning puts the relational and systemic aspects of it at the center of a new basic research agenda. This agenda foregrounds the need for empirical approaches that include longitudinal portraits of particular learners and the learning opportunities they encounter and create within and across settings. Particularly important is the need to begin to unpack and define informal teaching interactions and other dimensions of sociotechnical systems that inspire learning, as well as attend to how variations in privilege can constrain or make possible opportunities over time (Gutiérrez and Penuel 2014; Lee 2010).

As a hybrid, distributed learning environment, DYN gave our research teams a rich opportunity to contribute findings and new design-relevant theoretical ideas relating to these questions. The goal of this chapter is to highlight what we learned and point to some directions for future research. Our analysis has a dual focus: (1) the social and material *catalysts for participation* embedded in DYN that enabled engagement and artifact creation and that positioned learners as developing designers, authors, activists, editors, social leaders, artists, and engineers; and (2) the *learning pathways* of youth who were developing particular profiles of expertise and interests over time and across settings. This dual focus builds on a conceptualization of learning as lifelong, life wide, and life deep, where opportunities arise and are created over time, in and out of school environments, with strong connection to cultural values, social practices, and personal relationships (Banks, Au, Ball, et al. 2007; Barron 2006; Bell, Bricker, Reeve, et al. 2010; Bransford, Barron, Pea, et al. 2006). In the next section, I elaborate on our findings around these two analytic themes and then offer some directions for future research.

CATALYSTS FOR IMAGINATIVE PARTICIPATION

By any measure, participation in DYN during the three years of our study led to significant growth in expertise. Most entering sixth graders at Renaissance Academy Middle School had experience creating PowerPoint presentations, but very few reported repeated, engaged production with any digital media or considered themselves expert with the tools of the trade. As the cohort of students we followed moved from sixth into seventh and then eighth grade, they dramatically increased the frequency of their experiences creating digital media. This was true across different genres of production, including publication (making a website, creating a podcast), expressive endeavors (designing a logo, developing a song), and computational activities (building a simulation, programming a robot). At the beginning of sixth grade, 83 percent of the students in the cohort we focused on reported no sustained experiences in any genre of creative production; by graduation, 77 percent reported sustained experience with at least one genre, and 20 percent reported this level of involvement for all three. Within DYN, depth of production experience was linked to teaching others, confidence in collaborative work, and a view of one's self as able to come up with new ideas. Compared to our Silicon Valley sample, by the close of eighth grade the Renaissance group had accrued significantly greater breadth and depth of expertise. How can we account for this high and atypical level of production, particularly given the challenge that mentors sometimes faced in motivating project work? What specific opportunities catalyzed project creation and participation in the community?

Varied and Distributed Approaches to Inspiring and Showcasing Work

Within DYN, multiple participation structures provided focused opportunities to generate ideas and refine skills. We saw mentors blend aspects of formal learning in classrooms and apprenticeships using a range of demonstration and work sessions reminiscent of what has been found in studies of pedagogies common in the visual arts (Hetland, Winner, Veenema, et al. 2007). *Workshops* offered demonstrations, suggested readings, and provided models of adult expertise and practices to which their learning could aspire. *Forums* introduced important issues, invited reflection through production, and provided a setting to share work. The school-based *media arts classes* offered up compelling projects and ensured that everyone had an opportunity to engage with mentors. The *online space* offered a place for anytime posting, sharing of work, and exchanging of commentaries. Less-frequent events such as signature projects and contests were also consequential. *Signature longer-term projects* introduced new mentors and provided opportunities for cross-cohort collaborative engagement around a more intensive production experience. *Contests* were used in pods and in classes to generate enthusiasm for production and to heighten joint attention to norms and dimensions of quality in contest contributions. *Showcasing* of quality work was done through multiple online venues and through behind-the-scenes interviews that provided a glimpse into the histories, persons, and inspirations for creating. The diversity, redundancy, and quality of opportunities for engagement increased the probability that learners would be able to find people, projects, and tools that connected to their varying interests and personal preferences (Azevedo 2012) for forms of production, content, and social interaction.

Intentional Positioning for Participation

Equally important were the unique forms of mentor positioning and modeling that took place within and across the varied activities. We know from prior work that teaching practices that emphasize intellectual authority, accountability to others, and responsibility for problematizing content have been shown to lead to higher levels of engagement (Engle 2006; Engle and Conant 2002; Esmonde 2009). Much of this empirical work has taken place in classrooms where the subject matter is mathematics, literature, or science, with a focus on how positioning students in various ways as more or less competent, authoritative, and poised for a positive future shapes learning opportunities. Our analysis went across the formal and informal spaces at DYN and identified a number of novel forms of positioning that engaged learners and connected them to deeper ideas. These forms included (1) *identifying future pathways*—for instance, marking fields where a more diverse workforce is needed and inviting students to begin developing expertise now that might open doors for participation; (2) *reframing personal characteristics* as positive rather than negative—for instance, reframing a tendency to be unfocused as a tendency to be creative; (3) *recognizing expertise* through roles—for instance, asking members to speak at forums, to participate in committees, or to lead workshops; (4) *inviting social analysis* through reflection and critique, with a focus on stereotypical representations in the media; and (5) *recruiting bystanders* by offering personal invitations to take part in opportunities, with a focused attempt at involving girls in game design. DYN mentors brought to their interactions with students their own histories of being mentored, drawing on approaches that they had found personally transformative. Over time, the strategies for positioning learners as leaders, critics, social advocates, and creators became increasingly varied and intentional as mentors collectively tackled challenges they were experiencing, a practice supported by the DYN leadership. More broadly, we found evidence of frequent explicit invitations to create reflected in repeated mottos such as "be a voice, not an echo," "lead yourself, lead your world," and "remix your world"—messages that encouraged exploration and the uptake of tools to create digital artifacts. These ideas were physically embodied in posters that adorned the walls, showcasing DYN students at work as collaborators, authors, researchers, and creators and thus signaling welcome and "fit," or what has been called "ambient belonging" in recent papers (Cheryan, Plaut, Davies, et al. 2009). In addition to these forms of positioning, mentors and visiting artists modeled the behaviors, most notably collaboration and dedication to creating original work, that motivate and sustain production and illuminate pathways of interest-driven work.

LEARNER PATHWAYS

Ecological and sociocultural theories of learning and development take as a core premise the idea that learners are active in partially creating the opportunities they come to participate in. We chose to follow a small group of DYN members over time in order to understand these dynamics more deeply and to generate ideas about how these choices might be categorized and followed. Central to this approach is understanding the ways that learners see themselves in relation to their choice-based activity. From a sociocultural perspective, *identity* (or one's sense of one's present and future place in the world and connection to others) has profound implications for how one engages in learning settings; conversely, the ways in which learning settings engage individuals has important implications for how they view themselves and the domains that they are studying (Nasir 2011; Oyserman and James 2011). Our analysis focused on how issues of identity and the evolution of learning partnerships across time and DYN spaces played important roles in sustaining engagement in digital projects.

Imagining Future Selves

Our case study portraits were replete with examples of reflective meta-awareness—of selves in development—and our analysis suggested that interest-driven creative projects where students took on specific content-creation roles provided a catalyst for future relevant perspectives and goals. Freedom from grades and external evaluations in the pods offered permission for students to be more experimental, and choice of content and form allowed students to set their own goals and, as Maurice put it, "actually try to learn." We found that the form and content that these self-making, artifact-creating activities took on varied significantly, emerging from personal experiences, histories, and concerns in interaction with the new ideas and relationships that learners were encountering in the DYN spaces. We documented invitations to participate as game designers, become advocates of social causes, become talk-show hosts and social critics, and engage in song making and poetry writing. These invitations were often contextualized in terms of broader social movements of the past and the present and were linked to possible futures that could be crafted by youth. Although the form of appropriation was unique, the processes of imagining and building—whether putting together code to make a game, creating a slide show of admired political or pop-star heroes, building a social network site to encourage youth political awareness, or shooting an original movie script—often involved self-relevant content. The resulting product exhibited newfound skills that were often then incorporated into a sense of self as game maker, social network creator, video editor, musician, or poet. Not only did learners take on these practice-linked identities, but they also reflected on their possible future selves in doing so (Markus and Nurius 1986), imagining themselves as older and looking back at their middle school selves, the experiences they had accrued, and how these experiences were consequential for their future pathways. This phenomenon of projecting and articulating a possible future self—or *prolepsis*, to use Michael Cole's (1996) term—should be considered an important marker of a generative environment, and we can find backing for this idea in recent scholarship on literacy and learning. Research on informal learning in the visual arts (Heath 2004, 2005), musical apprenticeships (Mertl 2009), sports (Heath 1991; Nasir and Hand 2008), out-of-school science (Calabrese-Barton and Tan 2010; Heath 2012), and various digital hobbies (Barron 2006; Ching and Kafai 2008) has shown that the choosing and developing of active roles on authentic projects can lead to a cascade of other positive interactions. Shirley Brice Heath (1997, 1999) has documented changes in the language practices of youth who participated in arts programs. These changes reflected more attention to possibility, conditional thinking, and contingency; strategies for getting clarification from others; and perspective taking. In theorizing the learning of migrant youth attending a university-sponsored course, Kris Gutierrez (2011) articulates the construct of a collective third space that consciously brought together historicizing literacy practices and personal biography to link the past and present to imagined futures. Taken together, these findings foreground the relational aspects of interest-driven learning. How learners are treated as current and future participants and how they are helped to understand the role of the present and the past are central to their framing of challenges and possibilities for their own contributions.

Evolving Personal Learning Ecologies across Settings

Documenting the expansion of possible imagined selves as linked to particular role-based design practices leads us to the need to understand how engagement is sustained over time and the ways that adults can intentionally broker and coordinate continued opportunities to learn. Without the resources to maintain engagement over time, interests may dissipate. For this analysis, a relational perspective with a dual focus on learners and their social partners is needed. Our second related cluster of important findings from our study of DYN at Renaissance Academy has to do with the small but significant moves that allowed learning to be self-sustaining and how these choices related to adult and peer relationships. These moves included (1) *creating personal projects* alone or with others that might have begun inside DYN but evolved to emerge in new forms and in other settings based on interests; (2) *recruiting support* from mentors, parents, and teachers; (3) *sharing expertise* with family and community either by spontaneous decision or by invitation. The catalysts that initiated generative cycles of designing work, learning to build, demonstrating skill, benefiting from constructive feedback, and being able to show one's product led some students to evolve and develop projects outside of DYN. In turn, personal projects brought new opportunities to learn, social recognition, and invitations to share. We found evidence that students became increasingly socially connected around their projects through online and physically co-located spaces. Though our quantitative reports reflect the belief that the growth of technical expertise was due largely to people connected to DYN rather than to family members, our qualitative data suggest that family members were also significant learning partners. Parents who recognized the technical expertise their kids were developing connected them with opportunities to use that expertise to help others or to continue learning. These connections included providing ideas for using their skills to create gifts for others, to help out with church-based projects, or to do research on Internet security and privacy laws. Parents gave project-specific feedback and more general encouragement to persevere in the face of challenges. They also shared their own technical skills, including word processing and photo editing. These parenting practices are similar to the ones we documented among parents in Silicon Valley (Barron, Martin, Takeuchi, et al. 2009). Specific disciplinary work-based expertise varied across the Chicago and Silicon Valley communities, and thus the content of what was shared differed intergenerationally. For example, some Silicon Valley parents were professional programmers or designers, and they shared knowledge about the fundamentals of their disciplines as well as more general perspectives on technical innovation; their teens often took up these conceptual tools and values in their personal projects. On the other hand, we did not see examples of Silicon Valley teens building social networks to generate political discussion—though some were active on online sites that focused on open-source code or technical knowledge sharing more generally. Variation in ideational content of projects reflects the connection between learners and the ideas they encounter in their local or global networks.

LOOKING AHEAD

This book has made the argument for the value of intentionally designed digital media learning spaces. The need will be ongoing and increasingly important as opportunities for work and learning are tied to the capability to use, adapt, and create networked resources. In the hybrid DYN model, the multiple interacting features at work together created a dynamic, creative ecology where young people were positioned to find ideas and projects that were personally relevant, interesting to them, and generative for their developing identities. Given these multiple interacting dimensions of DYN, we don't attempt to make specific claims about which dimensions were the most important for the learning we observed—it is wiser to conceptualize them as a system (A. Brown 1994). In fact, DYN needs to be seen as one very generative node in learners' broader ecology. Families, other community-based programs, school classes, and friendship groups contributed to the learning we documented. At the same time our findings point to areas of research that might be addressed in future studies. Three directions stand out: (1) conceptualizing and supporting hybrid roles for educators; (2) diversifying how we assess the growth of learners; and (3) developing metrics to assess the quality and diversity of social resources within and across learning environments to advance equity.

Conceptualizing and Supporting Hybrid Roles for Educators

Our findings suggest that defining new forms of pedagogy, hybrid roles, and interactional practices for educators is both a major challenge and an opportunity for the field of informal learning (also see Chan, Rhodes, Howard, et al. 2012; Erickson, McDonald, and Elder 2009). One of the reasons why the informal space is undertheorized is that it looks very different from our culture's prototype for organized learning—the school classroom. In nonschool spaces, learning objectives are not uniform, and lesson plans are typically not in sight. Attendance is not required and often not systematically tracked. Explicit assessments are often neither welcome nor suited for these places where more free-form learning flourishes. Adult roles are hybrid and flexible, and interactions relate as much to personal learning biographies as to anything else. Because of these features, the quality of relationships within informal spaces is at the heart of learning. We need to know more about how face-to-face and online interpersonal interactions between educators and youth best recruit joint attention, engagement, and trust. Earlier studies of urban community-based organizations identified a number of characteristics of "wizards"—adults who lead youth-oriented organizations and are able to earn the loyalty and respect of the youth they serve (McLaughlin, Irby, and Langman 1994). These characteristics include positive perception of and emphasis on youth assets rather than problems, personal connections to neighborhoods, a willingness to work for little pay, a sensibility of giving back to their own communities, and a belief that they can make a difference in young people's futures. Despite these general characteristics, the conclusion is that these adults are so unique and their vocations so highly personal that it is challenging to think about how to support newcomers in this role. Our portraits and analysis of how DYN mentors came to engage in learning partnerships with the youth we studied are consistent with this general characterization of effective mentors. However, our research also suggests that contrary to the notion that high-quality mentorship is found rather than developed, collective work to codevelop one's practice can be a powerful way for adults to generate new ideas about varied ways to position mentees for leadership, teaching, and the imaginative work of coenvisioning their possible futures. It was powerful for mentors to articulate collectively their own personal learning biographies in shaping mentoring practices and goals and to reflect on ways to connect to kids. A more differentiated and detailed taxonomy of learning partnership categories and interactional practices to elaborate on those we documented in this book would be useful to the field of informal learning as researchers work to conceptualize and quantify the varied ways that learning happens inside and through relationships across personal learning networks. Particularly important is the work conceptualizing how to help mentors develop repertoires of relational practices that embody the forms of positioning that we observed work in the shorter and longer term to inspire engagement and to build learners' resilience in the face of obstacles.

With respect to pedagogies that invite digitally mediated production, frameworks grounded in specific disciplines, both digital and analog, are needed to deepen our ability to imagine new approaches to pedagogy as well as to document and analyze what is learned from them. A quick look at the literature provides a few useful examples. For example, Lissa Soep and Vivian Chavez (2010) describe a set of practices they call "collegial pedagogy" that support the learning of young journalists apprenticing in NPR's Youth Radio program. Youth Radio participants are in their late teens and early twenties, and they go through a series of increasingly intensive experiences that prepare them for their reporting work. They begin in classes and are introduced to genres of reporting through peer mentors. Later they work more with adults and are paid as interns to produce material. Youth and adults engage in collaborative framing and construction of original work, but the young journalists ultimately have editorial power. In this setting, the negotiation of stories is central, and the importance of a long view is increasingly critical given the longer digital afterlife of published work. This well-articulated model of how to work with youth developed over time and drew on established practices of documentary newsrooms. Another recent example comes from the adaptation of a studio art analytic framework to study and redesign approaches to teaching game design (Sheridan 2011). The studio art framework utilized hundreds of hours of recorded studio teaching practice to define major pedagogical approaches and associated habits of mind. Ethnographic work showed that the digital arts environment was overly weighted toward a habit of mind they called envisioning, which involves imagining next steps in making a product. This insight led to design ideas about how learning three-dimensional modeling might be better supported if the habit of mind they called observation, or looking closely in order to see things that are not normally perceived, was brought to the fore instead. This work also led to a critical evolution to include youth mentorship as a key component of the learning space, establishing the "Studio Mentorship Model." Other outstanding models of art-based and networked hybrid spaces can be found in established and innovative programs such Artists for Humanity (see Heath 2014), which provide multiple paths to leadership and expertise. The Fifth Dimension and the Intel Computer Clubhouses also provide models to build from, and what we have learned from those models needs to be synthesized (Cole 1996; Kafai, Fields, and Burke 2010). As we have learned from studies of project-based learning, defining learning-appropriate goals that are linked to experiences and formative assessment is key for growth.

Diversifying How We Assess Learners' Growth

There is a significant need to develop assessment approaches that go beyond academic skills to include growth in interests, self-efficacy for generating new ideas, future plans in relation to possible selves, repertoires of collaborative practices, and learning partnerships. These outcomes are not typically tracked and are not easily measured, but they are important. They map onto the kinds of inter- and intrapersonal competencies being highlighted in recent synthesis publications focused on the future of work and learning (Pellegrino and Hilton 2012) and connect with positive outcomes called out in the youth development literature, such as initiative—the capacity to direct attention and effort toward challenging goals (Larson 2000). These outcomes are also consistent with the categories of learning theorized to result from engagement with participatory cultures (Grimes and Field 2012; Jenkins, Clinton, Purushotma, et al. 2009). Over the three years of our study, we saw students continue to develop learning partnerships outside the school walls, in part by sharing their developing technical expertise, media projects, and ideas online, in their homes, and in local community centers. Being able to measure growth in learning, teaching, and collaborative partnerships could provide important tools for community-based interventions where a goal is to bridge digital divides linked to differences in resources for learning. Efforts to measure changes in interest highlight the importance of alignment between theories of how it is developed and how it is assessed (Renninger and Hidi 2011).

The collaborator and creator role challenges documented in our work provide a compelling rationale for more research that can help us understand sources of variability in the growth of repertoires in collaborative practices (Mercier, Tyson, Mertl, et al. 2008; Miller, Sun, Wu, et al. 2013) and the role that productive failure might play in their development (Kapur 2008). To develop this line of work, we need empirical approaches that offer the possibility of going beyond individual units of analyses to measure the quality of collaborative engagement and a growing capacity to manage and monitor joint attention to a collective project. Video-based records of interaction and measures of the quality of solutions to problems that are known to benefit from collaborative work have been used in past research and might be adapted to digital media projects (Barron 2003).

Although repertoires of collaborative practices are important, so are processes and measures related to identity. At DYN, the topics of gender and racial identity, history, and social analysis showed up in different ways across the pods and projects. Importantly, as we noted in the introduction, the DYN environment was multidimensional, and not all mentors or youth brought the same concerns or had the same interests in social analysis. However, the fact that these explicit conversations about gender and racial identity were happening reflected an opportunity that is rarely made available—but should be. Na'ilah Nasir's (2011) work on racial identity suggests that resisting and wrestling with stereotypes can be an important process for youth who experience prejudice on a daily basis and may even serve to build resilience in the face of affronts reflected in hostile interpersonal interactions (Sue 2010) or in stereotype threats (Steele and Aronson 1995). A research agenda on how to nurture complex multidimensional selves is needed. There is evidence based on more quantitative studies that the variety and specificity of positive possible selves is associated with a range of benefits, including self-regulation, academic persistence, and attention to health (Oyserman and Fryberg 2006). Experimental work suggests that interventions that connect possible selves with ideas for self-relevant learning can increase students' capacity to enact strategies that advance their goals (Oyserman, Bybee, and Terry 2006). Longitudinal work is beginning to show connections between ideas about the future and the pursuit of those ideas years later (Beal and Crockett 2010; Tai, Liu, Maltese, et al. 2006). Taken together, these findings point to the need for studies that look more closely at how practice-linked identities (Nasir and Cooks 2009) lead to sustained engagement over time, both through social relationships and the small moves that relate to proximal learning goals.

Developing Metrics of Out-of-School Opportunities to Learn

In addition to diversifying how we assess growth, developing new ways to measure opportunities to learn outside of school is an important area for future research.

Studies of family expenditures on child enrichment resources show an increasing gap related to parents' income (Duncan and Murnane 2011). Economists are beginning to show regional differences in intergenerational mobility, adding urgency to the need for studies that document the distribution of high-quality learning opportunities at the local geographical level (Chetty, Hendren, Kline, et al. 2013). In addition to developing approaches to measure available learning resources, it is important to investigate the actual quality and quantity of out-of-school learning activity (Bohnert, Fredricks, and Randall 2010; Gee 2008). Sociological approaches that conceptualize access to expertise in terms of various kinds of social, cultural, or technical capital and then chart how learners convert and mobilize such capital provide some ideas for how to begin to tackle both measurement challenges. For example, Cecilia Rios-Aguilar and her colleagues (2011) offer a framework for combining sociocultural constructs such as funds of knowledge with sociological notions of capital. They suggest that taking this approach seriously requires that formal and informal educators be considered to hold functional social capital and that research attend to how power relations allow capital to be activated or not with respect to learning and occupational goals. Taking a network approach to thinking about capital raises the possibility of defining important subtypes of human, social, or cultural capital in order to assess the diversity and expertise of social networks within learning environments over time. For example, we might develop measures of "inspirational capital" that reflect a learner's access to people, tools, organizations, and experiences that encourage original work and the development of personal projects. This would provide an opportunity to design studies that investigate interventions that lead to associated changes in personal learning ecologies as measured by the breadth, depth, and quality of learning partnerships. The conceptual and visualization approaches and associated technobiographies we shared for Calvin, Maurice, Ruby, and Michael represent prototypes of a useful type of research tool for documenting learning across settings and time. The next phase in our program of research will involve developing quantitative metrics based on these technobiographies that reflect changes in social networks and the diversity and depth of learning activities across settings. Visualizations like these can also provide formative data that might help mentors and family members to reflect on a child's learning ecology in order to broker and coordinate connections to generative resources.

VISIONING AND REVISIONING

Although out-of-school learning opportunities are on the rise as research and policy-makers recognize the benefits they bring (Hirsch, Deutsch, and DuBois 2011; Hirsch, Mekinda, and Stawicki 2010), there is a danger that nonschool time will be co-opted by school agendas or that more informal spaces will become subject to too much structure and lose their attraction. The collection of pedagogical approaches we saw emerge in DYN across the three years we observed Renaissance Academy speaks to the intentionally experimental culture nurtured by the DYN leadership. The leadership team was drawing on ethnographic work and their own observations to continuously assess, adapt, and establish new routines and practices as the need was perceived. DYN's permeable boundaries provided connections with additional artistic and professional communities and thus offered additional resources. All these approaches are attributes of what has been called a "learning organization" (Senge 1990), and studies of organizations in domains as diverse as business and scientific labs suggest that connecting with diverse communities, establishing practices for recognizing good work or progress, and fostering collaborative interactions are associated with innovation (George 2007; McLaughlin and Talbert 2001). Recent publications on the need for new models of design and implementation research for school reform (Gutiérrez and Penuel 2014; Penuel, Fishman, Cheng, et al. 2011) highlight the potential of partnerships that are grounded in the perspectives of both practitioners and researchers. Similar models are needed for out-of-school learning environments and for efforts that attempt to connect learning opportunities across settings (Ito, Gutiérrez, Livingstone, et al. 2013). In the time that it took to write up this book, the DYN model rapidly progressed. In the final chapter, we discuss how DYN was scaled up to reach many more students and additional communities, increasing the importance of the online space for connecting learners and the need for professional development for mentors, while simultaneously opening up new opportunities for research.

11

SCALING UP

Nichole Pinkard and Caitlin K. Martin

Our initial work at Renaissance Academy was an incredible success, but the fact that it was a charter school suggests that most of these students had involved parents who purposefully applied for their children to attend this unique school. Until we can completely figure out how to make this stuff available to *all* kids attending *all* public schools, then we haven't yet reached our end goal. We're still on the journey. At the core, I'm a technologist, and—we have to keep innovating.

—Nichole Pinkard, DYN internal program interview, 2011

The previous chapters have documented the growth and evolution of the Digital Youth Network in the program's first years. Through all of the changes DYN has gone through, its mission to address one of the nation's most significant and enduring questions has remained the same: How do we produce reliably excellent learning opportunities that allow children growing up in urban America to become digital media citizens?

After the three years of research reported in this book, the DYN team accepted the challenge that many successful design interventions face—to scale up. Using the learning ecologies framework for guidance and partnering with local and national organizations, we aimed to take the work we did in one charter school on the South Side of Chicago and make it successful in diverse communities and contexts for learning. In order to provide continued opportunities for Renaissance Academy graduates as well as new opportunities for other students, we adapted pieces of the existing DYN learning model and sought out new methods of implementation across various learning spaces in the city of Chicago.

In this chapter, we describe these new spaces and the corresponding evolution of DYN learning model components—in particular the online community, the artifact-based curriculum, and the skilled mentorship model. This continued work has been made possible through grants from the MacArthur Foundation's Digital Media and Learning Initiative as well as through new grants from the Bill and Melinda Gates Foundation and the US National Telecommunications and Information Administration. We include this final chapter with the hopes that it will offer the beginnings of a roadmap for how the DYN practices described in this book might be adapted and extended to similar efforts around the country.

NEW SPACES FOR LEARNING

As of 2012, DYN programming was offered in twenty-two public spaces throughout Chicago. DYN expanded its charter-school programming to six schools, including University of Chicago Charter Schools and Chicago International Charter Schools. In addition, the YOUmedia program offered DYN opportunities in four city libraries, and the Broadband Technology Opportunity Program extended DYN after-school pods to twelve neighborhood schools and community centers. In the next two sections, we describe these new DYN efforts.

YOUmedia

In 2008, through support from the MacArthur Foundation's Digital Media and Learning Initiative, DYN partnered with the Chicago Public Library (CPL) to explore the question of whether a set of activities could be created to engage public high school students across the city of Chicago enough to come to the downtown library regularly to explore themes in books through the creation and showcasing of collaborative digital media artifacts. The pilot project challenged students to create digital projects centered around the novel *The House on Mango Street* by Sandra Cisneros. Students' projects included photo diaries of Chicago neighborhoods, PSA videos related to themes in the novel, and podcasts of thematic poetry with original score accompaniment. Based on the pilot program's success, the MacArthur Foundation, the Pearson Foundation, the Entertainment Technology Center at Carnegie Mellon, and the Institute of Play supported DYN and CPL to create a drop-in teen learning space designed to connect high school students, books, media, mentors, and institutions and to inspire collaboration and creativity with digital media. The initial program, located in a five-thousand-square-foot space in the main downtown CPL branch, expanded to include three additional libraries in 2011 that targeted students in underserved neighborhoods with support from the Broadband Technology Opportunity Program.

Teens can use the YOUmedia space much like the drop-in Computer Clubhouse model described in earlier chapters (Resnick and Rusk 1996), where they have access to a safe and comfortable environment, adult mentors, and technology equipment. Teens at YOUmedia also have access to the same intensive learning opportunities available to Renaissance Academy students. DYN mentors and CPL librarians lead ten-week workshops to help teens build their digital media skills and create digital artifacts. At least two classes are offered each day at the YOUmedia spaces, including digital photography, video production, graphic design, spoken word, podcasting, and gaming and blogging together (an adaptation of the game design pod at Renaissance in which youth publish critiques of existing games as well as create their own). These classes are interwoven with shorter workshops focusing on genres of creative content expression, including fan fiction, poetry, spoken word, and debate. Teens learn how to use a variety of digital media tools, such as still and video cameras, drawing tablets, and video- and photo-editing software. YOUmedia also provides an in-house recording studio that features keyboards, turntables, and a mixing board. The program has multiple performance spaces designed to seed both focused one-time design projects and ongoing work.

The focused projects capitalize on unique opportunities made possible by local organizations that offer collaboration and resources. For example, through a collaboration with the Museum of Contemporary Art, students worked to understand and remix the work of artist Mark Bradford and received formative commentary directly from the artist. Ongoing projects include *Library of Games*, a blog and podcast dedicated to digital game design that includes interviews with professional designers and commentary on youth work and process, as well as the Lyricist Loft, an open mic for high school spoken-word artists, singers, and emcees. Youth artists are able to perform their work and have it videotaped and produced in a space for and about public expression. YOUmedia also has built-in certifications through an online badge system (described later in the chapter) to help students identify goals and progress on different paths of learning across modes of communication.

Even as YOUmedia has introduced a new population to DYN, it has also enabled some Renaissance graduates to stay connected. Follow-up surveys with students who had attended Renaissance Academy for middle school found that some, including Kiley, Evan, and Zach, had continued DYN participation through workshops at YOUmedia (see box 11.1).

A two-year evaluation of YOUmedia (Sebring, Brown, Ehrlich, et al 2013) funded by the MacArthur Foundation and conducted by the Consortium on Chicago School Research found that the program was primarily used by students who lived on the south side of the city (58 percent). Sixty-five percent of YOUmedia participants identified as African American (compared to 45 percent of Chicago Public High School students), 13 percent as biracial/multiracial, 12 percent as Latino/a, 7 percent as White/

BOX 11.1

In a follow-up survey of graduates in 2010, Kiley (one of our nine focal case students at Renaissance Academy) talked about using YOUmedia space to learn more during the summer before her first year of high school: "During my long, drawn-out summer break, I spent the majority of my time at the YOUmedia space downtown. I also volunteered to help out in the summer program at Renaissance Academy, editing footage from the competitions. From volunteering and spending time at the [YOUmedia] space, I learned how to design and create logos using Photoshop. I had a chance to interview and record contestants and get their input on the competition."

Caucasian, and 3 percent as other. The evaluation identified a number of positive results of YOUmedia participation, including that the majority of all students at all levels of participation reported improved digital media skills, improved academic skills (such as schoolwork, writing, and communicating with adults), and increased awareness of post high-school opportunities.

The report also described challenges faced by YOUmedia, some similar to those we have mentioned in chapter 8 and elsewhere in the book. One such challenge was the difficulty of balancing a youth-driven approach with an adult agenda for learning. Another ongoing challenge, one faced by many drop-in programs for youth including DYN pods at Renaissance, was how to engage youth participation. At YOUmedia there is first the question of how to recruit teens to attend, which includes how to make youth across the city aware of what is available to them in their public libraries. And then there is the question of how to sustain voluntary participation across ten-week workshops and beyond, moving youth from consumers to producers, from "hanging out" to "geeking out" (Ito, Baumer, Bittanti, et al. 2010). Some youth consistently participate in workshops and media production, but others use the space only as a comfortable, safe place to hang out after school, where they can be with their friends and play games. How to encourage all youth to take full advantage of the various learning opportunities available to them through YOUmedia remains a persistent issue. More and different ways to trace and understand participation over time and across different levels of intensity, such as longitudinal case studies of youth, are needed for learning spaces such as YOUmedia; these would allow us to understand individual learners and the learner community in spaces that welcome hanging out in addition to providing opportunities to mess around and geek out.

BOX 11.2

YOUmedia Internet Links

YOUmedia Chicago, http://youmediachicago.org
YOUmedia Signature projects, http://YOUmedia.tumblr.com/signature_projects
Final Report: Teens, Digital Media, and the Chicago Public Library, http://ccsr.uchicago.edu/publications/teens-digital-media-and-chicago-public-library

B-TOP Internet Links

B-TOP, http://www2.ntia.doc.gov/
Smart Communities, LISC Chicago, http://www.lisc-chicago.org/Our-programs/Smart-Communities/

DYN Online Community and Professional Development Links

Remix Learning, http://remixlearning.com
Learning Labs initiative, http://www.imls.gov/about/learning_labs.aspx

Broadband Technology Opportunity Program

In 2010, DYN partnered with Local Initiatives Support Corporation (LISC/Chicago) and its Smart Communities Program to develop the Broadband Technology Opportunity Program (B-TOP) for Chicago Public Schools. The B-TOP, initiated by the US government, funds projects that focus on increasing broadband Internet adoption and usage in areas that have traditionally been underserved. As of 2012, DYN had launched programs in five Chicago communities chosen by the city government. DYN after-school pods were offered at six neighborhood middle schools and six community centers within these neighborhoods. These organizations served African American and Latino students, most of whom received free or reduced-price lunch.

Twenty mentors rotated through the five communities each week; two pods were offered two days a week at each location. The program cycled through five six- to eight-week projects over the course of an academic year, with a focus on video production, digital design, digital photography, and digital music. Game design and robotics were not offered through B-TOP due to the expense of the robotics equipment, which was not included in the grant, as well as the difficulty finding mentors with the background needed to teach the material (reflecting the challenge described in chapter 8 related to supporting computational fluencies). As part of the grant, laptop carts were supplied in order to provide one-to-one access during DYN activities, but students did not have guaranteed access to the laptops in the spaces at other times.

Though there was no formal research component to this work, we saw promising results in participation. In 2010, the first year of the program, the two hundred students involved in the B-TOP DYN programming collectively created 750 videos and 1,373 blogs.

The Importance of Developing a Community

Targeting more informal community learning spaces in addition to the traditional school spaces has brought new challenges for DYN leadership and mentors. One important and immediately apparent issue was the need to develop an overall sense of community within these new spaces, together with a culture that values creative production skill. Unlike at Renaissance Academy, there was no preexisting shared community already in place in these new spaces—the YOUmedia library spaces were available to all teens across the city, and the neighborhood schools varied in their programmatic and community cohesion. As illustrated in the previous chapters of this book, the successful implementation of DYN at Renaissance was tightly connected to the specialized culture developed there over time and the shared values, interests, and identities related to digital media that emerged as a result.

In addition to training new skilled mentors and developing the modular artifact-driven curriculum, the DYN team is discovering how to tap into existing interests and relationships and to develop new cultures of participation and practice in these new communities and learning spaces.

ONLINE COMMUNITY

One approach to supporting a specialized community and building cultural capital around digital media across new spaces has been the adaptation and expansion of the shared learning network, Remix World. At Renaissance Academy, Remix World was a space for communication and showcasing that supplemented face-to-face time. Now that mentors are dispersed in different locations across the city, the Remix World social learning network is crucial as a location for youth and mentors to connect and access design tools and as a tool to help youth to visualize and share potential trajectories of learning.

At Renaissance, students could see potential developmental trajectories through the structure of the courses and pods and could interact with DYN mentors at the school. In other words, they were in contact with adult professionals, knew what programming was available to them, and could choose whom to go to if they wanted to learn more. One of the most valuable affordances of the close-knit community at Renaissance Academy was the modeling of creative work by older students, which then motivated younger students to articulate their own goals and pursue similar paths.

During the first year of DYN implementation at Renaissance, for example, a group of eighth graders became experts in digital video. In the process, they built relationships with mentors, had access to equipment, and were responsible for documenting school events. At their graduation from middle school, unbeknownst to either the eighth graders or the mentors, a group of seventh graders filmed the ceremony and later sold DVDs of the event. The new videographers told mentors, "We want to be the next." These visible trajectories at Renaissance motivated students to participate.

Some formal implementations of this idea are still in existence—a YOUmedia Junior Mentors program, for example—but the same informal but visible connections are often not in the new spaces because DYN programming and mentors might be at a specific location only once a week. They can no longer be the sole access to content knowledge, creative projects, community feedback, and tools of production.

DYN leadership therefore redesigned Remix World to be a space where pathways would be more broadly visible for a range of different learners across the city and where youth can participate over time, in and out of the actual physical locations where they initially became affiliated with DYN. The site articulates various pathways for becoming experts in different modes of communication in different ways, helping youth learners to identify learning goals and available resources, to track where they are, and to establish what they have to do to achieve their goals.

The current iteration of Remix World is developed and run through Remix Learning, a privately held company founded by Pinkard and DYN co-founder Akili Lee in 2010. The platform still includes profile pages, groups, access to mentors, and the ability to share and comment on projects and have discussions, but it has been expanded to enhance pathway visualization through a self-paced student curriculum, learning badges, and assessment rubrics, and it now has embedded flash-based design tools to enable students to do projects on their own time. The learning pathway framework is based around the learning "entry points" "I want to be" (role driven), "I want to make" (artifact driven), and "I want to do" (activity driven) (see figure 11.1).

Learning badges are available in different topic areas, helping youth learners navigate through the virtual space to create and achieve their own learning goals. In this context, badges are virtual markers that indicate identity and accomplishment gained through learning experiences and activities. They can play a critical role in learning as outward expressions of interest, sense of self, and skills. In some cases, the badges can mean increased access or opportunities within a DYN space, such as the ability to check out equipment or the invitation to co-lead a workshop. Some badges are awarded by DYN mentors (skills and quality), others are awarded by the community (helping others), and still others are awarded automatically according to a student's time spent and degree of participation (see figure 11.2). Rubrics provide students with specific criteria and the ability to assess their own work using a common framework of quality evaluation.

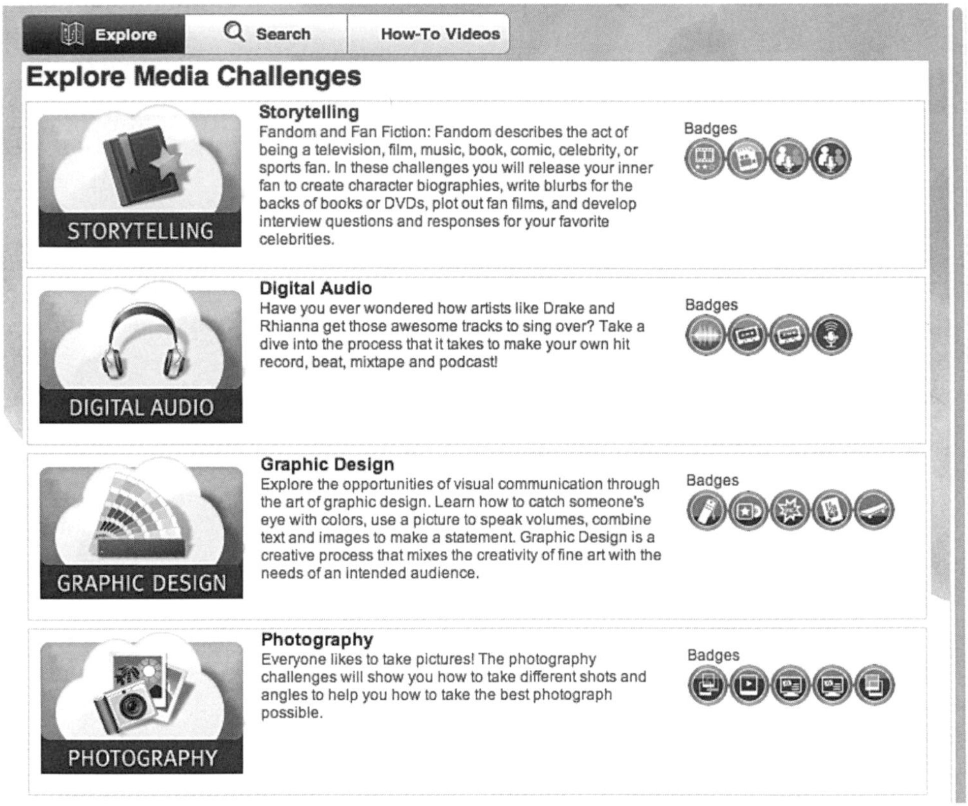

FIGURE 11.1
Self-paced learning pathways and badge-driven challenges available through iRemix.

Remix World is also being connected more broadly to the city of Chicago. In partnership with CitySpan Chicago, high school students now have access to an enhanced version of the site, which cross-references all digital media learning events and opportunities across the city. This work is part of the Chicago Learning Network, funded by the MacArthur Foundation and developed by DYN and the Electronic Learning Record. Ultimately, the Chicago Learning Network is envisioned as a set of standards that people can use across learning environments. It will create a shared understanding of work and a common language across public formal and informal learning spaces citywide. Youth will be able to search opportunities in and out of school and across the city, participate in various components, share work, receive badges and assessment, and develop portfolios of learning over time.

BADGE TYPES

SKILL-BASED

- relate directly to core mechanics or key skills in a given domain
- should have clear connections to "doing"
- require evidence in the form of artifacts
- are granted by meeting predetermined production-oriented targets that are then confirmed by a teacher or mentor
- may combine both active creation and reflective components
- can reward mastery as well as proficiency

COMMUNITY

- should encourage or reinforce social norms and practices or reward specific attributes or behaviors that are valued by the community (for example: good collaborator, inspirational poster, expert feedback)
- characteristics are preprogrammed in the system; more can be added as community behavior and badge use becomes more established
- can be granted by any member in the community who has gained the privilege to grant that particular badge (i.e. some community badges may be only granted by established community members)

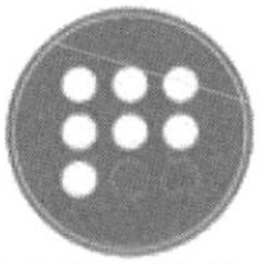

AUTOMATIC

- should encourage or reinforce social norms and practices
- do not require human intervention once targets have been programmed
- reward smaller-scale and more granular activity
- focus more on achieving quantitative goals, such as most [X], first [X], or 100th [X] in a specific time frame
- can be unexpected, leading to an early low-barrier sense of accomplishment, and possibly provide entry points into more sustained involvement

FIGURE 11.2
DYN Remix World badge types.

ARTIFACT-DRIVEN CURRICULUM

Mentors initially shared and modified the processes and practices of the DYN curriculum at Renaissance Academy through informal conversations. However, as the DYN program moved into the school day and new mentors joined the team, the DYN leadership recognized the necessity for a more formal record of how the program was developing and what structure was guiding it. As mentors spread into different spaces, this documentation became even more critical.

Even before the decision was made to scale up, the existence of Remix World and the ongoing professional development sessions worked to support the growing documentation of DYN practices, lessons, projects, and evaluation criteria. These documents, which covered in-school media arts classes and after-school pods, were collected and used to design modular eight-week workshops, which are used in the B-TOP after-school pods, in the charter-school day classes, and at the YOUmedia library spaces. The project-based modular curriculum is regularly updated and modified for new learning spaces based on student ages and interests, and community resources.

The curriculum is designed so that different individuals in different spaces can easily choose and implement what makes sense with respect to their communities, spaces, time, and abilities. We wanted to be able to say, "Here are a set of modules that someone can pick and choose from without having to worry about whether he or she has done all the prerequisites." The full curriculum is currently accessible to mentors and youth on the private Remix World site, and there are plans to make it available in print and via an app for mobile devices that can include more embedded media, such as mentor and youth commentary and examples of student work.

SKILLED MENTORSHIP MODEL

Through all of the growth described previously, skilled mentors remain the cornerstone of DYN programming. In 2010, twenty new mentors were brought in and trained to implement DYN programming across the different school, library, community, and online spaces. As of the spring of 2013, many staff from the core group remain involved, taking on new roles and responsibilities. Brother Mike moved into the role of DYN's associate director and is the lead mentor for YOUmedia. Asia is the media arts coordinator and a lead mentor in the school programs. Raphael left the program to pursue his own video-production work but remains involved with the DYN community. Tene Gray is now the DYN director. Lee has taken on the roles of director of digital strategy and development for DYN and CEO of Remix Learning. Tracy Lee Edwards and Darrel Johnson, former teachers at Renaissance, are now curriculum developers for DYN.

The DYN professional development model described in chapter 3 remains intact. Mentors come into the DYN community with their own specialty skill sets and portfolios of work and are responsible for sharing their expertise with other mentors. At the same time, they learn and continue to adapt the core DYN practices. All mentors participate in weekly three-hour professional development workshops—two face-to-face sessions per month and two online sessions per month on the DYN mentor online learning network. In their workshops and at the online professional development site, they share new curriculum documents and lesson plans, reflect on their practices, learn from and comment on others' experiences, share student work, pose questions, and receive professional feedback.

The DYN curriculum is very explicit about the artifacts that youth learners should be able to create in each mode of communication, exactly how DYN should teach the subject matter, and what the important project deliverables and dimensions of assessment are. This explicitness, in turn, allows the mentors a better understanding of how and to what purpose things are being taught and a common language and set of materials with which to discuss them.

Mentor roles have evolved as they have moved into more and different learning spaces throughout the city. They continue to offer workshops and instruction both during and after school and in more flexible spaces such as YOUmedia; they evaluate student work, create lesson plans, and offer one-on-one work with youth learners. At the same time, they are more mindful of not just guiding students along developmental learning pathways, but really supporting them to seek out resources and opportunities for learning on their own time across different spaces. An important new task is to understand the new communities into which DYN has moved and to adapt DYN practices and curriculum modules to fit them—in other words, to unpack the relevant cultural components for each particular environment.

Most recently, DYN mentors are being recruited to conduct professional development for outside entities thinking of replicating related programs beyond the Chicago area. There are plans to expand these efforts and to have DYN mentors conduct a series of summer workshops for formal and informal educators and for others who are interested in adapting this work for their own communities across the United States. In addition, led by Gray and in collaboration with the National Writing Project, the DYN mentor professional development model has been adapted for national organizations seeking to run their own versions of YOUmedia. This work is part of the Institute of Museum and Library Science and MacArthur Sponsored Learning Labs initiative.

SUMMARY

As the previous chapters have illustrated, Renaissance Academy was the primary setting for a unique learning environment. The DYN leadership recognized that the context was not easily replicable and instead sought to articulate the pieces of the model that were transferable in order to provide similar learning opportunities elsewhere. The practices of seeding creative production and supporting student identities as digital media citizens highlighted in chapters 4 and 5 are still at the core of DYN's mission. Youth's appropriation of creative production for themselves through informal interactions and across settings, as highlighted in chapter 6, is still the intended outcome. The modular curriculum is assembled around project-based assignments. Contests and connections to the broader community are cornerstones of the YOUmedia program, including an annual citywide spoken-word contest and collaboration with the Chicago Museum of Contemporary Art. The enhanced and evolving online learning community seeds new project work and offers a venue for communicating with mentors and for sharing work, both of which are important to supporting student identities. Regular forums to showcase student work remain part of the design process at the middle schools and community spaces, and new venues have emerged at YOUmedia, including the weekly blog and podcast at *Library of Games* and the weekly open mic at the Lyricist Loft.

The idea behind seeking out new spaces for learning was to give more kids across the city a vision of what is possible and ideas for how to get there. Despite the inherent challenges in this type of work—including the need for continuous adaptation and evolution to keep up with changing technologies and communities and the difficulty of engaging youth to participate in a sustained and deep way—we are encouraged by the results of these efforts. Through new partnerships and expansions into new public spaces across the city, a documented modular artifact-based curriculum, ongoing professional development with skilled mentors, and expanded online portals for learning pathways, we attempt to spark engagement and participation for more students across the city of Chicago. We have seen signs of success on the South Side and in other diverse communities around the city. We believe that similar successes can be created elsewhere. Through this book and our continually evolving, ongoing work, we are making a call to teachers, mentors, administrators, researchers, students, and organizers to work together to design, adapt, implement, remix, and create learning opportunities that enable every child to be a powerful and conscious producer and consumer of digital media.

NOTES

1. In 2008, the USI was integrated into the newly created Urban Education Institute.

CHAPTER 2

1. We did collect data on home access to technological tools such as printers, cameras, computers, and the Internet. Our first survey, administered in the early fall of 2006, when the students in the cohort we studied were beginning the sixth grade, revealed that 93 percent of the students had at least one working computer at home besides their DYN laptop (about half of the students, 48 percent, reported one computer; 28 percent had two; and 17 percent had three or more), and 85 percent had Internet access at home. These rates of computer and Internet access are comparable to national averages (Lenhart and Madden 2005). With respect to other technological tools, 85 percent of students in the cohort reported having a printer at home, 65 percent had a digital music device, 52 percent had a digital camera, 54 percent had a scanner, and 41 percent had a video camera.

2. Pseudonyms are used throughout the book to protect the youths' privacy and identity.

3. As we described in chapter 1, the DYN program exists in several middle and high schools in Chicago. Our research took place at Renaissance Academy, a small, urban middle school serving approximately 140 students in grades six through eight. We selected Renaissance Academy as the focal point for our research for two main reasons. First, our coauthor and collaborator Nichole Pinkard had longtime ties to the school and had an intimate understanding of its goals and structure. Second, two of us (Brigid Barron and Kimberley Gomez) had independently been working in the school in the 2005–2006 academic year before the grant was written. Pinkard had invited Barron to collaborate based on her prior work in Silicon Valley that investigated middle school students' history of experience in building and creating with technology; she had invited Gomez to help document what was happening on the ground. These prior pilot studies at Renaissance Academy allowed the research team to establish relationships with mentors and school staff, making it a natural choice for the three-year longitudinal study.

4. This trip was partially funded by a National Science Foundation CAREER Grant awarded to Barron that included funds for teacher–educator workshops focused on learning across setting and time (NSF grant REC-238524).

CHAPTER 3

1. This chapter refers to iterations of professional development during the initial pilot year of DYN (2005–2006) and during the first two years of the research (2006–2008). We focus in particular on the two years captured during the research period, a time we used to better understand how to design professional development for artists working as mentors and teachers.

CHAPTER 5

1. In order to reflect the informal nature of students' language and style in online posts, we have copied them verbatim, without correcting misspellings and leaving abbreviations intact.

CHAPTER 7

1. The initial sixth-grade survey focused on documenting student learning ecologies and technological expertise, so we are able to share changes over time for some of these measures. Later surveys included more noncognitive measures as we refined our instrument based on new research in the field and on findings from our qualitative work that indicated development and outcomes in areas such as creative self-efficacy, frequency of online activities, sharing work and ideas, and civic participation. Although we report these results for eighth grade, we do not have comparison measures from the beginning of sixth grade.

2. Home income level was not collected for individual students; a proxy was instead determined based on student eligibility for subsidized school lunch. Students who qualified for free or reduced-price lunch were classified as lower income; those who paid full price were classified as higher income.

3. Repeated measures ANOVA with time as the within-subjects factor, main effect of time ($F(1,38) = 148.68$, $p < 0.001$), pretest $M = 2.88$, $SE = 0.34$, post-test $M = 8.98$, $SE = 0.41$. Neither gender nor family income was significant as a between-subjects factor.

4. Repeated measures ANOVA with time as the within-subjects factor, main effect of time ($F(1,39) = 46.21$, $p < 0.001$), pretest $M = 0.33$, $SE = 0.14$, post-test $M = 3.00$, $SE = 0.37$. Neither gender nor family income was significant as a between-subjects factor.

5. Chi square analysis, $p < 0.05$.

6. Repeated measures ANOVA with time as the within-subjects factor, main effect of time ($F(1,39) = 185.43$, $p < 0.001$), pretest $M = 0.13$, $SE = 0.05$, post-test $M = 4.33$, $SE = 0.32$. Neither gender nor family income was significant as a between-subjects factor.

7. Repeated measures ANOVA with time as the within-subjects factor, main effect of time ($F(1,28) = 9.33$, $p < 0.01$), pretest $M = 2.32$, $SE = 0.21$, post-test $M = 2.86$, $SE = 0.21$. Neither gender nor family income was significant as a between-subjects factor.

8. Chi square analysis, $p < 0.05$.

9. Chi square analysis, $p < 0.001$.

10. Chi square analysis, $p < 0.01$.

11. Chi square analysis, $p < 0.001$.

12. Repeated measures ANOVA, main effect of time ($F(1,38) = 193.13$, $p < 0.001$), marginal interaction between time and engagement group ($F(1,38) = 3.25$, $p = 0.08$).

13. Repeated measures ANOVA, main effect of time ($F(1,27) = 19.17$, $p < 0.001$), significant interaction between time and engagement group ($F(1,27) = 12.57$, $p < 0.01$).

14. Average degree of agreement with two statements ("I feel that I can be creative" and "I feel that I can come up with interesting new ideas," alpha = 0.93) was 4 or higher on a scale from 1 (disagree strongly) to 5 (agree strongly).

15. Chi square analysis, $p < 0.05$.

16. Chi square analysis, $p < 0.05$.

17. Chi square analysis, $p < 0.01$.

18. Chi square analysis, $p < 0.001$.

19. Univariate ANOVA, higher engagement $SE = 0.43$, lower engagement $SE = 0.45$, marginal effect of engagement group ($F(1,45) = 3.21, p < 0.09$).

20. Chi square analysis, $p < 0.01$.

21. Chi square analysis, $p < 0.05$.

22. Chi square analysis, $p = 0.06$.

23. Chi square analysis, * indicates $p < 0.05$; *** indicates $p < 0.001$.

24. Chi square analysis, $p < 0.001$.

25. Univariate ANOVA, Palm $M = 6.79$, $SE = 0.72$, Renaissance $M = 3.17$, $SE = 0.23$, main effect of school ($F(1,399) = 221.46, p < 0.001$).

26. Chi square analysis, $p < 0.05$.

27. Chi square analysis, $p < 0.001$.

28. Univariate ANOVA, Palm $SE = 0.11$, Renaissance $SE = 0.30$, main effect of school ($F(1,415) = 23.86, p < 0.001$).

29. Reported that his or her parents use computers as a productivity tool as part of a larger job (e.g., is an author and uses word processing, is a financial planner and uses record-keeping software).

30. Reported that his or her parent's job was defined by technology or that the computer was the parent's primary tool (e.g., works as a Web designer, networking consultant, computer programmer, engineer).

31. Univariate ANOVA, main effect of parent technology job focus ($F(5,395) = 15.80, p < 0.001$); marginal effect of school ($F(5,395) = 3.41, p < 0.07$).

32. Chi square analysis, $p < 0.001$.

33. Chi square analysis, $p < 0.01$.

34. Univariate ANOVA, Palm $M = 5.84$, $SE = 0.14$, Renaissance $M = 8.75$, $SE = 0.40$, main effect of school ($F(1,400)=46.34, p < 0.001$).

35. Univariate ANOVA, Palm $M = 1.80$, $SE = 0.11$, Renaissance $M = 2.89$, $SE = 0.32$, main effect of school ($F(1,399)=11.02, p < 0.01$).

36. Chi square analysis, * indicates $p < 0.05$.

37. Univariate ANOVA, Palm $M = 0.44$, $SE = 0.08$, Renaissance $M = 2.43$, $SE = 0.20$, main effect of school ($F(1,390) = 86.31, p < 0.001$).

38. Univariate ANOVA, Palm $M = 3.08$, $SE = 0.56$, Renaissance $M = 2.77$, $SE = 0.16$, marginal effect of school ($F(1,389) = 3.54, p = 0.06$).

39. Chi square analysis, $p < 0.001$.

40. Chi square analysis, $p < 0.01$.

41. Chi square analysis, $p < 0.01$.

42. Number of people whom students considered an important source of learning about technology, from a list that includes mother, father, guardian, sister, brother, other relative, adult at community center. Univariate ANOVA, Palm $M = 2.00$, $SE = 0.08$, Renaissance $M = 1.56$, $SE = 0.20$, main effect of school ($F(1,346) = 4.00$, $p < 0.05$).

43. Number of types of people students taught about technology, from a list that includes mother, father, guardian, friend, brother, sister, grandparent, other relative. Univariate ANOVA, Palm $M = 1.43$, $SE = 0.09$, Renaissance $M = 3.17$, $SE = 0.24$, main effect of school ($F(1,402) = 47.23$, $p < 0.001$).

44. Chi square analysis, $p < 0.001$.

45. Chi square analysis, $p < 0.001$.

46. Chi square analysis, $p < 0.01$.

47. Chi square analysis, $p < 0.05$.

REFERENCES

Adams, Marilyn J. 1990. *Beginning to Read: Thinking and Learning about Print*. Cambridge, MA: MIT Press.

Amabile, T. 1996. *Creativity in Context: Update to the Social Psychology of Creativity*. Boulder, CO: Westview Press.

Amabile, T. 1998. How to kill creativity. *Harvard Business Review* 76 (5): 76–87.

Amabile, T., C. Hadley, and S. Kramer. 2002. Creativity under the gun. Special issue on the innovative enterprise: Turning ideas into profits. *Harvard Business Review* 80 (8): 52–61.

American Association of University Women (AAUW). 2000. Educational software and games: Rethinking the "girls' game." In *Tech-Savvy: Educating Girls in the New Computer Age*, ed. AAUW, 29–37. Washington, DC: AAUW Educational Foundation.

Annenberg Institute for School Reform. 2004. *Professional Learning Communities: Professional Development Strategies That Improve Instruction*. Providence, RI: Brown University. Retrieved August 7, 2011, from http://www.annenberginstitute.org/pdf/ProfLearning.pdf.

Armenta, A., A. Serrano, M. Cabrera, and R. Conte. 2012. The new digital divide: The confluence of broadband penetration, sustainable development, technology adoption, and community participation. *Information Technology for Development* 18 (4): 345–353.

Attewell, P., and H. Winston. 2003. Children of the digital divide. In *Disadvantaged Teens and Computer Technologies*, ed. P. Attewell and N. M. Seel, 117–136. Münster, Germany: Waxmann.

Azevedo, F. 2012. The tailored practice of hobbies and its implication for the design of interest-driven learning environments. *Journal of the Learning Sciences* 22 (3): 1–49.

Balsamo, A. 2010. Design. *International Journal of Learning and Media* 1 (4): 1–10.

Bambino, D. 1995. Blooming questions. Retrieved April 29, 2011, from http://www.nsrfharmony.org/protocol/doc/blooming_questions.pdf.

Bandura, A. 1997. *Self-Efficacy: The Exercise of Control*. New York: Freeman.

Banks, J., K. Au, A. Ball, P. Bell, E. Gordon, K. Gutiérrez, S. Brice Heath, C. Lee, Y. Lee, J. Mahiri, N. Nasir, G. Valdes, and M. Zhou. 2007. Learning in and out of school in diverse environments: Life-long, life-wide, life-deep. Seattle, WA: Center for Multicultural Education, University of Washington.

Bargh, J. A., and Y. Schul. 1980. On the cognitive benefits of teaching. *Journal of Educational Psychology* 72 (5): 593–604.

Barron, B. 2003. When smart groups fail. *Journal of the Learning Sciences* 12: 307–359.

Barron, B. 2004. Learning ecologies for technological fluency: Gender and experience differences. *Journal of Educational Computing Research* 31 (1): 1–36.

Barron, B. 2006. Interest and self-sustained learning as catalysts of development: A learning ecology perspective. *Human Development* 49 (4): 193–224.

Barron, B. 2010. Conceptualizing and tracing learning pathways over time and setting. *NSSE Yearbook* 109 (1): 113–127.

Barron, B., and L. Darling-Hammond. 2008. How can we teach for meaningful learning? In *Powerful Learning: What We Know about Teaching for Understanding*, ed. L. Darling-Hammond, B. Barron, P. D. Pearson, A. H. Schoenfeld, E. K. Stage, T. D. Zimmerman, G. N. Cervetti, et al., 11–70. San Francisco: Jossey-Bass.

Barron, B., C. K. Martin, and E. Roberts. 2007. Sparking self-sustained learning: Report on a design experiment to build technological fluency and bridge divides. *International Journal of Technology and Design Education* 17 (1): 75–105.

Barron, B., C. K. Martin, E. Roberts, A. Osipovich, and M. Ross. 2002. Assisting and assessing the development of technological fluencies: Insights from a project-based approach to teaching computer science. In *Proceedings of the Conference on Computer Support for Collaborative Learning: Foundations for a CSCL Community*, 668-669. Hillsdale, NJ: Laurence Erlbaum Associates, Inc.

Barron, B., C. K. Martin, L. Takeuchi, and R. Fithian. 2009. Parents as learning partners in the development of technological fluency. *International Journal of Learning and Media* 1 (2): 55–77.

Barron, B., S. Walter, C. K. Martin, and C. Schatz. 2010. Predictors of creative computing participation and profiles of experience in two Silicon Valley middle schools. *Computers & Education* 54 (1): 178–189.

Baumeister, R. F., and M. R. Leary. 1995. The need to belong: Desire for interpersonal attachments as a fundamental human motivation. *Psychological Bulletin* 117: 497–529.

Beach, K. 1999. Consequential transitions: A sociocultural expedition beyond transfer in education. *Review of Research in Education* 24 (1): 101–139.

Beal, S. J., and L. J. Crockett. 2010. Adolescents' occupational and educational aspirations and expectations: Links to high school activities and adult educational attainment. *Developmental Psychology* 46: 258–265.

Beck, E. E. 2002. P for political: Participation is not enough. *Scandinavian Journal of Information Systems* 14: 77–92.

Bell, P., L. A. Bricker, S. Reeve, and H. T. Zimmerman. 2010. Understanding families' educational decision making along extended learning pathways. In *Learning in the Disciplines: Proceedings of the 9th International Conference of the Learning Sciences*, vol. 2, ed. K. Gomez, L. Lyons, and J. Radinsky, 141–148. Chicago: International Society of the Learning Sciences.

Bers, M. U. 2006. The role of new technologies to foster positive youth development. *Applied Developmental Science* 10 (4): 200–219.

Binkley, M., O. Erstad, J. Herman, S. Raizen, M. Ripley, M. Miller-Ricci, and M. Rumble. 2012. Defining twenty-first century skills. In *Assessment and Teaching of Twenty-First Century Skills*, ed. P. Griffin, B. McGaw, and E. Care, 17–66. New York: Springer.

Birch, S. H., and G. W. Ladd, eds. 1996. *Interpersonal Relationships in the School Environment and Children's Early School Adjustment: The Role of Teachers and Peers*. Cambridge: Cambridge University Press.

Bohnert, A., J. Fredricks, and E. Randall. 2010. Capturing unique dimensions of youth organized activity involvement: Theoretical and methodological considerations. *Review of Educational Research* 80 (4): 576–610.

Booker, K. 2004. Exploring school belonging and academic achievement in African American adolescents. *Curriculum and Teaching Dialogue* 6 (2): 131–143.

Braasch, J., K. Lawless, S. Goldman, F. Manning, K. Gomez, and S. MacLeod. 2009. Evaluating search results: An empirical analysis of middle school students' use of source attributes to select useful sources. *Journal of Educational Computing Research* 41 (1): 63–82.

Bransford, J. D., B. Barron, R. Pea, A. Meltzoff, P. Kuhl, P. Bell, R. Stevens, et al. 2006. Foundations and opportunities for an interdisciplinary science of learning. In *The Cambridge Handbook of the Learning Sciences*, ed. K. Sawyer, 19–34. New York: Cambridge University Press.

Brown, A. 1994. The advancement of learning. *Educational Researcher* 23 (8): 4–12.

Brown, J. S. 2000. Growing up digital: How the web changes work, education, and the way people learn. *Change: The Magazine of Higher Learning* 32 (2): 11–20.

Bruner, J. S. 1994. The "remembered self." In *The Remembering Self: Construction and Accuracy in the Self-Narrative*, ed. U. Neisser and R. Fivush, 41–54. Cambridge: Cambridge University Press.

Bryk, A., L. Gomez, D. Joseph, N. Pinkard, L. Rosen, and L. Walker. 2006. Activity theory framework for the information infrastructure system. Unpublished manuscript.

Burguillo, J. C. 2010. Using game theory and competition-based learning to stimulate student motivation and performance. *Computers & Education* 55 (2): 566–575.

Busch, T. 1995. Gender differences in self-efficacy and attitudes toward computers. *Journal of Educational Computing Research* 12: 147–158.

Calabrese-Barton, A., and E. Tan. 2010. We be burnin: Agency, identity, and learning in a green energy program. *Journal of the Learning Sciences* 19 (2): 187–229.

Calkins, L. M. 1994. *The Art of Teaching Reading*. Portsmouth, NH: Heinemann Press.

Camp, T. 1997. The incredible shrinking pipeline. *Communications of the ACM* 40 (10): 103–110.

Castells, M. 1996. *The Rise of the Network Society*, Volume 1 of *The Information Age: Economy, Society and Culture*. Malden, MA: Blackwell Publishing.

Cecil, N. L. 1995. *The Art of Inquiry: Questioning Strategies for K–6 Classrooms*. Winnipeg, CA: Peguis.

Center for Children and Technology. 2002. *Evaluation of the Intel Computer Clubhouse Network Year 2 Report*. New York: Education Development Center, Inc.

Chan, C., J. Rhodes, W. Howard, S. Schwartz, S. Lowe, and C. Herrera. 2012. Pathways of influence in school-based mentoring: The mediating role of parent and teacher relationships. *Journal of School Psychology* 51 (1): 129–142.

Cheryan, S., V. C. Plaut, P. Davies, and C. M. Steele. 2009. Ambient belonging: How stereotypical cues impact gender participation in computer science. *Journal of Personality and Social Psychology* 97: 1045–1060.

Chetty, R., N. Hendren, P. Kline, and E. Saez. 2013. *The Economic Impacts of Tax Expenditures: Evidence from Spatial Variation across the US*. Retrieved on January 5, 2014, from http://obs.rc.fas.harvard.edu/chetty/tax_expenditure_soi_whitepaper.pdf.

Ching, C. C., and Y. B. Kafai. 2008. Peer pedagogy: Student collaboration and reflection in a learning through design project. *Teachers College Record* 110: 2601–2632.

Cochran-Smith, M. 2002. Inquiry and outcomes: Learning to teach in the age of accountability. *Teacher Education and Practice* 15 (4): 12–34.

Cochran-Smith, M., and S. L. Lytle. 1999. Relationships of knowledge and practice: Teacher learning in communities. *Review of Research in Education* 24 (1): 249–305.

Cole, M. 1996. *Cultural Psychology: A Once and Future Discipline*. Cambridge, MA: Harvard University Press.

Cole, M. 2006. *The Fifth Dimension: An After-School Program Built on Diversity*. New York: Russell Sage Foundation.

Cosmic Log. 2007. Kids rule in robotics. *MSNBC.com*, April 16. Retrieved January 15, 2012, from http://cosmiclog.msnbc.msn.com/_news/2007/04/16/4350784-kids-rule-in-robotics.

Cross, S., and H. Markus. 1991. Possible selves across the lifespan. *Human Development* 34: 230–255.

Czaja, R., and R. Cummings. 2009. Designing competitions: How to maintain motivation for losers. *American Journal of Business Education* 2 (7): 91–98.

Darling-Hammond, D., and M. McLaughlin. 1995. Policies that support professional development in an era of reform. *Phi Delta Kappan* 76 (8): 597–604.

DeBell, M., and C. Chapman. 2006. *Computer and Internet Use by Students in 2003*. Washington, DC: National Center for Education Statistics.

Delpit, L. 1995. *Other People's Children: Cultural Conflict in the Classroom*. New York, NY: The New Press.

DiMaggio, P., E. Hargittai, C. Celeste, and S. Shafer. 2004. Digital inequality: From unequal access to differentiated use. In *Social Inequality*, ed. K. Neckerman, 355–400. New York: Russell Sage Foundation.

DiSalvo, C., and J. Lukens. 2009. Towards a critical technological fluency: The confluence of speculative design and community technology programs. In *DAC '09: Proceedings of the 2009 Digital and Arts and Culture Conference*, 1–5. Davis, CA: University of California at Davis.

Drucker, P. F. 1998. *On the Profession of Management*. Cambridge, MA: Harvard Business School Press.

DuBow, W. 2011. *NCWIT Scorecard: A Report on the Status of Women in Information Technology*. Boulder: National Center for Women & Information Technology.

Duncan, G. J., and R. J. Murnane. 2011. The American dream, then and now. In *Wither Opportunity?*, ed. G. J. Duncan and R. J. Murnane. New York: Russell Sage.

Elder, G. H. 1995. Time, human agency, and social change: Perspectives on the life course. *Social Psychology Quarterly* 57 (1): 4–15.

Engle, R. A. 2006. Framing interactions to foster generative learning: A situative explanation of transfer in a community of learners classroom. *Journal of the Learning Sciences* 15 (4): 451–498.

Engle, R. A., and F. C. Conant. 2002. Guiding principles for fostering productive disciplinary engagement: Explaining an emergent argument in a Community of Learners classroom. *Cognition and Instruction* 20 (4): 399–483.

Erickson, L. D., S. McDonald, and G. H. Elder. 2009. Informal mentors and education: Complementary or compensatory resources? *Sociology of Education* 82 (4): 344–367.

Esmonde, I. 2009. Ideas and Identities: Supporting Equity in Cooperative Mathematics Learning. *Review of Educational Research* 79 (2): 1008–1043.

Furrer, C., and E. Skinner. 2003. Sense of relatedness as a factor in children's academic engagement and performance. *Journal of Educational Psychology* 95: 148–162.

Gee, J. P. 2000. Identity as an analytic lens for research in education. *Review of Research in Education* 25 (1): 99–125.

Gee, J. P. 2004. *Situated Language and Learning: A Critique of Traditional Schooling*. New York: Routledge.

Gee, J. P. 2008. A sociocultural perspective on opportunity to learn. In *Assessment, Equity, and Opportunity to Learn*, ed. P. Moss, 76–108. Cambridge, UK: Cambridge University Press.

George, J. M. 2007. Creativity in organizations. *Academy of Management Annals* 1 (1): 439–477.

Goldman, S., A. Booker, and M. McDermott. 2008. Mixing the digital, social, and cultural: Learning, identity and agency in youth participation. In *Youth, Identity, and Digital Media*, ed. D. Buckingham, 185–206. Cambridge, UK: Cambridge University Press.

Gomez, L. M., K. Gomez, and B. R. Gifford. 2010. Educational innovation with technology: A new look at scale and opportunity to learn. Aspen Institute Congressional Conference Program Papers, Education Reform Seventeenth Conference, "Transforming America's Education through Innovation and Technology," August 16–21, Whistler, British Columbia.

Goodenow, C. 1993. The psychological sense of school membership among adolescents: Scale development and educational correlates. *Psychology in the Schools* 30: 79–90.

Gray, T., N. Pinkard, K. Gomez, and K. Richards. 2008. Developing instructional practices of mentors through the creation of professional learning communities. Paper presented at the annual meeting of the American Educational Research Association, New York, March 24–28.

Green, M. 1995. *Releasing the Imagination: Essays on Education, the Arts, and Social Change*. San Francisco, CA: Josey-Bass Publishers.

Green, P. J., B. L. Dugoni, and S. J. Ingels. 1995. *Trends among High School Seniors, 1972–1992*. Washington, DC: US Department of Education, Office of Educational Research and Improvement, National Center for Education Statistics.

Greenhow, C., B. Robelia, and J. E. Hughes. 2009. Learning, teaching, and scholarship in a digital age. *Educational Researcher* 38 (4): 246–259.

Griffin, P., B. McGaw, and E. Care, eds. 2012. *Assessment and Teaching of Twenty-First Century Skills*. New York: Springer.

Grimes, S., and D. Fields. 2012. *Kids Online: A New Research Agenda for Understanding Social Networking Forums*. New York: Joan Ganz Cooney Center.

Grover, S., and R. Pea. 2013. Computational thinking in K–12: A review of the state of the field. *Educational Researcher* 42 (1): 38–43.

Gutiérrez, K. D. (2011). Teaching toward possibility: Building cultural supports for robust learning. *PowerPlay: A Journal of Educational Justice* 3 (1): 22–38.

Gutiérrez, K. D., and W. R. Penuel. 2014. Relevance to practice as a criterion for rigor. *Educational Researcher* 43 (1): 19–23

Haney, W. 1985. Making testing more educational. *Educational Leadership* 43 (2): 4–13.

Hargittai, E. 2005. Survey measures of Web-oriented digital literacy. *Social Science Computer Review* 23 (3): 371–379.

Hargittai, E. 2011. Minding the digital gap: Why understanding digital inequality matters. In *Media Perspectives for the 21st Century*, ed. S. Papathanassopoulos, 231–239. New York: Routledge.

Hargittai, E., and A. Hinnant. 2008. Digital inequality: Differences in young adults' use of the Internet. *Communication Research* 35 (5): 602–621.

Hargittai, E., and Y. P. Hsieh. 2012. Succinct survey measures of Web-use skills. *Social Science Computer Review* 30 (1): 95–107.

Harré, R., and L. Van Langenhove, eds. 1999. *Positioning Theory: Moral Contexts of Intentional Action*. Oxford: Blackwell Publishers.

Heath, S. B. 1983. *Ways with Words: Language, Life, and Work in Communities and Classrooms*. Cambridge, UK: Cambridge University Press.

Heath, S. B. 1991. "It's about winning!": The language of knowledge in baseball. In *Perspectives on Socially Shared Cognition*, ed. L. B. Resnick, J. M. Levine, and S. D. Teasley, 101–124. Washington, DC: American Psychological Association.

Heath, S. B. 1997. *Language and Work: Learning and Identity Development of Older Children in Community Settings*. George Miller Committee Lecture. Urbana: University of Illinois.

Heath, S. B. 1999. Dimensions of language development: Lessons from older children. In *Cultural Processes in Children Development: The Minnesota Symposium on Child Psychology, 29*, ed. A.S. Masten, 59–75. Mahwah, NJ: Lawrence Erlbaum Associates.

Heath, S. B. 2004. Risks, rules, and roles: Youth perspectives on the work of learning for community development. In *Joining Society: Social Interaction and Learning in Adolescence and Youth*, ed. A. N. Perret-Clermont, C. Pontecorvo, L. B. Resnick, T. Zittoun, and B. Burge, 41–70. New York: Cambridge University Press.

Heath, S. B. 2005. Strategic thinking, learning environments, and real roles: Suggestions for future work. *Human Development* 48 (6): 350–355.

Heath, S. B. 2012. Seeing our way into learning science in informal environments. In *Research on Schools, Neighborhoods, and Communities: Toward Civic Responsibility*, ed. W. F. Tate, 249–268. New York: Roman & Littlefield and American Educational Research Association.

Heath, S. B. 2014. Creative "garages" for community and economic youth development. In *Designing Educational Programs with Children and Youth: Alternative and Flexible Contexts for Learning. NSSE Yearbook*, ed. J. Vadeboncoeur. New York: Teachers College Press.

Henwood, F., H. Kennedy, and N. Miller. 2001. *Cyborg Lives: Women's Technobiographies*. York, UK: Raw Nerve Books.

Herrenkohl, L. R., and V. Mertl. 2010. *How Students Come to Be, Know, and Do: A Case for a Broad View of Learning*. New York: Cambridge University Press.

Hetland, L., E. Winner, S. Veenema, and K. M. Sheridan. 2007. *Studio Thinking: The Real Benefits of Visual Arts Education*. New York: Teachers College Press.

Hidi, S., and K. A. Renninger. 2006. The four-phase model of interest development. *Educational Psychologist* 41 (2): 111–127.

Hirsch, B. J., N. Deutsch, and D. DuBois. 2011. *After-School Centers and Youth Development: Case Studies of Success and Failure*. New York: Cambridge University Press.

Hirsch, B. J., M. Mekinda, and J. Stawicki. 2010. More than attendance: The importance of after-school program quality. *American Journal of Community Psychology* 45: 447–452.

Hitlin, P., and L. Rainie. 2005. Teens, technology, and school. Washington, DC: Pew Internet & American Life Project, August 2.

Holland, D., W. Lachicotte Jr., D. Skinner, and C. Cain. 1998. *Identity and Agency in Cultural Worlds*. Cambridge, MA: Harvard University Press.

Holland, D., and K. Leander. 2004. Studies of positioning and subjectivity: An introduction. *Ethos* 32 (2): 127–139.

Humphrey, N. 2004. The death of the feel-good factor? Self-esteem in the educational context. *School Psychology International* 25 (3): 347–360.

Hurn, C. 1985. Changes in authority relationships in schools 1960-1980. *Research in Sociology of Education and Socialization* 5: 31–57.

Ito, M., S. Baumer, M. Bittanti, d. boyd, R. Cody, B. Herr-Stephenson, H. A. Horst, et al. 2010. *Hanging Out, Messing Around, and Geeking Out: Kids Living and Learning with New Media*. Cambridge, MA: MIT Press.

Ito, M., K. Gutiérrez, S. Livingstone, B. Penuel, J. Rhodes, K. Salen, J. Schor, J. Sefton-Green, and S. C. Watkins. 2013. *Connected Learning: An Agenda for Research and Design*. Digital Media and Learning Research Hub.

Jenkins, H., K. Clinton, R. Purushotma, and A. J. Weigel. 2009. *Confronting the Challenges of Participatory Culture: Media Education for the 21st Century*. Cambridge, MA: MIT Press.

Jocson, K. M. 2009. Steering legacies: Pedagogy, literacy, and social justice in schools. *Urban Review* 41 (3): 269–285.

John-Steiner, V. 2000. *Creative Collaboration*. New York: Oxford University Press.

Kafai, Y. B. 1995. *Minds in Play: Computer Game Design as a Context for Children's Learning*. Mahwah, NJ: Lawrence Erlbaum Associates.

Kafai, Y. B., D. A. Fields, and W. Q. Burke. 2010. Entering the clubhouse: Case studies of young programmers joining the online Scratch communities. *Journal of Organizational and End User Computing* 22 (2): 21–35.

Kafai, Y. B., and K. A. Peppler. 2011. Youth, technology, and DIY developing participatory competencies in creative media production. *Review of Research in Education* 35 (1): 89–119.

Kafai, Y. B., K. A. Peppler, and R. N. Chapmen, eds. 2009. *The Computer Clubhouse: Constructionism and Creativity in Youth Communities*. New York: Teachers College Press.

Kahne, J., N. Lee, and J. T. Feezell. 2011. Digital media literacy education and online civic and political participation. *International Journal of Communications* 6 (1): 1–24.

Kapur, M. 2008. Productive failure. *Cognition and Instruction* 26 (3): 379–424.

Kapur, M., and C. K. Kinzer 2009. Productive failure in CSCL groups. *International journal of CSCL* 4 (1): 21–46.

Kerawalla, L., and C. Crook. 2002. Children's computer use at home and at school: Context and continuity. *British Educational Research Journal* 28 (6): 751–771.

Kruse, S., K. S. Louis, and A. S. Bryk. 1994. *Building Professional Community in Schools: Issues in Restructuring Schools*. Madison: Wisconsin Center for Education Research.

Larson, R. 2000. Toward a psychology of positive youth development. *American Psychologist* 55: 170–183.

Lee, C. D. 2010. Soaring above the clouds, delving the ocean's depths: Understanding the ecologies of human learning and the challenge for education science. *Educational Researcher* 39 (9): 643–655.

Lenhart, A., and M. Madden. 2005. *Teen Content Creators and Consumers*. Washington, DC: Pew Internet & American Life Project, November 2.

Lepper, M. R., G. Sagotsky, J. L. Dafoe, and D. Greene. 1982. Consequences of superfluous social constraints: Effects on young children's social inferences and subsequent intrinsic interest. *Journal of Personality and Social Psychology* 42 (1): 51–65.

Levy, F., and R. Murnane. 2004. *The New Division of Labor: How Computers Are Creating the Next Job Market*. Princeton, NJ: Princeton University Press.

Linde, C. 1993. *Life Stories: The Creation of Coherence*. New York: Oxford University Press.

Livingstone, S. 2002. *Children's Use of the Internet: Reflections on an Emerging Research Agenda*. New York: Sage.

Livingstone, S. 2012. Critical reflections on the benefits of ICT in education. *Oxford Review of Education* 38 (1): 9–24.

Margolis, J., R. Estrella, J. Goode, J. J. Holme, and K. Nao. 2008. *Stuck in the Shallow End: Education, Race, and Computing*. Cambridge, MA: MIT Press.

Margolis, J., and A. Fischer. 2003. *Unlocking the Clubhouse: Women in Computing*. Cambridge, MA: MIT Press.

Markus, H., and P. Nurius. 1986. Possible selves. *American Psychologist* 41 (9): 954–969.

Martin, C. K., and B. Barron. 2009. Learning to collaborate through multimedia composing: Repertoires of Collaborative Practice Symposium In *Computer Supported Collaborative Learning Practices: CSCL 2009 Conference Proceedings*, ed. C. O'Malley, D. Suthers, P. Reimann, and A. Dimitracopoulou, 25–27. New Brunswick, NJ: International Society of the Learning Sciences.

McFarlane, A. 2010. Behind the public face of Kew: Education and conservation in the Millennium Seed Bank. *School Science Review* 91 (336): 43–47.

McLaughlin, M., M. Irby, and J. Langman. 1994. *Urban Sanctuaries: Neighborhood Organizations in the Lives and Futures of Inner-City Youth*. San Francisco: Jossey-Bass.

McLaughlin, M., and J. Talbert. 2001. *Professional Communities and the Work of High School Teaching*. Chicago: University of Chicago Press.

Mercier, E. M., B. Barron, and K. M. O'Connor. 2006. Images of self and others as computer users: The role of gender and experience. *Journal of Computer Assisted Learning* 22 (5): 35–348.

Mercier, E. M., K. Tyson, V. Mertl, B. Barron, L. Herrenkohl, N. Nasir, and R. Pea. 2008. Repertoires of collaborative practice: A theoretical introduction. In K. Tyson (chair) Meta-Collaboration: The Role of Individuals' Theories of Collaboration in the Development of Collaborative Capabilities. Symposium presented at the annual meeting of the American Educational Research Association, New York, NY, March 24–28.

Mertl, V. 2009. "Don't touch anything, it might break!" Adolescent musicians' accounts of collaboration and access to technologies seminal to their musical practice: Repertoires of Collaborative Practice Symposium. In *Computer Supported Collaborative Learning Practices: CSCL 2009 Conference Proceedings*, ed. C. O'Malley, D. Suthers, P. Reimann, and A. Dimitracopoulou, 25–27. New Brunswick, NJ: International Society of the Learning Sciences.

Messick, S. 1994. The interplay of evidence and consequences in the validation of performance assessments. *Educational Researcher* 23 (2): 13–23.

Miller, B., J. Sun, X. Wu, and R. C. Anderson. 2013. Child leaders in collaborative groups. In *International Handbook of Collaborative Learning*, ed. C. Hmelo-Silver, A. O'Donnell, C. Chan, and C. Chinn, 268–278. London: Taylor & Francis.

Nanotechnology Now. 2007. More than 10,000 students from 23 countries combine sports and technology at the FIRST Championship. *Nanotechnology Now*. Retrieved August 25, 2013, from http://www.nanotech-now.com/news.cgi?story_id=21915.

Nardi, B. A., and V. O'Day. 1999. *Using Technology with Heart*. Cambridge, MA: MIT Press.

Nasir, N. S. 2002. Identity, goals, and learning: Mathematics in cultural practice. *Mathematical Thinking and Learning* 4 (2–3): 213–248.

Nasir, N. S. 2011. *Racialized Identities: Race and Achievement among African American Youth*. Stanford, CA: Stanford University Press.

Nasir, N. S., and J. Cooks. 2009. Becoming a hurdler: How learning settings afford identities. *Anthropology & Education Quarterly* 40 (1): 41–61.

Nasir, N. S., and V. Hand. 2006. Exploring sociocultural perspectives on race, culture, and learning. *Review of Educational Research* 76 (4): 449–475.

Nasir, N. S., and V. Hand. 2008. From the court to the classroom: Opportunities for engagement, learning, and identity in basketball and classroom mathematics. *Journal of the Learning Sciences* 17 (2): 143–179.

Nasir, N. S., and G. B. Saxe. 2003. Ethnic and academic identities: A cultural practice perspective on emerging tensions and their management in the lives of minority students. *Educational Researcher* 32 (5): 14–18.

National Research Council. 2012. *Education for Life and Work: Developing Transferable Knowledge and Skills in the 21st Century*. Washington, DC: National Research Council.

National Research Council, Computer Science and Telecommunications Board. 1999. *Being Fluent with Information Technology*. Washington, DC: National Academy Press.

National Science Board. 2012. Science and Engineering Indicators 2012. Arlington, VA: National Science Foundation (NSB 12-01).

New London Group. 1996. A pedagogy of multiliteracies: Designing social futures. *Harvard Educational Review* 66: 60–92.

Newmann, F. M., and G. G. Wehlage. 1995. *Successful School Restructuring: A Report to the Public and Educators*. Madison: Wisconsin Center on Education Research.

Newstetter, W. C. 2000. Guest editor's introduction. *Journal of the Learning Sciences* 9 (3): 247–298.

Noddings, N. 1992. *The Challenge to Care in Schools*. New York: Teachers College Press.

North Central Regional Educational Laboratory and the Metiri Group. 2003. *enGauge 21st Century Skills: Literacy in the Digital Age*. Naperville, IL: North Central Regional Educational Laboratory; Los Angeles: Metiri Group.

Osterman, K. F. 2000. Students' need for belonging in the school community. *Review of Educational Research* 70: 323–367.

Oyserman, D., D. Bybee, and K. Terry. 2006. Possible selves and academic outcomes: How and when possible selves impel action. *Journal of Personality and Social Psychology* 91 (1): 188–204.

Oyserman, D., and S. Fryberg. 2006. The possible selves of diverse adolescents: Content and function across gender, race and national origin. In *Possible Selves: Theory, Research, and Applications*, ed. C. Dunkel and J. Kerpalman, 17–39. Hauppauge, New York: Nova Publishers.

Oyserman, D., and L. James. 2011. Possible identities. In *Handbook of Identity Theory and Research*, ed. S. Schwartz, K. Luyckx, and V. Vignoles, 117–148. New York: Springer.

Pace, J. L., and A. Hemmings. 2007. Understanding authority in classrooms: A review of theory, ideology, and research. *Review of Educational Research* 77: 4–27.

Papert, S. 1980. *Mindstorms: Children, Computers, Powerful Ideas*. New York: Basic Books.

Partnership for 21st Century Skills. 2004. *Learning in the 21st Century*. Washington, DC: Partnership for 21st Century Skills. Retrieved December 1, 2011, from http://www.p21.org.

Partnership for 21st Century Skills. 2009. *P21 Framework Definitions*. Washington, DC: Partnership for 21st Century Skills. Retrieved August 13, 2013, from http://www.p21.org/storage/documents/P21_Framework_Definitions.pdf.

Pellegrino, J. W., and M. L. Hilton, eds. 2012. *Education for Life and Work: Developing Transferable Knowledge and Skills in the 21st Century*. Washington, DC: National Academies Press.

Penuel, W., B. Fishman, B. H. Cheng, and N. Sabelli. 2011. Organizing research and development at the intersection of learning, implementation, and design. *Educational Researcher* 40: 331–337.

Pianta, R. C., and M. Steinberg. 1992. Teacher–child relationships and the process of adjusting to school. *New Directions for Child Development* 57: 61–80.

Pinkard, N., and K. Austin. 2011. Digital Youth Network: Creating new media citizens through the affinity learning model. *International Journal of Learning and Media* 4 (2). Retrieved on September 1, 2013, from http://www.mitpressjournals.org/toc/ijlm/2/4.

President's Council of Advisers on Science and Technology. 2010. Prepare and inspire: K-12 education in science, technology, engineering and math (STEM) for America's future. Report to the president, September 2010. Prepublication version retrieved on January 15, 2011, from http://www.whitehouse.gov/sites/default/files/microsites/ostp/pcast-stemed-report.pdf.

Purcell, K., A. Heaps, J. Buchanan, and L. Friedrich. 2013. *How Teachers Are Using Technology at Home and in Their Classrooms*. Report. Washington, DC: Pew Internet & American Life Project, February 28.

Reich, R. 2002. *Bridging Liberalism and Multiculturalism in American Education*. Chicago: University of Chicago Press.

Renninger, K. A., and S. Hidi. 2011. Revisiting the conceptualization, measurement, and generation of interest. *Educational Psychologist* 46 (3): 168–184.

Resnick, M., and N. Rusk. 1996. The computer clubhouse: Preparing youth for a digital world. *IBM Systems Journal* 35 (3–4): 431–439.

Resnick, M., N. Rusk, and S. Cooke. 1998. The computer clubhouse: Technological fluency in the inner city. In *High Technology and Low-Income Communities: Prospects for the Positive Use of Advanced Information Technology*, ed. D. Schon, B. Sanyal, and W. Mitchell, 266–286. Cambridge, MA: MIT Press.

Rhodes, J. E., and S. R. Lowe. 2008. Youth mentoring: Improving programmes through research-based practice. *Youth & Policy* 99: 9–16.

Richards, K. A., and K. Gomez. 2011. Participant understandings of the affordances of Remix World. *International Journal of Learning and Media* 2 (2–3): 101–121.

Riel, M. 2005. Building communities of learners online. In *Online Learning: Personal Reflections on the Transformation of Education*, ed. G. Kearsley, 309–320. Englewood Cliffs, NJ: Educational Technology Publications.

Riel, M., and L. Harasim. 1994. Research perspectives on network learning. *International Journal of Machine-Mediated Learning* 4 (2–3): 91–114.

Rigney, D. 2010. *The Matthew Effect: How Advantage Begets Further Advantage*. New York: Columbia University Press.

Rios-Aguilar, C., J. Kiyama, M. Gravitt, and L. Moll. 2011. Funds of knowledge for the poor and forms of capital for the rich? A capital approach to examining. *Theory and Research in Education* 9 (2): 163–184.

Rogoff, B. 2003. *The Cultural Nature of Human Development*. New York: Oxford University Press.

Rogoff, B. 2008. Observing sociocultural activity on three planes: Participatory appropriation, guided participation, and apprenticeship. In *Pedagogy and Practice: Culture and Identities*, ed. P. Murphy, K. Hall, and J. Soler, 58–74. London: SAGE Publications, Ltd.

Ruíz-del-Solar, J., and R. Avilés. 2004. Robotics courses for children as a motivation tool: The Chilean experience. *IEEE Transactions on Education* 47 (4): 474–480.

Rutter, M. 2000. Resilience reconsidered: Conceptual considerations, empirical findings, and policy implications. In *Handbook of Early Childhood Intervention*, 2nd ed., ed. J. P. Shonkoff and S. J. Meisels, 651–682. New York: Cambridge University Press.

Schank, R. 1994. Goal-based scenarios. In *Beliefs, Reasoning, and Decision Making: Psycho-logic in Honor of Bob Abelson*, ed. R. C. Schank and E. J. Langer, 1–32. Hillsdale, NJ: Lawrence Erlbaum Associates.

Schwartz, D. G. 2003. Agent-oriented epistemic reasoning: Subjective conditions of knowledge and belief. *Artificial Intelligence* 148 (1): 177–195.

Sebring, P., E. Brown, S. Ehrlich, S. Sporte, E. Bradley, and L. Meyer. 2013. *Teens, Digital Media, and the Chicago Public Library*. Chicago: University of Chicago Consortium on Chicago School Research.

Senge, P. M. 1990. *The Fifth Discipline*. London: Century Business.

Shapiro, R. B., D. C. Nacu, and N. D. Pinkard. 2010. SPACE and RemixWorld: Tools to support a community of practice for new media education. Paper presented at the Games, Learning, and Society Conference, Madison, WI, June 9–11.

Sheridan, K. M. 2011. Envision and observe: Using the Studio Thinking Framework for learning and teaching in the digital arts. *Mind, Brain, and Education* 5: 19–26.

Smitherman, G. 1997. "The chain remains the same": Communicative practices in the hip-hop nation. *Journal of Black Studies* 28 (1): 3–25.

Soep, L., and V. Chavez. 2010. *Drop That Knowledge: Youth Radio Stories*. 1st American ed. Berkeley: University of California Press.

Stanovich, K. E. 1986. Matthew effects in reading: Some consequences of individual differences in the acquisition of literacy. *Reading Research Quarterly* 21 (4): 360–407.

Steele, C. M., and J. Aronson. 1995. Stereotype threat and the intellectual test performance of African Americans. *Journal of Personality and Social Psychology* 69 (5): 797–811.

Stokes, D. E. 1997. *Pasteur's Quadrant: Basic Science and Technological Innovation*. Washington, DC: Brookings Institution Press.

Sue, D. W. 2010. *Microaggressions in Everyday Life: Race, Gender, and Sexual Orientation*. Hoboken, NJ: Wiley.

Tai, R. H., C. Q. Liu, A. V. Maltese, and X. Fan. 2006. Planning early for careers in science. *Science* 1: 1143–1144.

Thoman, E., and T. Jolls. 2008. *Literacy for the 21st Century: An Overview and Orientation Guide to Media Literacy Education*. Malibu, CA: Center for Media Literacy.

Torrance, E. P. 1974. Interscholastic brainstorming and creative problem solving competition for the creatively gifted. *Gifted Child Quarterly* 18 (1): 3–7.

Tzou, C., G. Scalone, and P. Bell. 2010. The role of environmental narratives and social positioning in how place gets constructed for and by youth. *Equity & Excellence in Education* 43 (1): 105–119.

Urban Dictionary. 2013. Retrieved August 25, 2013, from http://www.urbandictionary.com/define.php?term=jappin.

U.S. Census Bureau. n.d. *American Fact Finder*. Retrieved November 25, 2012, from http://factfinder2.census.gov/.

Van Galen, J. A., ed. 1996. *Caring in Community: The Limitations of Compassion in Facilitating Diversity*. Albany: State University of New York Press.

Vansteenkiste, M., and E. L. Deci. 2003. Competitively contingent rewards and intrinsic motivation: Can losers remain motivated? *Motivation and Emotion* 27: 273–299.

Waller, W. 1932. *The Sociology of Teaching*. Chicago: University of Chicago Press.

Walter, S. E., K. Forssell, B. Barron, and C. Martin. 2007. Continuing motivation for game design. In *CHI '07 Extended Abstracts on Human Factors in Computing Systems*. New York: Association of Computing Machinery.

Warschauer, M. 2003. *Technology and Social Inclusion: Rethinking the Digital Divide*. Cambridge, MA: MIT Press.

Warschauer, M. 2006. *Laptops and Literacy: Learning in the Wireless Classroom*. New York: Teachers College Press.

Warschauer, M., and T. Matuchniak. 2010. New technology and digital worlds: Analyzing evidence of equity in access, use, and outcomes. *Review of Research in Education* 34 (1): 179–225.

Watkins, C. 2012. Digital divide: Navigating the digital edge. *International Journal of Learning and Media* 3 (2): 1–12.

Webb, N. M. 1989. Peer interaction and learning in small groups. *International Journal of Educational Research* 13: 21–39.

Wenger, E. 1998. *Communities of Practice: Learning, Meaning, and Identity*. Cambridge, UK: Cambridge University Press.

Wentzel, K. R. 1997. Student motivation in middle school: The role of perceived pedagogical caring. *Journal of Educational Psychology* 89: 411–419.

Wertsch, J. V. 1998. *Mind as Action*. New York: Oxford University Press.

Wiggins, G., and J. McTighe. 2005. *Understanding by Design*. Exp. 2nd ed. Alexandria, VA: Association for Supervision and Curriculum Development.

Wing, J. M. 2006. Computational thinking. *Communications of the ACM* 49 (3): 33–35.

Wing, J. M. 2011. Research notebook: Computational thinking—what and why? *The Link: The Magazine of the Carnegie Mellon University School of Computer Science* 6: 20–23.

Wortham, S. 2004. From good student to outcast: The emergence of a classroom identity. *Ethos* 32 (2): 164–187.

Zywica, J., K. A. Richards, and K. Gomez. 2011. Affordances of a scaffolded-social learning network. *Horizon* 19 (1): 33–42.

INDEX